TEWA WORLDS

TEWA WORLDS

AN ARCHAEOLOGICAL HISTORY OF BEING AND BECOMING IN THE PUEBLO SOUTHWEST

SAMUEL DUWE

THE UNIVERSITY OF
ARIZONA PRESS
TUCSON

The University of Arizona Press
www.uapress.arizona.edu

We respectfully acknowledge the University of Arizona is on the land and territories of Indigenous peoples. Today, Arizona is home to twenty-two federally recognized tribes, with Tucson being home to the O'odham and the Yaqui. The university strives to build sustainable relationships with sovereign Native Nations and Indigenous communities through education offerings, partnerships, and community service.

© 2020 by The Arizona Board of Regents
All rights reserved. Published 2020
First paperback edition published 2025

ISBN-13: 978-0-8165-4080-8 (hardcover)
ISBN-13: 978-0-8165-5689-2 (paperback)
ISBN-13: 978-0-8165-4141-6 (ebook)

Cover design by Carrie House, HouseDesign LLC
Cover art: *Tsi Ping / Flint Mountain #1* by Mateo Romero
Interior design and typesetting by Sara Thaxton
Typeset in Adobe Caslon Pro and Interstate

Unless otherwise noted, all photographs and illustrations are by the author.

Publication of this book was made possible in part by subsidies from the University of Oklahoma, and by the proceeds of a permanent endowment created with the assistance of a Challenge Grant from the National Endowment for the Humanities, a federal agency.

Library of Congress Cataloging-in-Publication Data are available at the Library of Congress.

Printed in the United States of America
♾ This paper meets the requirements of ANSI/NISO Z39.48-1992 (Permanence of Paper).

For Kate and Ben

CONTENTS

	Preface	*ix*
	Acknowledgments	*xvii*
1.	Always Becoming	3
2.	The Tewa World	28
3.	Archaeological Encounters	59
4.	Winter and Summer People	100
5.	The Center and the Edge	142
6.	The Walls Are Never Vagrant	186
7.	Seeking Life	226
	References	*243*
	Index	*273*

PREFACE

In the open country of northern New Mexico the relationship between space and time feels compressed and uniquely connected. Unexploded pieces of ordnance, artifacts of Cold War–era Los Alamos National Laboratory, rest on the same thin soil as centuries-old broken pottery made by Pueblo hands. Hispanic and Pueblo families gather together on feast days while tourists watch, hesitant but fascinated, from the periphery of the village's plaza. And casino gaming funds hydrological and anthropological research to establish and reclaim the Pueblos' ancestral rights to land and water. This is today's setting for the complex and enduring Tewa world, the cosmological center of New Mexico's six Tewa-speaking Pueblo peoples.

Situated in north-central New Mexico, the Tewa world is a land of deep contrasts and expansive vistas. A series of snowcapped mountains rise from the high desert hills and plains and the dark green canopies of cottonwoods trace the paths of life-sustaining water. For the Tewa Pueblos, the land and the people are inseparable. The people, whose village homes are at the center of the world, are interconnected within a dynamic cosmos of mountains, lakes, springs, hills, shrines, plants, and animals. Tewa social organization and ontology—the system of Tewa being—are mapped onto this landscape, and so are Tewa history and memory. This is the landscape where the Tewa, after centuries of living in disparate villages across a vast territory, reunited and found their center places. It is where their process of becoming a new and unique society began.

Over the past four centuries this enchanting landscape has also been traveled by conquistadors and atomic physicists, tourists and academics, artists and hippies. Tewa lifeways have transformed since the first Spanish entradas. And violence, oppression, revolt, conversion, factionalism, reconquest, and the eventual urbanism and commercialism of twenty-first-century America have all affected Tewa life. Yet Tsikumu, the Tewa's sacred peak of the west, endures, towering over the Walmart Supercenter in Española (figure 1).

The history and cosmology of the Tewa world challenge Western ideas of the relationship between time, space, and place. The archaeological record of old villages, fields of corn and cotton, and shrines reveals not just traces of the past but also places in the present that are imbued with power and meaning and connectedness with one other and with the Tewa people. The Tewa world, then, encapsulates both Tewa being and becoming. This world tells a story of ancient ties to space and place in northern New Mexico and an ongoing movement and adaptation to the often-dramatic contingencies of climatic and social change. It is a space that was and is created by the Tewa and a place that continues to shape the lives and histories of the people.

FIGURE 1 Tsikumu, the sacred Tewa peak of the west, viewed from Española, New Mexico, January 2017.

Through the lens of an archaeologist I seek to write one of many histories of the Tewa world. But this volume appears at a turbulent moment in American archaeology. It is a truism that anthropology is a colonial discipline, and southwestern archaeology is hardly exempt from this critique. For the past 140 years non-Indigenous researchers (like me) have enthusiastically crisscrossed the Pueblo world, building our careers on writing and debating narratives of the past, and we have sometimes prioritized universal human knowledge over our ethical obligations to the people we study and with whom we work. As an Anglo man from the Upper Midwest who has spent over a decade exploring sensitive aspects of other people's history and culture, I often wonder: Who am I to comment on Tewa history? And does writing with an authoritative voice simply add to the tall stack of books and papers written by anthropologists who have co-opted Pueblo narratives and beliefs for a larger scholarly discourse, at best, and their own personal gain, at worst?

These are fair questions, and ones that, frankly, I didn't anticipate addressing when beginning this project in 2007. When I first received funding to begin fieldwork in the Rio Chama valley, I set out to explore the valley's culture history as a way to "fill in the gaps" of our knowledge of human history in northern New Mexico. My theoretical focus addressed questions pertinent to other southwestern archeologists working in late pre-Hispanic contexts, of the consequences of population coalescence and the formation of identity. I slowly began to appreciate the rich, living social landscape and sacred geographies of the Tewa world, and I realized the importance of identifying and mapping these places as a way to more fully understand how this world came to be. I also devoured the gold mine of ethnographic literature for its valuable information to be used as analogy, although I was still naïve about Pueblo ethnography's unsavory past. And while some Tewa communities knew of my research, I acted largely independently; as I was not excavating, there was no formal consultation process. My resulting dissertation is in retrospect flawed: my discussion, while drawing heavily from the ethnographic writings, is strangely devoid of modern people, those for whom this history is their heritage. My description of Tewa history ends with the arrival of the Spanish, and it ignores the following four centuries, as well as the continuity between the past, present, and future.

My ideas of Tewa history, and the role that anthropologists should play in studying it, were challenged when I was asked to participate in archaeological research funded by the Tewa village of Ohkay Owingeh to establish the Pueblo's tenure to water rights in the Rio Chama valley. My training, which emphasized the archaeologist as an objective arbiter, initially made working in an applied context feel uneasy; however, my unease was replaced with a feeling of purpose and meaning when discussing the vital importance of this research with members from the Pueblo. I was filled with anxiety and then gratitude as the tribal council deliberated and approved the publishing of our work in academic journals. I was overcome with a similar feeling of anxiety upon completing research related to our 2016 field school excavations at Palisade Ruin. Santa Clara Pueblo requested that we not curate any material and instead rebury the artifacts where they were found. While ethically and legally this was the right decision, the act of carefully removing provenienced sherds and flakes from small plastic bags and mixing them together for a return to the earth made me feel something I hadn't experienced before while doing archaeology: a physical manifestation of the tension between gaining academic knowledge and securing the well-being of an Indigenous community.

This tension is not abating anytime soon. Yet in this book I take a hopeful approach. I now firmly believe that the business of archaeology is as much about the present (and future) as it is about the past, and as such archaeology has a responsibility to both acknowledge and benefit descendant communities. My thinking is informed and bolstered by a growing cohort of both Indigenous and non-Indigenous scholars engaged in collaborative archaeologies, a group that is finding common ground between seemingly disparate systems of belief. Rather than throw archaeology away as a rusted tool of settler colonialism, it can be used to establish the deep histories and land tenure of Pueblo people, reestablish connections and ensure access to sacred places, and protect these places for future generations. I do not dismiss the reasons I began this project in the first place—it is after all a fascinating history of migration, coalescence, and survivance located amidst a beautiful landscape—but I find that our archaeological histories can be much more robust, and interesting, when they holistically bring together both the ancient and the modern.

This book would undoubtedly be a more accurate representation of Tewa history if Tewa community members had been more involved in developing research goals or had co-authored this finished work. Indeed, it might have taken a much different shape, or it might not have been written at all. However, a decade of research left me with a story to tell of how Tewa ancestors came together in northern New Mexico to forge a new type of society and continued to endure after four centuries of colonialism. My main contribution, I hope, is to bridge the wide gulf between the present and the past in scholarship relevant to Tewa history, a scholarship that includes both detailed twentieth-century ethnography and a long history of archaeological research. To date there has not been a study that attempts to write a history that gives weight to the deep past, colonial encounters, and modern challenges. The unintended consequence of these subdisciplinary and temporal (history/prehistory) barriers is to divorce the Tewa people from their land and history. As such, the primary goal of this book is to view the long arc of Tewa history as a continuous journey, understood through my understanding of Tewa philosophical principles that emphasize continuity through change.

At its heart this book presents a culture history of the northern part of the Tewa world, the Rio Chama valley. The Chama has been an integral part of the Tewa world for at least eight centuries and was the place where disparate peoples came together, settled, and coalesced to form a new type of village life. After a long while the Tewa moved to join their relatives at villages along the Rio Grande. But they never "left" the Chama, and over the past five centuries they have maintained an enduring presence, both physically through refuge and pilgrimage and spiritually through memory and song. While I hope my approach of tracking a continuous Tewa history is beneficial to Tewa communities by providing archaeological evidence of their long tenure in the region, I acknowledge that my primary audience is southwestern archaeologists and state and federal land managers. Tewa perspectives challenge traditional Western assumptions regarding origins (chapter 4), ethnogenesis (chapter 5), and abandonment (chapter 6). They also, as discussed in chapter 7, provide a framework for moving forward. I hope that the following chapters allow archaeologists and land managers to appreciate something the Tewa have always known: the Tewa have strong and deep ties to places that extend beyond the modern reservation boundaries, and these places need to be protected and made accessible to Tewa community members.

While I have tried to be respectful of Tewa concerns, the following history necessarily touches on three matters that require mention and sensitivity.

The first is the acknowledgement that there is no one Tewa world but instead a multilayered mosaic of six contemporary villages (Ohkay Owingeh, Santa Clara, San Ildefonso, Pojoaque, Nambé, and Tesuque; map 2) that each have unique histories, futures, and engagements with the land. Extending into the past, there must have been many middle places and worlds established on the path of becoming. Anthropologists have often explored Tewa lifeways and histories as though they were a monolith and have privileged select ethnographies, particularly Alfonso Ortiz's (1969) *The Tewa World*, as representing the entirety of Tewa cultural diversity. Although I draw deeply from Ortiz's work because of its strong connections to the Chama, I realize that Ortiz, a cultural anthropologist from Ohkay Owingeh, characterized the Tewa world from his village's perspective and also through the lens of mid-twentieth-century structuralism. Rina Swentzell (1991:178), from Santa Clara Pueblo, explained that "there is never one truth" in the Tewa world. Access to knowledge is shaped by experience, history, society membership, gender, age, and kinship, and therefore it is problematic to take one person's account—Ortiz's or mine—as speaking for all Tewa people. I acknowledge my intellectual debt to Ortiz in the title of this book, but I also pluralize "world" to account for the dynamic diversity of today and yesterday. Future scholarship should recognize the diversity of the Tewa world and work with individual Tewa communities to explore their histories.

The second matter of concern is the use of Pueblo ethnography, which I draw on to understand the connections between people past and present. While engaging with ethnography has recently once again been championed by archaeologists as a way to humanize the past, my discussions with Pueblo community members and feedback from concerned anthropologists have opened my eyes to ethical issues of citing and using ethnographic description. Many Pueblo people find twentieth-century ethnography invasive and offensive. Pueblo ethnography is filled with transcriptions of songs and prayers and images of alters and shrines that were never meant to be seen beyond the purview of a society or a village, not to mention by the world of academia or the general public. And the methods used to obtain information were often, at best, ethically suspect. While much of this literature is freely available, a new book that cites and celebrates it (without context) can open old wounds. A good argument for exercising caution is that this knowledge belongs to the village from which it originated, and therefore its use should be restricted to descendant communities (Tosa and Seowtewa 2019). However, this literature has already shaped a century of archaeological research, and extracting ethnographic analogies from archaeological interpretation is now difficult. I'm not sure if I get it right, but I address this issue by drawing on only the very basic outlines of Tewa social and ceremonial patterns and by not discussing the intricacies of the doings themselves. I also commit to representing Tewa history as accurately as possible and to intervening in the traditional culture history that has often been skewed by Western bias.

And finally, the third important matter in writing this history addresses the sensitive nature of information gathered during fieldwork, particularly my documentation of sacred geographies that include blessing features archaeologists call *shrines*. Knowledge of the location and context of these geographies is essential to establishing the Tewa's long and continued tenure in the region and helps public land administrators and the general public appreciate the need for continued access to and protection of these places. However, Tewa community members have expressed their concern that revealing the locations of shrines will make them vulnerable to disturbance and desecration. I respect these concerns by including no images of these places and by obscuring their locations by creating schematic maps.

To close, let me stress that the Tewa know their own history, and in this book I attempt to neither challenge nor "test" the validity of their traditions or beliefs. Traditional and archaeological knowledge claims can be explored together to understand a broader perspective of Tewa history. It is my hope that the following chapters find, or at least seek, harmony between both perspectives in the larger story of the Tewa world.

Norman, Oklahoma
October 2019

ACKNOWLEDGMENTS

Two events fundamentally shaped the writing of this volume. The first was working on Ohkay Owingeh's water case, *New Mexico v. Aragon*, in 2012–2013. Although I was just a small part of the larger project, I witnessed firsthand how archaeology has real consequences, a lesson that altered how I view the archaeology of northern New Mexico and the discipline as a whole. I am very thankful to Sunday Eiselt and Andrew Darling for asking me to join them and to members of the Pueblo for their kindness and interest. The second event was participating in the seminar "Pueblo Movement and the Archaeology of Becoming" at the Amerind Foundation in 2017, a gathering of both Pueblo and non-Pueblo archaeologists, anthropologists, and community members who sought to emphasize continuities in Pueblo history. I immediately realized that this is the kind of work I want to be part of and the company I want to keep. I am grateful for the unique perspective of Joseph (Woody) Aguilar and the mentorship of Robert Preucel and for both my old and new friends who continually challenge my thinking.

The idea of working in the Rio Chama valley was originally proposed by Severin Fowles, who has remained a central figure in my career since he invited me out to Taos in 2000. Bradley Vierra gave me the opportunity to do my first archaeology in Tewa country at Los Alamos National Laboratory in 2005. The next summer I spent a transformative weekend with Richard Ford, Kurt Anschuetz, and Scott Ortman as Kurt and Dick introduced us to the Chama. This is where I first learned to identify shrines and agricultural features, and I am very grateful to Kurt and Dick for continuing to teach me how to engage with Tewa history. I am thankful to my dissertation committee at the University of Arizona, under whose guidance I performed a great deal of work on this project. Barbara Mills, E. Charles Adams, Daniella Triadan, and Sev Fowles expected my best and sometimes got it, improved my arguments and analysis, and offered endless encouragement. On the interpretation of Tewa history I have also benefited from conversations with many friends, too many to list here. Also, I'd be remiss if I didn't thank my wonderful colleagues at Eastern New Mexico University and the University of Oklahoma.

The field and laboratory studies that form the foundation for this book would not have been possible without the kindnesses of many people and institutions, including Michael Bremer (Santa Fe National Forest), Paul Williams and Merrill Ayers (Bureau of Land Management), Jonathan Van Hoose, Jeremy Decker, and John Mueller (U.S. Army Corps of Engineers), James Walker (Archaeological Conservancy), David Eck (New Mexico State Lands Office), Julia Clifton (Museum of Indian Arts and Culture), David Phillips (Maxwell Museum of Anthropology), Hector Neff (California State University, Long Beach), Brad Vierra (formerly of Los Alamos National Laboratory), Ronald Towner and Jeffrey Dean (Laboratory of Tree-Ring Research, University of Arizona), and the wonderful folks at Archaeological Records Management Section (ARMS).

Woody Aguilar, Kurt Anschuetz, Maren Hopkins, Kate Newton, and Bob Preucel each read one or more chapters of this book. Bruce Bernstein and an anonymous reviewer read the complete draft for the University of Arizona Press. The comments I received from all were incredibly insightful and made this a better book. Any errors or omissions are on me. I also wish to thank Allyson Carter, Scott De Herrera, and the staff of the University of Arizona Press for trusting me to make some tough deadlines and for their support of the project.

I am very grateful that Mateo Romero, of Cochiti Pueblo, allowed me to use his striking painting for the cover of this book. His rendition of Tsipin (Cerro Pedernal) captures the beauty of the Chama Valley and offers a meaningful Pueblo counterpoint to a landscape that has traditionally been painted, and made famous, by non-Pueblo people.

Financial support for research and writing was provided by a dissertation improvement grant from the National Science Foundation (#0741708), the Fred Plog Memorial Fellowship, Emil W. Haury Fellowship, Florence C. and Robert H. Lister Fellowship, and two junior faculty fellowships through the

University of Oklahoma (the College of Arts and Sciences and the Office of the Vice President for Research). Publication of this book was made possible by subsidies provided by the University of Oklahoma through the Office of the Vice President for Research, the Office of the Provost, the College of Arts and Sciences, and the Department of Anthropology.

Last, I give my greatest thanks to my family for their love and support. To my parents, Michael and Janis, who have always supported me, even going so far as to join me in the field when I needed a hand. And of course to Kate, for being my rock and inspiration for the more thoughtful parts of this book, and to Benjamin, who has spent his first three years putting a smile on my face.

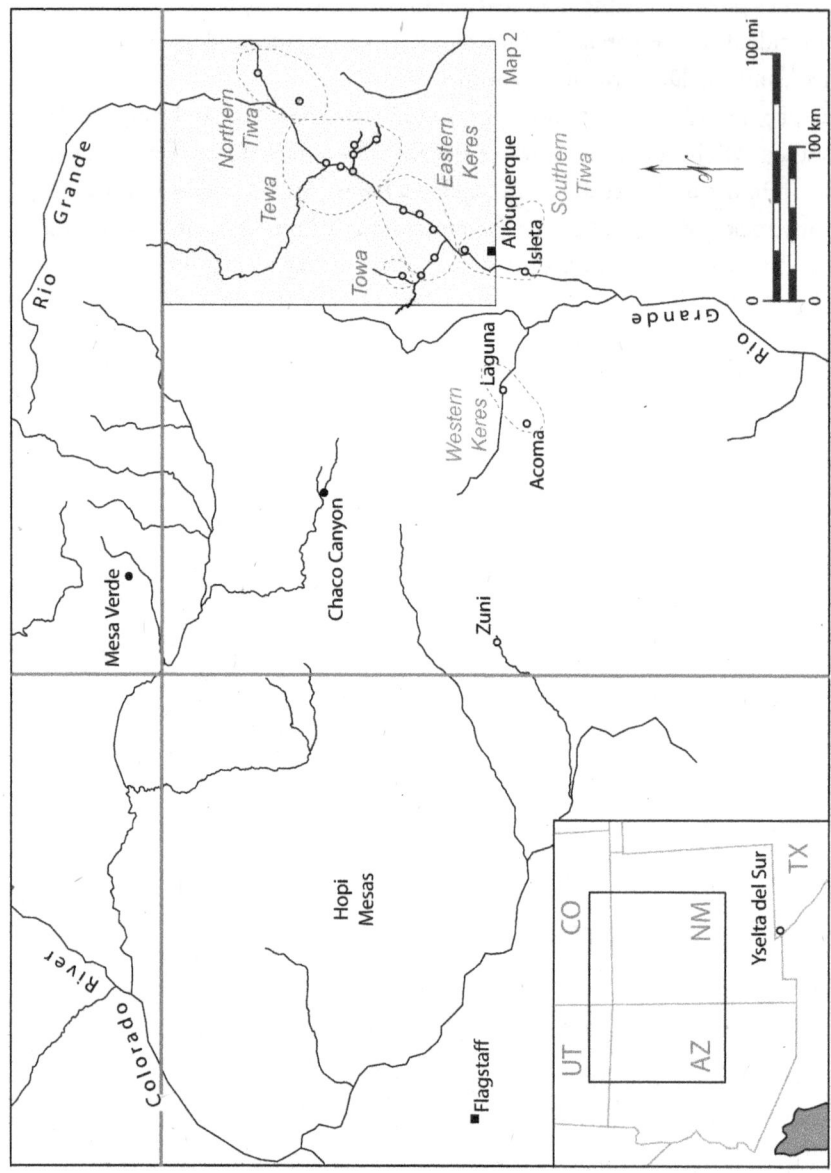

MAP 1 The Pueblo world, including modern Pueblo villages and archaeological locations mentioned in the text.

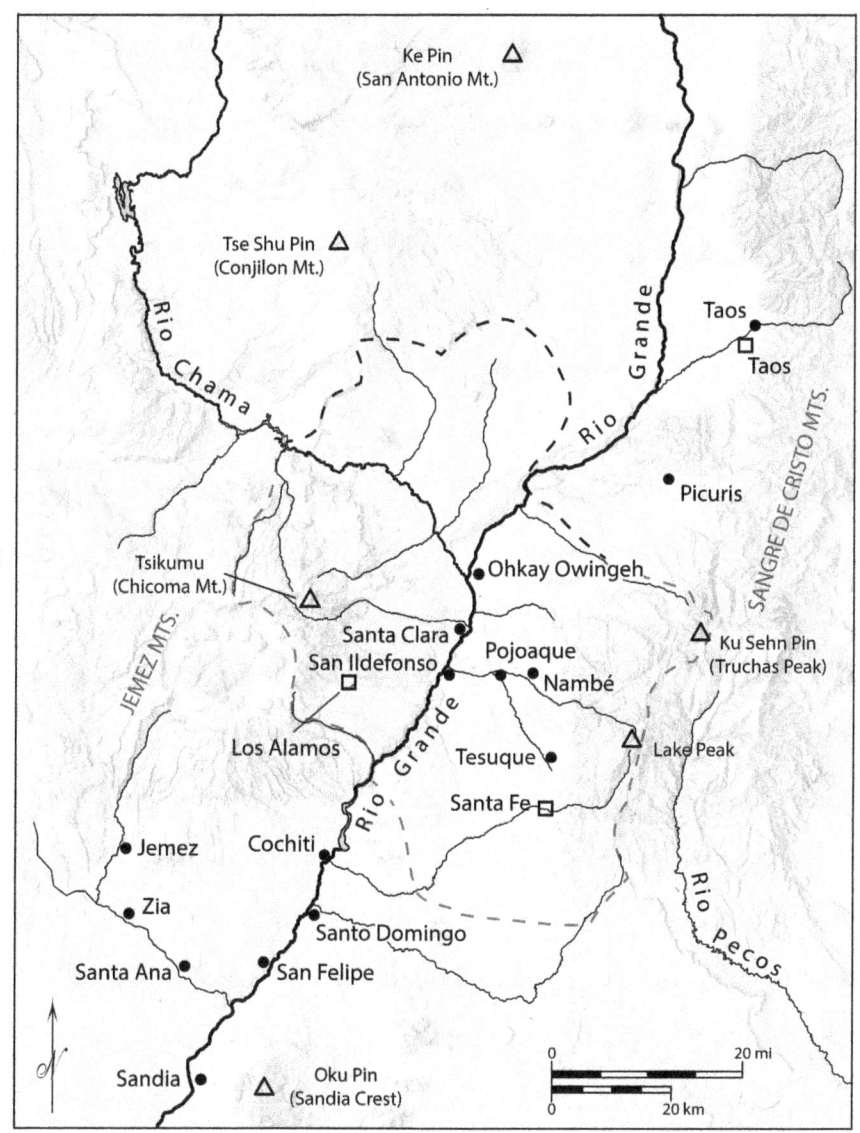

MAP 2 The Tewa world, including the Tewa and neighboring Pueblo villages, sacred peaks, and an outline (after Anschuetz 2010) of the Tewa's historic territory.

TEWA WORLDS

CHAPTER 1

Always Becoming

In the tall meadow grass outside the National Museum of the American Indian, a few hundred meters away from the gleaming dome of the United States capitol, sit five structures made of earth, wood, rock, and straw. Conceived and built in 2007 by the Tewa artist Nora Naranjo Morse, of Santa Clara Pueblo, and commissioned by the Smithsonian Institute, the sculptures represent important aspects in Tewa oral tradition: Father, Mother, Little One, Moon Woman, and Mountain Bird (figure 2). The most striking aspect of this installation, titled *Always Becoming*, is the way it contrasts with the timeless and enduring neoclassical architecture of Washington, DC. The structures, by design, are meant to weather and erode and eventually melt back into the earth, from which they were made.

Always Becoming, as both a title and a project, encapsulates the very heart of Pueblo being and becoming. The world is never static but is in a constant state of flux. It is continually re-created and transformed through the crossing paths of interconnected beings and energies of the world. The sculptures were built by many hands, including Naranjo Morse's family and friends and volunteers from around the globe. Once constructed, the cold winters and hot summers of the Potomac have eroded and changed the shape and color of the sculptures, and burrowing mason bees have drilled into the adobe surfaces. Squirrels, hawks, and insects have made their homes in the earth and wood. This occupation of the sculptures has not been limited to the animal world. During the frigid cold of President Obama's first inauguration, a homeless man crawled into one of

FIGURE 2 *Always Becoming*, April 2018. Photograph by William Reitze.

the structures and built a fire from sticks and a brochure. When confronted by a security guard his response was, "Hey, man. I am just trying to get warm." In this way the sculptures, according to Naranjo Morse, remind "us that the pieces are alive and are responding to the continuous interaction from their environment" (Naranjo Morse et al. 2012:148). They also recall Native (and perhaps all) peoples' ongoing growth and transformation. The sculptures, like life, are shaped by both past experiences and present, as well as future, encounters.

People, like the sculptures, are made from and of the earth. They emerge into this world and will eventually return, a cyclical pattern of movement that defines all life. While people are distinct in the world, they are not removed from it. The essential essence of life, in Tewa called *powaha* (water-wind-breath), touches and flows through people, and also the squirrels, birds, bees who make the adobe structures their home (Swentzell 1993:141). To recognize this interconnectedness and to achieve balance and harmony with the powaha, and between the polarizing elements of the universe, defines the "ideal beingness" of Pueblo existence (Naranjo and Swentzell 1989:258). Because the world and its people are in constant flux, so is the achievement of this harmony. Therefore, the process of finding this harmony in a changing world, termed *seeking life*, is the most basic concept in Pueblo thought (Laski 1958; Naranjo and Swentzell 1989:257–258).

Always Becoming also represents the constant engagement, and re-engagement, of people and their world through the principles of renewal and stewardship. Over the past decade the structures have been allowed to evolve and transform as the adobe falls and melts into the surrounding soil. But the structures have also been cared for, most recently in the autumn of 2015 when Naranjo Morse and her team replastered the sculpture and added additional elements. The sculptures, like all Pueblo places, are conceptualized as the intermingling of the beings of the world and are never abandoned. Pueblo places are remembered through story and song and also by visiting and caring for these places to reestablish connections with land. The world is constantly in flux, and so are people's relationships with the places that trace their history, shape their present, and guide their future journeys.

And finally, becoming, by its very nature, is never complete. The Pueblo people are often viewed, both by the public and sometimes even by anthropologists, as artifacts of a bygone era. Many Pueblo people live in the same places their ancestors many centuries removed lived, and to visit a pueblo is to see adobe structures and traditional pottery. The fact that one can visit Taos Pueblo or Acoma's Sky City and marvel at the soaring architecture is a testament to the incredible endurance and flexibility of the Pueblos in the face of nearly five centuries of colonialism. To seek life requires finding harmony between not just the people and the world but also between ancient traditions and twenty-first-century America. *Always Becoming* demonstrates this by placing ephemeral Pueblo architecture in the center of one of the world's most powerful and influential capitals. It flips the colonial enterprise on its head by establishing a Pueblo place in the heart of the colonizers' land and expands the boundaries of the Pueblo world far beyond the arid lands of the American Southwest.

■ ■ ■

The goal of this book is to present a history of how people came together to build, and continue to build, the Tewa world over the past eight centuries in northern New Mexico. Yet writing this history is hardly a new endeavor, and students of the Pueblos (including the Tewa) have grappled with similar questions of historical contingency and process across the American Southwest for over a century. Indeed, the Southwest was one of the crucibles where American anthropology and archaeology were forged in the early twentieth century and has been a battleground of theory and method ever since. Known as a "laboratory of anthropology" (Fowler 2000), southwestern anthropologists were deeply influenced by the fact that the Pueblo people have lived continuously at many of their villages for over seven centuries, and in the greater Southwest for millennia before that. The nascent field of anthropology and its four fields (archaeology, sociocultural, biological, and linguistics) worked closely together to study the Pueblo people and their history. In the years since, anthropology has become more fractured and specialized, yet an emphasis on the relationship between the Pueblo present and the past has remained, first through the enormous value of ethnographic fieldwork to interpret archaeological data and more recently through collaborative research between archaeologists and the Pueblo people.

Throughout its past, southwestern archaeology has attempted to understand the dynamic processes and events of Pueblo history through multiple and shifting theoretical paradigms, each with specific emphases and degrees of success. Archaeologists have relied on a theoretical smorgasbord that draws widely from the social sciences and humanities, including cross-cultural models, environmental interactions and adaptations, and postmodern theory. However, considerably less attention has focused on understanding the Pueblo past through the Pueblos' own philosophy, ontology, and cosmology—the Pueblo being and becoming illustrated by *Always Becoming*.

In her critique of the processual archaeology of the 1980s, Rina Swentzell (1991:177), from Santa Clara Pueblo, questioned "why Southwest archaeologists have not seriously considered the knowings (the philosophical assumptions, myths, and languages) of the Pueblo people" when interpreting the material record. She concludes, "philosophically, Southwest archaeologists and Anasazi (Pueblo) people are from distinct worlds." Her critique centered on the concept of truth. From Swentzell's perspective, archaeologists tend to accept the existence of an absolute truth (a real world observable by science) that can be uncovered through the collection of enough facts (and artifacts). The Pueblos, on the other hand, view truth as dynamic, multifaceted, and relative. There is never one truth, but many, just as there are multiple levels of being and a multitude of middle places. Swentzell developed this argument further to implore archaeologists to take Pueblo views of the cosmos and history seriously, not just as alternative histories but as fundamental philosophical and ontological principles, to understand the Pueblo past.

As an Anglo-American archaeologist—an outsider—I'm fully aware that I can only begin to grasp the faintest outline of Pueblo perspectives of their worlds, and that it is both challenging and uncomfortable to use these perspectives to understand Pueblo histories. But I argue that archaeologists might try. The potential results are twofold. The first is that by doing so we can write more robust, and more complete, histories of the Pueblo people. Pueblo perspectives challenge our fundamental assumptions about time, space, and the fluidity and interconnectedness of the world. In the following chapters I specifically focus on how we can reframe our understanding of origins, ethnogenesis, and abandonment in Tewa history. The second potential result of incorporating Pueblo perspectives is avoiding the pitfall inherent in southwestern archaeology, as well as all of anthropology, of divorcing living people from their deep and complex histories. By emphasizing continuities, as well as change, archaeologists can begin to appreciate aspects of Pueblo history that are beneficial to the Pueblo people today. These aspects include establishing the deep histories and land tenure that far exceed modern reservation boundaries and to ensure continued access to and protection of these places, now and for future generations.

In the next chapter I introduce the Tewa Pueblos and begin to explore their deep connections to a remarkable landscape, both today and in the past. But first it's important to put my project in context. Tewa history does not exist in a vacuum, nor is this volume the first to grapple with the challenges of taking Pueblo philosophy and history seriously. In the following pages I ask: What does an archaeology informed by Pueblo views of the world look like? I start by providing an introduction to the Pueblos, followed by a brief history of anthropological and archaeological research in the Southwest. Then I discuss how southwestern archaeologists, spurred by legal mandates and collaborative relationships, have begun to transform their views of Pueblo history and the nature of southwestern archaeology. I end by presenting a framework of what a possible archaeology of becoming would look like—ideas that inform and guide my exploration of Tewa history for the remainder of this book.

PUEBLO WORLDS

The Pueblo people have fascinated Europeans and their descendants since the first encounters in the sixteenth century. The Spanish, after successfully striking rich deposits of silver in Northern Mexico, began to set their sights on the north at mid-century, particularly as fabulous tales of the golden cities of Cíbola began to trickle through the colonial administration and aristocracy in the early years of New Spain (Riley 1999). The initial expeditions, most famously by Francisco Vásquez de Coronado in 1540–1542, encountered numerous small communities of maize-growing village agriculturalists whom they termed *Pueblos* (from the Spanish word for "town") to distinguish them from neighboring nomadic peoples, such as Apache and Plains tribes (Riley 1995). The Pueblos inhabited many villages spread along an arc stretching from modern-day northern Arizona to northern New Mexico and encompassing the flanks of towering mountains, the fertile valleys of the Rio Grande and its tributaries, and the tops of arid mesas. The Pueblos shared similar subsistence strategies (primarily maize agriculture in a semiarid region), architecture (stone or adobe "apartments" centered around central plazas), and social and ceremonial organization. In fact, because of these similarities the Pueblos were colonized and later administrated under the same generalized guidelines used throughout Spanish dominion of the Colony of Nuevo México (Simmons 1991), established in 1598.

The Spanish soon discovered much more diversity among the Pueblos than initially assumed. Because earlier encounters with the Tewa during Spanish incursions up the Rio Grande were friendly, Juan de Oñate, the governor of the first successful colonial enterprise, chose to establish his first headquarters at Ohkay Owingeh in 1598. The villagers' acceptance of the Spanish colonization of Ohkay contrasted greatly with Oñate's reception at Acoma five months later. Acoma's resistance, and the subsequent massacre by the Spanish of its people, brought to light the inherent tensions between the Pueblos and the Spanish as well as the diverse responses among Pueblos to the existential threat of colonization. Each Pueblo village, or group of villages, was autonomous in its decision-making. It quickly became apparent to Oñate, and to later Spanish administrators, that the Spanish were immersed in a complex and fluid social network of competition and alliances. The fluidity of these networks is well demonstrated by the Pueblo Revolt of 1680 in which the Pueblo villages set aside their differences and presented a unified front to drive the Spanish out of New Mexico for twelve years (Knaut 1995). However, when the Spanish came back to reconquest the colony, old alliances and complex relationships among the Pueblos emerged as villages either helped or fought the colonizers based on their individual interests (Liebmann et al. 2005). Therefore, the Pueblo Southwest was (and is) a collage of many different worlds with striking similarities.

Anthropologists, arriving in the late nineteenth century, also observed a similar pattern by conceptualizing the Pueblos as a unified culture area with historical and ethnic distinctions. The most apparent diversity is in language (Dozier 1970:181), as there are four language families spoken: Tanoan (including Tewa, Tiwa, and Towa languages among the Pueblos of the Rio Grande), Keresan (the language of five Rio Grande villages and Acoma and Laguna to the west), Zuni (a language isolate), and Hopi (part of the Uto-Aztecan family spoken among the Hopi villages). Pueblo linguistic diversity suggests a complex history of origins and movement. The grouping of villages who share language indicates a shared culture history (map 1). Anthropologists have also noted a diversity in social organization that crosscuts language (Eggan 1950). The western Pueblos of the Hopi villages, Zuni, Acoma, and Languna, are organized by matrilineal clans and households with matrilocal residence patterns. The Rio Grande (or eastern) Pueblos are more diverse but are generally organized by patrilineal dual division, or a mixture of both dual division and clan systems. But in spite of this variance in language and social organization there remains a curious homogeneity in ceremonialism, cosmology, and ontology. In fact, the content of Pueblo ceremonialism is nearly identical for each village, and rather it is the order of emphasis of rites performed that makes each unique (Parsons 1933:6). This homogeneity may stem from intense social networks across the Pueblo world, common histories, or a shared subsistence pattern of maize agriculture in a semiarid landscape. The last practically requires an ethic of achieving balance and harmony between people and their world, a foundation principle for all Pueblo life.

Much has happened over the past four centuries (the subject of chapters 6 and 7), but the Pueblos have managed continual occupation of the same land in the face of Spanish, Mexican, and American colonization. The modern Pueblo world comprises approximately sixty thousand people (based on the 2010 U.S. Census), many of whom live in thirty-one villages and on reservations spread over a roughly 400-mile crescent from Taos in northern New Mexico to Hopi in northern Arizona (map 1). Some villages, such as Ohkay Owingeh, have been continuously occupied for over seven centuries (Ellis 1989). Yet it is important not to fall into the trap of thinking that the Pueblos practice a pristine pre- or non-Western lifeway, historically or currently, and that they are artifacts of earlier times. This was certainly the assumption made by early anthropologists and the general public and represented in twentieth-century literature (see Aldous Huxley's depiction of the Pueblos in *Brave New World*). The Pueblos are thoroughly engaged in modern American life. A poignant example of this is from Severin Fowles's (2013:191) description of the feast day of San Geronimo celebrated by Taos Pueblo immediately following the September 11, 2011, terrorist attacks. The celebration involves a pole climb in which ceremonial clowns, called Kossa, climb a 100-foot pole in the center of the plaza, symbolizing the emergence of the people into this world. On the feast day following 9/11, the Kossa who reached the top of the pole unfurled a large American flag. This juxtaposition of American patriotism with timeless Pueblo tradition illustrates the tensions and negotiations the Pueblo people face today, and have faced throughout the historic period. In fact, as I argue throughout this book, these negotiations are based on a philosophy of establishing harmony, or *seeking life*, that has been a hallmark of Pueblo culture history extending far back in time.

WAYS OF KNOWING THE PUEBLO PAST AND PRESENT

Our understanding of the Pueblo people comes from many sources, including historic documents and the writings of Pueblo scholars and community members. But the bulk of our knowledge is subsumed under the umbrella of anthropology. The study of the Pueblo people beginning in the late nineteenth century fundamentally shaped the nascent discipline of anthropology. Upon winning the Mexican-American War, the United States in 1848 annexed what is now the American Southwest and California. Mexico itself had only recently gained its independence from Spain in 1821, and within a span of three decades, the region's residents (including the Pueblos) were governed by three consecutive states. Some of the earliest encounters U.S. citizens had with ancestral Pueblo places were through military expeditions (Snead 2001), but it was in the post–Civil War years that American institutions, particularly those on the East Coast, began to view the Southwest and its inhabitants with increasingly intense interest. Some of the fervor stemmed from the "discovery" of the Cliff Dwellers in southern Colorado in 1875 (Fowler 2000:50–70). In a captivating story, Richard Wetherill and Charlie Mason, cowboys from Mancos, Colorado, lost their cattle in a blinding snowstorm in December 1888. From high on a mesa the two men caught a fleeting glimpse of Cliff Palace through the wind and snow and became the first European Americans to view the massive thirteenth-century Puebloan habitations of Mesa Verde. Their story was highly publicized and helped catalyze a rush to systematically loot relics from Cliff

Palace and other sites and put them on display for fascinated attendees at the 1893 Chicago World's Fair.

Meanwhile, scholarly programs were initiated in the 1870s to 1880s by people like Frederic Ward Putnam (from the Harvard's Peabody Museum of Archaeology and Ethnology) and John Wesley Powell (the Smithsonian's Bureau of American Ethnology) and were rooted in collecting relics and material information about living Pueblo people, including biological and linguistic data (Fowles and Mills 2017). Also included was the newly formed Archaeological Institute of America, which sponsored the work of Adolph Bandelier, who spent multiple field seasons centered in Santa Fe in the 1880s (Snead 2001:9–10). Bandelier surveyed the region widely, providing the foundation for future anthropological research in New Mexico and across the American Southwest. Private patronage also played a part in the growth of southwestern archaeology, such as the Hemenway Southwestern Archaeological Expedition, led by Frank Hamilton Cushing, which surveyed both people and archaeology in Arizona and New Mexico. James Snead (2001) recounts the competitive environment of institutions and their motivations in southwestern archaeology and anthropology at the turn of the nineteenth century that would continue for decades. The amount of research was enormous and laid the foundation for the anthropological understanding of the Pueblo world.

Rina Swentzell's critique that southwestern archaeologists have not taken Pueblo concepts seriously when interpreting the past can be applied to much of the history of research in the region. It is also important, though, to recognize the inherent tension that has always been present in southwestern archaeology regarding the validity of connecting the present and the past and how these connections have been accepted and dismissed throughout its history. Certainly the earliest scholars, such as Cushing (1890) and Jesse Walter Fewkes (1900), practiced a holistic, evolutionary brand of anthropology inspired by Lewis Henry Morgan that worked from the present to the past and incorporated Pueblo knowledge (Fowler 2000). Although Cushing and Fewkes were primarily interested in the contemporary beliefs and practices of Zuni and Hopi, respectively, these early anthropologists also engaged in archaeological and linguistic research. Their belief, along with their contemporaries' (Mindeleff 1900; Mindeleff 1891), was that the material record was helpful in understanding the development of modern Pueblo people at multiple scales, from the village to individual clans and societies. The same can be said about Bandelier's (1892) survey of Pueblo archaeology in northern New Mexico. His work drew on the knowledge of the Pueblo people themselves, with a humanist touch, and was expressed in his 1890 publication of *The Delight Makers*, a fictional account of the experiences of ancestral Keresan people in Frijoles Canyon (part of the present-day Bandelier National Monument). These early approaches relied on close (albeit often unacknowledged) working relationships between anthropologists and Pueblo people (Colwell-Chanthaphonh 2010; Schachner 2018). They also assumed an unbroken connection between the present and the past.

As southwestern archaeology matured through the first decades of the twentieth century, the gulf between the Pueblo present and past began to widen, and the connections and continuities began to fray. Anthropology as a field was becoming more specialized, although for the first half of the twentieth century archaeologists and ethnographers were still working closely together, compared with other areas in North America (Fowles and Mills 2017:13). However, upon publication of Clark Wissler's (1917) rejection of the continuity between ethnography and the past, archaeologists became wary of the direct historical approach. There was increasingly less room for Pueblo voices in the culture historical "New Archaeology" practiced by Alfred V. Kidder (1924) and Nels Nelson (1916), which prioritized the delineation of materially based regional traditions (Anasazi, Hohokam, Mogollon) and precise chronological control. Severin Fowles and Barbara Mills (2017:14) note that, in effect, southwestern archaeologists were creating a new object of study—prehistory—that was divorced from history and also from the Pueblo people and their knowledge. The effects of this change continue to be felt today in how the Pueblo past is discussed by the public ("the mysterious disappearance of the Anasazi") and by archaeologists, who have historically focused more on Pueblo history prior to Spanish contact and less on the colonial period.

Southwestern archaeology found its footing just as Pueblo ethnographers entered a productive period through the mid-twentieth century, inspired in large part by a Boasian perspective and a need for systematic empirical research (Basso 1979). Many classics were written, including Ruth Bunzel's (1932) and Alfred Kroeber's (1919) work at Zuni, Robert Lowie's (1929a, 1929b) and Mischa Titiev's (1944) at Hopi, Leslie White's (1935, 1942, 1962) on the Keresan Pueblos, and Elsie Clews Parsons's on the Tewa and many other Pueblos (e.g., 1923, 1925, 1929, 1933). Some of this work was highly comparative (Eggan 1950; Parsons 1996[1939]) and explored the broad similarities and differences across the Pueblo word. It also crafted an idea of Pueblo life that has both aided and distorted (Lekson 2018:21) archaeological understanding of the past. While most southwestern archaeologists celebrate this robust body of ethnography, twentieth-century anthropology was highly exploitative of Pueblo knowledge, and particularly of Pueblo people, who were believed to be rapidly assimilating or abandoning their traditions (Brandt 2002). Early encounters with anthropologists led Pueblos to be ever more cautious in their interactions with outsiders, even as increasing numbers of ethnographers arrived (Brandt 1980).

By the 1960s, archaeology and ethnography had entered a stage of transformation. Ethnography's transformation came in the form of a rupturing of the insider/outsider dichotomy of mid-twentieth-century anthropology as Pueblo community members became trained anthropologists (Norcini 2007). Two prominent Tewa anthropologists, Edward Dozier from Santa Clara and Alfonso Ortiz from Ohkay Owingeh, received criticism in their hometowns for having divulged ceremonial secrets, even as their work was hailed as groundbreaking anthropology (Norcini 2007; Whiteley 1999). Significantly, Ortiz's work was among the last academic ethnographies of a Pueblo community. By the 1970s and 1980s, the Pueblos had begun to establish their own cultural heritage programs and to reject research (both ethnographic and archaeological, as well as others) that did not benefit the community (Brandt 2002; Kuwanwisiwma 2018). The Pueblos' caution when addressing research, combined with political activism and ethical and theoretical changes in the field, signaled a "death" of ethnography of the Pueblos as it had traditionally been practiced (Whiteley 1993). Nearly all ethnography practiced today is applied in nature, controlled by and in service to the Pueblos. This work is closely associated, or is part of, collaborative archaeological projects that once again attempt to tie together the present and the past.

The 1960s also brought processual archaeology to the Southwest, which refocused researchers to view Pueblo history as a series of case studies to build general anthropological theory. Questions included scales (and types) of sociopolitical and ceremonial complexity (Adams 1991; Johnson 1982; Mills 2000), the adoption of agriculture (Matson 1991), and human-environment relationships (Dean et al. 1985), among others. Processual archaeology, although drawing on both Pueblo and global ethnography as "middle range theory," was materialist and often relied on environmentally (or some other external factor) driven models. Significantly, Lewis Binford's (1962:218) critique that "historical explanations" were inadequate to account for culture process and provided an additional barrier to connecting the Pueblo present and the Pueblo past. Events of vital concern to the Pueblo people, such as migration and finding their middle places, were viewed not as historical processes in themselves but as the effects of larger cultural processes. This approach, coupled with the perspective held by some archaeologists of Pueblo ethnography that Pueblo voices were not representative of the past because of colonial and modern change (Upham 1987), further removed Pueblo representation in archaeological discussion.

At this juncture Rina Swentzell wrote her constructive critique. She concluded with a series of questions that presage the direction southwestern archaeology has taken for the past twenty years.

> Is it possible for *both* the Pueblo people and the archaeologists to uncover, in a partnership mode and a creative act, the patterns of human existence in the prehistoric Southwest? Is it possible for both reason and intuition to be used simultaneously? For such to happen, however, archaeologists, because they are presently in charge of digging and interpretation, must use "feminine" aspects of their beings to include Pueblo people in the process of linking present Pueblo knowledge with scientific evidence for a more holistic sense of Anasazi life and culture. Unexpected patterns and truths might even emerge. (Swentzell 1991:180)

It is remarkable how Swentzell's short essay, buried in a local New Mexico archaeological publication, anticipated the future direction of anthropological theory and archaeological practice. In subsequent years, two major developments began to shape southwestern archaeology. The first is a theoretical movement beyond processualism toward perspectives that embrace Indigenous narratives (Atalay 2012; Smith and Wobst 2005; Watkins 2000), postcolonial critiques (Liebmann and Rizvi 2010), and the writing of history (Fowles and Mills 2017). These new narratives acknowledge, as Swentzell (1991:178) states, that archaeologists have imposed Western biases and ideologies on Pueblo history. For example, Fowles (2013) focuses on Pueblo *doings*—an Indigenous conception—rather than religion, which is an artifact of the post-Enlightenment West. While religion is seen by archaeologists as being apart from, though connected to, other elements of society, doings break down the lines between these elements. To dance in the plaza or pray at a shrine is not to practice religion but instead to have "a heightened awareness of interconnectedness and relations between things" (Fowles 2013:103).

The second development is the acknowledgment by anthropologists that Pueblo philosophy and concepts of history and archaeological interpretation are coequal forms of knowledge. This acknowledgment began in earnest with the passing of Native American Graves Protection and Repatriation Act (NAGPRA) in 1990, which requires both archaeologists and museums to consult with tribes and gives Native people a stake in both previously collected material and future archaeological research. The consultation process is based on establishing cultural affiliation between modern and past people and gives oral tradition the same weight as archaeological evidence. Consultation compelled archaeologists to re-engage with living people and their concepts of history and initiated relationships that have strengthened into fully collaborative endeavors. Chip Colwell-Chanthaphonh and T. J. Ferguson (2008) discuss how the collaboration and coproduction of knowledge between archaeologists and Native American groups has been transformative. Through work with the Hopi (Colwell and Koyiyumptewa 2018; Dongoske et al. 1993; Ferguson et al. 1996), Zuni (Ferguson and Anyon 2001), Acoma (Garcia and Anschuetz 2019), and Jemez (Tosa et al. 2019), among others, archaeologists are incorporating Pueblo history into traditional archaeological discussions. Anthropology is not dead, but in this new framework much of the work traditionally performed by ethnographers is now practiced by archaeologists and their Pueblo collaborators. The resulting research, as demonstrated below, includes much more than simple narratives of the past but instead is imbued with moral and philosophical principles to live life in the present.

THE CONTINUOUS PATH

The fundamental shifts in research conducted by southwestern archaeologists over the past two decades have been profound. Research has begun to rely on Pueblo historical tradition as well as Pueblo philosophy to guide fieldwork and interpretation. Archaeologists have ample help in developing a new approach through rereading ethnography, absorbing the lessons taught by Pueblo scholars and artists, and collaborating with the Pueblo people, which provide direction in the writing of history. But at the end of the day we as archaeologists stare across a daunting chasm. On one side is the knowledge (and acknowledgement) of Indigenous conceptions of the world. On the other side is the meager material culture that constitutes the archeological record. How can we cross the divide? And how can we observe, analyze, and write about the past in ways that are relevant to the Pueblos today?

One way to traverse old divides between prehistory and history, archaeology and ethnography, is to view ethnographic and historic accounts not as simple analogies but as homologies, the result of shared and complex historical trajectories (Whiteley 2015, 2018). And these histories are not ones of unilinear descent or of branches in dendritic models but are the ongoing contact and convergence of people with different traditions, like a rhizome or a braided stream, whose descendants are rooted in multiple societies (Ferguson et al. 2013; Fowles 2018; Hays-Gilpin and Gilpin 2018a). Following Swentzell (1991), we can take this further: processes of being and becoming Pueblo, while manifested in historically contingent ways, may apply generally to the Pueblo past, present, and future. Thus there is power and relevance in using modern Pueblo knowledge and beliefs to understand the processes of history deep into the past.

This approach, which accepts not only Pueblo historical narratives but also theories of history as valid ways to interpret the past, will raise suspicion among some southwestern archaeologists. Traditionally, archaeologists have taken two general approaches to using ethnography and incorporating Pueblo voices to understand the past: they can either be used at face value, or they cannot (Spielmann 2005). In fear of the tyranny of the ethnographic present (Whiteley 2004), archaeologists are wary of assuming similarity between the present and the past. The concern is that the gulf between Pueblo archaeology's focus on the pre-Hispanic period and the ethnography of the twentieth century is much too wide and that four centuries of European colonization has wrought dramatic transformation in subsistence and land use, demography, social and political and ceremonial systems, and language (Dozier 1970). From this perspective, European colonization is sometimes seen as corrupting a pristine Pueblo world, destroying its people and ways of living and infiltrating those who remained with foreign religion, economics, and social ideas. The effects of colonization have not only been the preoccupation of archaeologists but ethnographers as well, for Elsie Clews Parsons (1996[1939]:1104) devoted an extended discussion in *Pueblo Indian Religion* to parsing out foreign elements in Pueblo ethnography to determine precontact beliefs.

The argument against continuity between the present and the past, therefore, is that great change occurred over the past four centuries and that the modern people are no longer representative of their ancestors. But from a Pueblo perspective change and continuity are linked. In fact, *it is through the processes of change that we best see these continuities.* In a recent volume (Duwe and Preucel 2019), archaeologists and Pueblo scholars and elders explore the inherent dynamism of movement in Pueblo life and history. Each Pueblo people has oral traditions that recount an emergence in the far north or west and a subsequent migration to their prophesied middle place. Along the way, and in concert with archaeological data, the people changed, for "as clouds shift and seasons change, so do human thoughts and human-made processes" (Swentzell, quoted in Naranjo 2009:4). Fluidity of movement and change is something that happened, continues to happen, and is a bedrock principle of Pueblo thought (Naranjo 1995). The Pueblos view continuity through an ancient and fundamental set of philosophical principles that guide the people on a never-ending and directed journey toward an ideal existence. Both the people today and their ancestors have followed this path. As Paul Tosa and Octavius Seowtewa (2019:255), from Jemez and Zuni, respectively, explain, "While our clothing and pottery have changed over time, our culture remains the same."

Support for the antiquity of modern Pueblo philosophy, espoused in *Always Becoming*, is best expressed in the emergence and migration traditions. When the people emerged into this world, they were considered "unripe" or not yet fully formed (Ortiz 1969:16–17). The people were then sent to find their middle places, and along the way began the process of becoming by meeting and separating, suffering loss, and overcoming adversity. The history of the ancestors is recorded in what archaeologists consider *sites*: ancestral villages, shrines, and fields. Beyond reminding the people about their history, these places are imbued with critical meaning about how to survive in the world today (Silko 1995:158). They also provide examples of morally and philosophically appropriate behavior that continue to guide the Pueblo people on their endless path.

The antiquity of this philosophy is also supported through comparative ethnography. All Pueblo people share concepts of being and becoming and comparable ideas of the size, shape, and nature of the world. This fact was marveled at by Parsons (1933:6), who viewed all Pueblo beliefs as practically identical. It was the combination and emphasis of the elements of these beliefs that constituted difference. How far into the past these concepts extend leads to a whole other discussion, although one could make an argument that these concepts go as far back as some 1,500 years with the emergence of fundamentally Pueblo traits: a reliance on maize agriculture (Reed 2000), the creation of architectural form and orientation (Lipe 2006; Van Dyke 2008), and a common iconography (Hays-Gilpin and Hill 1999). Irrespective of its antiquity, shared philosophy among Pueblos suggests that these concepts were present *at least* as recently as the Four Corners diaspora of the thirteenth century, when the Pueblo people separated and traveled to establish their modern middle places (Preucel and Duwe 2019).

AN ARCHAEOLOGY OF BECOMING

Mirroring contemporary debates on the "crisis of representation" and the growing doubts about the generalizing principles of anthropology (Marcus and Fischer 1986:8), Swentzell (1991:180) states that "it cannot be denied that modern Pueblo people are closer to the sensibilities of the Anasazi world than are the Western-European archaeologists." She goes on to argue that archaeologists have dismissed Pueblo ways of knowing in the writing of history as insufficient as hard evidence or scientific proof. This is ironic because these archaeologists, while suppressing the intuitive knowledge of the Pueblos, have in turn interpreted the past through the lens of their own Western biases and projected those biases onto their own archaeological reality. "Pieces of what archaeologists perceive in their interpretations *might* correspond with what the Anasazi/Pueblo people see as reality," Swentzell (1991:179) explains, "but seeing the entirety, with all its sensibilities and understandings, is impossible." She goes on to implore archaeologists to look beyond a positivistic approach, writing that "the focus on the material as opposed to the spiritual world is part of scientific thinking. Yet, traditional Pueblo people are intensely spiritual" (Swentzell 1991:178–179).

To guide my own thinking, I find it useful to return to the beginning of this chapter and use *Always Becoming* as an illustration to outline possible goals. I focus on four interrelated categories: (1) the world is always in a state of flux, (2) people and their worlds are interconnected, (3) people are constantly engaged with their larger worlds through stewardship and renewal, and (4) that the process of becoming is never complete.

THE WORLD IS IN A CONSTANT STATE OF FLUX

Movement, rather than stasis, is essential to the health and well-being of the Pueblo people (Naranjo and Swentzell 1989). As discussed earlier, Pueblo history tells the stories of people in constant flux, forever undergoing re-creation and transformation (Swentzell 1993:141). Yet at the same time "the ancient people perceived the world and themselves with that world as part of an ancient, continuous story composed of innumerable bundles of other stories" (Silko

1995:158). Pueblo history and Pueblo ways of knowing stress the concept of *continuity through change*.

Thinking about history as a continuous story is considerably different from the traditional view that privileges periodic transformation over transformative continuity, as exemplified by archaeology's use of chronologies and classification systems. In 1927 leading archaeologists working across the American Southwest devised the Pecos Classification, which organized Pueblo history into discreet time periods associated with specific material culture traits (Woodbury 1993). Archaeologists, who were creating intricate pottery seriations (Kidder 1936), soon incorporated the new field of dendrochronology to begin building high-resolution regional and intersite chronologies and thereby cemented the Pecos Classification into Western calendric time (Haury 1935). The system they created incorporated both concepts of cultural evolution and material-based culture areas. For example, the Pueblo III period (1100–1350), also called the Great Pueblo period, is characterized by cliff dwellings, standing masonry architecture, black-on-white pottery, and extended burials. The subsequent Pueblo IV period (1350–1600), or Regressive Pueblo period, includes large villages that surround a plaza, increased competition, and red, orange, and yellow pottery. For the past ninety years, archaeologists, regardless of their theoretical orientation, have continued to use this classification system and have focused on the transition between these periods rather than the dynamism within or the continuity between them. In the case of the Pueblo III–Pueblo IV transition, a time of perennial interest (and a focus of this volume), debate has centered on how to best explain this transformation, either through historic processes of movement or through evolutionary and environmental processes (Ortman 2012). Only recently has attention been paid to the experience of the people themselves, either migrants or their new neighbors.

Southwestern archaeologists have also contributed to widening the gulf between the present and the past—and the break in the continuous path—by constructing the concept of prehistory. In the early years, southwestern archaeologists sought to differentiate and distinguish themselves from historians as trained prehistorians (Fowles and Mills 2017:27). With few exceptions, the bulk of subsequent archaeological research has focused on pre-Hispanic contexts, with colonial archaeology having been mostly ignored until recently. This focus on prehistory to the dismissal of the colonial era is also reflected in the Pecos Classification, where a single time period, the Pueblo V (1600–present), refers to all of Pueblo history after Spanish colonialism. This is in a classification system based on high-resolution temporal control, and it is telling that it virtually ignores the great changes cited by archaeologists who are suspicious of ethnographic analogy (Upham 1987). Besides leading to incomplete and fractured scholarship, the history/prehistory divide also denies Pueblo people agency in telling their histories and determining their futures (Lekson 2009; Schmidt and Mrozowski 2013) and "continues to render Indian experiences of the present or Indian aspiration for the future opaque" (Ortiz 1977:22).

An archaeology of becoming, then, must be centered on the continuity and the unbroken connection between the Pueblo past, present, and future. This means focusing holistically on the entirety of Pueblo history and giving equal weight to the happenings before and after European colonization, including the experiences of the Pueblo people today. As we will see later in the chapter, the Pueblo people experience history not as events remembered in the past but as referents for present and future action. Recent archaeological research demonstrates that through their long history, and particularly through colonial encounters (Aguilar and Preucel 2019), Pueblo people acted on their deeply ingrained philosophy as a strategy for survivance in a world that was constantly in flux.

We should also be cognizant of the ways in which our chronologies and classifications impose a model of stasis and change foreign to Pueblo belief. Fowles and Mills (2017:49) note that the distinction between history and prehistory separates humanity into two categories of people: historic societies that embrace change and whose citizens create meaningful action and prehistoric societies that are populated by anonymous masses who endlessly and conservatively repeat tradition. Change, for prehistoric societies, takes the form of external events such as drought, disease, and population pressure. But if we take the Pueblos' history seriously, change was an ever-present reality that the Pueblo people embrace as they journey through a constantly transforming world. Swentzell (1993:145) writes that the Pueblos "did not settle in place for a long time, but rather emulated the movement of the seasons, winds, clouds, and life cycles by moving frequently. They responded to the movement of floods, droughts, and social tensions. The movement of clouds told them how they should move on the ground." Pueblo history is one of disparate people coming together and moving apart, always in a state of becoming. A good metaphor is a braided stream where local traditions and histories flow alternatingly apart and together or cross paths. Pueblo people are thus linked together through crosscutting ties of movement, contact, borrowing, and diffusion (Ferguson et al. 2013).

And last, while chronologies may be unavoidable, we can seek to explore the fluidity of Pueblo people within the periods and phases. For example, the Pueblo IV period is characterized by aggregation of people in very large villages and the concurrent reorganization of social life to accommodate this change (Adams and Duff 2004). Traditionally, archaeologists have assumed that the Pueblo people valued residential stasis and that their normal state of affairs was to make a home in a fixed place for a long period of time. The large pueblos built at the beginning of the period incrementally grew until they were eventually abandoned because of environmental change or Spanish imposition. Village life appears to have taken the form of short-term sedentism in which people built, occupied, and left these places in a fluid continuum (Anschuetz 2007b). Movement and flux were the rule rather the exception, and settling down in village life simply a pause along a continuous path (Fowles 2011).

THE INTERCONNECTEDNESS OF PEOPLE AND THEIR WORLDS

Like Naranjo Morse's sculptures, the Pueblo people are literally of the earth. In every Pueblo emergence tradition the people enter this world from a lower plane (Parsons 1996[1939]). Emerging from a lake or a spring—often depicted as a birth—the unripe people set out to understand this new land and relied on animals and spirits to help them find their way to the middle place. These early relationships act as charters that structure the whole of Pueblo cosmology and ontology: the Pueblo people are but one part of an interconnected world.

Pueblo ethnographers (through the Pueblos themselves) have been stressing this oneness for well over a century. Frank Cushing wrote the following about the Zuni.

> The *A-shi-wi*, or Zuñis, suppose the sun, moon, and stars, the sky, earth, and sea, in all their phenomena and elements; and all inanimate objects, as well as plants, animals, and men, to belong to one great system of all-conscious and interrelated life, in which the degrees of relationship seem to be determined largely, if not wholly, by the degrees of resemblance. In this system of life the starting point is man, the most finished, yet the lowest organism; at least, the lowest because most dependent and least mysterious. (Cushing 1883:194)

For the Pueblos the world is an interconnected whole of which humans are one component. Also included are plants, animals, shrines, celestial bodies, and topographic features. The innate interconnectedness between people and their worlds is not an abstract idea but rather is conceptualized as pathways of energy. The Tewa call this energy *powaha*, which translates to "water-wind-breath" (Swentzell 1989). Powaha circulates throughout the world in a prescribed manner, radiating in multiple directions, both horizontally and vertically, from the underworld to the sky and from the sacred peaks that bound the world to the heart of the earth at the middle place. It passes between the inhabitants (both human and nonhuman in the world) and in the places in which they construct.

Acknowledging and establishing a harmonious existence with this interconnected world represents the "ideal beingness of Pueblo culture" (Naranjo and Swentzell 1989:258). Balance is difficult to achieve because the world is filled with dichotomies, which are recognized by all Pueblo people, including north/south, summer/winter, farming/hunting, female/male, and life/death (Ortiz 1972). Pueblo culture sees these opposites as complementing each other rather than competing with each other. For example, the qualities of both men and women are viewed as essential to the well-being of the community, and an ideal leader is strong enough to encapsulate both (Parsons 1929), as expressed by the Tewa phrase "be a woman, be a man" (Ortiz 1969:36). These dualities, particularly the distinctiveness yet complementarity of summer and winter, permeate Pueblo social and ceremonial life from Hopi (Titiev 1944:173) to Taos (Bernardini and Fowles 2011). The Tewa are perhaps the most overt in their expression of duality, explicitly dividing their villages into two halves: the Summer and Winter People (Ortiz 1969).

An archaeology of becoming must emphasize complementarities over competition. This does not dismiss the inherent tensions that compose the world. But because the world is constantly in flux, the connections between the people and their cosmos, as well as the relationships between dialectic forces, are continuously negotiated and transformed. The Tewa call the process of finding balance and harmony in this changing world *seeking life*, and it is the basic concept in Pueblo thinking (Laski 1958; Naranjo and Swentzell 1989:258). The search for this balance can be viewed as a kind of theory of Pueblo history, as the people have sought to find harmony during the great migrations of the past, Spanish colonization, and the contemporary challenges of the twenty-first century. Applying the concept of seeking life into the past gives Pueblo people voice and agency.

Also, the inherent interconnectedness of Pueblo worlds mirrors recent discussions regarding archaeology's "ontological turn" (Alberti 2016). Through incorporating Pueblo ways of knowing, archaeologists are beginning to reconsider the entangled relationships between Pueblo and non-Pueblo actors, including the connections between humans and plants, animals, and spiritual beings (Fowles 2013). These studies critique the Cartesian dualities of mind/body and nature/culture and stress a Pueblo ontology significantly different from the Western world's. In this vein, interconnectedness challenges us to rethink ideas of Pueblo landscapes. For much of the history of southwestern archaeology, and particularly through the lens of processual archaeology, the land beyond and between Pueblo villages was viewed as an economic resource, a barrier to overcome, or a measure of site distribution (Anschuetz et al. 2001). Cultural meaning has focused on villages, relating them to but setting them apart from the larger world (Fowles 2009:449). The Pueblos, on the other hand, view people, buildings, and landscapes as part of a whole, that together define their existence and beliefs.

> Harmony, balance and nurturing are also pervasive qualities in the natural and man-made spaces of the Pueblo. In the Western world, significant spaces are the man-made ones. The traditional Pueblo focuses on the natural environment and the negative spaces created by the human-made environment. The plaza or outdoor communal space is more important than the defining walls and as important as the shrines which contain the openings into the underworld. The shrines and their opening are important because they connect the interior of the earth with the human-defined space of the plaza and, then, with the sky. (Naranjo and Swentzell 1989:260–261)

From this perspective there is no separation between people, villages, or landscapes. Ortiz's (1969) discussion of the Tewa world where the people have "mapped" their social and ceremonial organization onto the valley, hills, and mountains of northern New Mexico demonstrates this interconnectedness (chapter 2). Archaeologists are beginning to draw on this and other models to embrace the interconnectivity of Pueblo landscapes to explore the ever-changing shape and nature of Pueblo worlds and histories, including identifying the relationship between ancestral villages, shrines, fields, springs, hills, and mountains (Anschuetz 1998a; Bernardini 2018; Fowles 2009, 2010; Hedquist et al. 2018; Snead 2008). One important aspect of this work is the understanding that these sacred places and archaeological sites are not relics but integral and connected parts of modern Pueblo worlds.

ENGAGEMENT, RENEWAL, AND STEWARDSHIP

Through engaging with Pueblo communities, archaeologists are learning to rethink the meaning of material evidence of the past, which they have traditionally called *sites*. This is because these places are not simply the remains of past behavior but are instead conceptualized by Pueblo people as intentional markers that ancestors left so future generations could remember their past and find their way in the present. The Hopi call these places *footprints* that track their complex and nuanced clan migrations (Ferguson and Colwell-Chanthaphonh 2006:95). Similarly, the Zuni characterize material culture (what archaeologists call *artifacts*) as *memory pieces* in which ancestors memorialized history (Ferguson and Colwell-Chanthaphonh 2006:162). Damian Garcia and Kurt Anschuetz discuss how these places—called *footprints, fingerprints, impressions*, and *imprints*—show Acoma's people the location of where ancestors traveled (footprints), what they did during their lives (fingerprints), and the moral lessons to be passed on to following generations (impressions and imprints). According to Garcia and Anschuetz (2019:45), "Archaeological artifacts, features, and sites are cherished because these resources describe how the ancestors engaged in the greatest event imaginable on the most holy of stages: the *becoming* of the Acoma Pueblo within its cultural landscape."

For the Pueblos, then, the places where their ancestors traveled, lived, and prayed are not relics of the past but are meaningful locations in the present and future. These places and their associated stories are guides for appropriate moral behavior and are also lessons for how to sustain the health and well-being of the community (Cajete 1994; Silko 1995). Collaboration between archaeologists and Pueblo communities has hence emerged from a shared belief by both of the need to protect and preserve these places for future generations and to share this knowledge with their people and, if appropriate, with the larger public. These collaborations are also tied into an ethnic of stewardship and responsibility to take care of the land for future generations (Ferguson et al. 1996).

Traditionally, southwestern archaeologists have viewed ancestral places, particularly villages, as abandoned places that were left because of a failure of Pueblo people to adapt to environmental or social change (Hunter-Anderson 1979; Stuart and Gauthier 1981; Titiev 1944). Through listening to Pueblo people, these abandonment narratives are slowly giving way to the idea that people did not fail but instead made choices to move on their paths of becoming (Duwe and Preucel 2019). Recent collaborative research has demonstrated that these ancient homes have never been forsaken by the spiritual beings, and powaha, which flows through them. Tosa and Seowtewa (2019:255) explain: "We are instructed to speak to the ancestors at our old villages, to sing and listen to the elders, to learn. 'The spirits are waiting, they are waiting for you to come,' we say."

In the Pueblo world, history is measured by space, not time (Ortiz 1977). Pueblo history literally "is the land" (Ferguson and Colwell-Chanthaphonh 2006), and visiting places ensouled by ancestors is to experience that history anew and to renew the world (Ortiz 1991:7). Because these are living places, they directly influence the lives of those who visit them. A Hopi consultant explained that "the house is alive. You feed it for strength, like you feed yourself. The home itself is a person" (Hays-Gilpin and Gilpin 2018a:135).

In an archaeology of becoming, then, we must view our work as firmly rooted in the present with implications for the future. Not only is this the way the Pueblos view the footprints of their ancestors and the shrines that are forever acting as "nodes" in an interconnected meshwork of being (sensu Ingold 2011), there are also real political ramifications in the reports and articles we write. In the Southwest these are most visibly expressed in conflict over land and water. But there are also more nuanced consequences in maintaining the connections between the Pueblos and their homelands.

BECOMING IS NEVER COMPLETE

Last, the processes of becoming, and its associated philosophy, have no end point. Southwestern archaeologists, with their focus on prehistory, have traditionally viewed the history of the Pueblo world as ending with Spanish colonization (Lekson 2009:247). The subsequent Historic period has thus been seen as corrupted, with the Pueblos being tainted by the introduction of a new religion and social and political life and by population devastation. Through an increased engagement with Pueblo people, archaeologists are faced with an important question: When are the Pueblo people?

Through the course of this chapter I hope to have shown that modern Pueblo philosophy is both applicable and appropriate in understanding the actions and agency of Pueblo people in the past. I should note, though, that these concepts are not just simply traditions that are maintained by a few elders and scholars, holdouts from a past that is being rapidly consumed by modernity. While the loss of cultural knowledge in the present day is an alarming reality, and one that is actively being addressed through programs in language revitalization and the education of youth in traditional ways (Benjamin et al. 1996; Clark and Gumerman IV 2018), the change that has been experienced by the Pueblo people over the past four centuries has also been done in a Pueblo way. To answer the question posed above: the people today are as much Puebloan as their ancestors were, and as their future children and grandchildren will be. The process of seeking life between the tensions of the world is never ending.

These tensions have involved balancing new realities with ancient traditions and have included the coming of the Spanish and the introduction of capitalism (Suina 2019). In reaction to both events, Pueblos fiercely guarded certain elements of society while giving way to new alternatives for other elements. Harmony and balance were sought in a flexible and adaptive way. Seeking balance has also taken the form of reinterpreting traditional Pueblo culture in the present, strikingly represented by Pueblo artists such as Naranjo Morse and the sculptures of *Always Becoming*. Jason Garcia, from Santa Clara Pueblo, takes this a step further and juxtaposes tradition with popular culture (Bernstein 2012:132). He and others continue to evolve a ceramic medium that was so well seriated by Alfred Kidder in the 1920s.

One source of tension immediately relevant here is the century-long conflict and cooperation between anthropologists and the Pueblo people. While anthropology and archaeology were once the handmaidens of colonial enterprise, current research seeks to find a balance between the intellectual goals of archaeologists and the intellectual and spiritual needs of Pueblo communities. An archaeology of becoming, then, needs to be flexible, adaptive, and open to possibilities, some of which might be uncomfortable and challenging. If it is, "unexpected patterns and truths might even emerge" (Swentzell 1991:180).

■ ■ ■

The long arc of southwestern archaeological history has once again returned to seeking the voices and experiences of the Pueblo people to more fully and meaningfully understand the past. But this archaeology of becoming is still yet aspirational, and unfortunately many of the archaeologists cited throughout this chapter continue to be regarded as doing "collaborative" or "social" research and not simply performing mainstream southwestern archaeology. However these approaches are increasingly becoming more common as both Pueblo and non-Pueblo students are taught to incorporate multivocality and Pueblo elders and scholars are seen as historical experts. Perhaps this archaeology can be viewed in the same way the Pueblos view their history: as an ongoing process to strive for a more perfect, and complete, balance and harmony (Naranjo and Swentzell 1989).

In the following pages I seek to write *a* history of the Tewa world through the lens of an archaeologist. I do not claim this history to be definitive or exclusive because, as Swentzell (1991:178) wrote, "there is never one truth" in the Pueblo world. Swentzell was referring to the countless truths that stem from the permutation of how simultaneous levels of existence in Tewa ontology play out among the varied histories and memories of the diverse Pueblo people. What I can provide, as a non-Pueblo archaeologist, is a cultural-historical context based on a physical record of observable material traces. These remains are interpretable using ethnographic, ethnohistoric, and historic information as well Tewa philosophical and historical perspectives. I hope these chapters are useful to the Tewa people in strengthening the bonds with their world that colonizers have tried to sever for nearly five hundred years. I also hope to contribute to an understanding of the long and complex Tewa history of northern New Mexico, a history that has fascinated and frustrated anthropologists for over a century.

CHAPTER 2
The Tewa World

John Peabody Harrington spent the autumn of 1910 hiking through the rugged hills and valleys of northern New Mexico. As a linguist working for the Bureau of American Ethnology, his task was to document and compile a compendium and atlas of place names of the Tewa villages (Harrington 1916). His work included interviews and field trips with consultants from multiple villages. The world he recorded is bound by four sacred peaks, with each village as the center. Between—in valleys and hills and mountains—are countless named places that act as places of remembrance, homes of ancestors, and spiritual nodes in an interconnected web of *powaha*. These places are inherently connected to the villages' citizens, who, deep in the past, began to map their gender and ceremonial organization onto this landscape (Ortiz 1969). The places Harrington recorded encompass historical, spiritual, and moral concepts and values written some eighty years before Keith Basso's (1996) classic work detailing similar phenomena among Western Apache landscapes. An important lesson, still relevant to anthropology and archaeology over a century later, is that the village is but the heart of a complex and interconnected world. To begin to identify and understand these diverse and nuanced landscapes through time is to understand the Tewa and their history. And to recognize that the Tewa world is both wide and deep.

The Tewa world roughly corresponds to the physiographic province that runs along the Rio Grande Rift valley known as the Tewa Basin (Kelley 1979).

The basin is one of deep contrasts and expansive vistas, from the tall and jagged Sangre de Cristo Mountains in the east to the volcanic summits of the Jemez Mountains and the broken topography of the Pajarito Plateau in the west. It runs as far south as Santa Fe and north past modern Abiquiu Reservoir and to the beginning of the Rio Grande Gorge (map 2). In some places only ten kilometers separate lush riparian environments lined with cottonwoods from snow-covered peaks that reach over twelve thousand feet in height. Much of the landscape is covered with piñon-juniper woodland interspersed with sandy badlands. Reptiles, amphibians, fish, and other aquatic life are found in the region's permanent and semipermanent creeks and rivers, and high-elevation plants and large game (deer, elk, and sheep) are found along the Jemez and Sangre de Cristo Mountain ranges. On the whole, the Tewa Basin has a semiarid climate, receiving between 25 and 50 centimeters of rain per year (Luebben and Brugge 1953:2), a factor that influences nearly every aspect of Tewa life.

The centers of this world, or rather many worlds, are located in six small communities that have traditionally spoken the Tewa language. From north to south they are Ohkay Owingeh (formerly San Juan Pueblo), Santa Clara, San Ildefonso, Pojoaque, Nambé, and Tesuque. This list, of course, does not include the Tewa-speaking community of Hano at Hopi's First Mesa, a move made by Tanoan (southern Tewa) people in response to Spanish hostilities in the late seventeenth century (Dozier 1954). Some Tewa villages are over seven centuries old, and the connectedness between the people and the land extends through time immemorial. Like other Pueblo people, the Tewa are traditionally village agriculturalists, making a living growing maize and inhabiting compact towns composed of adobe-built apartments (figure 3).

Although anthropologists have commonly grouped these villages as Tewa based on their shared language and culture and to differentiate them from their distantly related neighbors to the north and west, each village is autonomous in the governance of its people and associated lands. And the different dialectics of Tewa spoken among the villages speaks to a nuanced diversity of histories and cultural contacts. The diversity among the villages includes different ways that disparate people came together in the thirteenth and fourteenth century (Duwe and Cruz 2019; chapter 4). No less important are the Tewa's reaction and resilience during Spanish and American colonialism. For example, Santa Clara Pueblo was heavily affected by an influx of distantly related kin from the Galisteo Basin who fled the Spanish during and after the Pueblo Revolt in the late seventeenth and early eighteenth centuries (Dozier 1954). And one of these

FIGURE 3 View of Ohkay Owingeh in 1899. From "San Juan," by Adam Clark Vroman. National Anthropological Archives, Smithsonian Institution (BAE GN 02044B 06344500).

villages—Pojoaque, located north of Santa Fe—was left entirely by its residents during the same period. In the 1930s the people returned and reconsecrated the land and reestablished the village, building something new based on traditions that extend very far into the past (Catanach and Agostini 2019). Even with these differences, all Tewa people share experiences in, conceptions of, and their place within the world (Ortiz 1994).

The Tewa and their ancestors have lived in northern New Mexico for hundreds, if not thousands, of years. Theirs is a history of migrations and coalescence as they sought their middle places among the modern villages. But these villages are not remnants of the past, somehow frozen in time. The Tewa have endured nearly five hundred years of colonialism, beginning with the pillaging of Ohkay Owingeh by Vásquez de Coronado's men in 1541 (Simmons 1991) and the establishment of Governor Oñate's first colonial capital at Ohkay Owingeh in 1598 and then at nearby Yunque'owingeh the following year. The Tewa were leaders in subsequent Spanish resistance, and Po'pay, the revolutionary from Ohkay Owingeh, coordinated the Pueblo Revolt in 1680 with the other Tewa and surrounding Pueblo villages (Preucel and Aguilar 2018).

Beginning in the eighteenth century the Tewa had to contend with an increasing population of new neighbors, first Spanish and then Mexican and American. Mexican and American institutions introduced new forms of governance, policies, and economics as well as anthropologists. Yet through all this change the Tewa people maintained their connectedness with the land, their deep past, and their ancient ways. The fusion of continuity and change is readily apparent when attending a feast day. Late-model pickup trucks are parked outside the plaza. People are required to turn off their cell phones before watching the dances. And the bountiful spread that covers the tables in the houses are a mix of new and old: Pueblo maize, Spanish wheat, and Jell-O.

The purpose of this book is to demonstrate how this Tewa world, described and mapped by twentieth-century anthropologists and lived by the Tewa today, has a deep and interconnected history. This requires exploring what the Tewa call *nah poeh meng*, or "the continuous path," which connects the past, present, and future, a continuity based on timeless Pueblo philosophical and historical concepts described in the previous chapter. But the scholarship on the Tewa, like that of all the Pueblos, is deeply fractured. On one side of the gulf between the present and the past lies a growing body of archaeological research that documents the movement of Tewa ancestors, their settlement in northern New Mexico and the establishment of a unique society, and their ongoing adaptation and survivance in the colonial era. On the other side is a nuanced description and explanation of Tewa being and becoming in the twentieth century. The elements of Tewa social and ceremonial organization were first mapped by Harrington (1916) and then described by Elsie Clews Parsons (1929), but it was Alfonso Ortiz (1969), along with Richard Ford (1968, 1972a), who demonstrated how these elements united a divided society and are reflected in the society's physical world.

Of course, to understand Tewa history is to embrace both continuity and change, being and becoming. In the next chapter I examine the history of archaeological research for the Tewa and review the foundation of the culture history on which I subsequently build. But integral to our understanding of this process is the shape and nature of the Tewa world in more recent times. For although Tewa ethnography is centered in the mid-twentieth century, it describes a cosmos where the past, present, and future are experienced by traveling through and living in this remarkable landscape. Tewa ethnography offers not only a window into the meaning of places that archaeologist's term *sites*, but it also shows how these places are inherently connected to the structure and well-being of the people, as well as their ancestors and larger cosmos. Tewa ethnography is also problematic. The Tewa people have been uncomfortable and hurt when their privileged knowledge is made accessible to the public. And archaeologists struggle with an ethnographic record that seems frozen in time with little discussion of the mechanics of historical and cultural change. Regardless of its challenges, an engagement with Tewa ethnography remains necessary to understand the complex past, and possible futures, of the Tewa world.

ETHNOGRAPHY AND OTHER MATTERS OF CONCERN

The Tewa people, although practicing many traditional ways, are thoroughly modern and are one of the many communities that coexist in the complex cultural milieu of northern New Mexico. But their unique social organization, worldview, dynamic history, and persistence in the face of colonial rule have attracted the attention of outsiders for over a century. Most of our understanding of the Tewa comes from classical anthropological treatises, beginning with Adolph Bandelier's (1892) exploration of northern New Mexico in the 1880s, J. A. Jeançon's (1912, 1923) archaeological work that employed workmen from Santa Clara, and Harrington's (1916) atlas. This early work also contributed to understanding Tewa ethnobotany (Robbins, Harrington, and Freire-Marreco 1916), ethnozoology (Henderson and Harrington 1914), and language (Harrington 1910). More formal ethnographies were written in the years that followed, including Parsons's (1924, 1929) description of the social and ceremonial organization of multiple villages, Willard Hill's (1982) monograph of Santa Clara based on work in the early 1940s, and William Whitman's (1947) work at San Ildefonso. The 1960s brought more focused discussions on specific topics, including Edward Dozier's (1966) treatment of factionalism in Santa Clara, Randall Speirs's (1966) understanding of the Tewa language, Ortiz's (1969) exploration of cosmology and social organization at Ohkay Owingeh, and Ford's (1968, 1972a) research of the cultural ecology of Ohkay Owingeh. Florence Hawley Ellis (1968), through work related to Indian Land Claims, also details both ethnographic and historical information of the Tewa pueblos, work that continues through applied anthropology directed for the benefit of the Pueblos themselves (Walt 2014). This is by no means a comprehensive list of Tewa ethnography, but it certainly demonstrates the length and breadth of anthropological interest regarding Tewa communities.

As noted in chapter 1, the ethnographic record, although providing important information, is controversial for Pueblo people. Early anthropological research relied heavily on relationships with Tewa people, which provided a rich subtext for interpretation but often emphasized the gathering of sensitive information over the wishes of the community. This was well understood in 1910 when Harrington (1916:37) conducted extensive interviews with Tewa people "whose names for obvious reasons are not here given." What was obvious to him was that the Tewa were "reticent and secretive with regard to religious matters" and that the sharing of this privileged information, particularly in a book that all could read, violated the communities' trust and could place these divulgers of secrets in mortal danger. Among the Pueblos, knowledge is associated with ritual power, and therefore secrecy is a way to protect Pueblo traditions from Spanish missionization (Sando 1979), to preserve the political power of specific ceremonial sodalities within a village (Brandt 1980), and to shield the people from the prying eyes of anthropologists (Suina 1992). In a Pueblo village, no one person or society knows everything, and besides truth is ever changing. The bundling of information in the form of static ethnographic volumes was both a form of betrayal and antithetical to Pueblo epistemology and ways of being.

Early interactions with anthropologists led Pueblos to be ever more cautious in their contact with outsiders, even as increasing numbers of ethnographers arrived in the Rio Grande valley. Among these was Elsie Clews Parsons, who wrote extensively on Pueblo religious practices, including those of the Tewa (Parsons 1924, 1929). The Pueblos of the Rio Grande were rightly suspicious of her activities, and she therefore resorted to "secretive methods" and became "the most ruthless of detectives," inviting knowledgeable members of a village to locations away from the pueblo, where they were offered gifts and money (Gutiérrez 1996:viii). Parsons was aware of the questionable ethics of her research methods and tried to minimalize the persecution of her informants and the ensuing factionalism within the villages by never naming names (Strong 1996). But real harm was done, both to the fabric of these communities and to the relationship between the Pueblos and anthropologists. In fact, Ramón Gutiérrez (1996:v) gives an anecdote about how in the 1960s not a copy of Parsons's opus *Pueblo Indian Religion* (1996[1939]) could be found in the library of the

University of New Mexico; they had all been stolen and destroyed by Pueblo people as a strategy for cultural preservation.

These early encounters between anthropologists and the Pueblos established tensions that are still felt today: a struggle of power between obtaining intellectual knowledge for the benefit of all and retaining that knowledge for the well-being of the community. Tensions became particularly pronounced after World War II, when increased opportunities for higher education led to two Tewa men, first Edward Dozier and then Alfonso Ortiz, earning their doctorate degrees in anthropology and going on to teach at a university and to research their hometowns and other Pueblo communities. Both Dozier and Ortiz leveraged their cultural knowledge, linguistic fluency, and deep familial connections as "insiders" to produce important anthropological volumes. Dozier (1954, 1966), who worked at the Tewa-speaking village of Hano at Hopi and explored Tewa factionalism at Santa Clara, illustrated the importance of movement in Pueblo cultural change. Ortiz (1969, 1979, 1991) fundamentally changed our views of Tewa being through his work at Ohkay Owingeh. Transcending the insider/outsider dichotomy of mid-twentieth-century anthropology, their work was hailed as groundbreaking. In the foreword to Ortiz's *The Tewa World*, Fred Eggan (Ortiz 1969:xi) wrote that "once in an anthropological blue moon the right person comes along at the proper time and presents us with an account of a particular tribe or a particular problem which moves us to a new plateau. . . . Ortiz has delineated [the Tewa's] world view with the authority of a participant, and has related it to their social and cultural life with a clarity and economy which is as rare as it is impressive."

This complementarity of viewpoints was and is not without tension. Both Dozier and Ortiz received criticism back in their hometowns of their anthropological research. Although Tewa ritual was never his focus, Dozier's work was categorically dismissed and avoided, along with Parsons's book and Hill's work (1982), on whose project Dozier acted as a translator (Norcini 2007:143). But Ortiz, in his holistic cosmological treatment of the Tewa world, delved deeper into more sensitive issues, and he was accused of divulging ceremonial secrets.

Of particular concern was the publication of *The Tewa World*, a detailed account of Tewa social and ceremonial organization, as well as cosmographic principles, through the lens of Ortiz's upbringing and research at Ohkay Owingeh. It is a very different publication than Parsons's work. Absent are the detailed descriptions of doings and the graphic depictions of alters and masks. In their place is a more generalized discussion of the social and ceremonial hierarchy of a Tewa village, as well as its organization into the dualities of summer and winter. To demonstrate how an inherently divided pueblo ensures unity, Ortiz described how these horizontal and vertical organizational dimensions intersect through rites of passage and the annual works of the ceremonial leaders and how these same principles are reflected cosmographically. To me, an outsider, his approach appears to be one of treading carefully to not reveal too much, and he certainly did not expose more than Parsons did. But to some in the communities, because he was Tewa, this work was and is viewed as a betrayal (Johnson 1997). Through reading remembrances and talking to those who knew him, it seems that the reality is far more complicated. Although the criticisms weighed heavily on him, Ortiz remained welcomed by many in the village. He also cared deeply for his people and for Native Americans nationally, devoting much of his career to social and political issues facing Native people and mentoring students, mediating at Wounded Knee, and advocating for the return of Taos's Blue Lake (Jojola 1997; Whiteley 1999).

My prolonged discussion of Ortiz is for two reasons. The first is that the inherent tension in his life's work—balancing the sharing of knowledge with the outside world with ensuring the well-being of his community and the risks that involves—is something that anthropologists and archaeologists are grappling with in varying forms today. As anthropologists we can ask: Why are we so interested in Pueblo life and history? Who is our audience? And what is the benefit of acquiring and disseminating this knowledge? The second reason is that Ortiz's work, as well as the writings of early ethnographers, is fundamental reading for outsiders in understanding the Tewa, and in a general way, Pueblo culture. To ignore ethnography when writing an archaeological history would be academic malpractice; to embrace it raises ethical red flags, because even though the types of data collected and the motivations of the knowledge seekers varied considerably, much of this information was not meant to be shared.

Stealing books is no longer an effective tactic in a world where many of these monographs and articles are digitally and freely available. Archaeologists do, and should, struggle with their discipline's colonial and exploitative past. In regard to the use of ethnography, the key question becomes: Can ethnographic material be used to benefit the Tewa people today? I believe that the answer is a qualified yes. Ortiz's descriptions of the sacred geographies of the Tewa world demonstrate rights to an extensive landscape far beyond the boundaries of existing land grants. It also helps land administrators, particular of state and federal land, appreciate why Tewa people need continual access to these places, including their sacred shrines for prayers, gathering places to acquire wild plants for their ceremonies, and hunting grounds to procure the animals that are their livelihood. And it shows that the Tewa have a deep history in both northern New Mexico and the larger Southwest, recorded in place.

Through acknowledging anthropology's past, I believe that archaeologists can build on parts of this foundation of knowledge in positive ways, with the caveats that we are discreet with sensitive information and that we recognize it represents the intellectual property of the people we study. In this chapter, and in the remainder of this book, I draw deeply from the ethnographic record in an attempt to connect material traces of the past to a continuous Tewa history that extends from the time of emergence into the twenty-first century. I explore Ortiz's and others' work, particularly Ortiz's discussion of Tewa cosmology and cosmography, but only in the most general of terms and in ways that are necessary to relate to the archaeological record.

ORTIZ'S QUESTION

In *The Tewa World*, Ortiz asked a simple yet fundamental question: *How can a society be both united and divided at the same time?* This question holds special relevance to the Tewa, who order nearly aspect of their lives, both socially and symbolically, through the dual organization of summer and winter. Every Tewa person is either a Summer person or a Winter person, and the heads of the respective moieties alternate seasonally in directing the social and ceremonial life of the village. Each moiety has its own specific set of rites of passage, and each is responsible for seasonally specific ceremonies. The origin of the Summer and Winter People is recounted in emergence and migration traditions in which the Tewa arrived in this world from a lake in the distant north and were subsequently split into two groups. Each group traveled south on different paths to find the center of the world. They eventually came together, according the Ohkay Owingeh tradition, at the village of Posi'owingeh, in the Rio Chama basin, a major tributary of the Rio Grande. After a long time they left Posi'owingeh and founded the six Tewa villages known today.

The answer to Ortiz's question, described below, is that the Tewa world achieves integration and continuity through a number of mediations that crosscut Tewa social organization and the landscape. However, archaeologists (Anschuetz 1998a; Ortman 2012), historians (Barrett 2002), and the Tewa themselves (Naranjo 1995; Ortiz 1979) acknowledge that the Tewa world in the mid-twentieth century was the product of a complex history of migration, hybridization of diverse groups, coalescence of early Tewa peoples, colonization, and modernity. Working in a structuralist framework inspired by Fred Eggan and Clifford Geertz (Ortiz 1972), Ortiz's approach is almost ahistorical and lacks discussion of mechanisms for cultural change. Therefore, in the remainder of this book I critically expand on Ortiz's question and ask *how a society became both united and divided*. What are the histories of the Tewa's ancestors, the Summer People and the Winter People? How did they come together and negotiate the contours of the Tewa world? And how did Tewa villages persist at the very epicenter of centuries of colonial rule?

Addressing these questions requires context, and I am not the first archaeologist to be drawn to Ortiz's cogent model of the Tewa world, one that emphasizes space as well as time. An inherent strength of Ortiz's work is demonstrating that the social and supernatural categories of Tewa existence are "mapped" onto the physical landscape of northern New Mexico and are thus partially observable in the archaeological record. These features include shrines, hills, springs, mountains, and ancient villages. The following is a summary and discussion of Ortiz's work, which begins with the Tewa's origin story, both as an important history of emergence and migration in its own right and as a charter for the Tewa's social and ceremonial organization. Next, the implications of this history are explored in Tewa social and ceremonial categories and organization. Last, I relate how this organization is manifested onto the physical world of northern New Mexico, a stepping-stone to developing an archaeological history of the Tewa world.

Before beginning, a word of caution. Ortiz wrote *The Tewa World* from his perspective and research at Ohkay Owingeh. He chose his hometown because it is the largest of the Tewa villages, and it was also among the most conservative. Ohkay Owingeh was also geographically the farthest away from Keresan Pueblo influence and had a social organization similar to that of past generations (Ortiz 1969:3). Ortiz's broad sketch of Ohkay Owingeh's social and ceremonial hierarchy is based partly on historical reconstruction, as some of the social categories were no longer functional in the 1960s (Ford 1968:72). And one gets the impression, perhaps due to his structural analysis, that the organizational system he outlines is far too tidy. For me, this broad-brush approach doesn't diminish the power and importance of the work, but it should be read schematically and not as an exact record of mid-twentieth-century life at Ohkay Owingeh. The upshot is that *The Tewa World* represents Ortiz's theoretically and historically informed version of Tewa social and ceremonial organization at Ohkay Owingeh. While his discussion likely applies in a general way to the other Tewa pueblos, we should recognize that each village has its own histories, interactions with the landscape, and possible futures.

Last, in the following discussion I use the present tense when describing the Tewa world recorded by anthropologists in the twentieth century. I do this with the understanding that village life has changed markedly over the past century and that some of the old ways are no longer practiced, at least not in the same forms. But the alternative is a past tense that makes Tewa life feel dead and gone, which it most certainly is not.

IN THE BEGINNING

The Tewa know their own history. It is recorded in stories and songs and has been passed down through countless generations. And it is told in many ways (Ellis 1974; Ortiz 1969; Parsons 1929, 1994), reflecting the teller's village, their role in society, and their access to knowledge. The following version is recounted in *The Tewa World* (Ortiz 1969:13–16), which like much of Ortiz's work is based on an Ohkay Owingeh telling but synthesizes multiple voices.

Tewa history begins not with the creation of the universe but with how the people emerged into the world. The people were living in Sipofene, beneath Sandy Lake Place, far to the north of their present villages. Sipofene resembled this world, but it was dark, and people did not know death. Among the people were two supernatural beings: Blue Corn Woman, the summer mother, and White Corn Woman, the winter mother. These mothers asked one of the men present to venture out and find a way the people might leave the lake.

After journeying to the four cardinal directions (north, west, south, and east), the man found nothing but mist because the world was still unformed and "unripe." Therefore, the mothers sent him upward. In a clearing, he encountered animals, including mountain lions, bears, wolves, foxes, dragon flies, and bees. The animals rushed him and scratched him badly, and then they told him, "Get up! We are your friends!" They gave him a bow and arrow, a quiver, moccasins, leggings, and buckskin and tied feathers in his hair. Painting his face black, they told him he had been accepted by them. The man returned to the lake as Mountain Lion, also known as the Hunt chief, the first of the Made People (ceremonial leaders of the people).

The Hunt chief gave an ear of white corn to one of the other men and stated, "You are to lead and care for all of the people during the summer." He then handed an ear of white corn to another man and said, "You shall lead and care for the people during the winter." In this way the Summer and Winter chiefs were instituted and joined the Hunt chief as Made People.

Meanwhile, among the people under the lake were six pairs of Towa é, or little boys with warrior characteristics. A pair of Towa é was sent to the north, west, south, and east and zenith to explore this new world. Each pair found that the earth was still soft, or "unripe," but they also reported seeing mountains. The Towa é of the cardinal directions each picked up and threw mud and created four *tsin*, or flat-topped hills. Finally, the pair associated with the nadir ventured out and found that the ground had begun to harden. The people were heartened and began preparation to leave the lake. The Towa é journeyed forth to the tsin to act as guards for the people.

The people emerged from the lake and soon realized that they could not easily walk. The ground was still unripe. The Winter chief solved this problem by freezing the ground with hoarfrost. After much walking, the people began to fall ill and found that the corn mothers had been filled with stones and spines, and hence was the first appearance of witchcraft. After replacing these stones and spines with more blessed filling, the people continued to march but again fell ill. Upon returning to the lake, the Ke, or medicine man, was made to aid and cure the people and join the ranks of the Made People.

After beginning to journey once more, the people reached a great river. Magpie set his tail across the river, allowing the people to cross over. The Towa é, the Summer and Winter chiefs, and many of the people had crossed the river when Magpie removed his tail. Many people were left on the other side, and these were the ancestors of the non-Pueblo people of New Mexico: the Navajo, Ute, Apache, Kiowa, and Comanche. The people returned to the lake three more times because they felt they were not yet complete. On each return new Made People were instituted. These include the Kossa and Kwirana (clowns), who were created to uplift the spirits of the wandering Tewa after they came back to the lake dejected. Also, to ensure success in warfare, the Scalp chief was instituted, and then the Women's society to assist the Scalp chief. The people were finally complete and ready to begin their migration to find the middle place.

The Hunt chief decided to split the Tewa into two groups, the Summer People and the Winter People. Each was headed by the Summer and Winter chief, respectively. Each group was sent south, over opposite places on the landscape and on either side of the Rio Grande. The Summer chief and his people traveled along the Jemez Mountains in the west and subsisted on different kinds of fruits. The Winter chief journeyed through the Sangre de Cristo Mountains in the east and ate deer and elk. On their travels southward, the people stopped twelve times. Individuals who died on the journey were buried near the villages and stones were piled over the graves. These stops are represented by the ancestral Tewa villages on both sides of the Rio Grande.

In harmony with Tewa social and ceremonial organization, the two groups came together at the village of Posi'owingeh, in the Rio Chama valley where they prospered in their new lives and stayed for a long while.[1] Eventually, an epidemic decimated the village's population and the pueblo's elders decided to move. The people split into six groups, each group maintaining the Summer and Winter People. The chiefs and other Made People were replicated as well when the six modern Tewa pueblos were founded.

SUMMER AND WINTER PEOPLE

As told in the emergence and migration tradition, the dual-division of Summer and Winter People (what anthropologists have termed *moieties*) is the primary group membership among the Tewa, and it permeates all aspects of life (Ortiz 1965). The origin tradition specifies that the peoples are two populations with a shared history but different historical trajectories.

Every Tewa person identifies as a Summer or Winter person. This identity is bestowed through the paternal line but can be flexible in response to life events, such as marriage. Heading the Summer and Winter People, and the

---

1. Depending on the teller and their village, this place varies. For example, consultants from Nambé, San Ildefonso, and Ohkay Owingeh named the village of Tekhe'owingeh, located near Pojoaque Pueblo (Duwe and Cruz 2019), as the place where the two groups met (Harrington 1916). Ortiz (1969:16), writing another Ohkay Owingeh tradition, names Posi'owingeh in the Chama Valley. And Ellis (1989), citing stories from Ohkay Owingeh, names the villages of Yunque'owingeh and Ohkay Owingeh as representing the Summer and Winter People, respectively, who eventually came together at Ohkay when the Spanish arrived and established their colonial capital. In chapter 4 I argue that understanding the place where the peoples came together is not as important as understanding the process by which they did it. All Tewa migration traditions are clear that the Tewa are an amalgamation of distantly related groups of people who joined together to create Tewa society.

village itself, are two chiefs, who are featured prominently in Tewa tradition. The Summer and Winter chiefs are coequal in authority but alternate seasonally in leading village life. From March through October, the Summer chief is responsible for the important ceremonies conducted during the agricultural growing season. The Winter chief leads the village though the cold months (November through February) and offers assistance in hunting. The Summer chief leads two months longer than the Winter chief, likely because of the introduction of Spanish wheat, which expanded the agricultural season into the early spring (Ortiz 1969:174). Together, the Summer and Winter chiefs alternate in the selection of the Towa é, who, at Ohkay Owingeh in the 1960s, served one-year appointments. These roles include governing officials (the governor, his lieutenants, and the sheriff), Fiscales (assistants to the priest and the Catholic Church), and assistants to the Made People.

The Summer and Winter People do not function as a classical anthropological moiety in that this division does not restrict marriage partners (either through exogamy or endogamy). Rather it is social and ceremonial in nature, with each people (led by the Summer and Winter chiefs) responsible for seasonal works that renew the world and channel blessings to the village. The division is also materially nuanced. While some villages (such as Santa Clara and San Ildefonso) maintain two kivas (one for each moiety), others, like Ohkay Owingeh, have one communal kiva. However, attached to this kiva are Siponene, or chambers, reserved for each people. While any initiated Tewa of the Summer or Winter People may freely access the Siponene of their respective moiety, a member of the opposite moiety may never enter this space (Ortiz 1969:42). Also, moiety members are not geographically restricted and may live throughout the village.

The Tewa village, therefore, is both united and divided. This paradox is illustrated by a Tewa person interviewed by Ortiz (1969:16): "In the very beginning we were one people. Then we divided into Summer people and Winter people; in the end we came together again as we are today. But you can see we are still Summer people and Winter people." Earlier anthropologists had acknowledged and marveled at this fact (Parsons 1929), but Ortiz made this understanding of how unity can come from division his central research question. The Tewa, like all Pueblo people, place particular emphasis on the dualities of this world. South, west, summer, female, and life can be opposed to north, east, winter, male, and death. But these opposites are not seen as being in competition with each other but as complementary; one cannot be complete without both summer and winter, female and male. In fact, the acknowledgement of gender complementarity is particularly pronounced in a common Tewa phrase: "Be a woman, be a man" (Ortiz 1969:36). In this thinking, the Summer and Winter People are equally necessary for the health of the village. A village would not be a village without this inherent division.

One way Ortiz understood this unity was by examining temporality and the cycles of Tewa life. While at any one time the village is governed by one particular people, governance is equalized over the course of a year. Also, as discussed below, the Towa é, or the mediators between the common people and the Made People priests, are alternately appointed for one-year terms by the Summer and Winter chiefs. Another example is how particular identities are emphasized during the rites of passage through the life of an individual (Ortiz 1969:30–49). All babies in a Tewa village are given a name within the first four days following their birth, and this distinguishes them as Tewa, distinct from other people in the world. The next rite is "water giving," held in the first year of a child's life. This ceremony incorporates the child into their respective moiety, depending on the identity of the father, and is directed by either the Summer or Winter chief. Later on, when a child is between six and ten years old, the "water pouring" rite is conducted to mark the transition from early childhood to the life of the Dry Food People (common Tewa). At this ceremony, sex roles are differentiated. After ten years of age, children undergo the rite of "finishing" to initiate them into their moiety. Here again, sex roles are highly emphasized, with boys introduced to the deeper secrets of their moiety's ceremonialism. The roles and responsibilities learned at finishing remain with a Tewa for their whole life. However, "it is at death that the bond of moiety is broken and the solidarity of the whole society is emphasized again" (Ortiz 1991:12). In this way the *poeh* (path) of an individual Tewa's life mirrors the emergence and migration tradition. At birth, like emergence, all people are classified as Tewa with no other distinctions. Later on, and along the journey, a child takes one of two parallel paths as a Summer or Winter person, just as the people followed the routes to the middle place. At death the identity as Summer or Winter no longer matters—just as the people came together again as Tewa at their final destination.

THE SOCIAL ORDER

Tewa life is classified along two axes that are replicated at each village and have origins that extend back into deep time. The first, described above, is that every Tewa person belongs to either the Summer People or Winter People.

FIGURE 4 Tewa levels of being (after Ortiz 1969, figure 1).

The second is that regardless of moiety affiliation, each individual belongs to a specific rung in a social and ceremonial hierarchy. The Tewa divide and classify all social and supernatural existence into a hierarchy of six levels of being. The bottom three are categories of living people and the top three are supernatural. The lowest level is the Dry Food People, or the common Tewa who do not hold any social or ceremonial authority. The second level is the Towa é, who are recruited from the Dry Food People to perform year-long political work. The third level is represented by the Made People (Patowa), who act as social and ceremonial leaders of the people (figure 4).

The three upper categories are supernatural counterparts to the three categories of living people. Level 4, the Dry Food People Who Are No Longer, is made up of the souls of the deceased Dry Food People. Level 5, or the Towa é, is the supernatural counterpart to living Towa é, or the six pairs of brothers who journeyed out before the people at emergence and continue to watch over the Tewa from the tsin and mountains. And at level 6 is the Dry Food People Who Never Did Become. This level includes the souls of the Made People after death as well as all the deities in the Tewa world. Each category has referents in the emergence and migration tradition, and each is interconnected to the others, as well as to the moiety system. However, for sake of clarity, I discuss the three lower categories of human existence (and their supernatural counterparts) separately.

DRY FOOD PEOPLE

At the water pouring rite, a Tewa makes the transition from being an innocent child to becoming a socially aware person. The transition mirrors the tradition of the Tewa people emerging into this world and becoming "ripe," or with reason. The Tewa use the term *seh t'a*, which is translated as "dry food," from *seh* (a prepared dish, but can be extended to all matter) and *t'a* (hardened, dry, or ripe).

When referring to the emergence, the people became hardened matter as they began their path on the newly ripened earth (Ortiz 1969:16). And through the transition into reasoning children become Seh t'a (Dry Food) People as they begin their parallel path toward being members of Tewa society.

All Tewa people who emerged into this world, and those who are born today, began their early lives as Dry Food People. This category is for Tewa with no social or ceremonial authority, although they may achieve this later in life by becoming Made or, on a temporary basis, Towa é. As common Tewa, these people, although lacking the knowledge and skills to conduct and organize the works that maintain the balance of the world, are nonetheless integral in achieving these goals. All Tewa, often through their respective moiety, participate in dances, and the men have responsibilities in the kiva. But according to Ortiz's (1969:82) consultants, it is not good for one to be a Dry Food Person their whole life, and at the turn of the twentieth century nearly every adult at Ohkay Owingeh belonged to a group of Made People.

Upon death, the souls of the Dry Food People travel to the four directional shrines surrounding the village (see below) for a period of four days. They then are released to freely travel throughout the Tewa world as the fourth category of being, the Dry Food People Who Are No Longer. These souls, unlike those of Made People, do not return back to the primordial lake with the deities but instead continue to dwell in this world at ancestral villages and blessing places (Ortiz 1969:52). Because a soul may freely travel between these places, the myriad of shrines that cover the Tewa world may be visited to pay respects to the deceased. I will return to this point again when talking about the Tewa's ongoing engagement with their world.

TOWA É

The Towa é is an enigmatic category that demonstrates the fusion of traditional Tewa beliefs with Spanish political and religious concepts. Simply put, the Towa é are the executive arm of the Made People and are alternately selected by the Summer and Winter chiefs for one-year terms, historically, at Ohkay Owingeh. The Towa é comprise three groups. Spanish officials make up the first group, which includes the governor, his two lieutenants, and the *aguacil* (sheriff). These positions were introduced by the Spanish in the seventeenth century. The second group is the Towa é (War Chiefs), who assist and guard the Made People as well as coordinate ceremonial events in the village. The third is the Fiscales, who assist the Catholic priest and perform duties at the church. Based on the excavations of San Gabriel del Yunque (Ellis 1989), described in chapter 6, this group, too, may have had its beginning in the early seventeenth century.

The number of Towa é totals fourteen individuals, and they are selected by the Summer and Winter chiefs from the ranks of the Dry Food People. The selection process for the three groups alternates between the chiefs (Ortiz 1969:63). For example, in one year the Summer chief may begin the selection for the position of governor, and the Winter chief would then select the first lieutenant governor. This process continues for all three groups, with the Summer chief choosing the leader for all. In the subsequent year this process is reversed and the Winter chief begins the selection. Thus, within two years the selection of the Towa é is equally balanced between the moieties.

For a term that spans a calendar year, the Towa é sit "on cloud blossoms" (Ortiz 1969:67), meaning that they have temporary supernatural authority to aid in the work of the Made People and the village. The Spanish officials and the Fiscales are certainly historically recent in that they pertain to situations arising in the last four centuries (Ortiz 1969:71). The origins of the Towa é (the subcategory within the Towa é), however, are undoubtedly much more ancient. This group has two primary duties, and members are selected based on their knowledge and commitments to Tewa ritual (Ortiz 1969:69). The first duty is to coordinate all of the ceremonies planned by the Made People and participated in by the Dry Food People. This includes ensuring that all able Tewa are involved. The second duty is to serve as guards and lookouts for the Made People on all pilgrimages and at all retreats and when the Made People leave the village (Ortiz 1969:72). This role of lookout closely mirrors the Towa é in the emergence and migration traditions who, from the tsin (flat-topped hills), watch over and guard the people. The spiritual Towa é, the fifth category of Tewa being, are therefore the corporal Towa é's patrons. Ortiz (1969:61) explains that disentangling the complex history of the Towa é has been impossible but that based on a close association with Made People societies, this group likely has deep roots extending far back in time and may have once been a permanent category (Curtis 1926:4). With the arrival of the Spanish, these roles have been combined with other political positions in the last five centuries.

The Towa é as a group act as mediating figures in the village. Their main function is as an intermediary between the common Dry Food People and the Made People, the latter who as a rule do not directly interfere with daily life (Ortiz 1969:74). The Towa é transcend the moiety division, being from both the Summer and Winter People, and can directly intervene in the affairs of the village. They are also an important check on the Made People's authority. This is most dramatically demonstrated when the Towa é impersonate the Tsave Yoh, or the masked supernatural whippers who live under the tsin. Every year around the time of the Turtle Dance at the winter solstice the Tsave Yoh come to the village and flog those who have disobeyed the Towa é in the previous year, and this can include the Made People (Ortiz 1969:75). Therefore, the Towa é act both to execute the Made People's will for village life and to advocate on behalf of the Dry Food People.

MADE PEOPLE

The Made People (Patowa) organize and control all ceremonial activity of the village and are the power behind the Towa é. The term *Made People* can be translated as "completed" or "become," meaning that this category represents the apex of the social hierarchy of living people, the furthest along the path toward an ideal existence (Ortiz 1969:79). This category includes a diverse group of leaders, priests, and specialists who perform "works" organized by the Summer and Winter chiefs to ensure the health and well-being of the village, its people, and the world.

The Made People are organized into eight hierarchical groups, or societies (figure 5). Each group has a head, two lieutenants (a right and left arm), and multiple lay assistants. At the top of the hierarchy are the Summer and Winter chiefs, who represent the leadership of the moiety structure and alternate ceremonial control of the village throughout the year. The chiefs organize all major works, which are then followed by the other Made People societies and performed by the Dry Food People. While the Summer and Winter chiefs and their assistants necessarily need to be of their respective moiety, the members of the other six societies transcend this division and are "in the middle of the structure" (Ortiz 1969:91). Members are recruited from either moiety and perform their doings without bias to either Summer People or Winter People. These societies, besides assisting in guiding the village, people, and world through seasonal cycles, also perform specific tasks important for the welfare of the community. Made People who practice Bear Medicine, or the medicine men, cure the ill and confront witchcraft. Next are the Kossa and Kwirana, clowns, who serve important ceremonial duties, enforce traditional values, and entertain the people. They are followed by the Hunt society, which ensures success in hunting and organizes communal hunts. Last, the Scalp and Women's societies are closely related—the Scalp aided endeavors in battle and the Women's society assisted in these activities.

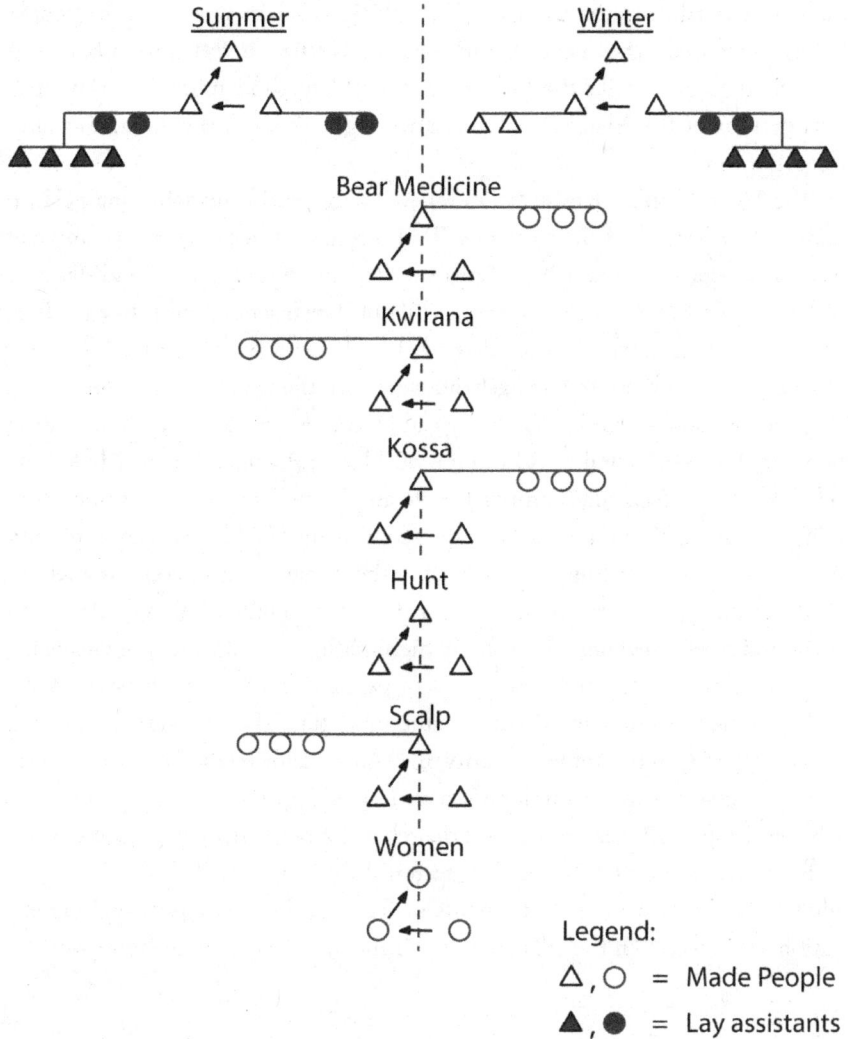

FIGURE 5 The Made People (after Ortiz 1969, figure 7).

Recruited from the Dry Food People, the Made People serve for life. Upon death, their souls travel backward along the original migration path and return to the lake of emergence. They join the Oxua, or cloud beings, who travel the entirety of the cosmos and bring rain and blessings to the people (Ortiz 1969:96). The Oxua are joined with other deities and constitute the ultimate category of Tewa being: the Dry Food People Who Never Did Become. This name is derived from the fact that although these spirits were with the people before emergence, they never became seh t'a (Ortiz 1969:91). The Oxua also includes high deities like the sun, moon, stars, plants, and animals and the specific patrons of the Made People societies highlighted in the emergence and migration traditions.

The Made People are essential in renewing the world and achieving balance between the Tewa and their cosmos. Their presence is also the key to answering Ortiz's question about how Tewa society can be both united and divided. The Made People are "those of the middle of the structure," and they mediate between various categories of existence in the Tewa world (Ortiz 1969:125). Because they represent the beings who were with the people before emergence, they are the most sacred human beings and therefore are tasked with mediating between the supernatural world and the world of the living. Also, the Made People mediate between the Summer People and Winter People. The importance of moiety distinction is balanced by the recruitment of Made People from both moieties and the overriding importance of the village and its people as a whole.

In summary, Ortiz examined and clarified long-standing questions of Tewa social and ceremonial organization. By highlighting both the unity of village life and the disjuncture of different classes of people, he asked the question: How can a people be united and divided at the same time? His conclusion was that inherent fluidity and complementarity of Tewa life allowed the Tewa to strive for a harmonious existence even though each Tewa village is inherently divided into what anthropologists call moieties. For archaeologists, Ortiz's greatest contribution was his focus on landscape. He masterfully demonstrated how the complex, multiscalar, and intersecting elements of Tewa social and ceremonial organization are reflected in the villages, hills, shrines, and peaks of the Tewa world.

TEWA COSMOGRAPHY

Based on the rich detail of his own fieldwork, as well as that of previous ethnographers (Dozier 1961; Parsons 1929), Ortiz (1969) sketched a Tewa cosmology that set the village as the "middle place" of a complex but structured world. For the Tewa the world is conceptualized as a sphere, with the earth as a pottery bowl and the sky as an inverted basket (Swentzell 1990). Horizontal space is bounded by the four cardinal directions: first by the four sacred peaks that bound the edges of the world and then by the hills that were erected by

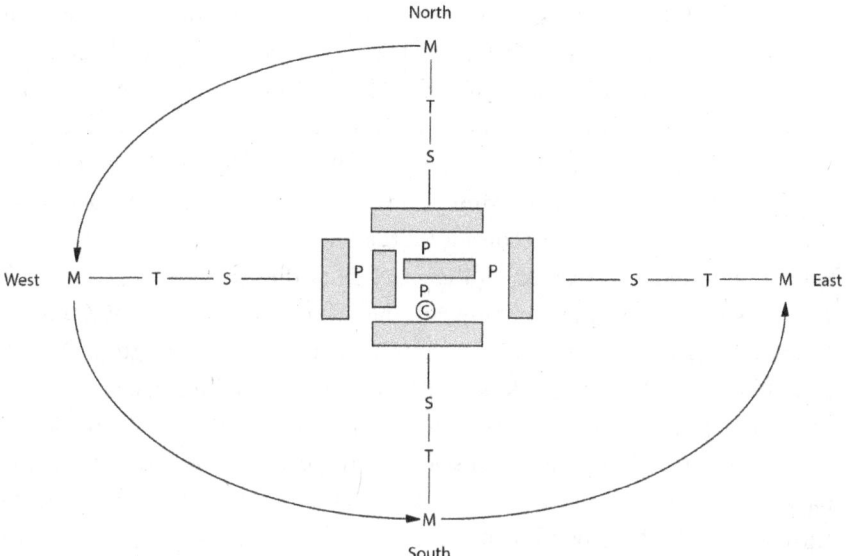

FIGURE 6 Alfonso Ortiz's model of the Tewa world (adapted from Ortiz 1969, figure 1). This includes three primary zones: the mountains (denoted by M), the tsin (T), and the village (including the shrines [S] that surround the village, the plazas [P], and the center [C]).

the Towa é (Parsons 1929). Vertically, the Tewa world is defined by three levels: the current world (middle) and the upper and lower worlds. The underworld is the same as the current (middle) world and is broken in topography. So is the upper world, although the Tewa have little concern in explaining this plane of existence (Ortiz 1969).

Long ago, the Tewa began to map their social and ceremonial system on their physical world of the Tewa Basin (Ortiz 1991). The Tewa world can be viewed as a tetrad of nested ecological zones that correspond to oral tradition, ceremonial beliefs, and social organization (figure 6). Each zone is defined by natural or cultural features that represent both a rung on the supernatural hierarchy as well as a stop on the mythical migration journey.

THE MOUNTAINS

The Tewa world is bound by four sacred peaks in northern New Mexico, which can be located on a topographic map. Harrington (1916:44) noted that the peaks are shared by Ohkay Owingeh, Santa Clara, and San Ildefonso. Ke Pin (San Antonio Peak, "Bear Mountain") in the north, Tsikumu (Chikoma Mountain, "Flaking Stone Covered Mountain") in the Jemez Mountains to the west, Oku Pin (Sandia Crest, "Turtle Mountain") to the south, and Ku Sehn Pin (Truchas Peak, "Stone Man Mountain") in the Sangre de Cristo Mountains to the east (map 2).[2] Tsikumu is in close proximity and acts as the pinnacle for each of these village's watershed and is thus considered the "mother mountain." For Tesuque, Nambé, and Pojoaque, located on the east side of the Rio Grande, Lake Peak in the Sangre de Cristos Mountains fills the role of mother mountain, though the mountains of the north, west, and south are the same (Harrington 1916:44; Ortiz 1969:141). While a quick perusal of Harrington's (1916) maps and associated place-name data verifies that the Tewa world and the known world are not correlates (the Tewa have extensive knowledge of the major features of the northern Southwest—e.g., a name for Yucca House in the Mesa Verde region [Ortman 2010]), the broad Pueblo conception of defining an edge as well as a center of the universe is strongly manifested by the Tewa. The northern, western, and eastern mountains appear to reasonably bound the Tewa historic land-use area, as recorded by early Spanish colonists (Barrett 2002). However, the southern peak, Oku Pin, is located near the present-day city of Albuquerque and is shared by Keresan and Tiwa pueblos to the south.

At the top of each of these mountains sits a *nan sipu*, or earth navel shrine (Parsons 1929:178). The Tewa believe these shrines are the homes of the Towa é, the spirits of the second supernatural level who lead the people through emergence and whose task it is to guard the Tewa world (Ortiz 1969:19). William Douglass (1912, 1917) observed and mapped the nan sipu on Tsikumu, describing it as a "World Center shrine." The nan sipu is different from other Tewa shrines because it acts to both bound the world and unify the many worlds of the Pueblo

---

2. There is some confusion about the northern peak. Harrington (1916:44) identifies the mountain as the distant San Antonio Peak, located near the New Mexico–Colorado border, while Ortiz (1969:19) authoritatively lists Tse Shu (Conjilon Peak), a much closer mountain located 20 km north of the Rio Chama, as *the* Tewa sacred mountain of the north. There are two possible reasons for this discrepancy. The first is that Harrington based his analysis on informants from multiple Tewa pueblos, including Ohkay Owingeh, Santa Clara, and San Ildefonso, and Ortiz limited his data to that of Ohkay Owingeh. The second is that the importance and location of sacred mountains can change with time. In the last fifty years Conjilon Peak has taken prominence as the northern peak at Ohkay Owingeh and continues in this role in the present day (Ortiz 1969:140; Kurt Anschuetz, personal communication 2010).

people. For example, from its center run multiple channels (or "rain roads") that point toward not only the Tewa villages of Ohkay Owingeh, Santa Clara, and San Ildefonso but also the Keresan pueblo of Cochiti, Jemez Pueblo, and the land of the Navajo. While the nan sipu on Tsikumu is best described, similar shrines exist (or did prior to twentieth-century destruction) on each sacred peak.

The sacred peaks and their associated nan sipu are the most powerful and dangerous places on the Tewa landscape. Their associations with rainmaking are particularly poignant, as mist and clouds are ubiquitous at these high elevations, and they have similar meaning for the Hopi and Zuni, where the Katsinas live (Fewkes 1922). The importance of these shrines for rainmaking is illustrated by Parsons (1929:178–179), who described the pilgrimage to the summit of Tsikumu after summer planting. The Made People sweep out the ritual roads that metaphorically lead to the pueblos; otherwise it will not rain. If a drought continues, they will return and sweep out the roads again, which witches have nefariously closed. It is not coincidental that the bases of these mountains (especially to the west and east) are the headwaters to some of the major waterways that sustain the Tewa villages.

Associated with the four sacred directional mountains are springs or lakes that represent the place of emergence and are portals to the underworld. These are home to the third and highest tier of supernatural entities, The Dry Food People Who Never Did Become. The most important of the supernatural entities, the Oxua (which include the spirits of deceased Made People), guard the entrances to these bodies of water. Similar pilgrimages for rainmaking were recorded from Nambé (Parsons 1929:179) and Ohkay Owingeh (Ellis and Hammack [1968], cited in Marshall and Walt [2007:F-5]) to Truchas Peak in the Sangre de Cristo Mountains in the east.

In the origin tradition, the Summer People traveled along the west side of the Rio Grande and were associated with the Jemez Mountains, and the Winter People traveled on the east side of the river and were associated with the Sangre de Cristo Mountains. The sacred mountains, Tsikumu and Truchas Peaks, part of the Jemez and Sangre de Cristo Mountains, respectively, appear to be imbued with duality. Parsons (1929:178) notes that on the annual pilgrimage to Tsikumu to pray for rain, the Summer chief arrives before the Winter chief. Additionally, Truchas Peak (or Lake Peak) is primarily a shrine of the Winter People (Ortiz 1969:165, n.3), although it is likely that the heads of both peoples ascended the summit. If this is true, this practice is in keeping with the Tewa cosmological conception of duality: although one people may temporarily be the leader, through a series of checks and balances all ceremonial and social life is balanced between the two over time and space.

THE HILLS

Between the mountains and the village lie the hills and mesas of Tewa country. These are the areas where both men and women hunt small game and forage for plants (food and medicinal/ritual herbs). This zone also includes land used for farming and is where the Made People conduct their doings for rainmaking (Jeançon 1923:53) and hunting (Parsons 1929). It is also the location of the tsin, directionally specific flat-topped hills, which are associated with the Towa é.

These hills, or tsin recalled from the Tewa emergence and migration tradition, were created by the Towa é. Pairs of Towa é ventured out into the unripe world and shot arrows to define the directions. They then threw mud to create the flat-topped hills of the directions, and upon the emergence of the people, took to the tsin to watch over and protect the Tewa. The tsin are therefore considered sacred because they are the homes of the Towa é. However, they are also foreboding places because it is believed that the Tsave Yoh, or masked supernatural whippers, inhabit the caves and tunnels within the hills (Ortiz 1969:19).

The tsin also help to define boundaries within the Tewa world. While the modern Tewa villages claim equal share to the sacred directional peaks, each village has its own specific set of tsin. Ortiz (1969:19) lists the tsin from Ohkay Owingeh: "The northern hill is Tema Yoh, located just above the small Spanish village of La Madera. A few miles to the southwest is Toma Yoh; Tun Yoh is between San Ildefonso and Santa Clara pueblos to the south, while Tsi Mayoh is near the Spanish village of the same name (the modern town of Chimayó), east of San Juan." Harrington (1916) describes San Ildefonso's tsin, which are different from the tsin of both Ohkay Owingeh and Santa Clara pueblos. The villages do, however, share the tsin of Tun Yoh, also known as Black Mesa, directly north of San Ildefonso. The geography of tsin highlights the specific cosmographies of Tewa villages.

This landscape, among and between the tsin, is filled with shrines, many of which are associated with hunting and farming. Hunting shrines made up of circular rock rings are located in areas where big and small game congregate (Ortiz 1969). Men coming and going from the hunt leave small offerings, such as cornmeal or animal bones (Parsons 1929:241). Shrines for agriculture can take the form of small boulder "field shrines" (Anschuetz 1998a) and large rock rings that anthropologists call world-quarter shrines. World-quarter shrines are used by the Made People to encourage rain and blessings to flow to the people (Jeançon 1923).

The landscape of the tsin is not exclusively the domain of men and ceremonial leaders. Ortiz (1979:284) describes this environment as a mediating area between the opposites of Tewa life. Women and Dry Food People may travel between the tsin to hunt and collect plants (Ford 1968:198), but they must be wary and watchful. Travelers who wander too close to the caves of the hills, where the Tsave Yoh live, risk being drawn into the labyrinths beyond; women and children are encouraged to be accompanied by men on these journeys (Ortiz 1979). The use of this landscape by both men and women makes the tsin sexually ambiguous, unlike the dangerous and forbidden mountains, which are restricted to men, and the village center, which is controlled by women.

The landscape of the tsin also mediates between the social and ceremonial levels of Tewa society (Ortiz 1979:284). Through their connection with the mythical Towa é, who from the tsin guard the Tewa people, the Towa é as a social category controls this sphere, as is made apparent with a specific shrine north of Ohkay Owingeh (Ortiz 1969). The Towa é act as middlemen between the common Dry Food People and the Made People by temporarily rising from the ranks of the Dry Food People to assist in the vital ceremonialism of Tewa life. They also serve as a check on Made People authority. Because this landscape is open to all classes of Tewa people, it represents a geographic metaphor of the tensions and balance, and also the ambiguity, of this intermediary space.

THE MIDDLE PLACE

The Tewa view the village as the heart of the world. It represents the middle place, where the Summer and Winter People come together, and acts as an axis mundi for both the horizontal and vertical dimensions of the cosmos. Ortiz (1969) originally described the village as encompassing two separate spheres: the heart of the village and its immediate environs. He later (1979:283) viewed the spheres as one inclusive microenvironment.

Archaeological mapping of ancestral villages (discussed in chapter 5) demonstrates that core aspects of Tewa communities have changed little from the mid-fourteenth century to the present day. The village is composed of a series of adobe-built apartment complexes (termed *roomblocks* by archaeologists) that surround an open plaza, or plazas. Within these plazas are round semisubterranean structures called *kivas* that serve as loci for ceremonial activity. Outside the plaza, beyond the roomblocks, are situated ash piles (what archaeologists call *middens*), which are places where the bodies of the deceased, the ash from the hearths, and discarded tools and other material from daily life are retired.

The plaza (*bupingeh*) is the most dynamic place in the Tewa cosmos and serves as the center of the world. The plaza itself is swept earth, and it is defined by the houses that represent the sacred peaks. In the plaza itself sits one or more kiva and the true center, the earth mother earth navel middle place (*Nan echu kwi nan sipu pingeh*), a small and innocuous shrine that takes the form of a loosely constructed circle of stones (Ortiz 1969:21) or a flat rock (Parsons 1929:247). The Tewa believe that from this shrine extends a tunnel into the heart of the earth (Ortiz 1969:21). And from the earth navel flows powaha (creative energy or breath), which connects all the entities in the world (Swentzell 1988), joining both vertical and horizontal axes. The plaza is therefore a microcosm of the Tewa cosmos.

The plaza is remarkable not for what it is, but for what it is not. It is a void area, "empty so that it may be full over everything—the sacred and the everyday" (Swentzell 1988:19). The Tewa spend much of their lives within the plaza and on the roofs of houses, especially during the warm summer months. Dances are held in the plaza, and the world is renewed through song and movement there (Sweet 2004). These community events bring together diverse people, which can be seen today at feast days. The plaza is a place of refuge and protection (Swentzell 1988:19), and it is never abandoned but always returned to (chapter 6). The plaza is "where the drama of human life is enacted" (Swentzell 1988:16) and is a central nexus where the relationships between people, spirits, and energy are constantly in flux. It represents a "healing place," where the ideal Tewa state of balance and harmony is sought and often achieved (Naranjo and Swentzell 1989).

The sacred landscape of the middle also extends to the ash piles and farmlands surrounding the village. A series of shrines, a type of *xayeh*, dot the landscape around the village. Xayeh is a broad category of spirits and associated objects that are endowed with sacredness due to their association with souls and the past (Ortiz 1969:20). The shrines surrounding the village, described in more detail in the next chapter, are places where the Dry Food People can access the network of powaha that flows through the world (Ortiz 1979:284). At these shrines members of the household, or *ma:tu'in* (Ford 2018), conduct special prayers for crop production, hunting, and the well-being of the group by depositing cornmeal or feathers (Ortiz 1979:284; Parsons 1929:134). These shrines also delineate the outer periphery of the middle place and act as a representation of the Tewa's four-directional cosmology, with major village shrines located at the cardinal directions.

These directional shrines, or *xayeh t'a pingeh* (soul-dwelling middle places), are particularly important to the Tewa because they are where the souls of deceased Dry Food People travel to after death. After four days the spirit of the deceased is met at the xayeh by the ancestral souls. The spirit is released and travels with the ancestral souls to all points in the Tewa world, including the mountains, hills, and other shrines (Ortiz 1969:52). This connection with the spirits of the deceased gives additional meaning to the placement of many of these xayeh on the ash piles where those who have passed are buried (Ortiz 1969:20).

Village shrines are regularly visited and cared for. Parsons (1929:239) describes how shrines are tended to with offerings of cornmeal and prayer feathers from an eagle or turkey. A Tewa consultant explained to Parsons that the prayer feathers are "like telephones" that carry messages to a distance, in this case a prayer for blessings (Parsons 1929:20). Offerings can be more specific, such as laying bones of deer and rabbits at a shrine for luck with hunting (Parsons 1929:134). Ortiz (1969: 54) explained how xayeh featured prominently in Tewa death rights. On the fourth day of mourning the deceased's family would hold a symbolic feast and then travel to the nearest directional shrine to drop the pot and scatter the food. A ritual would then be conducted to release the soul from the shrine and return it to the afterlife.

The middle place—the village and its immediate environs—necessarily belongs to all Tewa people. In contrast with areas of the Tewa world (the mountains and tsin) that are much more restricted to ceremonial specialists and men, the village is viewed as the domain of the Dry Food People and women. The village is viewed as the domain of women because of the Tewa belief that women know most about the home and family and the pan-Pueblo matrilineal ideology that women control domestic space (Ortiz 1979:284). As such, Tewa gender complementarity extends to the landscape, with women at the center and men on the edge. Without both the world would be incomplete.

DISCUSSION

In answering his question of how the Tewa can be both divided and united, Ortiz stressed how every aspect, and every dichotomy, of Tewa society is organized to achieve balance and harmony between the people and their world. In some cases balance and harmony is achieved through a mediating place or organization. In others it is through the temporal rhythms that define Tewa existence. The Summer and Winter People, unique in their historical paths, are united through their semiannual handing-off of office and through the existence of the Made People, who occupy a space "in the middle." The Made People also mediate between the world of the living and the spiritual plane. The inherent tension between the common Dry Food People and the ceremonial leaders, the Made People, is held in check by the Towa é. The Towa é also act as a bridge between traditional Tewa ways and the political, religious, and social changes brought about by European colonists. And the inherent strain between men and women is viewed as complementary, with leaders like the Made People embodying both male and female characteristics, for both are required to complete the whole.

These structures of mediation are also expressed in Tewa cosmography. The landscape of the tsin acts as an intermediate zone between the peaks and the village and holds places of male Made People and their associated spiritual beings and the homes of the Dry Food People and females, respectively. It is also most expressly seen in the village itself, which is the center of the world where all paths come together.

The act of being Tewa is to live with a primary aim to seek harmony between people and their larger world. However, no society is static, and the Tewa themselves understand that through movement the people have undergone great change since emergence and journeying to northern New Mexico. Over a century of archaeological research supports this claim, and people have lived in the region since Paleoindian times and also witnessed multiple waves of migration. The last eight centuries have been marked by population coalescence, conflict, and the emergence of new systems of village life. Beginning in the sixteenth century, the Tewa world was colonized by people from the other side of the globe. And the twentieth century brought new challenges with the introduction of Western capitalism and legal codes. What are the mechanisms for cultural change? And how did the world Ortiz described come to be?

What we need is a theory of Tewa history. In this regard it is fortunate that anthropologists have not been the only ones to define Tewa being and becoming, for the Tewa people themselves have written extensively on this and related topics. Tessie Naranjo (1995, 2008), Rina Swentzell (1988, 1991, 1993), Tito Naranjo (Naranjo and Swentzell 1989), Porter Swentzell (2018), and Gregory Cajete (1994) are all from Santa Clara and have contributed writings on Tewa being. Also included are the language preservation work by Esther Martinez (1982) and the activism and historical knowledge of Herman Agoyo (2002, 2005), both from Ohkay Owingeh. This is not an exhaustive list, and it leaves out the artists whose works convey similar meaning through different media. These scholars and community members cross disciplinary and cultural boundaries and offer something the ethnographic work on the Tewa cannot: fluidness and breadth.

The lessons from the writings of Pueblo people are reflected in chapter 1. The Tewa world interconnects and achieves balance between summer and winter, space and time, and past, present, and future. Therefore, in the remainder of this book I attempt to understand Tewa history through a Tewa ontological and cosmological perspective. I write a culture history of the Rio Chama valley that focuses not only on when and where people established their middle places at hamlets and towns (settlement and population reconstruction) but also on how they constructed their world. This history draws from the people's network of relations and interactions both within and without the Chama and their past and current connections with the shrines, blessing places, and natural features of the Tewa cosmos. I demonstrate that the Chama, and in extension the Tewa world, is an accretional landscape where disparate people with diverse traditions and histories came together through a process of negotiation to create a new society and a new identity. The world they created tied the Summer and Winter People together and influenced the lives of future generations, who commemorated and reinterpreted these places. This essential connection with the world allowed the Tewa to endure colonialism by reoccupying ancient villages and embarking on pilgrimages to ensure harmony in the midst of dissonance.

But, as Swentzell (1993:141) notes, "The achievement of harmony is transitory" and the world and its interconnectedness are in a state of "constant re-creation and transformation." The dualities that structure the Tewa world—summer and winter, female and male, life and death—are both complementary and a source of tension. The constant process of searching for harmony and balance between these opposites, known as "seeking life," is therefore the most basic concept of Tewa thinking (Naranjo and Swentzell 1989:258). To find balance among dialectic forces, such as the seasons or the sexes, is to acknowledge that these dichotomies complement each other as part of a larger whole. To seek life is to avoid stasis and to embrace movement and the transformation of life that results from the tension of opposites (Swentzell 1993:45). This fluidity of movement is both temporal (the seasonal transfer of authority between the Summer and Winter People) and spatial (the movement of people, animals, spirits, and blessings across the Tewa world).

The history of the Chama must have been replete with continual tensions, negotiations, and attempts to find harmony and balance. Key events where balance was sought include the coming together of the Summer and Winter People, the colonization by the Spanish, and the impositions of modernity. In this book I attempt to view Tewa history through the lens of seeking life to understand how Tewa society became both united and divided. This approach includes rethinking traditional ideas of identity and alterity, looking for complementarities over competition, and embracing the idea of movement as both a physical and a metaphorical concept. The inherent flexibility of Tewa life, including the concepts of movement and change—in conjunction with a deep connection to the places of the Tewa world—is a primary reason why the Tewa have endured into the twenty-first century (Ortiz 1994).

CHAPTER 3

Archaeological Encounters

In July 1776, as the ink was still drying on the U.S. Declaration of Independence that signaled the birth of a new nation, Spain was on the other side of the continent actively trying to strengthen the its political and economic future. Fray Silvestre Vélez de Escalante and his party departed Santa Fe to seek a path to California in hopes of connecting Spain's colonial interests and to protect against encroachment by other European powers. They never reached their destination—turned back by the wintery mountain passes near modern-day Salt Lake City—but on their circuitous return they explored a great swath of the Colorado Plateau and the Great Basin (Vélez de Escalante and Warner 1995). Their journey took them to ancestral Puebloan villages in the Four Corners region, and based on similarities in pottery and architecture, the region was declared "nothing else than the land by way of which the Tihuas [Tiwa], Tehuas [Tewa] and other Indians transmigrated to this kingdom" (Vélez de Escalante 1778:313). Vélez de Escalante's description of the region is the first mention of Tewa archaeology in the historical record and illustrates both the incredible geographic extent and the historical complexities of Tewa history.

The material traces of the past, of which there are many, have always been part of the lives of the denizens of the Tewa world. Of course, the Tewa regard ancient villages, shrines, and fields as living places. Yet these places have also been known by latercomers, particularly the Hispanic people who settled in the hills and valleys after the reconquest of New Mexico, beginning in the early eighteenth century. While we cannot know these later settlers' precise relationship with these archaeological places, we do know they were actively engaged with the material record. For example, the northern portion of Wiyo Pueblo, near Chimayó, has been mined extensively for adobe for centuries (Marshall and Walt 2007). Through the addition of life-giving water, old Tewa walls were reconstituted as Hispanic homes and churches. And these old homes continue to retain an intensely personal role in the lives and identities of many occupants (regardless of identity) in northern New Mexico.

The archaeology of the region was not a focus of historical interest until the field of anthropology "discovered" the Tewa homeland and the larger northern Rio Grande region in the late nineteenth century. Multiple occurrences catalyzed this research, including a burgeoning American archaeology, access to the region via railroad, and intense public interest. One hundred and forty years of subsequent research has elucidated a complex culture history that extends from the Paleoindian period to the present day. Interest in Tewa archaeology began to wane by the mid-twentieth century, but in the past twenty years it has witnessed a resurgence. Much of the current work has been prompted by collaboration, consultation, and intense interest in both the Tewa past *and* the present.

In the previous chapters I explored how southwestern archaeologists are currently taking Pueblo philosophy and ontology seriously when interpreting the past. I have also specifically detailed how the Tewa conceptualize their world in the mountains and valleys of northern New Mexico. We as archaeologists, even while acknowledging Pueblo philosophical and landscape principles, are left with a daunting task: bridging these rich modern and ethnographic descriptions with an often meager material record. How can we write histories that do not divorce the present from the past? And most important for the discussion in this chapter, what type of information is required to establish and interpret these connections through time?

In this chapter I apply the principles of an archaeology of becoming to begin to explore Tewa history. I briefly introduce the long history of Tewa archaeology and research in the Rio Chama valley. For it is in the Chama that I build on Ortiz's question of *how Tewa society became both united and divided*. My goal is to provide a history of the rich pictures that Ortiz paints of twentieth-century Tewa life and to bring together the sometimes disparate narratives formed from archaeological, historical, and ethnographic data. While this history may have many truths, my goal is to explore the continuous path of the Tewa people from the time of emergence to the twenty-first century. I then detail the decade of research I have conducted in this valley, addressing the middle places of ancestral villages, the larger sacred geography, and the movement of people and materials. I also explain the work of past anthropologists and historians and that of current colleagues, on whose research I rely heavily. This is the source material for the next three chapters.

ARCHAEOLOGY AND THE TEWA WORLD

Early on, outsiders saw that the Tewa had a long tenure in northern New Mexico, as documented by Vélez de Escalante's (1778) interpretations of Pueblo migration from the north and Harrington's (1916:38) observation that many places in the region had archaic (and ancient) names. But the first strong argument linking ancestral Tewa people to this landscape was made by Harry Mera (1934), who conducted a detailed investigation of historic and pre-Hispanic Tewa pottery and tracked its distribution across space. He found that these distributions geographically correlate to historic and ethnographic-era linguistic boundaries and that the world as conceptualized by the Tewa today dates to at least the fourteenth century, if not earlier. Mera's work, and subsequent synthesis of the northern Rio Grande culture history (Wendorf 1954; Wendorf and Reed 1955), bounded the early study of Tewa history in place, a view that would only be strengthened through the publication Ortiz's (1969) Tewa perspective. This view of an ancestral Tewa homeland continues to the present day as archaeologists acknowledge a very long and increasingly dynamic history of the region (Anschuetz 1998a; Anschuetz and Scheick 2006[1996]; Marshall and Walt 2007; Mathien 1994).

The history of archaeological research in the Tewa world generally tracks with that of the larger Southwest in its evolving theoretical and research perspective. This is due to the fact that Tewa archaeology played a central role in the development of both southwestern and American archaeology (Snead 2001). The excitement surrounding the Southwest as a laboratory of anthropology was stoked in the late nineteenth and early twentieth centuries by sustained and ambitious projects by Adolph Bandelier (1892) and Edgar Lee Hewett (1906). In the first half of the twentieth century these exploratory endeavors matured into a focus on identifying culture areas and chronologies, with Mera's (1934) dating of the Tewa homeland exemplifying this approach. While a culture history approach has never faded, processual approaches affected Tewa archaeology in the form of complex models seeking to understand human-environment interaction addressing questions of village formation (Hill et al. 1996; Kohler, ed. 2004) and population movement (Kohler et al. 2004). In recent years archaeologists have begun to incorporate Tewa knowledge and beliefs when attempting to answer historical and emic-based questions about the Tewa world (Anschuetz 2007a; Ortman 2012).

Regardless of theoretical persuasion, key questions regarding Tewa history have been remarkably consistent since the late nineteenth century. This stems from the fact that patterns in the material record—of settlement and chronological control—are relatively strong and that archaeologists have focused on times of great transformation, such as an apparent influx of migrants and the evolution of village life. In addition, the classifications and chronologies that were established by the mid-twentieth century have become firmly entrenched in how we think of the Tewa past. And this entrenchment, as I highlight in chapter 1, is problematic. Of particular concern is how these chronologies divorce the present from the past and make the "ancestral Pueblo" its own unique archaeological culture, somehow removed from the greater histories of living people. These chronologies also implicitly present Pueblo history as a series of progressive but static cultural periods, with change occurring only between these units of time and resulting from external stimuli. And, as Ortiz (1977) notes, the very idea of tracking Pueblo history through calendar time is in itself foreign, for the Tewa (and the Pueblo people more generally) view history as metaphorical and cyclical.

However, dividing the past into periods and phases may be a necessary archaeological crutch. Whereas general, region-wide chronological frameworks inadequately address nuanced and dynamic local histories, they do allow archaeologists a common frame of reference to compare material culture over time and space (Anschuetz 1998a). In the American Southwest the first well-established chronology was the Pecos Classification, which placed all Pueblo culture history into a general framework (Kidder 1927). The northern Rio Grande region, with its relatively late arrival or emergence of Pueblo culture compared with longer-established Pueblo cultures in the regions to the north and west, required a regionally specific chronology. Wendorf (1954), and later Fred Wendorf and Erik Reed (1955), defined the northern Rio Grande chronology based on five periods: (1) a preceramic period (that includes what is now known as the Paleoindian and Archaic periods), (2) the Developmental period, (3) the Coalition period, (4) the Classic period, and (5) the Historic period.

In this book I have decided to maintain this convention for the sake of dialogue but acknowledge that there is both continuity between these peri-

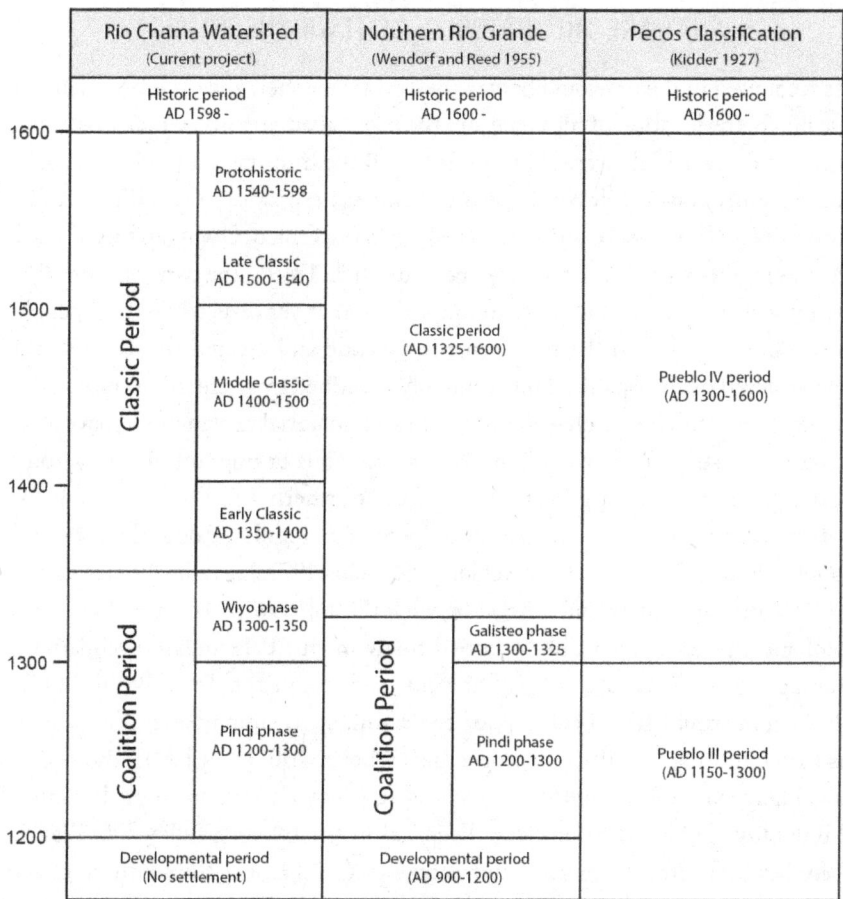

FIGURE 7 A comparison of the Pueblo culture history of the Rio Chama watershed (Current project), the northern Rio Grande region (Wendorf and Reed 1955), and Pecos Classification (Kidder 1927) frameworks.

ods (and with the present day) *and* dynamic change within them. I have also slightly adapted Wendorf and Reed's (1955) chronology to better fit the history of the Chama (figure 7). In lieu of a traditional culture history discussion for each period, I instead, for context, divide the following discussion into three perennial questions in Tewa archaeology, which will be addressed in the next three chapters: What are the histories of Tewa ancestors? How did they come together and negotiate the contours of the Tewa world? And how did Tewa society persist at the very epicenter of centuries of colonial rule?

WHAT ARE THE HISTORIES OF TEWA ANCESTORS?

As recounted in the previous chapter, the Tewa trace their ancestral homeland to the north, the location of Sipofene and the place of emergence. Upon arriving in this world, the people were split into two, and the Summer and Winter People subsequently traveled down the western and eastern sides of the Rio Grande, respectively. They eventually met, according to the Ohkay Owingeh tradition, at Posi'owingeh, in the Rio Chama watershed (Ortiz 1969). The core reality of this narrative is that Tewa ancestors comprised distinct yet distantly related people who came together in the northern Rio Grande and created the Tewa world encountered by the Spanish and eventually described by twentieth-century ethnographers. However, archaeologists, who seek material explanations, have long debated questions of Tewa origins as an indigenous or migrant phenomenon.

Certainly people have been living in the northern Rio Grande region for a very long time, with evidence of a sparse but regular Paleoindian period (9500–5500 BC) occupation (Acklen 1991; Ellis 1975:22; Lang 1980; Warren 1974). Kurt Anschuetz and Cherie Scheick (2006[1996]:173) argue that active geological processes have likely buried many in situ Paleoindian occupations, hampering our understanding of ancient land use in the Tewa Basin. While the region would have been a poor environment to support megafauna such as bison and mammoth (Anschuetz and Scheick 2006[1996]:221), the region was likely traveled through for millennia to procure obsidian from the Jemez Mountains and chert from Cerro Pedernal in the Chama Valley. Obsidian is found as far north as Colorado and as far south and east as the southern plains of New Mexico and Texas (Baugh and Nelson 1987).

The subsequent Archaic period (5500 BC–AD 900) was a time of increased land use (and likely increased population size) across the Tewa Basin. Although research on the Archaic is relatively new and ongoing, present data suggest that a dispersed population lived across a majority of the basin by the later years of this period (Vierra and Ford 2007). The area includes the Rio Chama watershed, where there is abundant evidence of Archaic land use (Anschuetz 1993; Schaafsma 1978), the Santa Fe area (Lang 1988; Post 1994), and the Pajarito Plateau (Vierra and Ford 2007). Research conducted in the piñon-juniper uplands of the Pajarito Plateau (Baker and Winter 1981; Biella 1992) reveals that middle- and late-Archaic hunter-gatherers intensively and systematically collected wild plants and animal resources seasonally, moving between high- and low-elevation resources (Vierra 2005).

Although the Developmental period (900–1200) is the first slice of time classically designated as "Puebloan," the earliest parts of this period were in many ways a continuation of the Archaic. Richard Lang (1992) suggests that the people of the Early Developmental period used the foothills of the Sangre de Cristo Mountains as part of their expanded territories to procure plants, animals, and raw materials, much as their Archaic counterparts did. Unlike in the Archaic period, however, the Pueblo occupation during the Developmental period was generally restricted to the southern portion of the Tewa Basin, to the areas adjacent to Santa Fe and Pojoaque (Boyer et al. 2010). Smaller numbers of people lived on the Pajarito Plateau (Biella 1979) and in the Santa Cruz valley (Marshall and Walt 2007) in the western and eastern portions of the basin, respectively. These settlements include both pit structures and associated surface architecture (Boyer 1998; Marshall et al. 1979). Anschuetz and Scheick (2006[1996]) suggest that the inhabitants of these sites were practicing an essentially Archaic lifestyle in the way they seasonally harvested wild foods and experimented with limited maize agriculture. However, by the Late Developmental period (1050–1200) the population had more than doubled (Ortman 2016a). Archaeologists have suggested that the increase in population might be related to the migration of people from the north or west, perhaps including Tiwa speakers from the San Juan Valley (Ford et al. 1972; Reed 1949). The majority of these residents lived in small hamlets under twenty rooms in size, with the notable exception of the Pojoaque Grant Site, which had twenty house units, one hundred rooms, and a great kiva (McNutt 1969).

The Coalition period (1200–1350) encapsulates the dramatic transformation of northern Rio Grande society from small scattered hamlets and villages to large and likely diverse villages (Cordell 1979; Habicht-Mauche 1993). The beginning of the period is heralded by the emergence of carbon-painted Santa Fe Black-on-white pottery as a regional northern Rio Grande tradition (Habicht-Mauche 1993; Kidder 1936; Wendorf and Reed 1955), a marked disjuncture from earlier mineral-painted wares (Ford et al. 1972). The Tewa Basin was also transformed by a large increase in population (Orcutt 1999; Ortman 2012) and subsequent changes in village size and composition (Cordell 1996), as well as an elaboration of ritual technologies (Wendorf and Reed 1955). Why did this dramatic change occur in the Coalition period, and what were its effects on the ancestral Tewa?

Explanations for this thirteenth-century transformation and population increase have traditionally been separated into two camps: either the increase was due to intraregional population growth and limited resettlement from surrounding regions (Boyer et al. 2010; Mera 1934; Steen 1977, 1982) *or* it was the result of the large-scale migration of foreign peoples, many likely originating from the northern San Juan and Mesa Verde region (Habicht-Mauche 1993; Harrington 1916; Jeançon 1923, 1925; Kidder 1924; McNutt 1969; Ortman 2012). Those arguing for local origins point toward a long and seemingly unbroken chain of cultural continuity from the Developmental period to the present day. This continuity is reflected in a long-lived and conservative Tewa pottery tradition (Schillaci and Lakatos 2017) and in settlement patterns and architectural forms (Anschuetz and Scheick 2006[1996]; Scheick 2003, 2005; Lakatos 2007). The contrasting argument points to large-scale population movement from the northern San Juan Basin to the northern Rio Grande region in the mid- to late thirteenth century (Jeançon 1923; Ortman 2012; Reed 1949). This migration was caused by extreme drought and social upheaval in the north, with tens of thousands of people joining their distant relatives across the Pueblo world (Ortman 2016a). Scott Ortman draws from biological, linguistic (Ortman 2012), and shared-metaphor (Ortman 2011) data and inferences to show how a massive population increase of migrants effectively overwhelmed the genes and language of local people and catalyzed the process of Tewa ethnogenesis.

Question of Tewa origins have been some of the most debated in the history of Tewa (and northern Rio Grande) archaeology and have become more heated and relevant with renewed interest in Pueblo movement (Duwe and Preucel, eds. 2019). In the next chapter I explore the competing arguments that archaeologists have made regarding Tewa origins and advocate for a "middle way": that Tewa society was formed through the amalgamation of both local and migrant communities (Anschuetz 2007b; Anschuetz and Wilshusen 2011). I argue that seeking origins is not the appropriate question in understanding the Tewa past, because in a dynamic Tewa philosophy of history there are no start and end points but rather a multitude of different histories of people who continuously seek life.

HOW AND WHY DID PEOPLE COME TOGETHER TO CREATE A NEW SOCIETY?

According to migration traditions from Ohkay Owingeh (Ortiz 1969, 1979, 1991), after traveling separate paths, the Summer and Winter People rejoined in the northern Rio Grande valley at Posi'owingeh. It was there that they built a new type of society, one based on harmony that balanced summer and winter, men and women, commoners and leaders, and the living and the dead. The village was the center of a well-ordered cosmos.

A similar transformation appears to have occurred across northern New Mexico by the mid-fourteenth century. Whereas populations in Coalition period lived in dispersed villages and hamlets over a large area, the subsequent Classic period (1350–1598) is defined by coalescence, or the restriction of the regional population into fewer, but larger, villages. This coalescence has been attributed to degrading environmental conditions as well as to increasing competition and conflict within the region (Fallon and Wening 1987; Jeançon 1923; Wendorf 1953), with places like the Chama Valley becoming population centers by the fifteenth century (Ortman 2016a). Village size increased dramatically in the early years of the Classic period, with villages of over one thousand ground-floor rooms becoming commonplace. While in some areas, such as the Rio Chama watershed, populations continued to increase (Ortman 2016a), the southern basin and the Pajarito Plateau (Orcutt 1991) actually witnessed a dramatic decrease in population as people coalesced to other areas of the Tewa Basin (including the Chama). This coalescence appears to have continued until Spanish contact in the late sixteenth century, when Tewa occupation was restricted to villages in the Rio Grande valley (Barrett 2002).

The Classic period is also the earliest that archaeologists have confidently assigned modern Pueblo identities onto the past. By the fourteenth century, pottery had undergone a sub-regionalization in style, and the region-wide Santa Fe Black-on-white transformed into distinct ceramic traditions, the most notable being glaze ware south of the Tewa Basin and a continuance of black-on-white pottery within the basin itself. The division of these traditions appears to correlate geographically with the distribution of historic Pueblo ethnic and linguistic boundaries: glaze ware is associated with the Keresan and Tanoan homelands and a black-on-white tradition (Tewa biscuitware) with the Tewa (Futrell 1998; Graves and Eckert 1998; Hagstrum 1985; Kidder 1936; Mera 1932; Shepard 1936). The most dramatic example of this boundary between glazeware and biscuitware is on the central Pajarito Plateau, where northern sites have very little glaze ware, in contrast with sites a few miles to the south that have assemblages made almost entirely of glaze ware. However, this pattern is complicated by the existence of glaze wares that were produced on the Pajarito Plateau in the sixteenth century at Puye, a village ancestral to Santa Clara

Pueblo—a possible consequence of the migration of Tano-speaking people into the Tewa Basin (Olinger 1991; Peckham and Olinger 1990). This possible ethnic boundary between ancestral Keres and Tewa people is also manifest in types of rock art on the Pajarito Plateau (Olsen 2004).

The divergence of ceramic types coincides with the apparent regionalization of social and ceremonial organization that resembles those of historic Pueblo groups. Villages in the Tewa Basin during the Classic period often have one to two large kivas that are similar to those used in historic Tewa moiety organization (Hawley 1950). In addition, ritual landscapes adjacent to these villages (Anschuetz 1998a; Snead 2008) are similar to those described by Tewa ethnographers (Ortiz 1969; Parsons 1929) and likely correspond in some way with how the Tewa mapped their lives onto the larger landscape. The reasons for this cultural florescence are debated. Archaeologists have explained these new types of village life (in both northern New Mexico and the larger American Southwest) in terms of population scalar stress (Johnson 1982) and the creation of integrative mechanisms to bind together disparate people (Adams 1991; Adler et al. 1996). Fowles (2004a) suggests that these functionalist models are too simplistic and do not account for how social and ceremonial systems can lead to *dis*integration as well. I explore the creation of new forms of village life in chapter 5 and discuss how the Summer and Winter People came together in the Chama Valley at Posi'owingeh and other villages in an ongoing process of seeking life.

HOW HAVE THE TEWA ENDURED FOUR CENTURIES OF COLONIALISM?

The Tewa recall in their traditions that after living at places like Posi'owingeh for a long while, the people were hit by an epidemic, and they left to found the modern villages along the Rio Grande (Ortiz 1969). The Tewa's unique social organization, both united and divided, was re-created at these new places, which were eventually encountered by the Spanish. Tewa scholars are adamant that their former homes were never abandoned, however, and they continue to act as living places where the souls of ancestors dwell and are nexuses for *powaha* (Swentzell 1988).

The third research question, relating to encounters with the Spanish in the mid-sixteenth century and the subsequent colonial period, has traditionally encompassed archaeological research of the Historic period (1598–). This research is the least developed in Tewa archaeology, whose focus for most of the twentieth century has primarily been on "prehistoric" periods. In the traditional chronology, "history" for the Tewa begins in 1598 when Juan de Oñate arrived at Ohkay Owingeh and a year later established the first capital of New Mexico, across the Rio Grande at Yunque'owingeh. Traditional Tewa chronology continues through the subsequent disruption of Tewa life, including a dramatic loss of life (Barret 1997), decreased opportunities for mobility (Barret 2002), the introduction of Catholicism and Spanish governance (Simmons 1991), the adoption of European plants and animals (Ford 1987), and the imposition of severe economic policy (Riley 1995). This intense period of dramatic cultural disruption was followed by the Pueblo Revolt era in the late seventeenth century (Knaut 1995), homesteading by Spanish colonists across the Tewa homeland a few decades later (Wozniak 1992:61), and the arrival of American colonists and, eventually, modernity. In short, the Historic period encompasses rapid and dramatic change that counters anything that came before it.

The majority of archaeology of the Historic period has focused on Tewa villages that were missionized by the Spanish, such as Yunque'owiunge (Ellis 1989), and it has emphasized the Spanish experience more than the Tewa experience. However, Richard Ford (1987) writes about how the residents of Ohkay Owingeh adapted to Spanish cultigens. Part of this focus on mission village was because by the seventeenth century Tewa life was centered at these places and there was no permanent settlement in the highlands that had been occupied in the preceding Classic period (Barret 2002). Archaeologists have questioned when, why, and how these larger homelands in the highlands were abandoned. In chapter 6 I explain the problems with this abandonment narrative in the context of Tewa concepts of time and space.

In recent years archaeologists have begun to realize the importance of addressing how the actions of Pueblo people in the Historic period shaped their futures and were a continuation of ancient traditions. Much of this work focuses on the Pueblo Revolt era, in which the Pueblo people actively resisted colonization and practiced survivance (Liebmann 2012; Liebmann and Preucel 2007). In this vein Joseph Aguilar's (Aguilar and Preucel 2019) recent research explores how the Tewa (and other Pueblo) people militarily resisted the Spanish reconquest of New Mexico in 1692 at Tunyo, or San Ildefonso's Black Mesa, while simultaneously seeking protection and strength (and an unbroken connection with ancient traditions) at ancestral villages on the Pajarito Plateau. Similarly, Bruce Bernstein and colleagues (2019) demonstrate how the Tewa were quick to adapt to colonial realities by accepting certain foreign elements, such as wheat agriculture, while at the same time keeping them separate and distinct from sacred Tewa cosmological and ontological systems. In chapters 6 and 7 I argue that the processes of becoming that have been so important for the Tewa through their migration and coalescence continued through the Historic period and into the present day.

ENTER THE CHAMA

These three perennial research questions form the backbone and structure of this volume, which attempts to understand how the Tewa have continued to seek balance and harmony in an ever-changing world. The Tewa world is hardly monolithic. While all of the modern Tewa villages share similar historical processes, language, and culture, each experienced the coming of the Summer and Winter People (Duwe and Cruz 2019) and Euro-American colonization (Catanach and Agostini 2019) differently. Hence each village has a unique relationship with its landscape and history. The differences in experiences have been noted by archaeologists, who have delineated a series of "districts" across the Tewa Basin to distinguish divergent settlement histories of the Rio Chama valley, the Pajarito Plateau, and the area surrounding Santa Fe, among others (Anschuetz and Scheick 2006[1996]). The upshot is that there is no one Tewa history, just like there is no one truth in the Tewa world. But because all Tewa history encompasses similar historical processes of becoming Tewa, each district can provide important insights about how this world came to be and continues to be.

This project focuses specifically on one corner of the Tewa world, the Rio Chama valley, and on the story of how the Tewa world has been integrally connected with its peaks and valleys for eight centuries. The Rio Chama is a major tributary of the Rio Grande, with its headwaters in the mountains of southern Colorado and its mouth near Ohkay Owingeh. The lower portion of the Rio Chama, from Abiquiú to the Rio Grande, runs through the northwest corner of the Tewa world. The Chama is fed by a number of small streams along this stretch—El Rito Creek, Rio Ojo Caliente, and Rio del Oso. Ancient homes and fields are perched on the alluvial benches that line these waterways. Farther afield, in the hills and mountains that surround the valley, sit shrines and hunting camps, clay pits and chert quarries.

While the Chama holds importance for all Tewa people, this landscape, as Jeançon (1923) noted through the statements of workmen from Santa Clara Pueblo, is particularly associated with Ohkay Owingeh. The evidence stems from the fact that according to Ohkay oral tradition, residents from the large villages of the Classic period moved to Ohkay and Yunque'owingeh (Walt 2014). Initiates would have been shown the boundaries of Ohkay's territory, a boundary that separated Ohkay from Santa Clara over the Jemez Mountains (Walt 2014). And Ohkay's connection with Tsikumu runs along a tributary of the Chama, the Rio del Oso, and the ancestral villages and shrines that line this creek tie Ohkay Owingeh to their landscape and history (Anschuetz 2014). I draw heavily on Ortiz's description of the Tewa world, which is written through the perspective of a man from Ohkay Owingeh. In his book and later writings Ortiz speaks of the Chama often, describing it as the place where the Summer and Winter People came together, where his ancestors lived and flourished, and where the people continue to return to sacred places. It seems therefore fitting to explore the history of the landscape of which Ortiz writes and which inspires my research.

The history of the Chama offers a unique opportunity to explore the relationship between Tewa emergence and migration traditions and the archaeological record. Unlike the eastern side of the Rio Grande, where Pueblo people had been living for hundreds of years (Marshall and Walt 2007), or the Pajarito Plateau to the south, which saw a substantial influx of people in the early thirteenth century (Ortman 2012), the Chama had no full-time settlement until the mid-thirteen century. In fact, the Chama Valley was only sparsely occupied until the early fourteenth century, when diverse groups began to settle in the upland and lowland areas. In the next chapter I argue that these groups represent the Summer and Winter People, who began a long process of cultural negotiation. The end result of these negotiations was the founding of very large villages by the mid-fourteenth century, including Posi'owingeh, which is recounted in Tewa tradition as the place where the peoples met. For two centuries these villages acted as important middle places in an ever-changing landscape, and the Chama became the largest population center in the Tewa world (Ortman 2016a). When the Spanish arrived in the sixteenth century, the Tewa were beginning to focus their residence on the Rio Grande, but their ancestral homes and sacred places continue to be visited and cared for by the people today. In this way the "sites" we study are not just markers of past occurrences but are instead living places that shape and structure the world and connect the past, present, and future.

The history of archaeological research in the Chama is long and storied. For the past 140 years the large villages of the Coalition and Classic periods—nearly permanent markers on the landscape—have received most of the attention. First recorded by Bandelier (1892) and Hewett (1906), these places were the focus of early excavation, such as Al Jeançon's work at Pesede'owingeh (1912) and Poshu'owingeh (1923) and Frank Hibben's (1937) excavation of Riana Ruin, as well as limited testing by others. In the 1930s Mera (1934) visited, mapped, and surface collected pottery from most of the ancestral villages in the Chama and the larger region to develop both the geographic boundaries and temporal depth of Tewa history in the "biscuitware area." At mid-twentieth century the large villages of the Classic period were subject to large-scale excavation. Archaeologists from the School of Advanced Research uncovered Te'ewi'owingeh and Kap'owingeh in a salvage project that had been catalyzed by the fear of destruction by a dam that was never constructed (Wendorf 1953). And the University of New Mexico (UNM) field school, directed by Florence Hawley Ellis, spent multiple field seasons at Sapa'owingeh (Ellis 1975) and Tsama'owingeh (McKenna 1970; Windes 1970). With shifting ethical and political considerations, as well as a focus away from the northern Rio Grande in the second half of the twentieth century, large projects have not happened since the 1970s. Archaeological work has instead focused on smaller-scale academic work at Ponshipa'akedi'owingeh (Bugé 1978, 1984) and cultural resource management mitigation at Howidi'owingeh (Fallon and Wening 1987).

Despite the impressive legacy of archaeological research in the Chama, the record remains in many ways uneven and undersynthesized. One reason is that much of the excavation happened in the first half of the twentieth century. Both Jeançon (1912, 1923) and Hibben (1937) did fine work for their era, but their methodologies and curation practices make quantitative analysis and regional comparison difficult. This problem of comparability extends through the middle of the century, when screening and representative collection and curation were not at modern standards (Peckham 1981; Wendorf 1953). Another major reason is that two of the largest villages in the Chama, Tsama'owingeh and Sapa'owingeh, were never substantially published. Ellis directed the UNM field school and conducted large-scale excavations. Until recently all we knew about this work took the form of teaching assistant reports (McKenna 1970), although this is changing, as both the notes and collections have become available for study (Eiselt and Darling 2013). It is also curious how a valley so important in northern New Mexico history has largely been forgotten, with synthesis and summary found only in the "gray literature," or government reports and legal documents (Beal 1987; Eiselt and Darling 2013). It is my hope that this volume begins to bring this important place in Tewa history to light for a larger audience.

In recent years archaeologists have begun to expand beyond large Tewa villages and into the surrounding landscape. Only about 10 percent of the valley has been systematically surveyed, and much of this takes the form of linear highway and powerline projects. The most substantial areal survey was done by Kurt Anschuetz (1998a), who explored the Rio del Oso valley and documented a vast landscape of villages, shrines, and agricultural fields. From this data, in conjunction with Tewa concepts, he developed a model of how the Tewa created a complex cosmology that allowed for movement and flexibility to creatively live in an arid and unpredictable environment (Anschuetz 2007a). Archaeologists have also begun to address the Tewa presence in the Chama during the Historic period, including reoccupation of and pilgrimage to ancestral villages (Anschuetz 1998a) and sheepherding (Kemrer 1992; Schaafsma 2002). The upshot is that while the villages are inherently important—they are middle places—the Tewa world encompasses a much larger landscape that has until recently been almost completely ignored.

A necessary dual focus on both the village and the larger landscape is particularly suited for the Chama. The majority of the valley is owned by federal land agencies (Santa Fe National Forest, Carson National Forest, Bureau of Land Management-Taos Field Office), with most privately owned property in the river bottoms. This particular land ownership affords researchers access to a broad landscape that is protected by both federal officers and site stewards. The valley's cultural material is also relatively well preserved; most of the pot hunting at the large villages likely occurred decades ago (Duwe 2011), and while unfortunate, it does not dramatically affect the integrity of these places.

THE PROJECT

While I draw heavily from over a century of archaeological research, this project centers on the field and laboratory work I have conducted over the past decade in the Chama Valley. In total, my project has focused on nineteen Tewa villages and their associated landscapes in the Chama Valley and two villages on the Pajarito

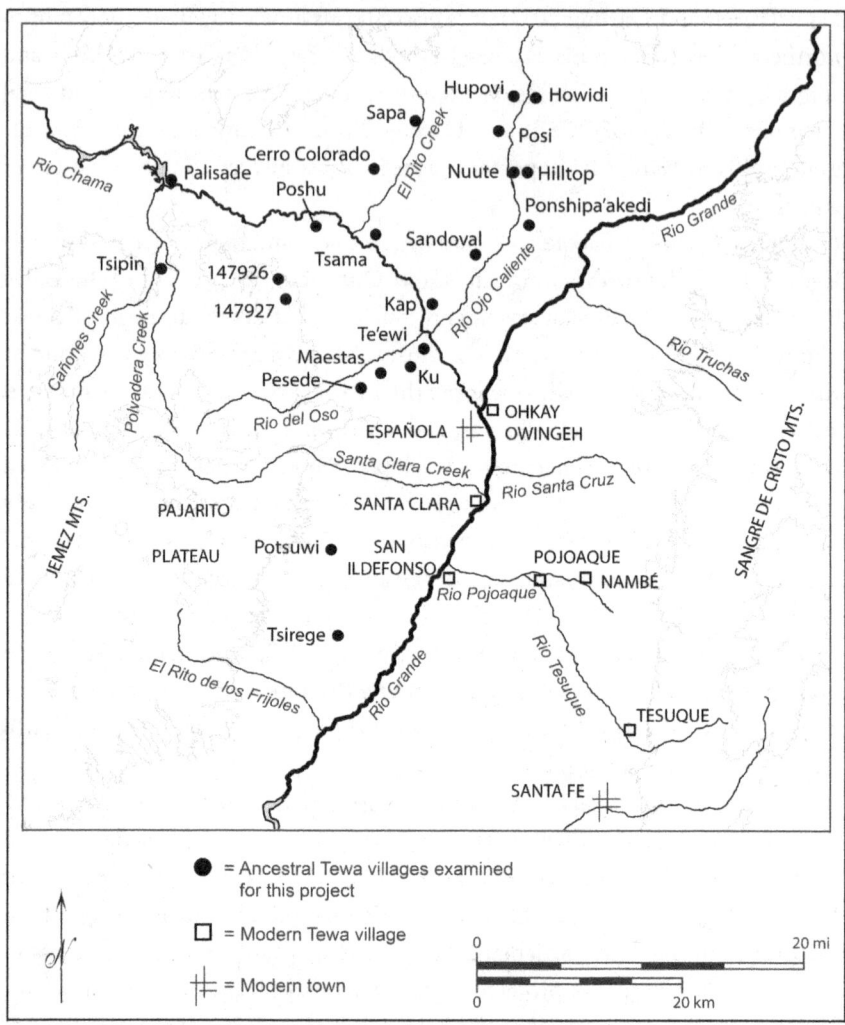

MAP 3 Location of Tewa villages examined in the current study.

Plateau (map 3). Over the past decade I and colleagues conducted various analyses, including architectural mapping, pottery analysis, chemical compositional analysis of ceramics, sacred geography survey, and dendrochronology (table 1).

The bulk of the research is the product of my dissertation research (Duwe 2011). My aim was to understand the creation and development of Tewa cosmology, and this required a detailed culture history of the Chama Valley.

TABLE 1 The methods used to examine twenty-one Tewa villages in the Rio Chama valley and Pajarito Plateau

VILLAGE	SITE NO. (LA)	DATES (AD)	MAP	POTTERY ANALYSIS	PROVENANCE STUDY	LANDSCAPE SURVEY
Howidi'owingeh	71	1377–1537	Drone (Duwe et al. 2016)	Surface/museum (Duwe 2011)	Duwe 2019	Duwe 2011
Potsuwi'owingeh	169	1348–1550	—	Museum excavated collections (Duwe 2011)	Duwe 2019	—
Tsirege'owingeh	170	1357–1600	—	Museum excavated collections (Duwe 2011)	Duwe 2019	—
Te'ewi'owingeh	252	1365–1600	Drone (Duwe et al. 2016)	—	Duwe 2019	—
Ku'owingeh	253	1366–1500	Total station (Duwe 2011)	Surface collection (Duwe 2011)	Duwe 2019	Duwe 2011
Poshu'owingeh	274	1375–1500	Drone (Duwe et al. 2016)	—	—	Duwe n.d.
Ponshipa'akedi'owingeh	297	1312–1550	Drone (Duwe et al. 2016)	Surface collection (Duwe 2011)	Duwe 2019	Duwe 2011
Nuute'owingeh	298	1350–1700	Drone (Duwe n.d.)	—	—	—
Pesede'owingeh	299	1365–1600	Total station (Duwe 2013)	Surface collection (Eiselt and Darling 2013)	—	Duwe 2011
Kap'owingeh	300	1300–1400	Total station (Duwe 2011)	—	Duwe 2019	Duwe 2011
Tsipinõwingeh	301	1317–1400	GPS (Duwe 2011)	Museum surface collections (Duwe 2011)	Duwe 2019	Duwe 2011
Sapa'owingeh	306	1385–1526	Drone (Duwe et al. 2016)	Museum (Duwe 2013.)	—	—
Cerro Colorado	370	1350–1425	GPS (Duwe n.d.)	—	—	Duwe n.d.
Hupovi'owingeh	380	1363–1550	Drone (Duwe et al. 2016)	Surface (Duwe 2011)	Duwe 2019	Duwe 2011
Posi'owingeh	632	1344–1500	Total station (Duwe 2011)	Surface (Duwe 2011)	Duwe 2019	Duwe 2011
Tsamaowingeh	908/909	1231–1550	Total station (Duwe 2011)	—	Duwe 2019	Duwe 2011
Palisade	3501	1312–1335	Total station (Duwe 2017)	Excavation (Duwe 2017)	—	Duwe 2017
Hilltop Pueblo	66288	1362–1600	Total station (Duwe 2011)	Surface collection (Duwe 2011)	Duwe 2019	Duwe 2011
Maestas Pueblo	90844	1250–1425	Total station (Duwe 2011)	—	—	Duwe 2011
Sandoval Pueblo	98319	1322–1394	Total station (Duwe 2011)	Surface collection (Duwe 2011)	Duwe 2019	Duwe 2011
LA 147926	147926	1250–1300	GPS (Duwe n.d.)	—	—	Duwe n.d.
LA 147927	147927	1300–1350	GPS (Duwe n.d.)	—	—	Duwe n.d.

Occupation dates were derived from a combination of dendrochronological and mean ceramic dating, and the end dates for occupation are ambiguous (see chapter 6).

Because of ethical and political concerns, the project practiced an ethos of surface archaeology, and no soil was disturbed. I relied on four datasets: (1) the mapping of visible village architecture, (2) the analyses of both pottery from surface contexts that was returned and previously collected material (to both date villages and to understand regional identities), (3) a pottery provenance analysis (including a clay survey), and (4) the survey of the sacred geographies that surround villages. I also performed a dendrochronological analysis of Tsipin'owingeh (chapter 4). I conducted three seasons of fieldwork (2007–2009) and addressed the majority of Coalition and Classic period villages in the valley.

Shortly after the completion of my dissertation I was invited to join a team of archaeologists to conduct research for Ohkay Owingeh regarding a water-adjudication case, *New Mexico v. Aragon* (Eiselt and Darling 2013). Our aim was to establish Ohkay's long tenure in the Chama and their ancestors' ancient water management practices. Because the disputed legal map overlaid nearly perfectly on my dissertation work, I was tasked with developing a momentary population model based on room estimates and chronology. This meant that I was able to use advanced technology (unmanned aerial vehicles, or drones) when I revisited villages and to conduct new research at additional villages, including site mapping, ceramic analysis, and sacred geography survey. Through this work I was able to refine a "pueblo decomposition model" (Duwe et al. 2016) to estimate room counts for use in population estimates. We also incorporated this data into the larger discussion of Tewa irrigation practices (Eiselt et al. 2017).

In past years I have conducted small projects to add to my dissertation data and have published the results. This includes fieldwork in 2015 that addressed how Tewa sacred geographies, and particularly ground cupules, changed through time (Duwe 2016). I also reanalyzed and reconceptualized the results of my pottery provenance study, with a discussion of changing scales of Tewa identity (Duwe 2019).

One of the most poorly understood periods of Tewa history in the Chama is the early fourteenth century, when various people settled in the region and began to negotiate a new type of village life. In 2016 I directed the University of Oklahoma field school to excavate Palisade Ruin. The village had been previously excavated in 1958 but was never backfilled or screened (Peckham 1981). In consultation with Tewa communities our aim was to disturb no new soil but instead to reexcavate the village, particularly the backdirt, and to conduct artifact analysis and site mapping. The artifacts were analyzed and then returned to the ground. These analyses (discussed in the next chapter) are insightful in understanding how various Tewa ancestors created their world.

Archaeology alone is not enough for understanding the continuous path of Tewa history being and becoming in the Chama. It is only one source of information about how the Tewa remember and continue to experience the deeds of their ancestors. Historical sources, ethnography, and, most important, the philosophy espoused by the Tewa today are all necessary for this understanding.

AN ARCHAEOLOGY OF TEWA BECOMING

In the previous chapter I explored twentieth-century Tewa ethnography, particularly Ortiz's model of the Tewa world, and argued that the system he described does not have a clear mechanism for historical and cultural change and is therefore divorced from the long arc of Tewa history. A similar argument could be made for Tewa archaeology, which has struggled with connecting the past with the present and incorporating Tewa knowledge into archaeological interpretation. Although early researchers such as Bandelier (1892) wove together ethnography, archaeology, and ethnohistory to write continuous histories of the Pueblos in northern New Mexico, the majority of archaeological work in the twentieth century focused on Tewa "prehistory." Twentieth-century research did not outright deny Tewa ancestry—it drew heavily from ethnography to make sense of a complex material record—but it did make the Tewa of the past an isolated study population only distantly related to living people today. We can see this divorcing of the present and past in multiple ways. The first is the use of material culture to describe people. A notable example is Mera's (1934) discussion of the "biscuitware area." Today many archaeologists, myself included, often discuss "ancestral" Tewa people, and I wonder if this has the same effect of separating the past from the present. The second way Tewa past and present are separated is in how the processes of historical change have been explained, with positivist economic and ecological models privileged over Tewa concepts of continuity. Discussions of the emergence of increasingly larger villages and complex social and ceremonial organization most clearly express the privileging of change over continuity (Kohler et al. 2004). And third, an evolutionary view of progress is embedded in the region's chronology, with the Classic period implicitly viewed as the apex of Tewa culture before Spanish colonization. The shift of population away from the Chama and other areas toward the Rio Grande is seen as an end of an era rather than as another moment in an endless cycle of movement.

Both archaeologists and the Tewa agree that the Tewa people have long lived in northern New Mexico and that Tewa history is dynamic and transformative. In this book I take an approach that embraces both continuity and change through the entirety of Tewa history. My underlying assumption is that Tewa philosophical concepts discussed today are very old and have acted as guiding principles for the Tewa since the beginning. Based on this continuity of belief, it is possible to tie together the present and the past as a continuous history that can include great change; in fact, these continuities allow us to explain the changes. By philosophical concepts I refer to those discussed in chapter 1: that the Pueblo people (including the Tewa) live in an interconnected world that is in a constant state of transformation as the people seek life by finding balance and harmony among opposites. This world is constantly renewed as the people live in and travel through their homeland and experience history in space rather than in time.

At the end of the day, interpreting this history rests on an often ambiguous material record that consists of fallen adobe walls and discarded pottery, shrines and agricultural features. From these, archaeologists can estimate village and regional momentary population (Duwe et al. 2016; Ortman 2016a), reconstruct social networks of connectedness and movement (Curewitz and Foit 2018; Duwe 2019), and understand the ways Tewa people constructed and conceptualized their larger worlds through time (Anschuetz 1998a; Duwe and Anschuetz 2013; Duwe 2016). These powerful analyses rely heavily on Tewa ethnography to inform interpretation of past events. But how can we as archaeologists begin to view past events as not simply informed by modern Tewa experiences but rather as a continuous path of seeking life throughout the entirety of Tewa history?

Fortunately, Ortiz (1969) provides a model that emphasizes both time and space and a map for how the Tewa lived and continue to live in their world. As discussed in the previous chapter, Ortiz described the Tewa world as fundamentally organized by opposites (summer/winter, commoners/leaders, female/male, life/death). The people achieve unity between these opposites through mediating social and ceremonial organization. Examples of these acts of seeking life include how the Made People act to balance the Summer and Winter People, how the power of the Made People is both expressed and held in check by the Towa é, and how traditional Tewa life is buffered by Towa é governance and Catholic officials. Larger dichotomies are also balanced through being Tewa, including finding harmony between males and females and the balance of the seasons to ensure that food and blessings reach the people.

While there are some aspects of Ortiz's model that are difficult to correlate with the archaeological record, his landscape perspective provides an important starting point to understand the nature of these mediations and where they take place. The Tewa world, as described in the previous chapter, is divided into a series of ecological zones that are associated with Tewa social and ceremonial life. Bounding the world are the mountains and their sacred peaks of the four directions. At the top of these peaks are the homes of the Towa é, and the springs and lakes on the peaks' skirts are guarded by the Oxua, or ancestral spirits of the Made People. This zone is exclusive to men and to the Made People and their assistants. It is here in the most dangerous and powerful place on the landscape that the balance between the people and their larger world is most pronounced, and where the doings that mediate this balance take place. Between the mountains and the village is the hilly badland area and the locale of the *tsin* (sacred directional hills). This is an intermediary, mediating zone between the dangers and power of the mountains and the middle place of the village. This area is controlled by men and ceremonial specialists (and their associated shrines) but is open to women and Dry Food People. Finally, at the heart of the world is the village and its immediate environs. The village is the domain of women and all the people and is the middle place and the nexus of where people, animals, plants, blessings, and spirits connect and depart. The village represents ultimate harmony because it is where "human life can be felt most intensely, because it is there where one can be in the connective flow of the universe" (Naranjo and Swentzell 1989:262). And, important for the current project, the village is also "where the past and future come together in the present" (Naranjo and Swentzell 1989:257).

As noted in the last chapter, Ortiz's model of the Tewa world, although informed by his deep understanding of Tewa society from growing up at Ohkay Owingeh, is a picture of life at one Tewa village in the 1960s and cannot be applied as an essentialized or timeless construct. It would be folly to simply "map" his model—a snapshot in time—unquestioningly onto the past, for to do so would be to ignore many hundreds of years of history. If we are interested in both continuity and change, we must acknowledge that through a history of seeking life the Tewa people have endlessly negotiated and renegotiated their world. From this perspective Ortiz's model is most useful to archaeologists as a guide for identifying the places where these mediations happen. We should expect that these elements, while interconnected, were and are always in a state of flux and that they developed during the Tewa's long tenure in northern New Mexico.

For this project I explore the question of how the Tewa became both united and divided by focusing on three separate but interconnected domains: (1) the histories of villages and the establishment and endurance of Tewa middle places that continue to be the focal point for seeking life, (2) the development of sacred geographies surrounding these villages and extending across the world and various elements of Tewa society that negotiated their cosmos and society, and (3) the movement and interconnectedness of people within an interconnected but ever-changing world.

MIDDLE PLACES

In Tewa cosmography the village is the middle, or heart, of the world. Six Tewa villages along the Rio Grande and its tributaries represent the most prominent current middle places. However, according to the Tewa, there can be multiple middle places and these places can shift through time. In fact, as discussed in the previous chapters, an ancestral village never ceases to be a middle place and remains an important nexus point for people and powaha.

Early in the twentieth century Jeançon (1923:1) lamented that "on the two sides of the Chama River, from its mouth to Abiquiú, a distance of about 25 miles, there are 10 or more ruins of which practically nothing is known." After nearly a century of archaeology this dearth of knowledge, in some regards, continues to be true. Early large-scale excavations at the village of Poshu'owingeh (Jeançon 1923) and Te'ewi'owingeh and Kap'owingeh (Wendorf 1953) helped archaeologists understand village form, pottery types, and general chronological questions. And Mera's (1934) regional survey established important baseline data for the boundaries and general scope and timeline of the Tewa presence in their larger homeland. In general most of this work was descriptive and sought to establish a basic culture history of the valley. Based on limited modern published excavations and a poorly resolved ceramic chronology, villages are often viewed as static, long-lasting, and permanent places. In recent years archaeologists in northern New Mexico have argued that villages are much more dynamic (Anschuetz 2007a; Duwe and Anschuetz 2013; Fowles 2011), yet we still know little about the nuanced histories of these places and people. How did villages change through time? What were the residents' identities? What types of mediating features were present? And what was their residents' relationship to one another and their surrounding worlds?

As the village is the heart of the Tewa world, the archaeology of these places is central to our understanding of Tewa history. I focused on three aspects of village history: mapping, pottery analyses, and population estimation.

VILLAGE HISTORIES AND MEDIATING PLACES

Traditionally, the principal element of Pueblo architecture is the room, which is used for both residence and storage (figure 8). Rooms are organized in contiguous, sometimes stacked, clusters or roomblocks that maintain shared walls, floors, and roofs. In northern New Mexico these architectural elements are built

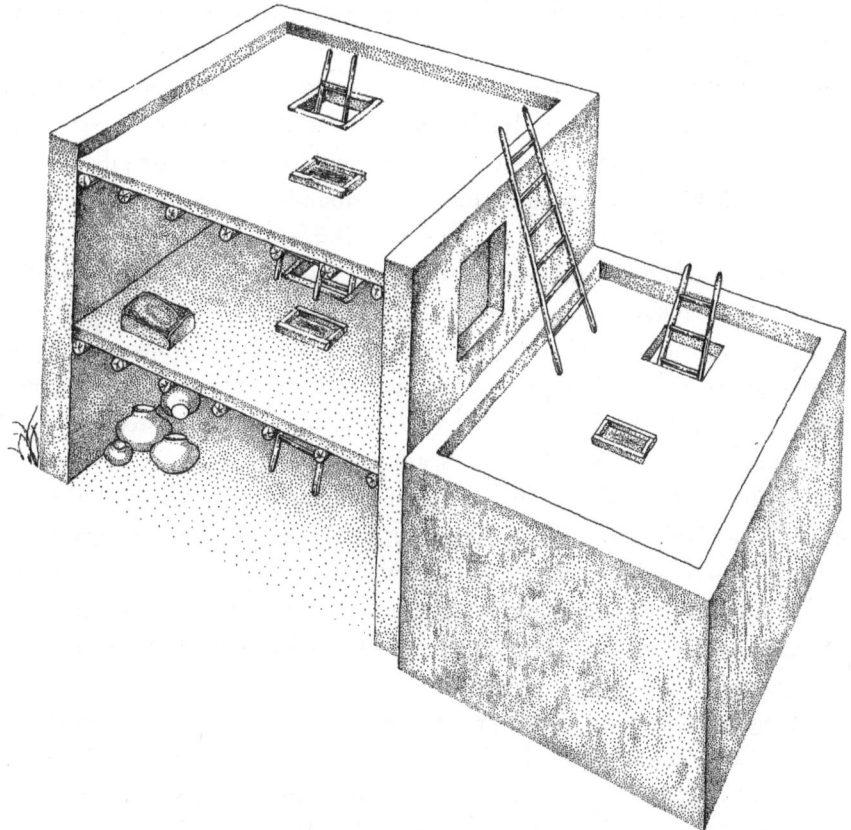

FIGURE 8 A cross-section of a pueblo roomblock (from Riggs 2001, figure 3.30). Courtesy of the University of Utah Press.

primarily with earth, stone, and wood. Walls are constructed using coursed adobe, with layer on layer of earth mixed with water and laid down to build walls upward (Duwe et al. 2016). The interiors of walls often display one or more layers of plaster (Stubbs and Stallings 1953:29). Vigas, or logs of local timber, serve as the main support members of the roof. The vigas are overlaid with latillas (poles of a smaller diameter) placed at right angles to the vigas and covered with a layer of thatching and dry adobe (Creamer 1993:20). Floors are nearly always composed of compacted adobe and are sometimes finished with stone or a clay slurry (Jeançon 1923:14).

Together these roomblocks resemble apartment complexes, and villages often have multiple complexes arranged around plazas. Described in the previous chapter, plazas, as negative and empty spaces, represent both the heart of the cosmos and the ethic of seeking life; it is a space that is continuously filled with people, spirits, and powaha and where relationships are constantly renegotiated (Swentzell 1989). Within the plaza is the true center, the earth mother earth naval middle place shrine, and also the kivas that act as a microcosm and a portal to the underworld. On the outer edge of the roomblocks lie the ash piles (middens), which serve as refuse areas and burial grounds. This outer edge defines the perimeter of the village and is ringed with shrines (see below).

Today these villages, although visited regularly, have returned to the earth as low piles of melted adobe covered in grass and shrubs. Because of the arid climate and relative protection of these places, we can learn much through examining what remains on the ground surface. I was interested in collecting two types of data. The first was to identify and define visible architecture, such as roomblocks, kivas, rock alignments, ash piles, and plazas. I used a Trimble Global Positioning System (GPS) and a total station to record these features in space (Duwe 2009; Duwe 2011). The information about architecture was particularly important in comparing changes within and between villages through time. A prominent example is the development of a general two-kiva pattern in the Classic period that is similar to the summer/winter moiety division in the twentieth century (chapter 5).

The second type of data was a product of attempting to estimate the number of rooms at each village. In the American Southwest, room number is often equated with population size. I was interested in creating detailed estimates that when combined with chronological control (see below) would show how each village was established, grew, and renegotiated through time. Using both a total station (Duwe 2011) and an unmanned aerial vehicle, Sunday Eiselt, Andrew

Darling, Chester Walker, Mark Willis, and I were able to create detailed (3 mm accurate) surface models of the eroded adobe architecture (Duwe et al. 2016). I then built a decomposition model to estimate the number of rooms present based on the volume of fill for each roomblock. Whereas previous archaeologists guessed the number of rooms, this model provides a standardized method for comparing village size through space and time, important information for understanding how people came together and moved apart during a dynamic Tewa history. I then applied this model to villages that had not been analyzed in the 2016 paper.

CHRONOLOGY AND IDENTITY

Beginning in the fourteenth century, Tewa ancestors began to distinguish themselves from their neighbors by creating a unique trajectory of pottery distinct from the glaze ware to the south and the black-on-white pottery to the north and west. This Tewa series of pottery was an outgrowth of the region-wide Santa Fe Black-on-white and includes a succession of black-on-white types produced through the coming of the Spanish in the sixteenth century and the development of red, black, and polychrome vessels in the Historic period (table 2). Early archaeologists closely associated this line of pottery with an emerging Tewa identity, with the aforementioned biscuitware area (the distribution of Abiquiu Black-on-gray and Bandelier Black-on-gray sherds) defining the Tewa world in the Classic period (figure 9). Besides denoting identity, Tewa pottery has also been integral in establishing the regional culture history. About a third of the painted pottery recovered at Pecos Pueblo was imported Tewa pottery, and through both seriation and stratigraphy Alfred Kidder (1936) began to contextualize these types in time. Numerous other syntheses and chronological revisions occurred through the twentieth century (Harlow 1973; Habicht-Mauche 1993), providing archaeologists with a relatively good resolution (within a century) to date villages using pottery alone.

This project relies on pottery analysis from twelve villages in the Chama and northern Pajarito Plateau to refine Tewa history by dating inter- and intrasite histories and to understand the fluid construct of the Tewa world by using pottery as a proxy for identity. I analyzed existing museum collections when they were available. When museum collections were not available, I collected pottery from the ground surface (see Duwe 2011 for a detailed methodology). Additional analyses were conducted through the *Aragon* case (Eiselt and Darling 2013) and through the 2016 University of Oklahoma field school (Duwe

TABLE 2 Decorated pottery produced by potters in the Tewa Basin from 1200 to 1760

TYPE	DATES (AD)	DESCRIPTION	REFERENCES
Santa Fe B/w	1175–1425	Primarily bowl form with dark gray carbon paint. Paste is characteristically blue/gray with sand, siltstone, or tuff temper. Geometric designs are applied to bowl interiors.	Habicht-Mauche 1993; Kidder and Amsden 1931; Sundt 1984
Wiyo B/w	1250–1475	Exclusively bowls with interiors polished and painted with dark black carbon paint. Soft paste tempered with fine volcanic material. Bold designs with thick lines are applied to bowl interiors.	Habicht-Mauche 1993; McKenna and Miles 1996; Mera 1935; Wendorf 1953
Abiquiu B/g	1375–1450	Almost exclusively bowls, light porous paste self-tempered with quartz sand and tuff or pumice. Sharp black carbon paint is applied on a thin slip and polished. Designs include zigzags, crosses, checkerboards, and hatched triangles.	Harlow 1973; Kidder 1931; Mera 1934
Bandelier B/g	1400–1550	Technology identical to Abiquiu B/g although also made in jar form. Paint and slip are applied to both the interior and exterior of bowls.	Harlow 1973; Kidder 1931; Mera 1934
Potsuwi'i Incised	1450–1650	Primarily jar form. Similar paste as Sanakwi B/c. Surface decoration entails incised lines in geometric patterns along the midsection, often with a mica wash. European vessel forms.	Harlow 1973; Mera 1932
Sankawi B/c	1525–1600+	Both bowls and jars. Slip and paste are pink, orange, and tan with sand or pumice temper. Thinner walls compared with earlier types. Designs are more complex than the biscuitwares and lines are thinly painted with carbon paint. Includes European vessel forms.	Breternitz 1966; Harlow 1973; Mera 1932, 1939
Tewa Polychrome	1650–1750	Evolved from Sankawi B/c, with the difference being the addition of red slip. Predominately jars. Geometric designs of fine-lined, widely spaced panel units with triangles and dots	Harlow 1973; Kidder and Amsden 1931; Mera 1932, 1939
Kapo Black/Tewa Red	1650–1760	Highly polished black surface and hard, thin walls. Identical types with Kapo Black being fired in a reducing atmosphere.	Frank and Harlow 1974; Harlow 1973; Kidder 1936; Mera 1939

FIGURE 9 A selection of Classic period Tewa vessels including (a) an unprovenienced Bandelier Black-on-gray bowl, Catalogue No. 36.2.1; (b) a Potsuwi'i Incised jar from Sapa'owingeh, Catalogue No. 69.36.61; and (c) a Sapawe Micaceous Washboard jar from Yunque'owingeh, Catalogue No. 66.105.15. Courtesy of the Maxwell Museum of Anthropology, University of New Mexico.

2017). I also relied on excavation notes (Eiselt and Darling 2013) and existing publications of the few sites that had relevant data (Ortman 2012; Wendorf 1953). See table 2 for sources.

The first goal was to critically evaluate the traditional static association between Tewa series pottery and Tewa identity. Examining both the distribution of pottery types and the diversity within each type (both technological and stylistic), I found that while this long tradition of pottery was undoubtedly made by the Tewa's ancestors, the Tewa world was in constant flux. This is reflected in changing and permeable boundaries between the Tewa and Keres people (Duwe 2011) and the multiple identities of people who settled the Chama and negotiated both their metaphysical and material worlds (Duwe 2016).

The second goal was to place Tewa villages, or components of these villages, in a chronological framework. This is helpful to understand both intravillage histories and the rates and directionality of population movement in the Chama Valley. Although pottery, particularly from surface contexts, offers a poor alternative to other higher-resolution methods like dendrochronology, the dearth of excavation makes ceramic dating a reasonable option. I used the mean ceramic dating method devised by Vincas Steponaitis and Keith Kintigh (1993) to estimate village chronologies (Duwe 2011; Duwe 2013). This method of ceramic dating requires two forms of information: ceramic frequencies for multiple assemblages (both inter- and intravillage) recorded during analyses and assumed dates of manufacture for all pottery types in the assemblage (derived from table 2). Mean ceramic dating is highly subjective, although the estimates produced clearly have interpretive value when synthesized with room counts to estimate momentary population.

I also supported my chronological interpretations by incorporating dendrochronology to pinpoint specific building events. I culled data for all known archaeological tree-ring samples collected in the Chama from the Laboratory of Tree-Ring Research at the University of Arizona and also collected and analyzed samples from Tsipin'owingeh, an important place discussed in the next chapter (Duwe 2011).

The resulting date ranges displayed in table 1 are primarily based on mean ceramic dating analysis and dendrochronology (Duwe 2011, 2013). I argue that the date ranges represent the times of major occupation of each settlement. These dates, of course, do not preclude habitation or visitation of these villages before or after the stated date range. For example, all of the Classic period villages have evidence of Coalition period pottery, a pattern noted in chapter 4, which suggests that the range of early settlement in the Chama was much more expansive than traditionally believed. Also, some of these villages have evidence (either through pottery or architecture) of revisitation in the Historic period (chapter 6), which I used as evidence that the Chama was never abandoned.

ESTIMATING POPULATION

The Tewa's ancestral villages in the Chama have long been regarded as some of the largest in the American Southwest. In fact, Pueblo Bonito, the famous great house in Chaco Canyon, could easily fit within the plaza at Sapa'owingeh. It is no wonder then that archaeologists have attempted to estimate the population of these places, particularly with the number and prominence of these ancestral villages in the Chama during the Classic period. For the present study this information is important to understand how the Tewa people settled the Chama and eventually came together at the middle places like Posi'owingeh. As middle places, the village is the nexus point where people, spirits, and powaha meet, and therefore we must account for the processes by which each village was established, grew, negotiated, and continually visited and returned to.

In the Southwest, population is often estimated by room count, with a variety of formulas equating population with room count (Duwe et al. 2016; Maxwell 1994). However, if we assume that the Tewa world was constantly in flux, then we must acknowledge that a large pueblo need not be fully occupied throughout the entirety of its life, but that it can grow accretionally (Riggs 2001) or can be occupied sparsely for long periods of time (Creamer 1996). The largest villages in the Chama have over one thousand ground-floor rooms, and it is unlikely these rooms were all inhabited at full capacity or simultaneously. Both previously excavated data and my ceramic analysis indicate that these villages were long lived, some over two centuries. Therefore it is important to translate room counts and occupational duration for each village into meaningful population estimates for chronological periods.

To model momentary village growth histories, I applied Scott Ortman's (2012) village growth model based on my calculated room counts and occupational durations (Duwe 2011, 2013). Ortman's model is based on his analysis of room count and chronological data from excavated villages in northern New Mexico. He found that this data generally fit a logistic S-curve pattern, meaning that after a village was established, there was a period of slow growth, followed by a period of rapid growth, and finally another period of slow growth. He calculated a series of proportional vectors that can be applied to the total number of rooms to estimate growth across multiple chronological periods. Ortman (2016a) later refined his methodology to incorporate Gaussian statistics for better chronological control, and I draw from his regional analysis of the Tewa Basin throughout this book.

The above exercise presented a momentary history of occupied rooms at each village. The next critical step was to convert these room counts to population estimates. While room counts are often used in southwestern archaeology as a proxy for population, I opted to estimate population based on roofed-over space (Naroll 1962). Following the methodology we used in our paper (Duwe et al. 2016), I multiplied room counts by an average room size observed in excavated villages in the Rio Chama valley (9.75 m^2 based on data from Howidi'owingeh [Fallon and Wening 1987]) and then divided this total area by an ethnographically derived estimate (10 m^2 per person) for roofed-over space.

These estimates provide me with a general guide to understand trends in population coalescence and settlement patterns. They are also empirically based, with stated assumptions that can be debated and refined. However, it is likely that the resulting estimates are far too high and that it would be difficult for the Chama to feed a population upwards of ten thousand people (Anschuetz 2007a).

Archaeologists do not have a good idea of the relationship between room counts and overall population and are likely overestimating population for two reasons. The first is our questionable assumption that there is a relatively continuous ratio of habitation to storage rooms through time (Anschuetz and Ford 2018:24). The Tewa people, living in a dynamic agricultural environment of unpredictable precipitation and frost cycles, likely would have overplanted in good years and stored multiple years of maize to buffer against climatic uncertainty (Anschuetz 1998a). Historical accounts explain how the pueblos in Tiguex province, near present-day Albuquerque, stored seven years worth of corn (Riley 1987:211, citing Hammond and Rey 1940:255–256), a similar estimate to the six years of surplus described by Fray Escalona at Ohkay Owingeh in 1601 (Hammond and Rey 1953:696). Storage, of course, requires space, and there is a markedly large increase in storage rooms across the region in the Classic period (Anschuetz and Scheick 2006[1996]:219). The upshot is that many of the rooms we count might have been housing maize instead of people, and storage needs may have continued to increase by the sixteenth and seventeenth centuries as people lived in increasingly larger villages during a time of unpredictable and dramatic climatic change (Van West et al. 2013).

The second reason population might be overestimated is that it remains difficult to model how and when people left these villages or the constant flow of people between large villages and small homesteads. Kurt Anschuetz (2007a) discusses how the Tewa people likely moved frequently across the landscape, in both highland and lowland areas, to make an agrarian living in an arid climate. Maize is planted in many dispersed fields to guarantee that it remains segregated by color, which also has the effect of spreading crops across multiple microclimates to ensure that some survive the frosts of cold-air drainages in the spring and fall and the torrential rains and hail of the summer monsoons (Ford 1980). This land-extensive practice also allows for fallowing, or resting, of the land (Anschuetz 1998a:479). Anschuetz (2007a) also argues that the massive villages we study today may have acted more as monuments to their persistence then testaments to large populations. These ancestral places are returned to again and again, either through pilgrimage or reoccupation (chapter 6). His discussion offers an important critique of how we have likely overestimated village and population size by not accounting for this fluidity of movement, summed up in the phrase "big sites are not necessarily so big, just as the small sites are not necessarily so small" (Anschuetz 2007a:188). Our models (Duwe 2011; Ortman 2012, 2016a) assume continuous growth and permanent settlement, an outgrowth of not being able to model seasonal patterns of movement and not being able to identify how people leave and return to a village. So please take these models with a grain of salt. However, until we can account for this fluidity, momentary population estimates offer an empirical, albeit relative, measure of how villages were built and moved through over the past eight centuries.

SURVEYING SACRED GEOGRAPHIES

Ortiz demonstrated that the Tewa world extends beyond the village to the mountains and valleys of northern New Mexico. This landscape, first recorded in the anthropological literature by John Harrington (1916), includes places of memory and nexuses between people, spiritual beings, and powaha. These places were created in the past, but they remain integral to the nature of the Tewa world today. And we can assume that because this world is in constant flux, exploring this landscape makes it possible to understand when and possibly by whom these places were established and how this world was negotiated as disparate people settled and forged a new life in the Chama. Therefore, a major source of data for this project is the survey of Tewa sacred geographies associated with ancestral villages.

Understanding that the Tewa created meaningful social and cosmological space through the creation of place is one thing (chapter 2), identifying and interpreting these places eight hundred years later is quite another. Many sacred places are archaeologically invisible. For example, the earth mother earth navel middle place, or sacred center of the village, is a small flat rock in the plaza (Ortiz 1969), and many Tewa shrines were composed of feathers that were strung in a juniper tree (Parsons 1929). Some sacred places have no human modification at all, like important topographic features such as springs (Walt 2014). Only the largest and most prominent, but not necessarily the most important, shrines are available for archaeological analysis. While identification of these places is difficult, we are fortunate to have multiple ethnographic descriptions of material manifestations of the cosmos (Ortiz 1969; Parsons 1929) and over half a century of collaborative relationships between archaeologists and the Tewa people. Richard Ford, and the knowledge he has gained by traversing the Chama with Tewa friends and colleagues, has been invaluable to researchers who are interested in understanding northern Rio Grande landscapes (Anschuetz 1998a; Eiselt and Darling 2013; Fowles 2009; Snead 2008).

METHODS

Colleagues and I surveyed the sacred geographies surrounding seventeen ancestral villages in the Chama dating from the Coalition period to the Historic period (table 3). The bulk of the research was part of my dissertation (Duwe 2011), with additional fieldwork in 2015 (Duwe 2016). Additional data were collected at Pesede'owingeh as part of the *Aragon* casework (Duwe 2013; Eiselt and Darling 2013). I focused primarily on Tewa shrines described in the ethnographic literature (see below). Crews ranging from one to four people systematically surveyed the landscape immediately adjacent to a site (within 0.5 km). For the sake of efficiency I conducted unsystematic survey beyond this distance up to 2 km from the village, to include hill tops, ridges, and other prominent features where the ancestral Tewa were likely to have built shrines. Using the shrine typology developed below, all potential shrines were recorded, photographed, and spatially located using a Trimble GPS. This information was then incorporated into a geographic information systems (GIS) database and synthesized with available chronological, architectural, and ceramic data to place these sacred geographies into a historical framework.

The survey focused primarily on shrines and other ritual landscape features surrounding the village. In relation to the conceptual world described by Ortiz (1969), the survey coverage for this project is small; I have left out the entirety of the mountains and the majority of the tsin. However, based on nuances in ritual landscapes expressed by the ethnographic-era Pueblos (chapter 2), the types, placements, and quantities of shrines immediately surrounding the village are directly related to both conceptions of the cosmos and social identity.

Shrines, like rock art, are notoriously difficult to date. I relied on both associated ceramic scatters and obvious architectural associations to assign shrines to both chronological periods and phases. At sites with multiple components, such as Tsama'owingeh (composed of both a Coalition period occupation and a large Classic period compound), it was difficult to delineate chronological components within the ritual landscape. For the most part, however, shrines and their associated ritual landscapes could be roughly dated to four periods: the Pindi phase of the Coalition period (1200–1300), the Wiyo phase of the Coalition period (1300–1350), the Classic period (1350–1598), and the Historic period (1598–).

I formulated the following shrine typology based on (1) previous landscape studies in the northern Rio Grande region (Anschuetz 1998a; Fowles 2004a, 2009; Snead 2008), (2) discussions about and hiking the landscape with Richard Ford, and (3) personal observation and ethnographic analogy. Two hundred and twenty-five shrines of eight types were recorded. For clarity I have divided my typology into two classes: (1) shrines located at or near the village and (2) shrines located in the surrounding tsin. Also, because of the sensitive nature of the places, I do not include any photographs and I have heavily schematicized maps of sacred geographies in the next three chapters.

VILLAGE SHRINES

Cupule shrines. The most common (n = 110) and easily identifiable shrine on the Tewa landscape is the cupule shrine, also known as a cupule boulder (Anschuetz 1998a). This type of shrine is found at thirteen of the fourteen sites where I conducted landscape survey, regardless of temporal or spatial constraints. First identified in the archaeological literature by Jeançon (1923) and later found across the northern Rio Grande region (Anschuetz 1998a; Fowles 2004a; Snead 2008), these shrines encompass a great deal of morphological variability. In general, however, the cupule shrine is often composed of a small- to medium-sized (50 x 50 x 50 cm) boulder, with anywhere from one to one hundred pecked

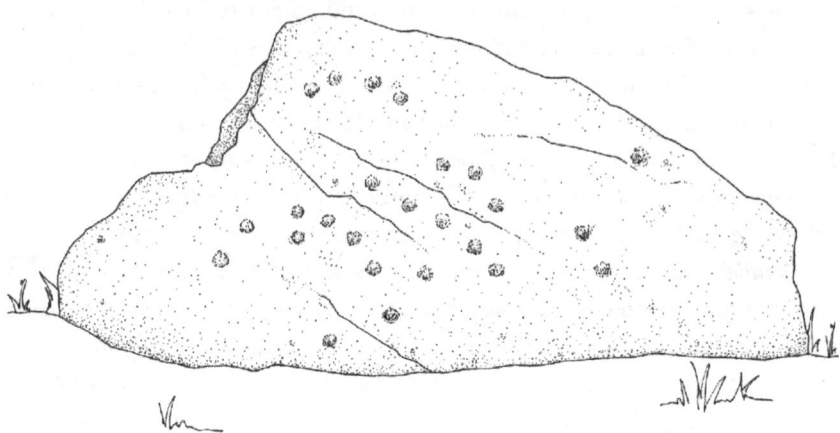

FIGURE 10 A drawing of a cupule shrine from the Taos region (from Fowles 2004a, figure 8.7). Courtesy of Severin Fowles.

cupules, or indentations, on the visible rock face (figure 10). On average, most cupules are 2–5 cm wide and 0.5–1 cm deep. Cupule shrines are primarily located on the edges of site architecture and were built on the tops of ash piles. Often, more prominent examples are placed at cardinal directions in relation to site architecture, but high concentrations of cupules are also found near formal entrances to a village.

Cupules are ubiquitous and often found in the presence of ground features characteristic of other Tewa shrines. These cupules shrines are also not restricted to boulders but are found on both rock outcrops and cliff faces. Parsons (1929:134) states that it was color and not shape that dictated rock choice for the ethnographic Tewa. The Tewa appear to have been pragmatic about rock choice as well, with basalt, granite, and volcanic tuff used in the creation of cupule shrines. Although rock choice is almost certainly a product of available minerals, one cannot discount the relative softness and ease of grinding the shrine itself. When a softer material is available (e.g., tuff versus granite), it is almost always used to a greater degree than the harder material (Duwe 2016).

Cupule shrines have clear analogies with Tewa landscape use in the twentieth century. Jeançon (1923:70), while excavating at Poshu'owingeh with workmen from Santa Clara Pueblo, learned that "at certain times of the years, and during certain ceremonies, it was and still is the custom for women to go at daybreak and pound on the rocks to attract the attention of the 'Sun god.' The same rocks were always used, and that accounted for the holes." Based on this statement, and the shrines' placement on the edges of the village, cupule shrines are almost certainly a type of *xayeh*, or household shrine, identified by Elsie Clews Parsons (1929, see chapter 2). These shrines were likely places to communicate with the larger cosmos. The cupule shrines' placement on the tops of ash piles, the traditional burial place for Pueblo people, is important. Ortiz (1969:52) describes how the directional shrines, or "soul-dwelling middle places," were places where the souls of the deceased Dry Food People (those without ceremonial or political authority) traveled after death. Once at the shrine, the spirit is met by ancestral souls who journey with the spirit to all points on the Tewa landscape, eventually returning to the place of emergence.

Cupule shrines appear to have substantial antiquity in northern New Mexico. This shrine type is found in the Rio Grande Gorge near Taos and based on repatination, likely dates to the Archaic period (Severin Fowles, personal communication 2011). In the Rio Chama watershed, cupules were ground into boulders that surrounded some of the earliest settled villages in the Chama, dating to the thirteenth century (chapter 4). Other early examples from the region come from T'aitöna (Pot Creek Pueblo), a large Tiwa village built in the late thirteenth century (Fowles 2004a, 2009), and the ancestral Tanoan site of Burnt Corn Pueblo (LA 359) in the southern Tewa Basin (Snead 2008). Although cupule shrines appear to have been present in the northern Rio Grande region for thousands of years, the meaning and intensity of their placement around Late Coalition period villages mark a strong contrast to earlier settlements. It appears that not only were the location and placement of cupule shrines a novel landscape feature in the late-thirteenth-century northern Rio Grande region, but this shrine type was also shared by both the ancestral northern Tiwa and Tewa.

Ground-slick shrines. The second class of shrines is nearly as common as cupule shrines but appears to be more spatially and temporally restricted. Ground-slick shrines, also called ground-slick boulders (Anschuetz 1998a; Fowles 2004a), are composed of small- to medium-sized (50 x 50 cm) cobbles and boulders with oblong slicks ground into the rock face. These slicks are highly standardized and measure approximately 16 x 8 cm. While some ground-slick shrines have only one slick, the majority have multiple slicks that are often clustered together. The depth of grinding is variable but often very shallow (< 0.5 cm). The majority of ground-slick shrines are found on the edges of ancestral Tewa villages and are often located near cupule shrines. However, while cupule shrines are placed in all directions (particularly emphasizing the cardinal directions), ground-slicks are often located in clusters to the east and west of the village proper.

Unfortunately, there are no clear ethnographic analogies for ground-slick shrines. Presumably based on their morphology, these slicks were used to sharpen axes and hoes—the instruments of agriculture—which is supported by ground-slicks amidst field systems in the Rio del Oso valley (Anschuetz 1998a). But these shrines almost certainly must have had ceremonial importance. Previous studies of northern Rio Grande shrines (Anschuetz 1998a; Fowles 2009; Snead 2008) have assigned ritual importance to ground-slicks, particularly based on their association with cupule shrines and other landscape features. Nowhere is this pattern demonstrated better than at Tsipin'owingeh, where entire rock outcrops are covered with both cupules and ground-slicks. The Tewa themselves revere ground-slicks as blessing places (Richard Ford, personal communication 2006), and therefore I consider this type of feature to be a shrine. A subset of the ground-slick shrine is a boulder with very deep slicks up to 3 cm deep. This previously unclassified shrine type is similar to ground-slick shrines in material and location but was found only at Pose'owingeh.

Ground-slick shrines appear to have been part of the Tewa landscape since the late thirteenth century, although their appearance on shrines at Chaco Canyon (Windes 1978) make ground-slicks a pan-Pueblo shrine type. In the Rio Chama watershed six ground-slick shrines were identified at Coalition period villages (chapter 4). However, within the study area this class of shrine is spatially restricted. Of the six sites spanning the years 1300–1550 in the Rio Ojo Caliente valley, only one, Posi'owingeh, was associated with ground-slick shrines. And these shrines were all located on the western edge of the village. Whether this pattern is a product of unique identities or possibly a manifestation of Tewa dual-division will be discussed in chapter 5. While cupule shrines are found across the northern Rio Grande region and may be pan–eastern Puebloan, ground-slicks are much more restricted. Snead (2008) found examples at Burnt Corn Pueblo, and this shrine type is ubiquitous on the Pajarito Plateau (Steen 1977).

Channels and serpent shrines. The pecking of long, narrow channels in the bedrock underlying and surrounding sites is a hallmark of pre-Hispanic and historic Tewa shrines and rock art on the Pajarito Plateau (Munson 2002; Olsen 2004; Steen 1977). These ground channels, often accompanied by a cupule at one end, are found only at one surveyed site in the Rio Chama watershed: Tsipin'owingeh ($n = 33$). Carved into the soft tuffacious rock surrounding the site, these channels are most likely symbolic representations of serpents. Snakes are important symbols of moisture and fertility in Pueblo societies across the American Southwest (Fewkes 1906). The *awanyu*, or feathered serpent, is a motif of Mexican origin (Hewett 1906) that became prevalent in Pueblo pottery (Mera 1934), kiva murals (Crotty 1995), and rock art (Munson 2002) in the Classic period. The appearance of serpent imagery coincided with changes in ceremonial life (Phillips et al. 2007) and likely with the worldview of fourteenth-century Rio Grande Pueblo people.

Channels found at Tsipin'owingeh display a great deal of variability, ranging in length from 10 cm to 3 m. On average, each channel is approximately 4 cm wide and 2 cm deep. Many channels are attached to one or more cupules, and some form branching and complex patterns. While many channels and channel-cupule combinations are abstract representations of serpents, others are recognizable to species.

Nonground shrines. The last type of village shrine is one with no apparent human modification at all. Parsons (1929:56) described many xayeh as simply a boulder or collection of upright stones. The majority of these shrines are lost to the archaeologist. There are, however, instances where a large boulder appears out of place and was likely transported to its current location.

While the category of nonground shrines is a catchall, variability in both morphology and spatial context suggests multiple functional types. Nonground shrines are often found in pairs and mark the entrance to the village at Howidi'owingeh, Ponshipa'akedi, and Tsama'owingeh. A similar pattern is found at T'aitöna in the Taos District (Fowles 2004a). At Ponshipa'akedi multiple elongated upright stones were found in a north-south line 200 m east of the village. Based on the size and shape, these stones are similar to racetrack markers described in Tewa ethnography (Ortiz 1969:123).

TSIN

World-quarter shrine. Although rock rings are an important type of Pueblo shrine that extends back to the eleventh century in the San Juan Basin (Windes 1978), the world-quarter shrine appears to be unique to the Tewa. This shrine type is composed of available stone (basalt, granite, or tuff) arranged in a ring 10–12 m in diameter with an opening oriented due east. Only one world-quarter shrine is present per village and is located, on average, approximately 500 m southeast of the village on a hill or ridge roughly at the same elevation as the village. The Tewa were pragmatic in their placement of these shrines and appear to have chosen their location based on topographic constraints rather than on strict orientation or distance from the village.

The name *world-quarter shrine* is a misnomer. The term was first used by William Douglass (1912) to describe the *nan sipu* (earth naval) shrine on the summit of Tsikumu, the sacred Tewa peak of the west. The nan sipu, described in chapter 2, is a large circular stone structure with multiple "rain roads" that channel blessings, moisture, and fecundity to the Tewa and neighboring Pueblo people (Douglass 1917). Although only the nan sipu on Tsikumu has been recorded, it is likely that this type of shrine was found on all four sacred peaks, representing the four cardinal Tewa directions, or quarters. In actuality, the world-quarter shrine is more akin to defining a center—based on its proximity to the village—than delineating an edge. When Jeançon (1923) excavated Poshu'owingeh, he used Douglass's terminology to describe the shrine type he found, and northern Rio Grande archaeologists have maintained the name *world-quarter shrine* for the past century. For the sake of clarity, I have preserved this nomenclature.

Twentieth-century ethnography fails to mention the presence, let alone the meaning, of the world-quarter shrine. This is most likely a consequence of Spanish, and later American, persecution of traditional ceremonial activity. The Tewa were forced to take much of their ceremonialism underground to avoid the ire of outsiders (Snead 2008). Ironically, it was an archaeologist who recorded the symbolic and functional aspects of the world-quarter shrine. Jeançon (1923), citing information from Aniceto Swanso, a man from Santa Clara Pueblo who assisted in excavating Poshu'owingeh, explained that the world-quarter shrine was primarily used to encourage rainfall. During a long drought, the Summer and Winter chiefs, along with their top lieutenants, would retreat to the shrine and "would stay there for four days and nights and make magic to bring rain" (Jeançon 1923:53). From this description archaeologists have learned two important points. First, the world-quarter shrine was a key component in the growing of maize for the Historic period Tewa. And second, the shrine, although beneficial to all the people, was the purview of the Made People, or Tewa ceremonial leaders. According to Jeançon (1923:53), "only a very few men knew the rain medicine," and thus the world-quarter shrine is in a very different class from the village shrines described previously. The shrine's position within sight of the village but far enough to keep ceremonial activities hidden is reminiscent of the private/public dichotomy of ritual demonstrated in multiple contexts, from plazas and temples in Peru (Moore 2009) to pottery designs among the Pueblos (Mills 2007). Perhaps the appearance of the world-quarter shrine in the Tewa world signifies a transformation of social and ceremonial organization to one that resembles the ethnographic Tewa, at least in terms of the establishment of the Made People as the de facto leaders of the village.

Anschuetz (1998a) proposed that the world-quarter shrine was a Classic period phenomenon that signaled the development of a Tewa landscape and people that were in the process of becoming. Many Classic period villages in the Rio Chama watershed appear to have a world-quarter shrine. I found or rerecorded a world-quarter shrine at each of the Classic period villages where I conducted landscape survey. However, although the world-quarter shrine is a hallmark of the Classic period, there is both direct and indirect evidence that this shrine type first appeared in the Wiyo phase (1300–1350). I cored a piñon beam located in the world-quarter shrine at Tsipin'owingeh (occupied from 1312 to 1350, appendix A) that yielded a cutting date of 1326. A world-quarter shrine is located 400 m southwest of Wiyo Pueblo (LA 253), a village that was contemporaneous with Tsipin'owingeh (Marshall and Walt 2007). Both of these sites were the largest villages (> 400 rooms) in the Tewa Basin during the Wiyo phase, and both were places where a large population and an uncertain climate led to the development of a more complex ritual landscape. Whether this transformation of landscape equates with a transformation of social and ceremonial organization will be addressed in the next chapter.

Circular shrines. World-quarter shrines are not the only type of rock ring structures in the hills surrounding a Tewa village. A small number (*n* = 4) of rock rings, measuring on average 2 m in width by 2 m in height, were found in the hills surrounding four Coalition and Classic period villages. Two Classic period shrines (from Ku'owingeh and Howidi'owingeh) had small openings oriented to the east.

Both Ortiz (1969) and Parsons (1929:241) discuss the function of circular rock ring shrines on the hills surrounding a village as being related to hunting. Ortiz (1969:24) states that these shrines are located in the hills where both big and small game congregate. Small offerings, taking the form of corn meal or animal bones, were made by men coming and going from the hunt (Parsons 1929:241).

MODELING LANDSCAPE THROUGH TIME

In the next three chapters I demonstrate how the number of shrines, the diversity of shrine types, and the standardization of shrine placement increase through time, with the large Classic period villages closely resembling Ortiz's twentieth-century model. But more important, I show that that the use of shrines is very old and it is the context and meaning of shrines that are in flux through centuries of becoming Tewa. While it is possible to associate the creation of shrines with specific chronological periods, shrines are living places that continue to be visited by the Tewa today. The sacred geography of the Chama is therefore accretional and forever acts as the nexus between the past, the present, and the future (see chapter 6).

MOVEMENT, IDENTITY, AND CONNECTEDNESS

Archaeologists have understood that by the fourteenth century the Pueblo people of northern New Mexico began to express subregionalism in material culture, suggesting the formation of societies and worlds similar to those of contemporary Pueblo people (Anschuetz 2015; Fowles 2004a; Mera 1934). Much of the work done by archaeologists on the material culture of the Pueblo has defined the larger Tewa world in relation to their neighbors to the south, west, and east. But little research has explored the internal dynamics of the developing Tewa world to understand how different communities formed, interacted, diversified, and moved along their paths of becoming. Defining these paths of movement, emerging and diversifying identities, and changing social connectedness is crucial to understanding how the villages in the Chama—a substantial population center by the fifteenth century—constructed and conceptualized their larger world.

One way to begin to address these questions of movement and interaction is to examine the production and distribution of pottery in and between two well-studied areas of the Tewa Basin: the Rio Chama valley and the Pajarito Plateau. If we can assume that the movement of pottery is indicative of some sort of social interaction (feasting, exchange, marriage), then documenting the flow of pots between areas becomes a proxy for social connectivity. I conducted a pottery provenance study of decorated pottery from thirteen villages from both the Chama Valley and the Pajarito Plateau (Duwe 2011, 2019). Because of the diverse geology of the region, I was able to differentiate pottery that was made locally from that which was imported in both areas and by doing so was able to estimate the frequency of nonlocal pottery across villages.

My central observation is that though Tewa pottery was produced in large quantities in both areas, the Rio Chama watershed and the northern Pajarito

Plateau exhibit different quantities of local and nonlocal pottery, which suggests varying economic and social relationships as well as histories of movement. Correlating the pottery data with population histories reveals that unique Tewa identities developed during the Classic period through the process of population coalescence—a process that continued through the Historic period and resulted in the diverse Tewa Pueblos of today.

SUMMARY

In the course of the next three chapters I tell a history of how the Summer and Winter People came together, created a new society, and endured centuries of colonization, all the while maintaining their connections with their ancestral homeland. Viewing this history as continuous—meaning that it connects the present with the past and extends to the future—allows me to understand how particular events (e.g., the negotiation of the Peoples, Tewa-Spanish relations) may have been conceptualized by people in the past, because these concepts are articulated by the Tewa today. Of course I am not Tewa, but I am moved by Rina Swentzell's (1991) plea that archaeologists take Pueblo views of history seriously. Also, emphasizing continuity works the other way as well: it connects the Tewa people today to their deep past and to their landscape.

The context for my study is the history of the Rio Chama valley, an important landscape for all Tewa people but specifically for Ohkay Owingeh. The Chama has long fascinated archaeologists, even as it has been understudied. I seek to write a culture history of the valley that takes seriously both Swentzell's (1991) and Ortiz's (1977) critiques that archaeologists and historians acknowledge Tewa views of history, time, and space. I draw from over a century of archaeological investigations and contribute additional data, including village mapping, ceramic analysis, landscape survey, and a pottery provenance study. I then interpret the data holistically, in light of ethnohistorical literature, Tewa ethnography, and modern critiques.

My discussion begins in the next chapter with a seminal moment in the Tewa's migration tradition: how the Summer and Winter People traveled separately and reunited in northern New Mexico. Following the ethic of seeking life, these journeys and encounters are not just historical events, they also shaped the very fabric and being of the Tewa world today and for the future.

CHAPTER 4

Winter and Summer People

Early in *The Tewa World*, Alfonso Ortiz (1969) made a fascinating decision. In providing historical context for his ethnography, he eschewed archaeological and historical knowledge of deep Tewa history—a sizable body of work by the 1960s and one with which he was very familiar (Ortiz, ed. 1972; ed. 1979)—and instead relied solely on stories about Tewa emergence, migration, and becoming. This made sense for the purpose of his argument. These stories provide a charter for Tewa social and ceremonial organization, a system he set out to describe and understand. But there was likely another reason: the Tewa already know their own history, regardless of archaeological interpretation. As Ortiz (1991:7) later explained, "The Tewa know not when the journey southward began or when it ended, but we do know where it began, how it proceeded, and where it ended. We are unconcerned about time in its historical dimension, but we will recall in endless detail the features of the twelve places our ancestors stopped. We point to these places to show that the journey did indeed take place. This is the only proof a Tewa requires."

This view, of course, is in stark contrast with how many archaeologists have studied Tewa and all Pueblo history over the past century. Archaeology by its very nature is inherently concerned with time in its historical dimension and definitely requires (ideally, quantifiable) evidence to support interpretation. In fact, of all aspects of understanding Tewa history questions of origins are most contentious. Archaeologists continue to debate whether Tewa ancestors migrated from the north or were indigenous to the Rio Grande valley. They have leaned on many forms of evidence, including architecture, settlement patterns, population estimates, skeletal morphology, and linguistics. And even with these data, much of it agreed on by all sides, different conclusions have been reached. Proof, for archaeologists, of how these journeys took place has been tough to come by.

As an archaeologist, I too am interested in the historical dimension. In fact, in the next chapter I put a date (circa 1350) to a pivotal moment of Tewa history: the coming together of the Summer and Winter People at the village of Posi'owingeh. I also value empirical evidence to support my arguments. But I see the irony that one of the absolute certainties in Tewa life, the migration of the Summer and Winter People from the north, is one of the most debated and poorly understood periods by archaeologists.

In this chapter I propose a way forward that takes a page from Ortiz's work. What if archaeologists were to privilege Tewa traditions of emergence and migration as a first principle? And what would an archaeology of the Summer and Winter People look like? This approach does not simply incorporate the Tewa's historical knowledge as another line of evidence in addition to settlement patterns and population data. Rather, Tewa stories act as a charter that serves as the bedrock to Tewa philosophy and guides archaeological interpretation. Through constant movement the Tewa people sought and found their middle places, all the while attempting to find balance and harmony between the tensions of the world. Tewa history has not one truth, but many, and these dynamic and multifaceted truths are expressed in how the Summer and Winter People traveled in, joined together, and built the Tewa world (Swentzell 1991). In this view, the inherent messiness of the archaeological record should be explored rather than debated.

After establishing the diverse histories of the peoples, I turn my attention to the Rio Chama valley, for it is there, according to Ohkay Owingeh's tradition, that the peoples traveled through and eventually came together. The Chama is unique in that unlike other neighboring areas there were no villages established there prior to the mid-thirteenth century, and for the next century it was a place where disparate people settled and flourished. I suggest that the people who settled there in the thirteenth and fourteenth centuries represent the Summer and Winter People who eventually joined and negotiated the Tewa society described by Ortiz. It was a society made up of people from many different places and that forged a world inseparable from the mountains and valleys of northern New Mexico.

One goal of this book is to answer the question of how the Tewa become both divided and united. As Ortiz did, I view the division of Tewa life into two moieties, the Summer People and the Winter People, as a historical explanation for how related yet separate people learned to coexist. Yet the two moieties do much more than just represent the encounter of two distinct populations in the northern Rio Grande valley. They also describe an ongoing process of seeking life that happened in similar ways across the Tewa Basin in the thirteenth and fourteenth centuries and that continues today through negotiations between the complementary opposites of the contemporary world.

ORIGINS

Who and *when* are the Tewa? This deceptively simple question lies at the heart of much of historic and recent archaeological scholarship. Can we consider the migrants from the Four Corners Tewa, or are they indigenous to the Rio Grande valley? What about the varied people who began to settle the Chama and the other parts of the Tewa Basin in the Coalition period? Or maybe the Tewa are the people contacted by the Spanish in the mid-sixteenth century. Or are they the men and women interviewed by ethnographers in the 1920s? What about the Tewa people today?

These are ultimately questions of origins and identities that have been pondered by outsiders since Silvestre Vélez de Escalante (1778) first noted similarities in material culture between the people of northwestern New Mexico and the people living in the Rio Grande valley. Archaeologists generally agree that by the fourteenth century ancestral Tewa people are clearly distinct from their neighbors to the north, south, and west (Mera 1934). While by no means as static and bounded as traditionally believed, this emerging Tewa world is supported by both distributions of material culture and specific Tewa traditions (chapter 5). However, questions of how the Tewa world came to be and how it relates to the world encountered by the Spanish and described by Ortiz (1969) have proven more difficult to answer. Tewa origins have been intensely explored, and yet this area of study has the most contentious aspect of Tewa archaeology. And archaeologists have undervalued and understudied the importance of the Historic period in demonstrating how Tewa identity has continually been renegotiated rather than corrupted by the coming of the Spanish (chapter 6).

Archaeologists over the past century have been keenly aware of the impact (or lack thereof) residential transformation and the settlement upheaval of the thirteenth century had on the formation of new Pueblo identities, including that of the Tewa. The response to this upheaval, caused in part by worsening climatic conditions, resulted in the migration of thousands of people to far-flung regions of the Pueblo world and the depopulation of much of the northern Southwest. Population coalescence occurred rapidly at multiple scales as Pueblo people began to build large plaza-centered villages and to create novel social and ceremonial systems of organization (Adams and Duff 2004). Perhaps not coincidentally, the population of the Tewa Basin more than doubled between 1275 and 1320 (Gabler 2009; Ortman 2012; but see Boyer et al. 2010), and within a century the large towns of the Classic period became important middle places for an emerging Tewa identity.

In recent years a new generation of scholars have revisited old debates about the origins of the Tewa people in regard to this migration event. These debates can be grouped into two categories: (1) in situ development of Tewa society in the Rio Grande valley and (2) large-scale population movement from the northern San Juan Basin, particularly the central Mesa Verde region. While both models acknowledge the social and demographic transformation that occurred in the Pueblo Southwest in the thirteenth century, they vary in emphasizing where and when the essential elements of Tewa language and culture were created and introduced.

The proponents of the in situ development model believe that Tewa society and language emerged from a protopopulation of ancestral Tanoan speakers (Tewa, Tiwa, and Towa) who had lived in northern New Mexico since at least AD 900 (Boyer et al. 2010; Mera 1935; Steen 1977; Wendorf and Reed 1955). Recently, researchers hypothesized that sometime around AD 900 the Tewa language diverged from the Tiwa language (Schillaci, Lakatos, and Sutton 2017), and the Tewa people began an unbroken chain of cultural continuity through the present day. This continuity is reflected in a long-lived Tewa pottery tradition (Schillaci and Lakatos 2017) as well as in a continuation of architectural forms in the northern Rio Grande valley that are substantially different from those in the Mesa Verde region (Lakatos 2007). Also, new research suggests that villages in the southern portion of the Tewa homeland dating to the Developmental period (AD 900–1200) have Tewa names and hence great antiquity (Schillaci, Lakatos, and Sutton 2017).

The contrasting model is of large-scale population movement from the upper San Juan Basin to the northern Rio Grande region in the mid- to late thirteenth century (Jeançon 1923, Ortman 2012; Reed 1949). This out-migration was caused by extreme climatic and social upheaval in the north, which led to the complete depopulation of the region (Ortman 2010, 2012) and the movement of tens of thousands of people who joined distant relatives across the Pueblo world (Ortman 2016a). These migrants spoke the Tewa language, a claim supported by Tewa place names remembered in the Mesa Verde region (Ortman 2012) and with shared Tewa metaphors between the archaeology of the Mesa Verde region and the northern Rio Grande valley (Ortman 2011). Additional supporting evidence includes shared sacred geographies between the regions (Ortman 2010), craniometric similarities (Ortman 2012), the potential introduction of particular domestic turkeys in the Rio Grande valley (Kemp et al. 2017), and the exchange of obsidian between the Four Corners region and the Rio Grande region (Arakawa et al. 2011). Evidence for the movement of people has historically and recently been the strongest argument for this migration, however (Ortman 2012, 2016a). Ortman (2012) suggests that a population of Tewa-speaking migrants began to settle in the northern Rio Grande region, particularly on the Pajarito Plateau in the western half of the Tewa homeland, in the thirteenth century. The migrant population may have totaled ten thousand (although some question the upper limit of these estimates based on limited arable land [Anschuetz 2007a]) and effectively overwhelmed the genes and language of indigenous populations (Ortman 2012).

I find these models intriguing, and I suspect that elements from both are accurate representations of the past. My view is echoed by recent researchers who have taken more nuanced positions about Tewa origins that acknowledge the convergence of multiple populations in the thirteenth century. For example, Michael Schillaci and Steven Lakatos (2016) reintroduce a hybrid model that acknowledges long-term and small-scale migration from the San Juan Basin and adjacent regions throughout the Developmental period, culminating in migration from the Mesa Verde region in the thirteenth century (Cordell 1979; Kidder 1924; Habicht-Mauche 1993). These people would have contributed to the northern Rio Grande valley's population growth and would have been incorporated into the existing ancestral Tewa world. And Ortman's position (2012), while advocating large-scale replacement of local tongues with the Tewa language and the eventual creation of a novel Tewa society, acknowledges the adoption of elements of existing Rio Grande peoples.

Even with these reasonable concessions, the two models remain sharply divergent. At issue is not just the geographic origins of Tewa ancestors as either indigenous to the region or migrants from the north but also the very mode of cultural change. Both recognize the stark difference between the great towns built at the beginning of the Classic period and the small hamlets and villages of both migrant and indigenous communities built a century earlier. These fourteenth-century towns were substantially larger (some with over one thousand residents) and closely resembled historic and modern Tewa pueblos (chapter 5). Researchers advancing the in situ hypothesis point toward the unbroken continuity in material culture (Lakatos 2007; Schillaci and Lakatos 2017) and substantial pre-1270 population (Boyer et al. 2010) to explain that Classic period Tewa society was the result of centuries of cultural development in the Rio Grande valley. In addition, there is archaeological evidence that supports strong continuities in settlement systems observed in archaeological assemblages from the southern portions of the Tewa Basin (Anschuetz and Scheick 2006[1996]) and from the Santa Fe area (Scheick 2003, 2005) from the late Developmental period onward. The Rio Grande Tewa would have accommodated refugees and incorporated them into their villages and lives, a process that perhaps encouraged coalescence (Schillaci and Lakatos 2016) that led to the creation of novel social and ceremonial organization (Moore and Boyer 2009). Proponents of migration explain this continuity, and the lack of a definitive Mesa Verde–style material culture, through other social processes: transformation and ethnogenesis. Ortman (2012) views the Mesa Verde migration as analogous to a later event of Tewa cultural revitalization—the Pueblo Revolt—and argues that the migrants purposely abandoned their current failed ways of living to return to an idealized past still lived by their distant cousins to the south and east. By adopting the Rio Grande Pueblos' lifeways, the migrants returned to the old ways to start anew, although they likely carried with them their previous ways of seeing and speaking about the world.

Debates of Tewa origins, then, can be generally summed up as arguments that emphasize either continuity or change. These arguments mirror the way archaeologists have explored origins on the grandest of scales: the origins of humanity through the (modern) human revolution and the Neolithic (agricultural) revolution. Clive Gamble (2007) argues that archaeologists have divided the past into static periods of time and have traditionally explained history as a punctuated equilibrium driven by often externally forced revolutions. While his examples center on the evolution of human cognition or the factors leading to domestication and the adoption of agriculture, similar concepts exist in the Southwest in how we explain the large-scale adoption of maize agriculture in the sixth century (Reed 2000), the shift from living in pit houses to aboveground pueblo architecture some three centuries later (Rocek 1995), and the reorganization of the Pueblo world in thirteenth century. Because traditional southwestern archaeological narratives view Pueblo history as a stepwise progression from simple to complex (Wendorf and Reed 1955) to simple again, with the coming of the Spanish (Lekson 2009), each narrative serves to both demarcate and explain disjuncture between relatively static periods of time. The transition from each static period of time can also be considered a sort of origin point for the Pueblo people, as climate change and population movement catalyzed Tewa ethnogenesis in the migration model. An alternative approach to revolution is to emphasize gradual change and continuity. This does not do away with established points of origins (European hunters/farmers or Pueblo hamlets/villages) but instead expects eventual change through the passage of time, a concept Gamble (2007:23) describes as "future-creep." In the in situ model, gradual change in Tewa culture is implied by a (predominately local) growing population that needed to adopt new types of social and ceremonial organization to accommodate new neighbors (Boyer et al. 2010; Moore and Boyer 2009).

Gamble points out that ideas of progressive culture change and the definition of points of origin are both artificially imposed on the past. Origins are particularly problematic, as they are defined by shifting contemporary archaeological and political concerns, and clear breaks between temporal periods always falter under scrutiny. He argues that historical change should instead be understood as a continuous process of the construction, negotiation, and renegotiation of identities of people in many times and many places. He views the past not as a series of step changes but as a gradient with an uneven surface that encapsulates both continuity and change (Gamble 2007:277). Based on what we know about the Tewa's own theory of history—a continuous but ever-changing path with many and varied truths—I wonder if the problem with Tewa origins, and the debates thereof, is actually in the question itself.

This is not to argue that the Tewa themselves do not have a clear concept of origins. As recalled in chapter 2, the Tewa emerged into this world from the distant north and were separated into two peoples who each took parallel journeys to seeking the middle place. Upon reaching what is now northern New Mexico, the Summer People and Winter People came together and built their homes and lives with a unique arrangement that was both united and divided. In its barest form, the Tewa's history details five core realities. The first is that the Tewa have always had a distinct cultural identity, even before emergence. Second, Tewa ancestors, while likely distantly related, have disparate histories and took separate paths prior to coming together in the middle place of the Rio Grande valley. Third, along their journey the people necessarily changed. Fourth, upon reuniting, the peoples negotiated a unique social and ceremonial organization. And fifth, becoming is never complete.

A search for archaeological origins appears to be antithetical to Tewa conceptions of history and identity. According to Ortiz (1991:7), "A Tewa is not so interested in the work of archaeologists. A Tewa is interested in our own story of our origin, for it holds all that we need to know about our people, and how one should live as a human. The story defines our society. It tells me who I am, where I came from, the boundaries of my world, and what kind of order exists within it; how suffering, evil, and death came into this world; and what is likely to happen to *me* when I die." Returning to the original questions of who and when are the Tewa, we can now see that these inquiries are impossible to answer. Broadly speaking, the Tewa have always been Tewa and can trace their ancestry through many lineages. At the same time, the Tewa are in a constant state of becoming and of negotiating their identities in a dynamic and interconnected world. The story of Tewa origins is continuously being written.

Instead of focusing on who the Tewa were and when they came to be, an alternative approach addresses a more crucial question: How did Tewa ancestors negotiate and renegotiate their world? I owe a large debt in my thinking to Kurt Anschuetz (2007b), who by the mid-2000s was unsatisfied with the reemerging Rio Grande/Mesa Verde dichotomy regarding Tewa origins. He suggested that both camps were simultaneously right and wrong: the Tewa's ancestors lived in both these regions and were jointly responsible for introducing critical elements for an emerging Tewa society. While this "middle way" is becoming increasingly accepted in the aforementioned hybrid models, Anschuetz took the next critical step in exploring how these disparate groups negotiated life in the northern Rio Grande region through the concepts of center and edge. He proposed that indigenous Rio Grande people, through their long-established settlement patterns and architectural forms, contributed to these negotiations by offering a conception of center that was subsequently adopted by Mesa Verde migrants. At the same time, the migrants introduced new concepts of edge, represented by directional shrine complexes observed in the Mesa Verde region

(Ortman 2010) but not present in the Rio Grande valley prior to 1250 (see below). Anschuetz developed this argument further by proposing that a key process in Tewa ethnogenesis was the unification of center and edge through the fundamental theme of movement, with new edges redefining the idea of center and vice versa (Anschuetz and Wilshusen 2011). While this hybridization of culture laid the foundation for the emerging Tewa world, the negotiation between center and edge is ongoing and never complete. The Tewa's emphasis on movement between the landscape's many centers and edges allowed for an inherent flexibility in how the people maintained access to their broad land base and sustained their identities within a constantly transforming world of social tension and climatic uncertainty.

In the following pages I demonstrate that Tewa history witnessed multiple episodes of the coming together of diverse people and many movements of the centers and edges and that these diverse people are conceptualized as Summer and Winter People in Tewa oral tradition. This shift in focus allows us to view Tewa history not as a series of events but rather as a process. This process is known as *seeking life* and the continuous transformation of society through movement and finding harmony among opposites.

THE ARCHAEOLOGY OF THE PEOPLES

Who are the Summer and Winter People? For the Tewa, historically and today, these groups form the primary group membership of the village, and every Tewa belongs to one or the other group (see chapter 2). This inherent division permeates all aspects of life and was the impetus for Ortiz's question of how a society can both be united and divided. Ortiz offers a historical explanation for this crucial duality, which is found in the Tewa's emergence and migration traditions. Upon emergence, the people were divided into two groups, each led by a chief, and the groups traveled separately to find the middle place. The Summer People traveled along the western side of the Rio Grande, eating fruits, and the Winter People journeyed along the eastern side, eating deer and elk. On their travels southward, the people stopped twelve times, and these twelve stops are represented as ancient villages. Eventually, the two people came together in the Rio Grande valley and built their homes with a unique social arrangement: each village was united *and* divided, as both the Summer People and the Winter People maintained their different identities but worked together for the benefit of the entire village. In subsequent years the Tewa established their historic and modern homes but have continued to maintain this unique arrangement to the present day.

Archaeologists have always been interested in Pueblo moieties, which are present in some form among all the Rio Grande Pueblos. For the Tewa, moiety organization is particularly strong, leading researchers to wonder how moieties developed, about their antiquity (in regard to alternative forms of village life), and about the implications for the culture history of the Pueblo Southwest. I address questions of Pueblo moieties (including the Tewa's Summer and Winter People) more fully in the next chapter, but for now it is enough to say that functionalist approaches to moiety formation based on population size do not adequately account for historical processes of movement and coalescence. Both models of Tewa origins clearly demonstrate that two generalized populations, first-comers and migrants, came into contact in the thirteenth-century Rio Grande valley. Although these models vary on the mode of cultural change and the primary geographic source population, both emphasize an exchange of genes and culture, leading to the eventual formation of Classic period village life. If we begin to take Ortiz's historical explanation of the history of the peoples seriously, I suggest that the archaeological record of the Tewa Basin supports the interpretation that these generalized groups of first-comers and migrants, as well as their negotiations, are remembered in Tewa cosmogony as the Winter People (first-comers) and Summer People (migrants).

This will not be a novel approach for southwestern archaeologists. I take cues from Severin Fowles (2013), who elegantly used migration stories of Summer and Winter People in his discussion of northern Tiwa Pueblo history, as well as Wesley Bernardini's exploration of a similar process among the Hopi (Bernardini 2011; Bernardini and Fowles 2011). I and others (Duwe 2011, 2014; Ortman 2018) have previously applied Tewa origin stories to histories of Tewa migration. Finding ways that Pueblo tradition and material evidence support a unified history, and then using Pueblo conceptions of migration and coalescence to inform our interpretation of the archaeological record, is a powerful tool. However, we must be careful to understand that Tewa traditions are highly metaphorical and not apply the Summer/Winter dichotomy too rigidly. As I show below, the histories of the Summer and Winter People may speak to a more generalized process of continued negotiation rather than to a series of single events, although these traditions do likely act to remember the different ways that Tewa ancestors entered the Rio Grande valley and made it their home.

The specific paths the Summer and Winter People took are recounted in a Nambé tradition recorded by Florence Hawley Ellis (1974):

> "The Tewa people came into the Rio Grande in two major groups, one arriving from the northwest (San Juan drainage) by way of the Chama Valley and the other coming up the San Juan River but eventually leaving it to cut across the Conejos and reach the Rio Grande in southern Colorado. They then followed the Rio Grande south to the western high foothills of the Sangre de Cristos, where they settled in a number of pueblos built on high ridges, far above water."

Those who journeyed down the eastern side of the Rio Grande and lived high on the flanks of the mountains are remembered as the Winter People in Tewa tradition (Ortiz 1969; Parsons 1994[1926]). The archaeology of the region supports this narrative. While the culture history of the eastern portion of the Tewa Basin extends far back to Clovis times (Warren 1974), occupation was generally sporadic and small in scale until AD 900. At the start of the Late Developmental period, the middle northern Rio Grande, along with much of the surrounding region, experienced an uptick of population. Scott Ortman (2016a) estimates that the area housed approximately nine hundred people in the years between 900 and 1050, but the population more than doubled by the end of the eleventh century. I follow others (Ford et al. 1972; Reed 1949) in thinking that this increase in population may be related to an early migration from the north or west, perhaps including Tiwa speakers from the San Juan valley, as demonstrated by ceramic evidence that suggests social ties to the west (Anschuetz and Scheick 2006[1996]:183). The majority of the residences were small Pueblo hamlets under twenty rooms in size (McNutt 1969).

The Winter People, then, were the first-comers. They likely shared a cultural affinity with other contemporary Tiwa-speaking people in the Rio Grande valley, such as people ancestral to Taos and Picturis (Fowles 2013), and may have produced the same Kwahe'e Black-on-white pottery (Schillachi and Lakatos 2016). However, in the thirteenth century the eastern side of the Rio Grande was affected by the demographic and social trends experienced by the entire region as migrants from the north and west entered the region. While population size remained steady in the first half of the thirteenth century, it tripled to roughly six thousand people by 1315 (Ortman 2016a). Populations were never large in this area, and this increase in numbers has been explained as the product of internal growth (Boyer et al. 2010; Schillachi and Lakatos 2017). During this period, however, a number of larger villages were built across the landscape, often on terraces overlooking drainages, that demonstrated considerable variability in architecture, with both L-shaped and C-shaped plaza pueblos (Dickson 1975). This heterogeneity in material culture suggests the possibility of multiple disparate people inhabiting the highlands in the southeastern portion of the Tewa world. Did this signal the coming of migrant populations, or the Summer People?

In the traditions recorded by Ellis (1974) and Ortiz (1969), the Summer People traveled from the northwest and are associated with the western side of the Rio Grande. Ortman (2012) attributes the fivefold increase in the number of people on the Pajarito Plateau in the thirteenth century to migrants moving from the Mesa Verde region, which I believe represent the Summer People in Tewa memory. These people would have been distantly related to the Winter People, or the Tiwa-speaking migrants who left the north three centuries earlier, but also distinct from them. While migrants from the Mesa Verde region likely brought concepts of placemaking (Ortman 2010) and aspects of social organization (Ortman 2018) with them on their journey to the Rio Grande region, they also left much behind, including much of the material culture of the north. Although there are some possible connections between the Mesa Verde region and the Rio Grande valley demonstrated in pottery style (Ortman 2012), much of the Rio Grande material culture displays continuities that extend deeply in time (Lakatos 2007; Schillaci and Lakatos 2017). This continuity has been explained as either evidence of a small migrant population that did not substantially influence life in the Rio Grande or as the migrants' rejection of their past through a revitalization movement that embraced the Winter People's ways of living.

These Summer newcomers likely dispersed from their original homes on the Pajarito Plateau and encountered the Winter People in other areas of the Tewa Basin. In a recent paper Patrick Cruz and I argue that these contacts and negotiations happened at many times and places (Duwe and Cruz 2019), just as each village remembers the places, and the contingencies, of this coalescence differently. There are multiple middle places (sensu Swentzell 1991). For example, traditions from Nambé, San Ildefonso, and Ohkay Owingeh recall the village of Tekhe'owingeh as the place where the peoples joined (Parsons 1994[1926]:15). Cruz believes that he has located this place as an early thirteenth-century Coalition period site near Pojoaque. Called the "Winter Village" by locals, Tekhe'owingeh represents a possible early encounter between the peoples on the eastern side of the Rio Grande. The Summer People's populations must have been small and likely readily adopted the cultural norms of their Winter People hosts. Conversely, Ortiz (1969), retelling Ohkay's traditions, discusses the middle place as Posi'owingeh in the Chama Valley. Rather than a history of one people joining another at their ancestral home, the history of the Chama, discussed below, is a story of the two peoples settling separately and coming together in a "new world" of sorts and eventually building Posi'owingeh in the mid-fourteenth century. And last, Ellis (1987) recalls a tradition from Ohkay Owingeh that describes the middle place as being the village of Ohkay itself. The coming together of the peoples was a direct result of colonization when Yunque'owingeh (Summer People) was ceded to the Spanish to build their capital and the people joined with their new neighbors at Ohkay (Winter People). The traces of these histories and identities can still be heard in the distinct Yunque dialect today (Richard Ford, personal communication, May 2018).

Based on these three examples, Tewa history witnessed multiple episodes of the coming together of diverse people, from the early parts of the Coalition period to the establishment of the Spanish colony in 1598. The recounting of multiple middle places likely represents the diversity in histories across a heterogeneous Tewa world. But it also suggests that the Tewa oral traditions are remembering a pattern of serial coalescence in which the Summer and Winter People, however defined, joined and rejoined multiple times (Duwe and Cruz 2019). This is particularly relevant when residents of Ohkay were consulted about each described middle place. While the Tewa's origin traditions are useful historical narratives for shaping archaeological questions, perhaps their true strength is in encapsulating a *process* of negotiation rather than a specific *event*. The basis for the Winter and Summer People may be in the generalized story of the settlement of first-comers and migrants in the Tewa Basin, but it continues to remain poignant in a Tewa perspective of seeking life that views history as a continuous transformation of society through establishing harmony among opposites.

If we take the Tewa's history seriously, then it becomes too simplistic to attribute Tewa origins to either migrants or indigenous people. However (and whenever) we define Tewa identity, the Tewa likely share cultural affiliation with Pueblo ancestors across the American Southwest, and Tewa identity and society can be traced to both in situ development and migration from the north. Once we accept that these negotiations occurred across the Tewa world, and that they are crucial to understanding the resulting Tewa identities, we can begin to focus on the unique historical contingencies of each area of the Tewa world. In the following sections I explore the settlement of the Chama Valley and the experience of both the Summer People and the Winter People settling and beginning the long process of negotiation, eventually leading to the village life of the Classic period.

SETTLERS OF THE CHAMA

Whereas much of the Tewa Basin, particularly the east side of the Rio Grande, was occupied for hundreds of years before the large-scale social and demographic changes of the Coalition period, a very different history took place on the northwestern frontier of the Tewa world. The Rio Chama valley, with its verdant, well-watered valleys, was settled relatively late in the mid-thirteenth century. However, within a hundred years the valley became a population center of the Tewa world and was the location, according to Ohkay Owingeh's tradition, where the Summer and Winter People came together to forge a new society.

In light of the complex and ancient history of the Tewa Basin, the most surprising aspect of the Rio Chama is the relatively late date of the first settlement in the valley. Over a century of archaeological survey has failed to yield a securely dated Developmental period occupation along the Rio Chama or its tributaries (Anschuetz 1998a; Beal 1987). Villages and hamlets dating to this time period, which are characteristically defined by mineral painted Kwahe'e Black-on-white pottery (Habicht-Mauche 1993:15), are found in relatively substantial numbers in both the Santa Cruz watershed (Marshall and Walt 2007) and Santa Fe areas (Anschuetz and Scheick 2006[1996]; Lakatos 2007) on the eastern side of the Rio Grande. In fact, there is no evidence of houses until the mid-thirteenth century. With only 10 percent survey coverage of the Rio Chama watershed, it is possible that some early villages remain unrecorded, but it is likely that the region was essentially unoccupied prior to 1200. This is not to say that Pueblo people did not know of the Chama. Stephen Post (2013) demonstrates that the valley was widely visited for hunting and procurement. The lack of settlement in the Chama Valley, with its ample arable lowland and upland resources, has been attributed to the presence of Gallina people to the north and west through the end of the thirteenth century (Beal 1987:18). However, it may be more likely attributed to low population densities in the region (Ortman 2016a) and the relatively cold temperatures of the valley compared with those of the Pajarito Plateau and along the Rio Grande (Anschuetz 1998a:84).

Whatever the reason for the late settlement of the Rio Chama watershed, the initial settlement of the Chama in the thirteenth century coincided with the depopulation of the northern San Juan region and the resulting residential and social upheaval that followed. The following is a discussion of the Pindi phase (1200–1300) of the Coalition period, defined by Fred Wendorf and Erik Reed (1955) and named after Pindi Pueblo near Santa Fe. This was a time when Pueblo populations increased across northern New Mexico and new types of communities and material culture expanded into the uplands and valleys. This expansion included the Chama Valley, a seemingly open landscape where multiple disparate people could settle and negotiate identities and cosmologies in the centuries that followed (map 4).

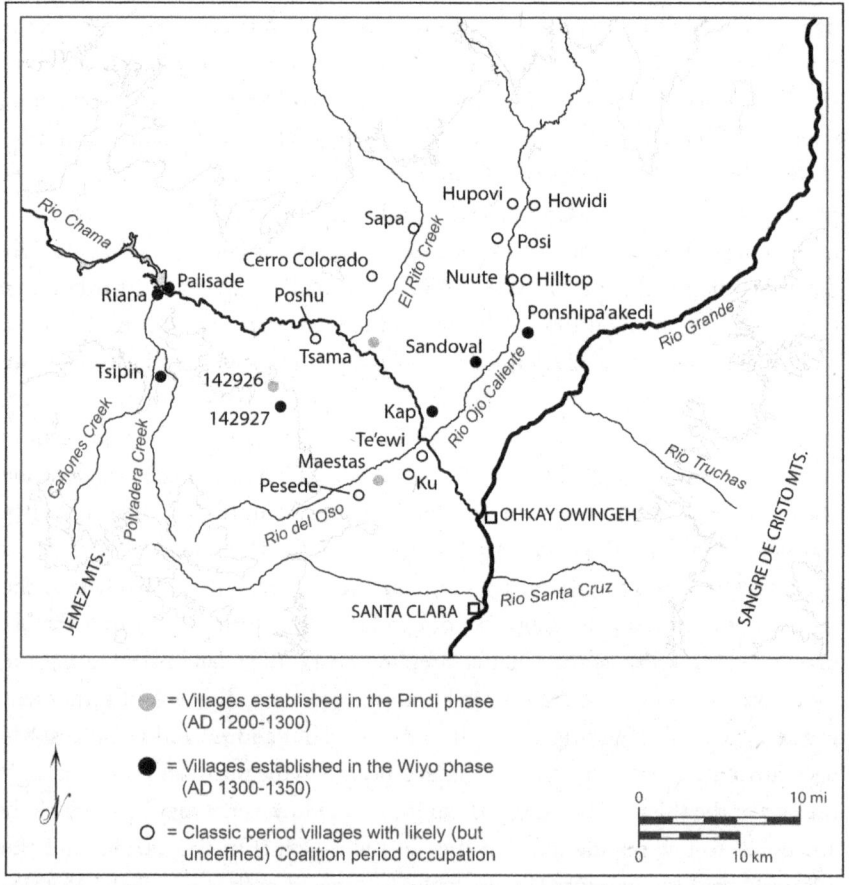

MAP 4 Map of Pindi and Wiyo phase villages in the Rio Chama watershed.

QUESTIONS OF IDENTITY

It is curious that the earliest example of sustained residential settlement in the Chama is also a place that was occupied through the coming of the Spanish. Tsama'owingeh (LA 908/909), located on a bluff overlooking the river plain in the central portion of the valley, was resided at by substantial numbers of people for nearly four centuries. In fact, Governor Oñate assigned a priest to the village in 1599, and the village lent the Chama a version of its name for Spanish cartographers (Riley 1995). Tsama'owingeh is a large village that was given two site numbers by Mera in the 1920s (figure 11). The first, LA 908, is a multiple-roomblock village that dates to the Classic and Historic periods (Greenlee 1933). The second, LA 909, is a much smaller 188-room (Duwe et al. 2016) pueblo that was built in the mid-thirteenth century (McKenna 1970; Windes 1970; Windes and McKenna 2006). Mean ceramic dating of excavated pottery (Greenlee 1933; Ortman 2012) places the estimated founding date of the Coalition period roomblock at 1251 (Duwe 2011). However, a beam with a cutting date of 1231 was uncovered inside the oldest kiva (Windes and McKenna 2006), which suggests a founding date in the 1230s. Portions of this Coalition period roomblock were excavated by Florence Hawley Ellis and the University of New Mexico field school in 1970. Unfortunately, a final report was never published, but preliminary reports by graduate students and subsequent reanalysis of site

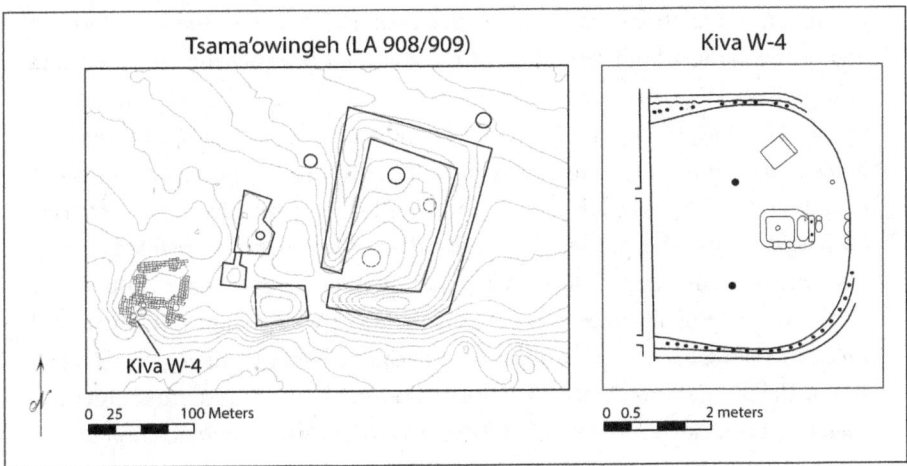

FIGURE 11 Plan of Tsama'owingeh and Kiva W-4. Map of the walls from the "West Pueblo" and the kiva are after Windes and McKenna 2006.

data (Ortman 2012; Windes and McKenna 2006) have provided architectural site plans and a curated ceramic assemblage.

The identity and origins of these first settlers of the Rio Chama watershed are difficult to assess. In many ways the architecture and layout of Tsama'owingeh appear to be similar to sites south of the Rio Chama watershed dating to the thirteenth century, including Forked Lightning in the Pecos district east of Santa Fe (Kidder 1958) and Pindi Pueblo near modern-day Santa Fe (Stubbs and Stallings 1953). The original builders of Tsama'owingeh may have identified closely with Coalition period villagers, or Winter People, to the south. Through the residential upheaval that resulted during thirteenth-century migration into the northern Rio Grande region (Anschuetz and Scheick (2006)[1996]), many of these people may have uprooted from their original homes and decided to settle in the wide-open landscape of the Chama.

However, there are also indications that the original settlers of Tsama'owingeh were coming from much farther afield. Ortman (2012:325) suggests that the earliest inhabitants of Tsama'owingeh were migrants from the northern San Juan region (the Summer People), based on his stylistic reanalysis of pottery from the West Plaza. According to Ortman, particular elements in Santa Fe Black-on-white pottery, such as framing lines and rim ticking, more closely match pottery motifs in the Mesa Verde region than those of the much closer Pajarito Plateau.

Of particular interest to the argument that Tsama'owingeh was established by migrant populations from outside the Tewa Basin is the D-shaped form of one of the earliest built structures at the site (and possibly the entire Chama Valley). Kiva W-4 measured approximately 2 x 3 m and had a vent tunnel oriented to the east (figure 11). The floor assemblage was composed of three post holes, a foot drum, and a subrectangular adobe-rimmed firepit-deflector-ashpit complex (Windes and McKenna 2006:247–249). And the kiva appears to have been used early in the village's history, based on its burnt and trash-filled context (Windes and McKenna 2006). A number of archaeologists have commented on the meaning of D-shaped kivas across the Southwest as conceptually related to the form of Chacoan great houses or sites in the Mesa Verde region (Bradley 1996). The proliferation of the D-shaped kiva form in the thirteenth century has therefore been viewed as part of a Chacoan or Mesa Verde revitalization movement (Bradley 1996:244–247; Saitta 1997:26). D-shaped kivas are not anomalous in the thirteenth-century northern Rio Grande region. Structures similar to Kiva W-4 have been found at Arroyo Hondo (Creamer 1993) and Pindi

Pueblo (Stubbs and Stallings 1953:14) in the Santa Fe area, Forked Lightening in the Pecos district (Kidder 1958:35–42), Kiva House near Cochiti (Kohler and Root 2004:125), on the Pajarito Plateau (Steen 1977), and at T'aitöna near Taos (Fowles 2013). However, Kiva W-4 at Tsama'owingeh appears to be one of the earlier D-shaped kivas in the region. While it is impossible to know, there is an intriguing possibility that the settlers of Tsama'owingeh were traveling from the north or west and creating a new life in a new world, using familiar historical motifs.

The Pindi phase in the Rio Chama valley cannot be understood outside the context of the northern Rio Grande region as a whole. Ortman's (2012) demographic comparison of the Mesa Verde and northern Rio Grande regions reveals that the Tewa Basin, and, specifically, the Pajarito Plateau, experienced substantial immigration originating from outside the northern Rio Grande region from 1280 to 1300. Concurrent with this population movement was the establishment of small villages in areas south of the Chama, including in the Rio del Oso valley (Anschuetz 1998a) and in the central lower Rio Chama valley (Bremer 1995a, b). Possibly the best known of these villages is Maestas Pueblo (LA 90844), located in the Rio del Oso valley (figure 12). Maestas Pueblo was a small village of thirty to one hundred rooms composed of adobe masonry apartments (Anschuetz 1993; Duwe 2011). The site's open plaza design and orientation to the southeast are reminiscent of the Wiyo phase (1300–1350) villages that appear within a quarter century of the founding of Maestas Pueblo. However, Maestas Pueblo's architectural layout and apparent lack of a kiva clearly sets it apart from contemporaneous villages like Tsama'owingeh. And, as will be discussed below, Maestas Pueblo has some of the clearest evidence of Tewa-like shrines in the drainage.

A focus on the big villages of the Classic period has been at the expense of understanding these early settlers. Maestas Pueblo was identified through systematic block survey (Anschuetz 1993), of which there has been little conducted in the Chama. At around the same time that Maestas Pueblo was recorded, Michael Bremer (1995b) located LA 142926 southeast of Abiquiú, a small linear roomblock covered with Santa Fe Black-on-white pottery (figure 12). I suspect there are many more late thirteenth-century villages located in the southern portion of the Chama Valley.

Identifying the identity of the settlers from Maestas Pueblo and contemporaneous small sites is challenging. Were these people migrants (Summer People) from the north or were they displaced or expanding Rio Grande

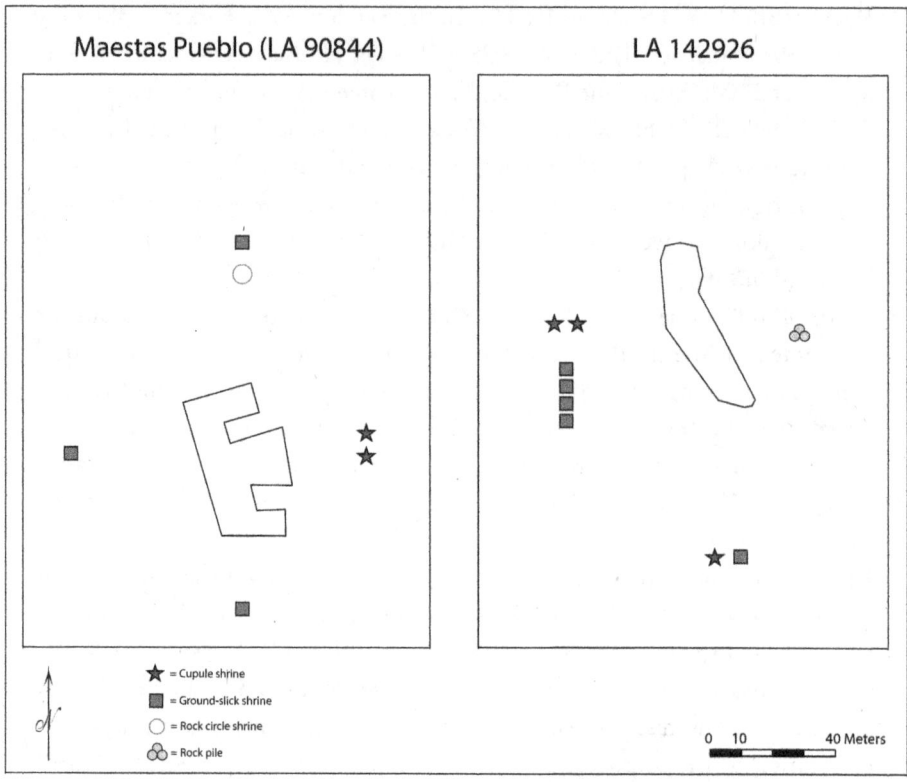

FIGURE 12 Schematic maps of the sacred geographies of (a) Maestas Pueblo and (b) LA 142926.

populations (Winter People)? Mapping the sacred geographies at and between these villages suggests that at least some of these people were migrants from the north and west.

EMERGING TEWA TRADITIONS

An integral part of Tewa identity is the construction of the landscape and the cosmos (Ortiz 1969). While we cannot expect to reasonably map twentieth-century cosmograms onto the distant past, identifying early examples of Tewa placemaking can provide important information regarding the identity of early settlers in the Rio Grande region, as well as how their worlds were actively becoming. We do know that migrant populations in the thirteenth-century

Four Corners region had well-established placemaking traditions, including shrines surrounding the village (Ortman 2010). We are less sure about what the landscapes surrounding Developmental period Rio Grande villages looked like, although this absence of information may be attributed to a lack of looking for shrines and other features. However, based on current information, no shrines or other ritual landscape features built prior to the late thirteenth century have been found at any ancestral Tewa site. James Snead (2008) identifies a similar pattern of the emergence of shrines in the late thirteenth century to the south and east of the Tewa Basin and attributes these new landscapes features to migrating populations, possibly deriving from the northern San Juan regional depopulation.

Identifying the earliest shrines in the Chama is difficult because there is no way to directly date these features and because some of the earliest sites are also the longest lived in. For example, Tsama'owingeh was established in the early to mid-thirteenth century, but it is a multicomponent village that was occupied through the beginning of the seventeenth century and continues to remain an important place of pilgrimage (chapter 6). During survey, I located ten shrines in the immediate area surrounding the village, including four cupule shrines, one ground-slick shrine, four nonground shrines, and a world-quarter shrine. Unfortunately, it is impossible to date shrines other than by association with ceramics and architecture, consequently these landscape features could not be assigned to specific occupations. While both cupule and ground-slick shrines are found at later Pindi phase villages, the world-quarter shrine most likely dates to the second quarter of the fourteenth century, based on a similar structure found at Tsipin'owingeh (see below).

Only additional field research at single-component Pindi phase sites will allow archaeologists the opportunity to better understand the ritual landscapes, and conceptions of space and placemaking, of the initial colonists of the Rio Chama watershed. We do, however, know that within a quarter century (circa 1275), the incoming settlers were actively constructing shrines surrounding their villages. These shrines, particularly the cupule and ground-slick types, were antecedent to those developed later in Classic and Historic period Tewa landscapes. The clearest examples of Pindi phase ritual landscapes in the Rio Chama watershed are in the Rio del Oso valley. Kurt Anschuetz (1998a), in a nearly full survey of the valley, recorded a total of 175 shrines located adjacent to villages and agricultural fields. Of those shrines, 24 dated to the Pindi phase and included both cupule and ground-slick shrine boulders. Maestas Pueblo, built around 1275 (Anschuetz 1993), followed this trend with ritual landscape that includes two cupule shrines and ground-slick shrines located on the west, south, and east sides of the site. A rock circle shrine, measuring 2 × 2 m, is located directly north of the village (figure 12). Similarly, LA 142926 to the west is surrounded by three cupules shrines and four ground-slick shrines on the west, south, and east (figure 12).

Pindi phase shrine types in the Rio del Oso valley are similar to some later Classic period village shrines, specifically cupule and ground-slick shrines. However, limited quantities and types of shrines, as well as a spatial context of landscape features, suggests that Pindi phase residents did not conceptualize the space surrounding their villages in the same way their descendants did. Certain features of the ethnographic Tewa landscape described by Ortiz (1969) are absent, including directional shrines. Anschuetz (1998a) argues that the placement of shrines is related to boundary maintenance in an ever more competitive world. In the Pindi phase, the Rio Chama watershed was occupied by a small population and access to agricultural land and other resources would have been unrestricted. These settlers were moving into a new and mostly empty landscape where pressure to define themselves both socially and spatially would have been low. This is a very different pattern from that in the Classic or Historic periods where very large villages were evenly spaced along major waterways. Boundaries, as functional field markers or as more abstract manifestations of identity, became much more important as the Rio Chama watershed became the center of gravity in the Tewa world, beginning in the fourteenth century.

Tsama'owingeh, Maestas Pueblo, and LA 142926 represent the earliest examples villages with associated sacred geographies in the Rio Chama watershed. Not coincidentally, the late thirteenth century was also the time when contemporaneous areas of the northern Rio Grande region began to experiment with new conceptions of space and place, including complex landscapes of cupule, ground-slick, rock circle, and nonground shrines in the Taos area (Fowles 2009) and the Galisteo Basin (Snead 2008). The origins of the Pindi phase settlers are currently unknown, but it is possible that they represent migrants from the regions north and west of the Tewa Basin who continued their ideas of the "villagescape" (Fowles 2009), similar to those expressed at Chaco Canyon (Marshall 1997; Stein and Lekson 1992; Windes 1978) and in the northern San Juan basin (Fetterman and Honeycutt 1987; Ortman 2010). For Maestas Pueblo and LA 142926, this suggests that the Summer People were present in the Chama in Pindi times.

While the settlers of the Rio Chama watershed were experimenting with new ways of creating space they were also participating in an ancient Rio Grande architectural tradition. The kivas of Tsama'owingeh (Windes and McKenna 2006) are a central focus in the earliest component of the site and are oriented to the east. Stephen Lakatos (2007) argues that the eastern orientation of pit structures/kivas is unique to the northern Rio Grande region (versus orientation primarily to the south in the northern San Juan region) and that this tradition has been maintained from AD 500 to today. He argues that the northern Rio Grande kiva form represents Pueblo cosmological elements such as the middle place and dualities (seasonally dividing the year along an east-southeast axis that points to the rising sun on winter solstice) that are vital to the historic Tewa. Therefore, while it is difficult to determine the origins of the settlers of the Rio Chama watershed in the Pindi phase, multiple cosmological traditions were possibly expressed concurrently in the thirteenth century. The negotiation of these new ideas has defined ancestral Tewa landscapes through the modern day.

A TURBULENT TRANSFORMATION

The early fourteenth century, which I define as the Wiyo phase (1300–1350) of the Coalition period, was tumultuous for the entire northern Rio Grande region. Population expansion into the Tewa Basin continued as the final wave of migrants entered the region (Orcutt 1991; Ortman 2016a). A dramatic region-wide climatic downturn between 1320 and 1360 (Orcutt 1991; Rose et al. 1981:104; Towner and Salzer 2013:58) may have acted as a catalyst for population coalescence, or the movement of people into fewer but larger villages, in the Wiyo phase (Crown, Orcutt, and Kohler 1996). The general shift from high-elevation mesa-top villages to low-elevation river-valley towns has been clearly documented on the Pajarito Plateau (Orcutt 1999), a patterns that Preucel (1987) attributes to increasing competition among different population centers. The process of coalescence appears to have been happening at a regional scale as well, possibly with people on the Pajarito Plateau moving north into the Rio Chama watershed, as evidenced by the northward flow of pottery (Duwe 2019).

The Wiyo phase in the Chama has been traditionally defined by a series of material elements first clearly described by Frank Hibben (1937) and his "biscuitoid" culture: the use of predominately Wiyo Black-on-white decorated pottery, quadrangular plaza pueblos, single east-oriented kivas, and defensive characteristics. The term *biscuitoid* comes from the physical properties of Wiyo Black-on-white, which is a transitional pottery type between the widespread Santa Fe Black-on-white and the much more localized Tewa biscuitwares (Abiquiu Black-on-gray and Bandelier Black-on-gray) that were produced beginning in the mid-fourteenth century (Shepard 1936). Hibben's (1937) description of life in the early fourteenth century was primarily based on three villages located along the Rio Chama: Kap'owingeh (LA 300; Luebben 1953), near the confluence of the Rio Chama with the Rio Grande, and Palisade (LA 3505; Peckham 1981) and Riana Ruin (LA 911; Hibben 1937), located on the northwestern frontier of Pueblo settlement in the region. These villages share unique features, including a three-walled room block with an ephemeral fourth wall, an orientation to the southeast, and an abundance of Wiyo Black-on-white pottery.

In the eighty years since Hibben's synthesis, archaeologists working in the Tewa Basin have learned that (1) population influx during the Wiyo phase was much greater than originally thought (Anschuetz 1998a; Beal 1987; Duwe 2011; Marshall and Walt 2007) and (2) architecture, ceramic, and ritual landscape patterns resemble earlier Four Corners (Trott and Taylor 1994) and contemporaneous and later Rio Grande (Marshall and Walt 2007) styles, suggesting that the population of the Tewa Basin was not as culturally homogenous as initially believed (Duwe 2011, 2016).

The first point, that Wiyo phase occupation of the Rio Chama watershed was much more extensive than previously thought, is demonstrated by the building of new villages along the previously uninhabited Rio Chama tributaries of the Rio del Oso and Rio Ojo Caliente, as well as peripheral areas of the region (figure 11). These new villages include Sandoval Pueblo (LA 98319), a 136-room village composed of two-room blocks oriented to the east, located along the Rio Ojo Caliente (Duwe 2011), and LA 142927, a small quadrangular site that is similar to Palisade and Riana Ruins (Bremer 1995b). And there is a likely a much larger Wiyo phase settlement pattern that is likely masked by the later and much bigger villages of the Classic period. Both Santa Fe Black-on-white and Wiyo Black-on-white pottery are found at every Classic period village in the Chama Valley (Duwe 2011; Fallon and Wening 1987; Ortman 2012; Wendorf 1953), and the Wiyo phase component of Ponshipa'akedi'owingeh is clearly visible (Duwe 2011). This persistent evidence of Wiyo phase material culture suggests that the population was larger than previously believed and that these new villages were anchors for eventual Classic period coalescence. While the size and histories of these places remain unclear, I have included these Classic period villages as possible Coalition period occupations in map 4.

The second point, concerning the apparent cultural heterogeneity, is particularly expressed through architecture. Although Hibben's biscuitoid pattern is strong, figure 13 demonstrates the range in architectural variability among Wiyo phase villages. Both Sandoval and Tsipin'owingeh are linear sites, versus the compact and quadrangular C-shaped villages, and Tsipin'owingeh was by far the largest settlement in the Rio Chama in the early thirteenth century with 450 rooms and thirteen kivas. These villages are all roughly contemporaneous, suggesting multiple groups of people residing in the valley. To Hibben and his contemporaries, Wiyo phase material culture represents a push of new settlers into the Rio Chama watershed (Hewett 1938; Hibben 1937; Mera 1934). It is difficult to argue to the contrary, as biscuitoid villages appear quite different from Pindi phase settlements. But how can we explain the heterogeneity among villages, particularly those that were built at the same time? In the following discussion I recall my and others' work at Wiyo phase villages and specifically highlight two remarkable but very different villages on the northwestern periphery of the Tewa world.

THE NORTHWEST FRONTIER

The upper reaches of the lower Chama, including the fertile, yet cold (Anschuetz 1998a:84), valleys of the Cañones and Polvadera Creeks and the rugged canyon country of the Chama, remained sparsely populated until 1312, when significant new settlements occurred on the northwestern frontier of the Tewa Basin. It is rare to be able to accurately date specific historical events in the northern Rio Grande archaeological record, but based on collected and available tree-ring dates, two important—but very different—settlements were built in 1312 in the far western area of the Rio Chama watershed: Palisade Ruin (LA 3505) and Tsipin'owingeh (LA 301). Palisade Ruin is a prototypical Wiyo phase site; its site plan was used in Hibben's (1937) initial classification of the period's material culture. Tsipin'owingeh, meanwhile, is a large, approximately 450-room linear pueblo with one great and twelve small kivas that in many ways stands out as an anomaly compared with contemporaneous settlements in the Rio Chama watershed and the Tewa Basin as a whole.

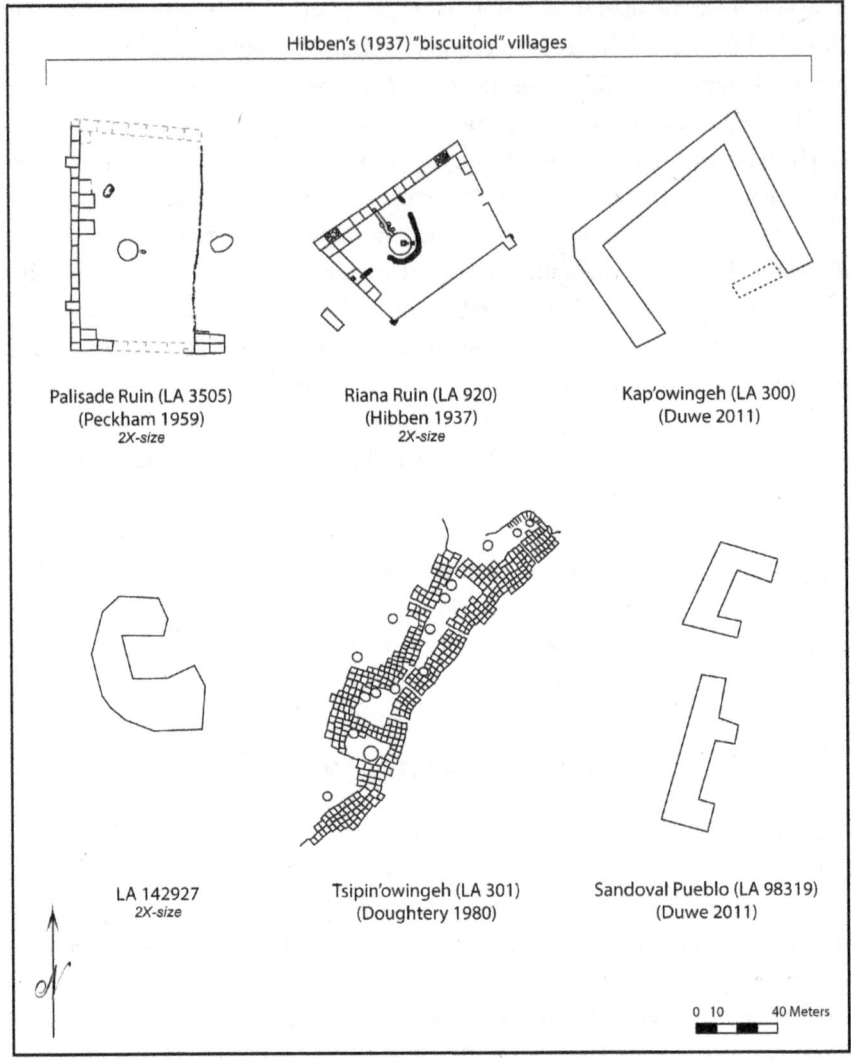

FIGURE 13 Plan maps of Wiyo phase villages in the Rio Chama valley.

Palisade Ruin is located on a high plateau overlooking the narrow neck of the Rio Chama canyon. The village is a small fifty-room U-shaped pueblo with a wooden fence, described as a palisade by the excavators, on the south side completing the quadrangle and enclosing a central plaza (figure 13). Based on a relatively large tree-ring sample, the village was built in 1312. And based on both tree-ring dates and the ceramic assemblage, it was likely only occupied for a generation (Klager 1980). The site, excavated by Museum of New Mexico in 1958 as part of a salvage project related to the construction of Abiquiu Reservoir, was revisited in 2016 by the University of Oklahoma field school. Because the excavations were never backfilled and the backdirt was never screened, our goal was to remap the village and to screen excavated dirt to recover artifacts (mainly pottery and lithic debitage) for analysis (Duwe 2017; figure 14). When combined with previously curated collections, which we reanalyzed, our project has allowed Palisade Ruin to be one of the best-understood Wiyo phase villages in the region.

Tsipin'owingeh is located 8 km south of Palisade Ruin on a highly inaccessible mesa that Mera (1934:4) categorized as "defensive." Based on available dendrochronological dates, the village appears to have been initially built between 1312 and 1314 (Klager 1980). Unfortunately, the wood beams with cutting dates lack provenience data, and it is impossible to identify the areas of initial occupation or architectural growth patterns. However, a second cluster of dates centers around 1325–1326 and biscuitware was identified on the ground surface, suggesting that people lived in the village through the beginning of

FIGURE 14 The 2016 University of Oklahoma excavations at Palisade Ruin.

FIGURE 15 The rubble of Tsipin'owingeh, looking south.

the Classic period (Duwe 2011). The village was built with locally available tuff-block masonry (figure 15) but also has hundreds of "cavate" rooms carved into the cliff edge east of the site, a great kiva, and a world-quarter shrine. A small adobe roomblock is also located to the north, which may represent a later occupation. Tsipin'owingeh was the largest site in the Rio Chama watershed in the first half of the fourteenth century, a claim contested only by the contemporaneous large site of Wiyo Pueblo, in the Santa Cruz valley on the east side of the Rio Grande (Marshall and Walt 2007). The village has never been professionally excavated but was mapped (Doughtery 1980; Duwe 2011) and surface collected (Trott and Taylor 1994). Kathryn Jerome (2018) analyzed approximately half of the 2,600 painted sherds collected from the ground surface, and Daniel Quintela (2018) examined all flaked stone material as part of the current project.

Architecturally—in size, site plan, and building material—Palisade Ruin and Tsipin'owingeh are starkly different places. Hibben (1937) explained the difference in architecture though his interpretation of the site's chronologies. Though Palisade Ruin was occupied in the Wiyo phase, he believed Tsipin'owingeh's occupation extended through the Classic period. While his assertion is correct based on biscuitware found at Tsipin'owingeh (Duwe 2011; Jerome 2018), Hibben did not yet have access to tree-ring dates that demonstrate both villages were built the same year. Robert Greenlee (1933) thought that these villages may have been built by different people, with Tsipin'owingeh having closer connections to the Jemez Mountains and the Pajarito Plateau to the south. The idea that the villages were built at the same time but by different people patterns well with what we know of contemporaneous architecture in the Chama and beyond. Palisade Ruin looks like a small replica of the contemporaneous village of Kapo'owingeh, suggesting a shared identity. Within the plaza is a single east-oriented kiva (Peckham 1981) reminiscent of an indigenous Rio Grande style (Lakatos 2007). So too is its C-shaped site plan, which is similar to that found in the middle northern Rio Grande (Dickson 1975). Tsipin'owingeh resembles both contemporaneous and later sites on the Pajarito Plateau. The linear site plan and multiple small kivas are similar to early fourteenth-century sites on the Pajarito Plateau (Trott and Taylor 1994). Some of the kivas are oriented to the south, a pattern closely aligned with the Mesa Verde region (figure 16). Furthermore, the surrounding sacred geography (described below) is heavily dominated by serpent imagery that is also characteristic of sites both north and south of Frijoles Canyon on the Pajarito Plateau (Munson 2002:156).

The differences between the two villages extend to the material culture, which shows that the residences of both places participated in unique social and economic networks. We were surprised to find that almost one-fifth (17 percent) of the painted pottery from Palisade Ruin was Pindi Black-on-white, a distinctive type of pottery characterized by white crushed pumice temper (Duwe 2017). Pindi Black-on-white is a variant of Santa Fe Black-on-white, which was produced in Santa Fe and the nearby Sangre de Cristo Mountains, the traditional home of the Winter People (Stubbs and Stallings 1953; Wilson 2007). Because biscuitoid villages like Palisade Ruin represent a wave of new settlement in the Chama, it suggests that these people originated from the eastern side of the Rio Grande. While Palisade Ruin is not unique in its connection to the home of the Winter People—Pindi Black-on-white constituted 32 percent of the painted pottery from Tsama'owingeh (Ortman 2012:322–323)—this pattern of a long-term connectedness with the Rio Grande villages becomes significant when compared with Tsipin'owingeh (1.9 percent). Tsipin'owingeh does not appear to have this same connection to the eastern portion of the Tewa Basin, but it does have higher percentages of both Vallecitos Black-on-white

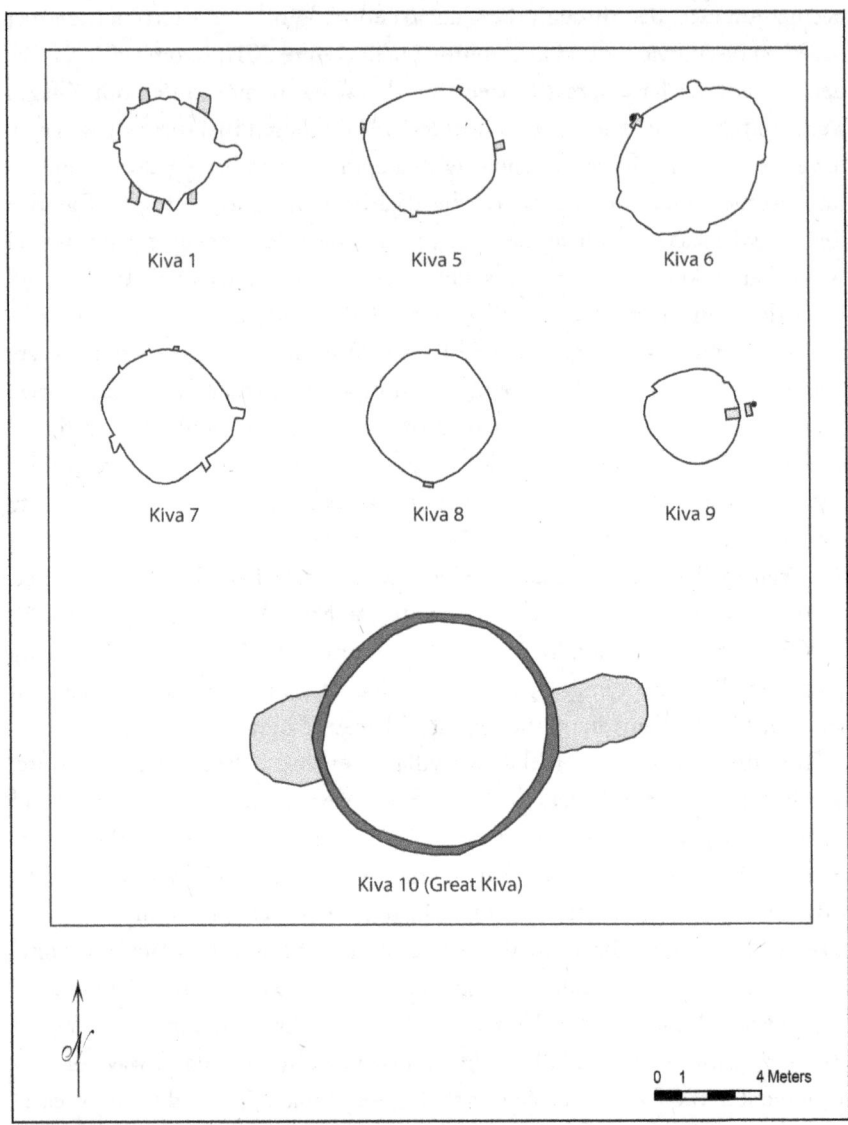

FIGURE 16 The kivas of Tsipin'owingeh (adapted from sketch drawings in Doughtery 1980).

(3.2 percent) and Jemez Black-on-white (0.6 percent), both made in the Jemez Mountains to the south (Jerome 2018).

This diversity between Palisade Ruin and Tsipin'owingeh, particularly in connection with places on the landscape, emerges from a comparison of the lithic assemblages from each village. Two important sources for stone tools are situated on the northwest edge of the Tewa world. Eroding from the flanks of Cerro Pedernal, or Tsipin in Tewa ("flaking stone mountain"), are beds of white, red, and black chert/chalcedony. The high-quality chert was mined at the source and also collected from small nodules found in the alluvial gravels in the vicinity of Abiquiu Lake (Smith and Huckell 2005; Warren 1974). The Jemez Mountains to the south are well known for obsidian and dacite materials, which are found at multiple sources, including at nearby Polvadera Peak (Shackley 2011). Both chert and obsidian were utilized by residents of the Tewa Basin, and the larger region, for thousands of years (Smith and Huckell 2005), and the lithic assemblages from both Palisade Ruin and Tsipin'owingeh contain both materials. However, when the debitage (a proxy for local production) between villages is compared, a pattern emerges of divergent landscape foci (table 3). The residents of Palisade overwhelmingly (77.3 percent) favored Pedernal chert, which is found in the local terrace gravels. Other material was also knapped, including orthoquartzite, dacite, and mudstone. Only very small quantities of obsidian (1.1 percent), likely originating from the Polvadera Peak, were identified, although finished obsidian tools were recovered (Duwe 2017). Conversely, the assemblage of Tsipin'owingeh is more diverse and favors Polvadera obsidian over Pedernal chert (Quintela 2018). This is surprising given that the name of

TABLE 3 Comparison of lithic material source from debitage between Palisade Ruin (LA 3505) and Tsipin'owingeh (LA 301)

MATERIAL	PALISADE RUIN	TSIPIN'OWINGEH
Pedernal chert	77.3%	8.9%
Polv. obsidian	1.1%	39.5%
Jemez obsidian	0	2.1%
Dacite	2.4%	0
Orthoquartzite	0.7%	0.5%
Mudstone	16.4%	1.6%
Other	2.1%	47.4%
Total	718	190

the village translates to "village of the flaking stone mountain," but it does suggest a strong connection to the Jemez Mountains and the south, perhaps even stronger than contemporaneous villages on the Pajarito Plateau had to these same sources where assemblages were composed of approximately 4–15 percent obsidian (Walsh 1998).

The heterogeneity of the Wiyo phase is seen not only in the diversity between villages but also perhaps within them as well. The predominate pottery, Wiyo Black-on-white, is viewed by archaeologists as a transitionary type between regional Santa Fe Black-on-white and more localized fourteenth-century wares. Wiyo Black-on-white pottery has classically been defined as exclusively produced as bowls, with polished interiors painted with dark black carbon paints, soft paste temper with volcanic material, and bold designs with thick lines (Habicht-Mauche 1993; McKenna and Miles 1996; Mera 1935). In reality, Wiyo Black-on-white is often defined by what it is not rather than by what it is: a locally produced Wiyo phase pottery that is neither the earlier Santa Fe Black-on-white nor the later biscuitware, nor any other type of contemporaneous pottery produced in the northern Rio Grande region. Archaeologists have long understood that Wiyo Black-on-white is messy and exhibits a high degree of stylistic (Luebben 1953) and technological (Wilson 2007) variability. Jerome (2018) recorded similar variability in paint and slip color, temper and paste, and vessel-wall thickness in pottery that I had previously recorded as Wiyo Black-on-white (Duwe 2011). While pots are not people, it is tempting to equate this heterogeneity in pottery with a heterogeneity of people who were learning and creating new pottery traditions as they also crafted new ideas of society and the cosmos. And this variability in pottery production is also present at both Palisade Ruin and Tsipin'owingeh, suggesting that none of these communities were homogenous wholes but rather dynamic places where people negotiated life in the Chama.

THE HETEROGENEITY OF THE COSMOS

The apparent heterogeneity of material culture between (and perhaps within) Wiyo phase villages is also manifested in sacred geographies. I chose four villages that encompass the geographic and spatial variability of the Rio Chama watershed and mapped the associated ritual landscapes (Duwe 2011, 2016). The area includes biscuitoid villages of Kap'owingeh, along the Rio Chama, and LA 142927, south of the Chama, and linear sites of Sandoval Pueblo in the Rio Ojo

Caliente valley, and Tsipin'owingeh. I and my survey crews also attempted to locate shrines at Palisade Ruin, but we were unable to do so. Maestas Pueblo, established in the Rio del Oso valley at approximately 1275, was also occupied to the mid-fourteenth century and into the Wiyo phase (Anschuetz 1993). In general, the shrines are similar to those of the earlier Pindi phase and later Classic period. As with the Pindi phase, there are few identifiable patterns and no evidence (besides at Tsipin'owingeh; see below) of the areas that Made People would have conducted their doings. There is also a diversity in the number, types, and places of these shrines, making the sacred geographies surrounding these villages as unique and diverse as other aspects of their material culture.

We know very little about the sacred geographies surrounding biscuitoid villages, as Riana Ruin was highly disturbed or destroyed in the building of Abiquiu Lake and the landscape surrounding Palisade Ruin was likely highly disturbed (Duwe 2017). Kap'owingeh, located on an alluvial bench overlooking the Rio Chama, exhibits some of the same shrine types found at other Wiyo phase villages, but unfortunately access to the landscape surrounding the site was limited to the south and west (figure 17). However, Kap'owingeh was built directly above a small cave that appears to have been the focal point of landscape ritual at the site. Although naturally occurring, the cave at Kap'owingeh was modified by human hands. Niches are carved into the cave walls and a petroglyph depicting a bird is located above the cave entrance. Caves were important places to the ethnographic-era Tewa, either as portals to the underworld or as the homes of dangerous mythical beings (Ortiz 1969; Parsons 1929). Villagers at the contemporaneous site of Tsipin'owingeh (discussed below) also modified natural caves for both functional and symbolic purposes. The location of Kap'owingeh, although situated on a prominent point with a viewshed that encompasses much of the Rio Chama valley, was almost certainly due to this cave. A series of forty cupules and seven ground-slicks were recorded on the exposed tuff bedrock surrounding and above the cave entrance.

The most complete landscape of this village type is LA 142927, which was first identified in the 1990s (Bremer 1995b). I identified two paired ground-slick boulders and a cupule shrine west of the architecture of the village (figure 17). This paucity of shrines is interesting when compared with linear villages like Sandoval or the much bigger Tsipin'owingeh (see below). The sample size of villages is small, but it suggests that biscuitoid villages had fewer and less diverse shrines. While the paucity of shrines at Palisade Ruin was attributed

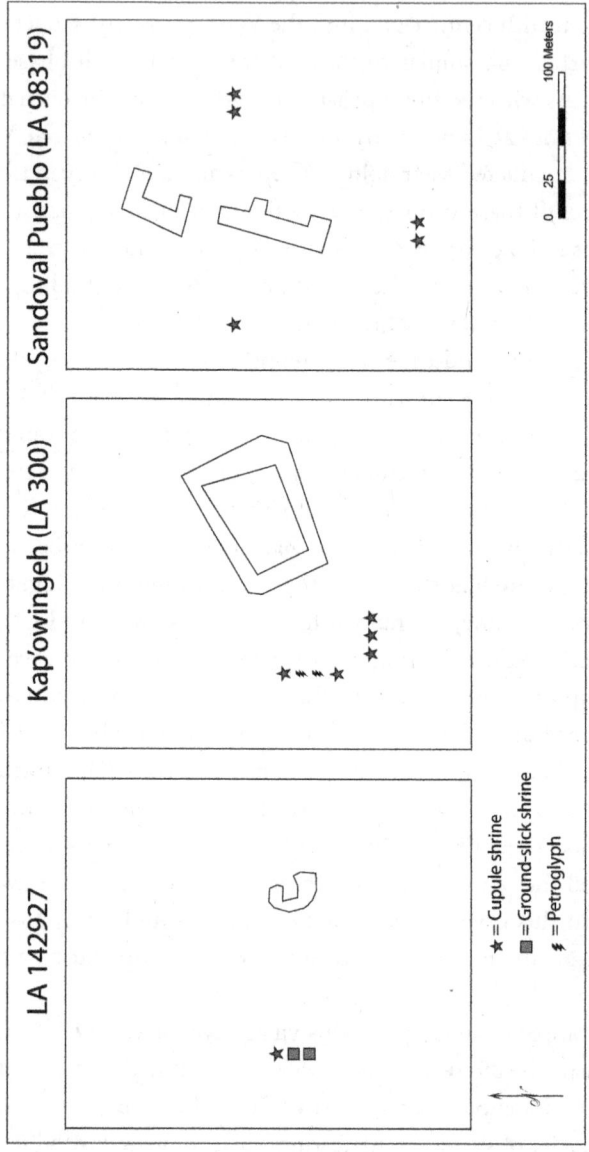

FIGURE 17 Schematic maps of the sacred geographies surrounding LA 142927, Kap'owingeh, and Sandoval Pueblo.

to landscape disturbance (Duwe 2017), it is possible there were few shrines to begin with and this may reflect diversity in landscape between multiple populations.

The biscuitoid villages appear to be different from other contemporaneous settlements, such as Sandoval Pueblo, located 5 km north of the confluence of the Rio Chama and the Rio Ojo Caliente. I found there a predominance of Wiyo Black-on-white pottery with smaller amounts of biscuitware, dating the village to 1300–1400 (Duwe 2011). A small village (136 rooms), Sandoval Pueblo is surrounded by six cupule shrines oriented to the west, south, and east (figure 17). These shrines are remarkable for the number and depth of cupules on each shrine. The southernmost cupule shrine at Sandoval Pueblo is composed of forty-two individual cupules ground to depths of up to 4 cm. If grinding depth is directly related to the amount of pecking performed, then the shrines at Sandoval Pueblo were either used for a long period of time or were intensely used over a short period. I have no doubt that Sandoval Pueblo was occupied through the end of the fourteenth century, based on a moderate amount of Abiquiu and Bandelier Black-on-gray pottery found at the village (Duwe 2011). Therefore, for a century these shrines were probably important places to the Classic period residents of the Rio Ojo Caliente valley. The small number of shrines and the intensity of their use suggest that that these six cupule shrine boulders were places of great importance. I interpret that the majority of archaeologically visible ritualized landscape activity at Sandoval Pueblo was invested in a limited number of shrines set near the middens surrounding the village. As such, the sacred geography of Sandoval Pueblo was similar to that of Maestas Pueblo in that it was primarily restricted to the scale of the village and the shrines were probably maintained by households.

The expansion of Wiyo phase settlers into the peripheral areas of the Rio Chama watershed includes a collection of villages near modern-day Abiquiu Reservoir. The area was first settled in 1312–1314 with the establishment of Palisade Ruin and Tsipin'owingeh. Tsipin'owingeh, easily the largest Wiyo phase site in the Rio Chama watershed, housed approximately four hundred people (Trott and Taylor 1994). The shrine assemblage surrounding the site, both in the number and the types of shrines present, is dramatically different from that of Maestas Pueblo, Kap'owingeh, and Sandoval Pueblo. Tsipin'owingeh is ringed by a large number of cupules, ground-slicks, channels, and serpents. The location of these shrines varies from the location of shrines around the other villages in the Rio Chama watershed. The shrines at Tsipin'owingeh are located on exposed tuffacious bedrock and not on individual boulders or cobbles, as they are at other villages. Because the site was only occupied for approximately forty years (Duwe 2011), the number of shrines at Tsipin'owingeh suggests an intensive use of the landscape.

Besides the quantity of shrines, the sacred geography of Tsipin'owingeh is unique in its high degree of serpent imagery. Serpent imagery, depicted in rock art and pottery of the Classic period, is uncommon in the Coalition period. While imagery of snakes could be attributed to the precocious nature of the site's landscape, illustrated in the building of a world-quarter shrine (see below), the preponderance of snakes could also relate to environmental woes experienced by residents of the northern Rio Grande region in the early fourteenth century (Orcutt 1991). Among the ethnographic-era Tewa (Parsons 1929:53), serpents are inherently tied to ideas of moisture and fertility, and similar concerns likely would have been found among the villagers of Tsipin'owingeh. Similar sorts of shrines and rock art found in Coalition period sites on the Pajarito Plateau, such as a large panel at LA 3851 with ground-slicks and channels (Munson 2002:156), adds weight to the interpretation that the original settlers of Tsipin'owingeh originated in the south and may have introduced new cosmological concepts in the Rio Chama watershed.

TRANSFORMATION

The second half of the Wiyo phase was a critical time of transition in the Rio Chama watershed. Populations appear to have continued to grow throughout the Rio Chama watershed in the first half of the fourteenth century. The largest village in the region, Tsipin'owingeh, underwent a substantial building event in 1325–1326. Because the tree-ring samples with cutting dates are unprovenienced, it is impossible to understand the specific nature of village growth. However, based on nineteen tree-ring samples that were collected from the roomblock architecture in 2009, both early and late-dated beams appear to be intermixed spatially across the site (Duwe 2011). It is likely that the 1325–1326 building event was a significant addition to the standing architecture, possibly representing the construction of additional stories and the influx of populations moving into the Tewa Basin (Trott and Taylor 1994). What is known is that the village's world-quarter shrine dates to this time period—a wood beam with a cutting date of 1326 was found imbedded in the stones of the shrine.

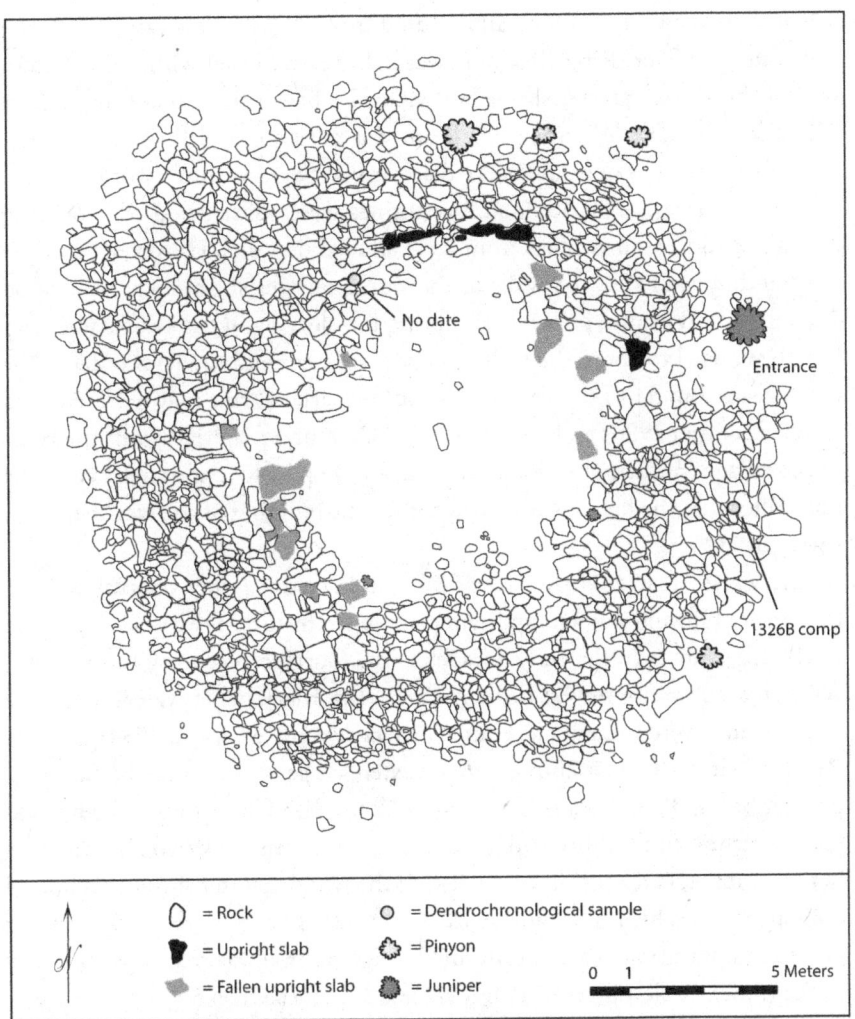

FIGURE 18 The world-quarter shrine of Tsipin'owingeh.

The world-quarter shrine at Tsipin'owingeh is located approximately 0.5 km southeast of the site on a small mesa connected to Pueblo Mesa by a narrow ridge (figure 18). The shrine conforms to the average shape, size, and orientation of similar shrines throughout the Rio Chama watershed. The Tsipin'owingeh world-quarter shrine is 12 m in diameter and was constructed from piled sandstone slabs. Wall height is 1.5 m on the northern portion of the shrine—considerably taller than similar shrines—with an opening, or entrance, oriented to the east. A piñon limb, cored in 2009 in collaboration with the Laboratory of Tree-Ring Research, was discovered buried within the eastern wall of the world-quarter shrine and yielded a bark ring and cutting date of 1326 (Duwe 2011). Whether this beam was cut and used for the construction of the shrine is debatable. The discovery of wood within a world-quarter shrine is unusual, as all other similar shrines were constructed of a low ring of granite and basalt cobbles from local alluvial deposits. However, based on the standing wall size, the walls of the world-quarter shrine may have stood 2 m tall. Wood beams, possibly cut during the clearing of the shrine area, may have been used to shore the walls composed of dry-laid sandstone slabs. The dated beam found in Tsipin'owingeh's world-quarter shrine may represent "old wood" (Schiffer 1986) and the reuse of architectural materials from the ruins of the village. But the shrine's distance from the pueblo lends credence to the possibility that the beam was indeed cut for the building of the world-quarter shrine in 1326.

The world-quarter shrine specifically addressed weather control and the bringing of rain and was an important place in the historic Tewa world (Jeançon 1923). The climate in the early decades of the fourteenth century was unstable across the entire Southwest (Orcutt 1991). The Rio Chama watershed, while warmer and wetter than the Four Corners region (Maxwell 1994) and the Pajarito Plateau (Gabler 2009), suffered extended periods of drought. Growing populations at Tsipin'owingeh and in the entire Rio Chama watershed would place moisture and fertility at the forefront of concerns for Wiyo phase settlers in the peripheral areas of the watershed. If the world-quarter shrine was indeed built in 1326, it is likely no coincidence that at the end of the large-scale building event at Tsipin'owingeh a shrine devoted to agricultural was erected within view of the (now) fertile valleys of Polvadera and Cañones Creeks.

Ethnographically, the world-quarter shrine was unlike the village shrines that immediately surround a village. Ceremonialism at the world-quarter shrine was practiced not by individuals or household groups—the Dry Food People (Ortiz 1969)—but by the leaders of the village and those with high degrees of ritual knowledge. Jeançon (1923:53) describes use of the shrine as part of a four-day retreat. The Summer and Winter chiefs, as well as the Kossa and Kwirana (Tewa clowns) and lay assistants, would pray for rain. The appearance of a world-quarter shrine at Tsipin'owingeh in 1326 suggests that this sort of ceremonial hierarchy, or one similar to it, may have been present in the latter part of the Wiyo phase.

While the world-quarter shrine at Tsipin'owingeh is the only dated shrine of its type in the northern Rio Grande region, it is by no means unique. In the Taos area, Fowles (2009) recorded an earthen-berm circle north of T'aitöna that is similar to a world-quarter shrine. Wiyo Pueblo, a five-hundred- to one-thousand-room village located across the Rio Grande in the Rio Santa Cruz valley (Marshall and Walt 2007), was likely occupied from 1300 to 1350 and is associated with a world-quarter shrine. Based on its association with the Wiyo phase village, the shrine is probably contemporaneous with Tsipin'owingeh's world-quarter shrine. Additionally, a shrine that resembles a world-quarter shrine was identified at Burnt Corn Pueblo in the southern Tewa Basin (Snead 2008), although its orientation is slightly different, as it is located approximately 300 m north of the village.

Tsipin'owingeh was probably not unique in its landscape transformation during the Wiyo phase. Ancestral Tewa sites across the Tewa Basin, especially those of large (>400 rooms) size, were likely undergoing similar changes in adapting to population, subsistence, and metaphysical pressures. However, Tsipin'owingeh provides an excellent case for how these factors contributed to a major step in the process of Tewa becoming. Within a quarter century similar processes would occur at the Classic period villages.

And then, by mid-century, Pueblo occupation of the upper lower Rio Chama valley ceased. The bellwether was Riana Ruin (and possibly some of its residents), which was the casualty of a catastrophic burning event that Hibben (1937) places around 1350. Kap'owingeh was also left and burned at this time (Luebben 1953). And although small quantities of Abiquiu Black-on-gray and Bandelier Black-on-gray pottery were found at Tsipin'owingeh, the main occupation of the site was likely finished by the mid-1300s (Trott and Taylor 1994). Archaeologists have traditionally struggled with interpreting evidence of violence among ancestral Pueblo populations (Walker et al. 2000). Finding a motive for arson at Riana Ruin, a site that was likely a defensive outpost at the entry to the Tewa world, appears relatively straightforward. The site was burned quickly and completely, the remains of an individual were found among the fallen roof timbers, and a ceremonial headdress—likely passed down through generations and of immeasurable value (Parsons 1933)—was discovered in the ashes of the kiva (Hibben 1937).

Riana Ruin, the evidence suggests, was the victim of an attack. The perpetrator remains unknown. Based on the transformation occurring across the northern Rio Grande during this time period, enemies may have come from outside the Pueblo area in the form of raids from the Plains (Wendorf 1953), or the villagers may have been the victims of perceived or real endemic violence (Fowles 2004b). Another possibility is that Pueblo people burned the village as an act of persecution of witchcraft (Darling 1998; Walker 1998). Whatever the reason, the ancestral Tewa population receded downriver by mid-century, where they settled the massive villages built in the Classic period.

DISCUSSION

The heterogeneity of material culture—including architecture, pottery, flaked stone, and sacred geographies—suggests that the Chama was settled by multiple groups of different people in the century prior to coalescing at the large Classic period villages. The first settlers established Tsama'owingeh in the 1230s, with smaller villages built on the south side of the Chama through the end of the century. The identities of these people are difficult to discern, but archaeologically they appear to have more in common with contemporaneous migrant communities across northern New Mexico. In the early fourteenth century many more people moved into the valley and founded villages that are strikingly different materially. Some, such as Palisade Ruin, have connections with the eastern portion of the Tewa world, while others, like Tsipin'owingeh, appear related to contemporaneous villages to the west. We know that by the mid-fourteenth century these people coalesced into very large villages, and therefore the development of these undeniably Tewa villages required the negotiation of the many people who had made their homes in the Chama.

Our expanding understanding of the diversity and extent of material culture challenges notions that Tewa origins and identity can be explained either as in situ Rio Grande development or as the result of migrations from the northern Southwest. Rather, the world-changing events of the thirteenth century—drought, social upheaval, diaspora—catalyzed movements of and encounters between peoples across much of the Southwest and, importantly, in northern New Mexico. When viewed through the lens of the Tewa's migration tradition—that of two distantly related yet distinct people traveling separately down the eastern and western sides of the Rio Grande—the newcomers (Summer People) and first-comers (Winter People) are both Tewa ancestors, and both contributed significantly to a new life in the middle place (Parsons 1994[1926]:15). Because the Tewa world is hardly monolithic, these encounters played out differently through space and time (Duwe and Cruz 2019). But the complementarity between summer and winter is reflected in nearly every aspect of Tewa life today (Ortiz 1969) and is reflected materially in the past through the hybridization of ancient Rio Grande notions of space and novel placemaking traditions.

The coming together of these disparate people was not just a single event but a continual process, a process that lasted over a century in the Chama itself. This is likely why it is so difficult to assign identity to settlers in the Pindi and Wiyo phases. While some migrants may have entered the Chama from the northwest, and some first-comers may have traveled west from the skirts of the Sangre de Cristos Mountains, many settlers probably had already begun the process of negotiation with their new neighbors in the early thirteenth century. There are indications that this happened on the east side of the Rio Grande at Tekhe'owingeh (Duwe and Cruz 2019) and on the Pajarito Plateau (Ortman 2012). When individuals from these many groups began to make their homes in the Chama, distinctions between indigenous and migrant, if they existed, were already blurred.

For Ortiz, the traditions recalling the journeys of the Summer and Winter People and their eventual coming together offer a historical explanation of the inherent dualities of Tewa life. An explanation I believe is supported through the material record. But for the Tewa, according to Tessie Naranjo (1995), the details of these journeys, such as specific sites, places, and dates—much of my discussion in this chapter—are not so important. She writes, "Any Pueblo person, who is asked to tell a story about our migration or about anything else, will tell a story and others will not contradict or correct it. All stories are considered valid. There is never one version of any story. There are many ways to describe an event" (1995:248). Instead of specific details, larger concepts of movement, placemaking, breathing, and dying are emphasized. These larger concepts are essential elements in the Tewa philosophy of seeking harmony and balance and embracing the transformation of life that results from the tension of opposites (Swentzell 1993:45).

Naranjo (1995:249) explains that archaeologists seek specific and detailed truths, while the Tewa tell generalized stories encompassing many truths, with one person's truth not invalidating another's. What is important are the larger processes of movement and transformation. Much of the debate about Tewa origins is focused on the details of population size and occupation dates, but movement and transformation certainly play a role in each model. The advantage of adopting the conceptual framework of Summer and Winter People is that our starting point is the assumption that multiple people contributed, and belonged, to Tewa society. Rather than focusing on which people (firstcomers or newcomers) contributed *the most* to the Tewa cultural identity, we can instead explore the historical contingencies of how these people interacted and negotiated their worlds. They engaged in a continual process of seeking life that took many forms, just as there are multiple truths and diversity among Tewa villages today.

Returning to the question posed at the beginning of the chapter: Who and when are the Tewa? To speak of archaeologically identifiable origins of the Tewa is difficult because there are many Tewa ancestors. If we accept the Tewa's model of Summer and Winter People, then neither group of people can be privileged over the other; they are considered today to be equal and complementary halves of a total whole. The negotiations among the people may have been rife with tension, and judging from the remains of Riana Ruin, not always peaceful. It is easier to identify patterns of difference in the material record than to understand how these negotiations occurred, but emphasizing continuities over change is a powerful direction for future research.

One could make the argument that what we consider *Tewa* was a process of ethnogenesis in the thirteenth and fourteenth centuries that resulted in Classic period village life. But as I'll discuss in the next chapter, these villages were in many ways the result of the continuation of the same processes that occurred earlier, and continue through to the modern day. In this way the Tewa are forever in a process of becoming, and therefore our discussions of origins seem foreign to Tewa scholars like Ortiz. Unlike him, I am interested in time in the historical dimension. But we can strive to acknowledge two important points. The first is that the Tewa have maintained a unique yet fluid identity since the time of emergence (Ortiz 1991:7). The people did not become Tewa somewhere along the journey but have always been Tewa, forever in a process of becoming. The second is that the certainty with which the Tewa speak of their origins is different from that of Western archaeologists. Tessie Naranjo explains the Tewa perspective this way:

> Truth for the non-Indian is outside of him/herself. For Pueblo people, it is again that larger idea of being one with everything so that the truth does not exist outside of the self. Each person is a center as is each Pueblo community. Perceptions from centers are not exclusive. Therefore, we speak with certainty

without accepting exclusive truths. Knowledge, for the Indian person, is something that comes from the person and the community. It arises from consensus. Movement is part of us. Explanations are not necessary—only stories which remind, acknowledge, and honor the power and force of movement. People have moved from place to place and have joined and separated again throughout our past, and we have incorporated it into our songs, stories, and myths because we must continually remember that, without movement, there is no life. (Naranjo 1995:249–250)

Recent research addressing the thirteenth and fourteenth centuries is expanding our understanding of the inherent messiness of the material record and making it more difficult to fit the data into traditional archaeological models. Perhaps by exploring this messiness through the process of movement and the continuous path of seeking life we too can accept, or at least acknowledge, nonexclusive truths in the becoming of the Tewa world.

CHAPTER 5

The Center and the Edge

When Adolph Bandelier climbed to the top of a steep terrace on the west bank of the Rio Ojo Caliente in the early 1880s, he was amazed at what lay before him: a series of massive adobe housemounds, which he estimated housed two thousand people, and an incredible vista where "the whole valley stretches out" (Bandelier 1892:45). He was also particularly struck by the number and size of the kivas, which he attributed to a complex social organization, and the amount and diversity of material culture exposed by pot hunters (figure 19). Bandelier believed that this place, called Posi'owingeh by his Tewa consultants (translated as "greenness pool height pueblo ruin" [Harrington 1916:165]), was clearly very old, inhabited before the Spanish conquest, but that it was also unambiguous about its cultural affiliation. He drew a direct connection between the village and the Tewa people he knew along the Rio Grande. Bandelier noted in particular the sacredness of the hot springs that lay at the base of the terrace (a portal to the underworld and a representation of the place of emergence [Walt 2014]) and the stories of Pose-yemu, the hero, who was born and raised there (Bandelier 1892:47). And of course Alfonso Ortiz (1969) later recounted how the citizens of Ohkay Owingeh believe that it was at Posi'owingeh that the Summer and Winter People came together to create a new type of village life.

Bandelier would not be the last archaeologist to climb that terrace. In the decades that followed, advances in archaeological dating and a growing con-

FIGURE 19 An artist's reconstruction of Posi'owingeh. Richard Schlecht, NG Image Collection.

sensus of a Rio Grande culture history placed the building and occupation of Posi'owingeh in the Classic period (Beal 1987). In this new chronology Posi'owingeh was but one of many very large plaza-centered villages established in the mid-fourteenth century in the Chama Valley and across northern New Mexico. These villages, the product of population coalescence, were associated with dramatic changes in social and ceremonial organization, changes that are seen in large dance plazas, big kivas, complex sacred geographies of shrines, and an incredibly diverse and complex material culture (Wendorf and Reed 1955:153). The Classic period is also the time when distinct subregional patterns began to emerge, most notably through pottery, which archaeologists believe are early hints of the formation of modern Pueblo, and importantly Tewa, identities (Futrell 1998; Graves and Eckert 1998; Mera 1934, 1935). In short, the Classic period villages in the Chama and the greater Tewa Basin look much more similar to historic and ethnographic-era Tewa pueblos than anything that came before, and they mark the formation and emergence of a materially unique identity. If we draw from Ohkay Owingeh's tradition, it appears that the Summer and Winter People came together at many of the large Classic period villages, not just at Posi'owingeh, in a process that marks a significant step along the path of Tewa becoming (Anschuetz 1998a).

In this chapter I explore the creation of Tewa village life that emerged when many people from the small Wiyo phase villages coalesced and built very large towns along the Chama and its tributaries. I show that many of the foundational elements of being Tewa, described in chapter 2, such as dual division organization and a social hierarchy and ethnic boundaries, were clearly emphasized through the building of these villages and reflect the union of the peoples recorded in Tewa tradition. But I also argue that while to archaeologists these changes at first blush appear to signal a great transformation, they were certainly not entirely new, for the building of places like Posi'owingeh was the culmination of hundreds, if not thousands, of years of Tewa history. And the process of becoming is never complete. Similar processes of identity formation continued to occur throughout the Classic period and have been noted by archaeologists and historians in the Historic and modern periods.

Archaeologists have rightly, I believe, considered that the early to mid-fourteenth century represents an important period of Tewa becoming. But to isolate these series of migration and coalescence events as a singular expression of Tewa ethnogenesis substantially limits our ability to understand the ongoing negotiation of peoples and their worlds. In the following pages I demonstrate how the history of the Classic period was incredibly dynamic and includes a constant movement of people (through coalescence and between villages), shifting identities and social boundaries, and emerging and diverse social and ceremonial systems. In short, the history of the Tewa people is best understood as one of constant and ongoing ethnogenesis, a fluid and ever-transforming process the Tewa call *seeking life*, as the people negotiated how to be both divided and united.

ETHNOGENESIS AND BECOMING

There is no question that the Pueblo world was transformed in the wake of the historical events of the thirteenth century. The depopulation of the Four Corners region led to mass migration of thousands to the south and east, and the subsequent coming together of people is correlated with significant changes in village life. Within these plaza-centered villages arose new ceremonial systems (Adams 1991; Crown 1994; Glowacki and Van Keuren 2011), social organization (Reid et al. 1989), pottery (Habicht-Mauche et al. 2006), social networks (Mills et al. 2013), and subsistence and agricultural practices (Anschuetz et al. 2017; Camilli et al. 2019). The break between this suite of elements and those that came before was dramatic enough to warrant Alfred Kidder (1927) and other leading archaeologists to demarcate the beginning of a new era—the Pueblo IV period—that extended to the coming of the Spanish in the sixteenth century. Similar trends happened in the Rio Grande valley, although slightly later, causing Fred Wendorf (1954) to devise a new yet parallel chronology with different terminology. His Classic period is roughly contemporaneous with the Pueblo IV period, and the two are often used interchangeably.

With an increased focus on topics such as identity and agency and an increasing acceptance to listen to Pueblo tradition and reread ethnography, archaeologists have characterized the Pueblo IV period as representing the creation of new Pueblo worlds (Adams and Duff 2004). The historic events of regional depopulation, migration, and resettlement into coalescent communities in the thirteenth and fourteenth centuries fundamentally altered community life from what it had been, and the resulting social organization expressed the beginnings of the modern Pueblo people. While earlier processual approaches viewed the causes of migration and coalescence as influenced by climatic instability (Matson et al. 1988; Stuart and Gauthier 1981), resource scarcity (Dean et al. 1985; Hunter-Anderson 1979; Kohler and Matthews 1988), and population pressure (Moore and Boyer 2009), these new social approaches, although not dismissing the challenges of farming in an arid environment, focused on the historical consequences of negotiating new societies.

Archaeologists have addressed in particular questions of how and why Pueblo people fundamentally reorganized their communities to embrace an ethic of community collectivism and social uniformity, the hallmark of the modern Pueblos. This is evidenced by the large plazas that center the village (areas of communal performance) and the florescence of new types of ceremonial organization that encompass the entire community (Adams 1991). This ethic, similar to the Tewa ethic described in chapter 2, is practiced at all the pueblos and emphasizes complementarity, balance and harmony, and, notably, the absence of overt forms of hierarchical leadership and centralized power (Parsons 1996[1939]). The communal village is in stark contrast with social life in the preceding centuries, such as the experimentation with urbanism, hierarchical government, and regional polity of the Chaco Phenomenon (Lekson 2012) or the household or lineage-centric aggregated villages of the thirteenth-century Mesa Verde region (Glowacki 2015). Severin Fowles (2012) proposes that the village life of the Pueblo IV period is emblematic of a reformation movement, a rejection of earlier theocracies, and a democratization of the cosmos.

The novelty of these new systems of organization, combined with the concurrent settlement of many of the modern Pueblo villages, has led some southwestern archaeologists to view the Pueblo IV period transition as a kind of ethnogenesis, or the creation of new ethnic identities. Ethnogenesis, as both a historical and a social process, has undergone a resurgence in the archaeological literature in varied contexts, from colonial encounters to deep antiquity (Hu 2013; Voss 2008, 2015; Weik 2014). These researchers focus on the historical processes and consequences of the creation of new ethnic identities, defined as beliefs of shared common ancestry through similarities in customs or "memories of colonization and migration" (Weber 1978, cited in Hu 2013). These processes may include the consequences of colonization, intersections at frontiers or borderlands, or the movement of people, among others, and focus on the negotiation of novel identities. From the broad strokes of Pueblo history painted in this volume, and the specific discussions of Tewa tradition and archaeology, ethnogenesis is a captivating frame for viewing the migration and coalescence of disparate people and the formation of new center places.

For example, Wesley Bernardini (2011) explores Hopi ethnogenesis as the convergence of two peoples with different historical trajectories: the Motisinom from the north and the Nùutungkwisinom from the south. Meeting at the Hopi Mesas, they reconciled their diverging ceremonial systems to forge a Hopi identity. Scott Ortman (2012), too, draws on an ethnogenetic framing to explain Tewa origins in the late thirteenth and early fourteenth centuries. He argues, as discussed in the previous chapter, that the drought and social unrest of the thirteenth century led to a rejection of the corrupt lifeways of the migrants leaving the Mesa Verde region and an embrace of older ways practiced by their distant relatives in the Rio Grande valley. This historical contingency explains that lack of material traces of the migrants' homelands as well as the new types of architecture, subsistence strategies, material culture, and settlement patterns. Kurt Anschuetz (2007b; Anschuetz and Wilshusen 2011) also explores Tewa ethnogenesis but emphasizes the importance of both indigenous and migrant people in its formation and its dynamic and ongoing processes. Although the study of ethnicity and ethnogenesis has been recast as social identity by some because of negative associations with historical uses of ethnicity (Preucel 2005a), similar ideas have been present over the past century of southwestern archaeology, from Harry Mera's (1935) discussions of the emergence of historic Pueblo linguistic and social boundaries in northern New Mexico to Andrew Duff's (2002) exploration of the formation of Hopi and Zuni identities.

These narratives are intriguing, particularly in how the material record and Pueblo tradition are in general agreement about key historical elements: great migrations, seeking and finding the middle place, and the coming together of disparate people to forge a new type of village life. However, the use of ethnogenesis to explain historical change seems to emphasize the stepwise transition between two relatively static, archaeologically constructed units of time—the transition between the Pueblo III and the Pueblo IV periods—more than change within these periods or continuity between them. I engaged in a similar critique in the previous chapter when addressing the problems of identifying origins and emphasizing change over continuity. While the Pueblo IV transition was undoubtedly crucial to the development of the Pueblos, it is certainly not the only one identified by archaeologists. For example, scholars working in the Historic period (Liebmann 2012; Liebmann et al. 2005; Preucel et al. 2002) argue that the social and residential upheaval of the Pueblo Revolt and its aftermath in the late seventeenth century directly led to the demographics and character of the modern Pueblos. This social upheaval included both the creation of new villages with diverse populations and the development of belief systems and a social organization that were both novel and purposely reminiscent of ancient (and non-Spanish) traditions. These ethnogenetic transformations have been claimed through the eighteenth and nineteenth centuries as well, with the development of *vecino* identities, or the hybridity of Native and Hispanic culture and class (Catanach and Agostini 2019; Jenks 2013).

Is it possible there are multiple instances of Pueblo ethnogenesis? Looking further back in time, we could also think about other transitions in the same light: the widespread adoption of maize agriculture (Reed 2000), the transition from pit house to pueblo (Rocek 1995), and the collapse of the Chaco Phenomenon (Lekson 2012). And in more recent history we see the dramatic changes in adapting to a Hispanic and an American landscape (Suina 2019). It appears that the Pueblos, like all people, are constantly remaking themselves and that their identities are fluid and never static. Returning to the lessons of chapter 1, this is exactly how the Tewa and other Pueblos view their own history: through the concept of always becoming and seeking life. The world is composed of the forever-fluid movement of people, things, spirits, blessings, and ideas. Perhaps we should begin to think of ethnogenesis not as an event that defines or explains great transitions but as an ongoing philosophy that guides Pueblo being and becoming (Anschuetz 2007b; Anschuetz and Wilshusen 2011).

This fluidity certainly defines Tewa history. In the last chapter I showed that Tewa origins cannot be attributed exclusively to either indigenous Rio Grande people or to migrants from the Four Corners region, but instead to both. These generalized groups encountered each other in the Tewa Basin throughout the thirteenth century. While archaeologists disagree about the nature of these interactions, there is no question that people and ideas mixed rapidly as migrants streamed into the northern Rio Grande valley. By rejecting the recent past and adopting much of the culture of their new neighbors who practiced something akin to the old ways, according to Ortman (2012), the migrants remade themselves and their society in this new homeland. Ortman sees a revolutionary analogy in the Pueblo Revolt and the purposeful shaking off of a corrupt lifestyle in favor of an old one. Though this is an intriguing idea, it may be an imperfect analogy, as the rulers of Mesa Verde were unlikely of the autocratic sort that defined Spanish colonizers, and therefore this process likely entailed more complex political, social, and ecological issues (Preucel 2013). Regardless, Ortman argues that Tewa ethnogenesis began through these interactions and the building of new types of villages that had Rio Grande–like elements that housed predominately migrant people. The initial negotiations and competition between these disparate yet distantly related people appear to have extended well into the fourteenth century. The Chama was settled by multiple populations who differentially engaged with one other and their landscapes throughout the 1200s. If ethnogenesis began when the people met and started to interact, then it continued for multiple generations. In fact, as this chapter will document, it was only at mid-fourteenth century, when the people from these Wiyo phase settlements coalesced and built very large villages, that we first observe settlement patterns, architectural design, material culture, and use of the landscape that resemble Ortiz's Tewa world. At the beginning of this period these ancestral Tewa villages began to produce and use similar material culture, namely pottery, whose distributions roughly correlate with historic and ethnographic sociolinguistic boundaries.

These villages represent something new and were the culmination of hundreds of years of Tewa history. And the subsequent Classic period was hardly static. Fred Wendorf and Erik Reed (1955:153), synthesizing the first seventy years of research conducted in the region, acknowledge that "all evidence indicates that this cultural expansion and florescence was still developing when it was abruptly modified by the impact of European culture." However, the nature of florescence, or ongoing ethnogenesis, has been obscured by lack of research and poor temporal resolution. In fact, many discussions of Tewa history present the Classic period, in the Chama specifically, as a relatively stable two centuries inaugurated by the building of massive villages and ended by their abandonment around the time of Spanish colonization (Beal 1987). Some archaeologists have noted a gradual process of coalescence (Mera 1934), but until recently few have acknowledged the dynamic movement of people, material, and ideas or the ever-changing nature of Tewa identity.

In this chapter I explore the culture history of the Chama Valley to emphasize both continuity and change. I begin by presenting the settlement history of the valley and by highlighting the multiple scales and types of movement. Through coalescence, seasonal mobility, and ongoing movement among villages the Tewa people were constantly negotiating their relationships with their people and the cosmos. Next, I demonstrate that being Tewa is largely contextual and ever changing and that, based on my pottery provenance and ceramic research, the villages of the Chama began to emerge as a separate social group in relation to other groups throughout the Tewa Basin. Finally, I focus on a central question of this volume: How did Tewa society become both united and divided? I explore the development of social and ceremonial organization that appears similar to that of historic and modern Tewa villages, including moieties and the ceremonial hierarchy. I argue that the roots of both extend deep into Tewa history, but it was through the historical contingencies of building large villages that the fundamental building blocks of Tewa social and ceremonial organization became expressed in unique ways. While becoming Tewa requires acknowledging both continuities and change, there are specific points in Tewa history where change occurred at a more rapid pace. I tie together the importance of coalescence in Tewa traditions with the material evidence to argue that while Tewa ethnogenesis is ongoing, the coming together of the Summer and Winter People laid the foundation for all future history.

MOVEMENT AND RETHINKING VILLAGE LIFE

The Classic period villages that line the waterways of the Chama are impressive and imposing places that captured the imagination of Bandelier and all later archaeologists. Even though the massive multistory roomblocks have collapsed and eroded, what remains are seemingly permanent monuments to two centuries of intensive occupation of the valley. The mounds of adobe are sometimes tall enough to garner their own contour lines on topographic maps, and the surrounding landscape remains verdant, as ancient agricultural technology retains lifegiving precipitation. For archaeologists, the Classic period has, true to its name, persisted as the central focus of Tewa culture history. In an older evolutionary narrative these villages represented the peak of Tewa society that was eventually corrupted by European conquest (Wendorf and Reed 1955). The material culture from this period simply dwarfs all else. These large towns were often built on (or of) earlier Coalition period villages, and a ubiquitous scatter of Tewa biscuitware pottery covers the thin soil between the piñons and junipers.

Despite the intense focus on the Classic period in the Chama, the era remains best defined by its bookends: the large-scale coalescence of people and the building of the large villages at the start of the period in the mid-fourteenth century and the depopulation of the valley at the end of the period beginning in the sixteenth century. The two centuries between these defining events are viewed as almost static. Archaeologists have postulated that these villages experienced growth and change, but an often unquestioned assumption of a sustained presence and demographic stability underlies our models of population size and settlement patterns (Duwe et al. 2016; Ortman 2016a). Archaeologists have assumed that the ancestral Tewa (and all Pueblo) people conceptualized village life as we in the West do today: as places of enduring sedentism where movement away (or "abandonment") is viewed as a failure to integrate a diverse society or as the consequence of external calamity. Success, then, is the ability to stay in place.

Recently, archaeologists working in northern New Mexico have begun to rethink the Pueblo village in light of the Pueblo's own philosophy of movement. Fowles (2011) engages with the paradox of Robin Fox's (1967:24) description of the Pueblos as "urbanized nomads," village agriculturalists who are constantly on the move. In Pueblo history the pathways between places (trails that carry people and channels flowing with *powaha*) are emphasized over the places themselves, and these networks of interconnectedness take material form in Pueblo cosmography. Fowles wonders if we can flip on its head the traditional assumption of residential stasis as the ideal nature. Perhaps stasis and village life were understood as disruptions within a normal state of perpetual movement. He asks, "Might villages have been conceived as mere way stations within the larger journey?" (Fowles 2010:50). At these "way stations" the Pueblos weathered sedentism through ritual: experiencing the perpetual movement of their ancestors through dance, pilgrimage to sacred places, and the recounting of past journeys through story and song. These ritualized expressions of movement were not just important for sustaining a philosophy of movement while residing in the village, they were also crucial for allowing residential movement to occur again.

Anschuetz (2007a), addressing the large Classic period Tewa villages of the Chama, demonstrates that even at the large villages movement never ceased. He argues that the large site footprints we map today are the result of the complex accumulation of the social actions of diverse people. While the village is a center place, it is not necessarily the population center. To adapt to climatic uncertainty, the Tewa employed a residential and organizational flexibility based on short-term sedentism to redistribute both populations and agricultural fields at smaller houses across their homeland. People built, lived in, left, and reoccupied the center places in a constant movement between the center and the edge. In this process, the people continually remade themselves (Duwe and Anschuetz 2013). Robert Preucel (1988) demonstrates a similar process on the Pajarito Plateau, where people moved back and forth between villages and field houses as a type of agricultural adaptation, a process of village succession in which some field houses became villages in their own right. Anschuetz suggests that the repetitive acts of building and maintaining the sheer size and scale of the large village's architectural footprint may have been more important than the occupation of these rooms (which was likely fluid and fleeting). In the context of continual movement, creating a coherent center place would have secured the legitimacy of their occupancy in the landscape, brought a sense of continuity, and marked the passage of time.

Both Fowles's and Anschuetz's critiques challenge archaeologists to reframe traditional notions of Pueblo village life by privileging movement over stasis and continuity over change. Unfortunately, much of this movement is beyond the grasp of my current data that examine the architectural footprint and (admittedly poor) chronologies of seventeen Classic period villages in the Chama Valley and the Pajarito Plateau (map 5). However, patterns do emerge of villages that were constantly being remade through the ebb and flow of people building, leaving, and returning to their middle places. The following is a culture history of the Classic period in the Chama Valley with particular emphasis on these fluid and ever-changing settlement patterns.

INITIAL COALESCENCE (1350–1400)

The Wiyo phase (1300–1350) appears to have ended with a major transformation. Many of the small villages established at the beginning of the fourteenth century, often hidden away in the peripheral canyons of the Tewa world, were depopulated (but not forgotten; chapter 6). The beginning of the Classic period (Wendorf and Reed 1955) is also when people began to move from the highland mesa tops on the Pajarito Plateau to the lowland areas, such as the Cochiti area (Orcutt 1999), the Rio Grande (Barrett 2002), and, based on the current data, the Rio Chama. These populations began to coalesce at very large sites in the mid- to late fourteenth century, with some villages growing to well over one thousand ground-floor rooms.

What is the cause of this apparent region-wide phenomenon? Janet Orcutt (1991) has explained that the early half of the fourteenth century was climatically unfavorable to Pueblo agriculture, based on Palmer Drought Severity Index (PDSI) data. It is a very real possibility that although Pueblo farmers used flexible and often successful farming techniques (Anschuetz 1998a), climatic realties resulted in a necessary resettlement to the verdant river valleys. Also, the end of the Wiyo phase was a time of apparent regional strife, with sites like

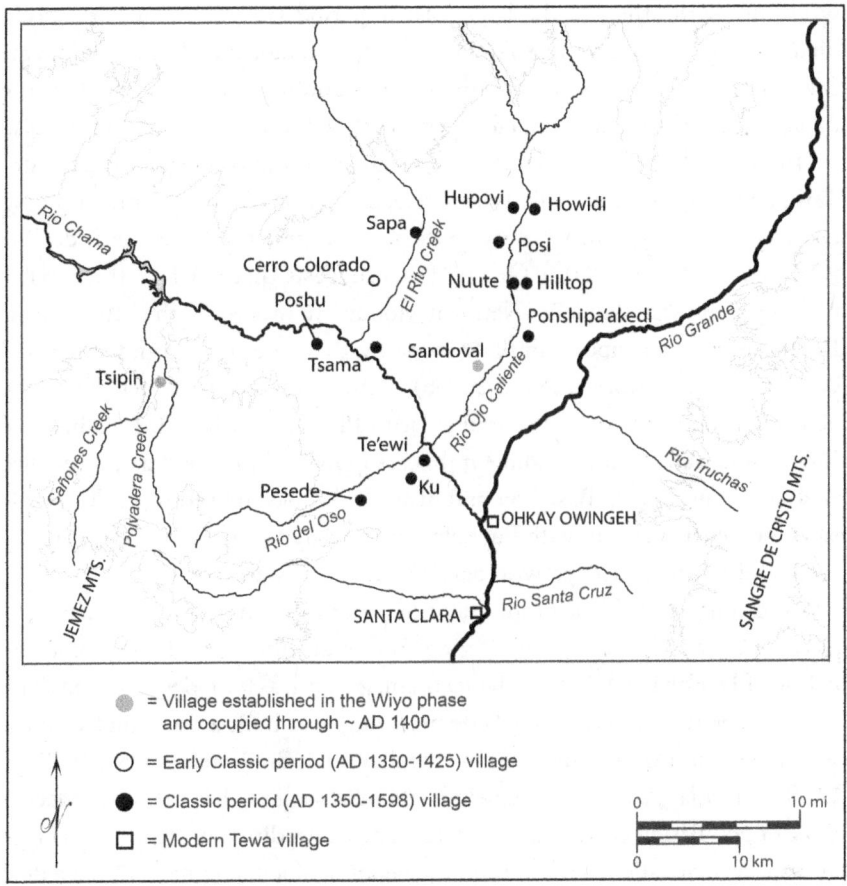

MAP 5 Classic period villages studied in this project located in the Rio Chama valley.

Riana (Hibben 1937) and Kap'owingeh (Luebben 1953) sacked at mid-century. The possibility exists that changing social boundaries and the threat of violence led to the population coalescence.

There are two distinct scales of population coalescence during this period. The first is coalescence within the Rio Chama watershed. People began to leave places in the peripheral areas of the Rio Chama watershed, or the areas in the uplands away from large watercourses, at the start of the Classic period (Mera 1934). While some of the evidence points toward a violent end, such as the burning of Riana Ruin, it is also likely that many of these people gathered peacefully with others at the large Classic period villages down at the river. That Wiyo phase villages like Tsipin'owingeh are retained in Tewa social memory (Richard Ford, personal communication 2009) further suggests that the inhabitants of these places joined larger ancestral Tewa communities to the east.

The second scale of coalescence was larger and encompassed the greater Tewa Basin. In the latter half of the fourteenth century, the population residing in villages on the Pajarito Plateau to the south experienced a dramatic decline (Orcutt 1991; Gabler 2009). Orcutt (1991) suggests that much of the population of present-day Bandelier National Monument moved south to the Cochiti Reservoir area, a proposal initially made by Bandelier (1892) and supported by Cochiti oral history (Preucel 2005b). Ortman (2012) speculates that many people on the northern and central Pajarito Plateau may have moved into the Rio Chama watershed, an argument that is supported by my pottery provenance analysis (Duwe 2019). Based on oral history, they also moved to the Tewa villages on the Rio Grande, with Puye closely associated with Santa Clara (Morley 1910) and Potsuwi'owingeh with San Ildefonso (Hewett 1906).

According to the Tewa origin tradition, after the Summer and Winter People journeyed down both sides of the Rio Grande, they joined together at the village of Posi'owingeh in the Chama drainage. Posi, as both dendrochronology and ceramic dating (Duwe 2011) demonstrate, was built around mid-century, with the earliest cutting date of 1344 (Smiley 1951; Smiley et al. 1953; Stallings 1937). The village's size and sprawling site plan suggest that this was indeed a place of population coalescence. The Tewa origin tradition explains how village life was dramatically transformed as the peoples joined together to build a dual social and ceremonial organization (Parsons 1929). Based on its multiple large kivas and ritual landscape (see below), it is possible that the material culture at Posi'owingeh expresses these same changes. But was Posi'owingeh the only site where population coalescence occurred? That is not likely, as hundreds, or possibly thousands, of people moved into the Rio Chama watershed. A large amount of architecture was necessary to accommodate these settlers in the latter part of the fourteenth century. Tree-ring dates illustrate large-scale building events from 1360 to 1370. We know that people moved into the Rio Chama and that populations coalesced internally within the watershed as well.

Although Tewa cosmogony tells us how the peoples came together at Posi'owingeh, what did the patterns of settlement and coalescence look like in other villages across the study area? While all of the large Classic period villages in the Rio Chama watershed were built by 1400, a comparison of architectural layout suggests very different settlement histories. Among fifteen villages studied in the Chama, two primary patterns in architectural site plan emerge: (1) the large, sprawling pueblo and (2) the compact, planned village. In short, patterns of Tewa coalescence, and their respective movement, were diverse and highly fluid.

The large, sprawling pueblo is characterized by Ponshipa'akedi'owingeh, Posi'owingeh, and Sapa'owingeh (figure 20). The unplanned nature of the roomblock placement suggests an accretional building sequence. Plaza space is rather informal and is shaped by the positioning of the roomblocks and kivas. Based on both pre-Hispanic Pueblo architecture studies (Cameron 1999) and ethnographic accounts (Fewkes 1900), the unplanned nature of the site architecture points to the aggregation of multiple groups of individuals over time. Ponshipa'akedi demonstrates this process, which for that village extended over a two-hundred-year period. Through the combination of high-resolution site mapping and controlled ceramic sampling, I chronologically seriated individual roomblocks by calculating mean ceramic dates (figure 21, Duwe 2011). There were three primary occupations through the village's history. The first dated to the Wiyo phase and the second and third began around mid-century. The pueblo appears to have been occupied through the early sixteenth century. A pattern of accretional growth and the aggregation of people into an existing Wiyo phase village clearly emerges at Ponshipa'akedi.

While the pattern at Posi'owingeh and Sapa'owingeh—very large accretional villages—is not as clear as it is at Ponshipa'akedi, both have evidence of an earlier Late Coalition period component. Multiple early cutting and noncutting dates were recovered at Sapa'owingeh, suggesting an earlier Wiyo phase occupation along El Rito Creek. A relatively large amount of Wiyo Black-on-white pottery, a type that dates to 1300–1350, is found in the Posi'owingeh ceramic assemblage (Duwe 2011). If Ponshipa'akedi began as a small Late Coalition period site and grew through population aggregation, then both Sapa'owingeh and Posi'owingeh may have had similar histories.

The second architectural type, the compact, planned village, is characterized by Ku'owingeh, Te'ewi'owingeh, Hupovi'owingeh, Howidi'owingeh, and Poshu'owingeh (figure 20). Based on mean ceramic dating calculated from analyzed sites (Ku'owingeh, Hupovi'owingeh, Howidi'owingeh, and Te'ewi'owingeh; Duwe 2011) as well as from available tree-ring dates and architectural analysis (Duwe 2011; Smiley 1951; Smiley et al. 1953; Stallings 1937), it appears that these villages were built as planned units and later than the sprawling sites (Duwe 2011). For example, Ku'owingeh is composed of two roomblocks joined around a central plaza. Ku'owingeh dates to 1376–1500 and was likely built as a planned village, based on mean ceramic dating (Duwe 2011) and despite

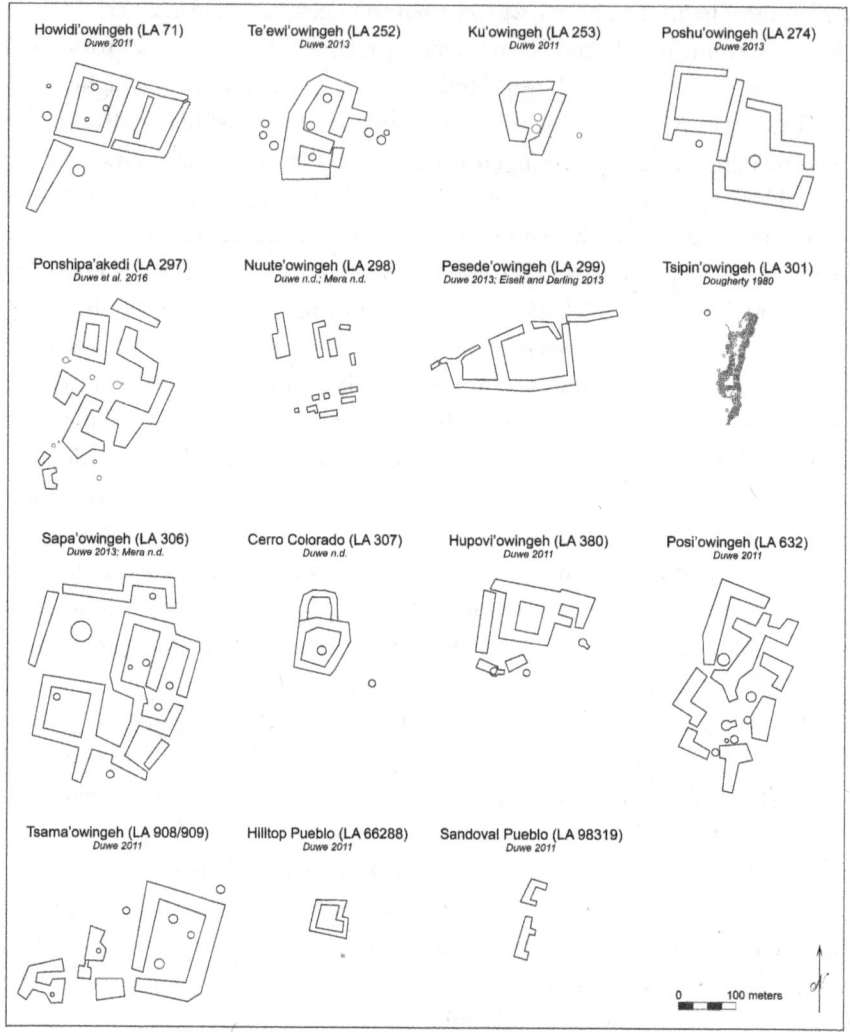

FIGURE 20 Architectural plans of fifteen Classic period villages in the Chama Valley.

the small quantities of Wiyo Black-on-white found there. When compared with sites like Ponshipa'akedi, however, the lack of occupational seriation at Ku'owingeh may be better viewed as a product of a large-scale, planned, and relatively short-lived occupation of the ancestral Tewa village.

The two types of Classic period settlements in the Rio Chama watershed—the sprawling, accretionally grown village and the compact, planned pueblo—

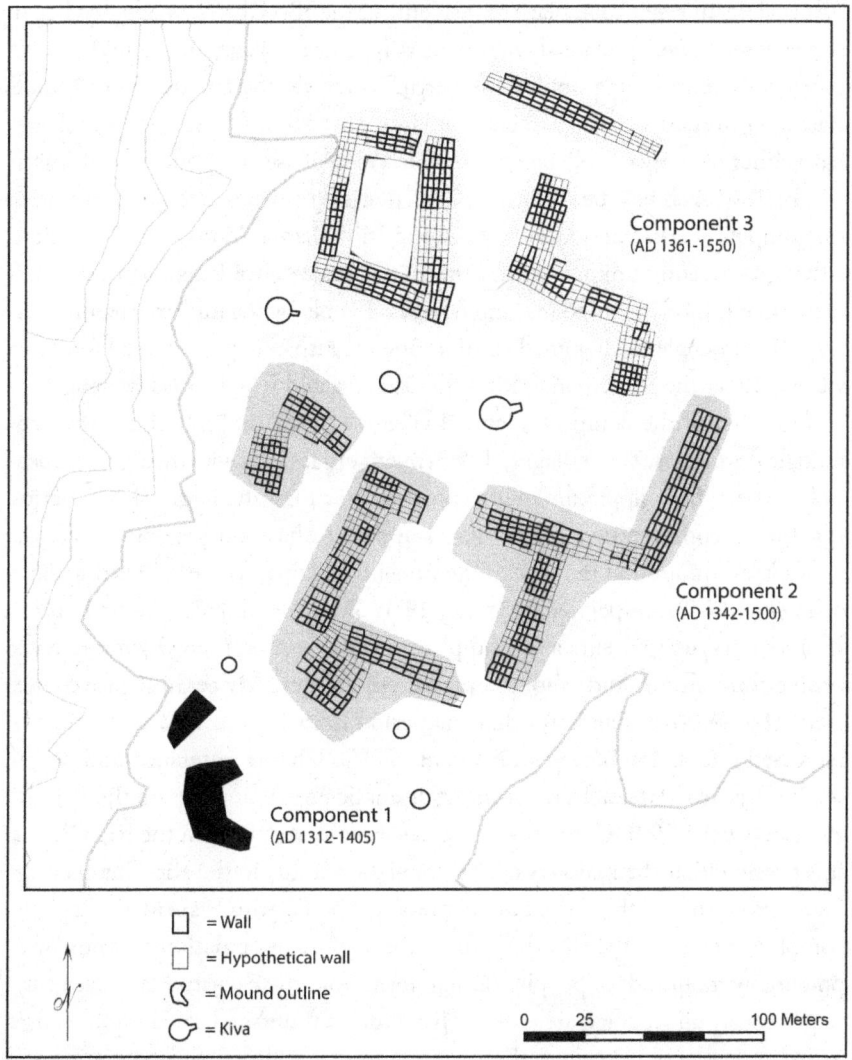

FIGURE 21 Intrasite chronology of building and occupation events at Ponshipa'akedi'owingeh.

represent two different types of village histories: the first is the product of disparate people joining together at the previously occupied Wiyo phase settlements and the second of people who moved to a previously uninhabited location and built a large new village that then grew over time. I speculate that the initial Tewa coalescence was a combination of two separate coalescence events. The first coalescent event took place as residents of the Rio Chama watershed began to coalesce at select previously occupied Wiyo phase villages in the mid- to late fourteenth century as populations began to recede toward the Rio Grande. Based on limited tree-ring dates, the large, sprawling Classic period villages have either securely established or possible Wiyo phase components. Additionally, Posi'owingeh has the earliest, at 1344, tree-ring cutting date samples among the sampled Classic period villages in the Rio Chama drainage. It is possible, although currently unknown, that the initial coalescence began as people left places like Kap'owingeh, Riana, and Maestas Pueblo by the mid-fourteenth century. These people likely joined communities of disparate people and built large villages along the Rio Chama, Rio Ojo Caliente, and Rio del Oso drainages.

But what of the compact, planned villages? Based on limited dendrochronological samples, two villages, Te'ewi'owingeh and Howidi'owingeh, appear to have been built approximately fifty years later than the large Classic period aggregated communities. Both villages appear to have undergone substantial building events around the turn of the fifteenth century, with early cutting dates of 1399 and 1401, respectively (Smiley 1951; Smiley et al. 1953; Stallings 1937). If this site type represents a second phase of coalescence, then where did these people come from? And who occupied these villages? My ceramic provenance study (Duwe 2019) illustrates that the period from 1350 to 1425 was a time of increased interaction between people in the Rio Chama watershed and people on the Pajarito Plateau. In this time of dramatic population loss on the Pajarito Plateau (Orcutt 1991; Ortman 2010) and subsequent growth in the Rio Chama, it is possible that the majority of the population influx in the Rio Chama originated from the south, in the upland mesas of the Pajarito Plateau. Perhaps the compact sites were the direct result of the regional population movement of potentially thousands of people coming north from the Pajarito Plateau, settling in previously unoccupied areas of the Rio Chama watershed, and building large, integrated villages. Although these newcomers were also likely negotiating and reorganizing their social and ceremonial organization, the planned nature of the sites suggests they were built with this organization in mind.

CONTINUED COALESCENCE (1400–1500)

Harry Mera, like his contemporaries (Hibben 1937), noted a dramatic shift in village size and location in the Chama, beginning in what would later be called the Classic period, as larger villages replaced smaller ones. But he also illuminated a trend that defines the culture history of the fourteenth through seventeenth centuries: the continual coalescence of people at fewer but much larger places. Working without the benefit of precise chronometric control, Mera believed that the initial Classic period villages were established by 1400. However, "within a hundred years at most a great change had taken place; peripheral sites, mostly defensive, had disappeared, and the population was largely concentrated in [villages] situated along the course of perennial streams" (Mera 1934:19). Mera believed that by the time of Coronado's expedition in 1541 "the entire Chama group had disappeared," as the Tewa continued to coalesce in places like Yunque'owingeh and Ohkay Owingeh and the other historic villages. In the next chapter I argue that this view was misguided, as the Spanish continued to encounter Tewa people in the Chama through the seventeenth century, but the overall coalescence at the Rio Grande appears to have been a very real process.

My population model—the synthesis of room estimates and mean ceramic dates and tree-ring dates—generally supports Mera's assertion (Duwe 2011; Duwe et al. 2016). In particular, there is a dramatic increase in population size through the end of the fifteenth century, with an associated rise in coalescence (figures 22 and 23). Many of the large villages established in the mid- to late fourteenth century continued to grow as smaller villages fell completely out of use. Villages established in the Wiyo phase, such as Tsipin'owingeh and Sandoval Pueblo, have little evidence of later Classic period pottery (Duwe 2011), and these places were, for whatever reason, not chosen for coalescence. A possible explanation is their location in high promontories, which would be unsuitable for expansion and access to water and farmland. Another curious example is the village of Cerro Colorado. Poorly understood, this pueblo, occupying a high mesa overlooking El Rito Creek, is covered almost exclusively with Abiquiu Black-on-gray pottery, which roughly dates the village to 1350–1425. Cerro Colorado appears to have been built during the initial coalescence of the valley, but occupation likely discontinued when its residents moved to the nearby village of Sapa'owingeh, the largest village in the Chama and one of the largest in the American Southwest (Beal 1987). By the end of the fifteenth century, settlement in the watershed consisted of eleven large villages housing thousands of individuals and many small seasonal occupations along the Chama and its tributaries. Although imperfect proxies for population size, the number of rooms estimated at many of these villages is enormous: Sapa'owingeh and Posi'owingeh had over two thousand rooms and four other villages had well over one thousand (Duwe

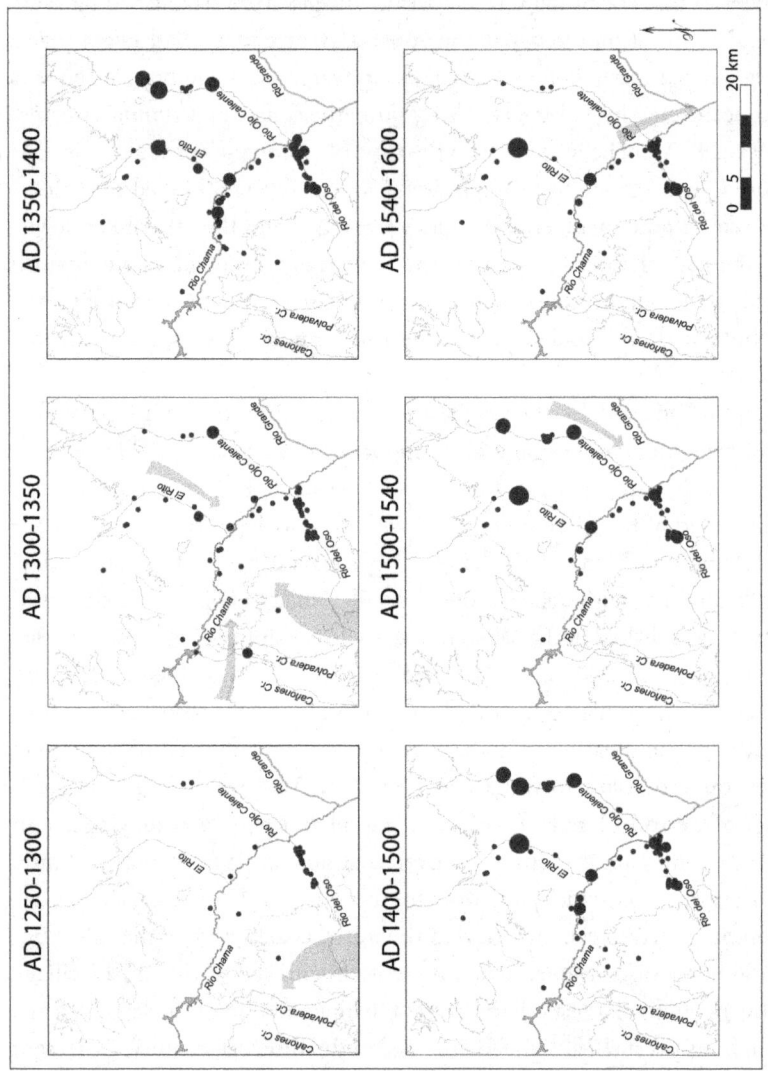

FIGURE 22 Population model of coalescence in the Chama Basin between 1250 and 1600, synthesized from Duwe 2011 and Duwe et al. 2016.

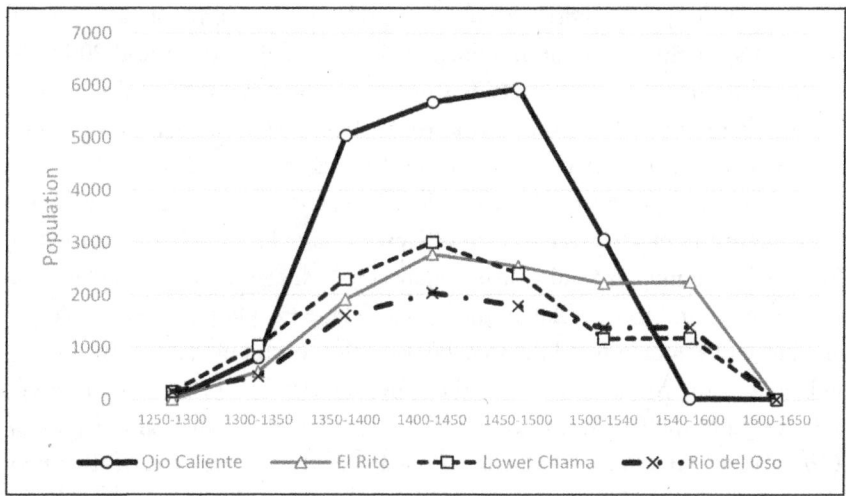

FIGURE 23 Momentary population estimate trends for large Classic period villages grouped by drainage.

et al. 2016). As discussed in chapter 3, we should take these population estimates with a large grain of salt. Unpredictability in precipitation as well as the effects of cold air drainage in the Chama and its tributaries likely limited agricultural productivity for populations this size (Anschuetz 1998a). Also, it is quite possible that we are overestimating these figures based on a faulty understanding of the ratio between storage and habitation rooms (Anschuetz and Ford 2018:24). Instead of focusing on the actual number of people living in drainages, it may be more useful to focus on trends and areas of population growth and decline, including processes of coalescence.

What was driving this coalescence? Certainly increased population, both through intrinsic growth (Maxwell 1994) and migration (Ortman 2016a), contributed to the numbers of people living at each center. But much of the coalescence at large villages and village clusters along drainages represents the restructuring of settlement patterns of existing people leaving smaller villages to live in larger ones. This is particularly true after 1480, when population appears to decline in the Chama but coalescence at a handful of villages continued. Archaeologists working in northern New Mexico have long been fascinated by coalescence in the region (similarly termed *aggregation* or *nucleation*) and have explained it either as an adaptation to climatic uncertainty where people began to pool labor and resources (Habicht-Mauche 1993) or as a response to an increasingly hostile and competitive social landscape where integrated communities of like-minded individuals sought protection in numbers (Fowles et al. 2007; Snead 2008). It may have been the case that outside threats (real or perceived) held fluid and fractious communities together, but Fowles (2004b) cautions against assuming that competition did not also arise within the villages themselves.

An alternative perspective is that coalescence may have been driven by a need to maintain the newly created form of Tewa village life. In chapter 2 I detail the immense number of individuals required to manage the village and ensure that blessings and fortune fall on the people. Made People supervise a series of annual "works" and ensured the well-being of the community, the Towa é work on behalf of the Made People, and the common Dry Food People are responsible for participating in a full calendar of social and ceremonial obligations (Ortiz 1969). At Ohkay Owingeh in the 1960s there were at least fifty-two Made People, including assistants. In the past when villages may have been made up of only a few hundred people, Made People would have comprised a large proportion of the overall population (Ortiz 1969:82). Perhaps the success of village life not only hinged on community protection and assistance but also on a critical mass of people to channel blessings to the people. Larger villages were more desirable than smaller ones, and the decline of regional population at the end of the century may have been a primary reason for coalescence.

The upshot is that the remaining Tewa villages grew not only by accepting individuals who left these smaller upland pueblos but also by accepting whole families or segments of communities. It remains an open question of how autonomous each village was in relation to others, particularly within neighboring pueblos, but below I demonstrate that each community had its own unique landscape and perhaps social and ceremonial hierarchy. If so, continued coalescence throughout the fifteenth century meant that negotiations between complementary people—a foundational idea in Tewa thought (Naranjo and Swentzell 1989)—led to the ongoing making and remaking of Tewa identity. Of particular interest is how the ethnographic literature describes the elements of Tewa village organization that allows for this dissolution and reformation. For example, factional differences between the Summer and Winter People can allow for the division of a village along moiety lines. Indeed, this scenario famously occurred at Santa Clara Pueblo in the early twentieth century (Dozier 1966; Hill 1982). Each moiety began to operate separately, including replicating the ceremonial positions of the other. Although this process was stopped short because of the limitations of life on the reservation, it is fair to assume that in the past this factionalism would have led to two independent communities, or the joining of those who left with other villages. For the latter, Richard Ford (2018) documents the Tewa social unit called the *ma:tu'in* (relatives). These groups represent the household and are the social and economic bedrock of a Tewa community. Although expressly not clans, they are named similarly to the clans among other Pueblo people, which would have facilitated visiting, trading, and moving into new communities among correspondingly named (and related, even through fictional kinship) ma:tu'in. In short, the Tewa have multiple ways to both leave and join a village.

Coalescence continued not only at the village level but also within distinct areas of the Chama where new identities may have formed. These villages appear to have been organized into clusters along the Rio Chama, Rio Ojo Caliente, and Rio del Oso. Sapa'owingeh, located along El Rito Creek, can be viewed as a cluster in its own right because of its immense size. Curiously, many of these villages are evenly spaced, particularly along the Rio Ojo Caliente where Ponshipa'akedi, Nuute'owingeh, Posi'owingeh, and the dual villages of Howidi'owingeh and Hupovi'owingeh are approximately 8 km apart. Ease of movement between equidistant villages and shared access to farmland and resources have led archaeologists to speculate that these clusters may have been organized as social units (Cruz and Ortman 2019; Fowles 2004b). A similar pattern of clustering occurs on the Pajarito Plateau, which Preucel (1987) believes was due to competition over limited resources such as agricultural land. Also, the Tewa today conceptually tie themselves to their landscape (and to one another) through an association with the river whose headwaters begin at a sacred peak and carry water and blessings down to the village. This connection is analogous to an "umbilical cord" (Anschuetz 2007a). If this same idea of connectedness can be projected onto the past, then perhaps ancestral villages along major waterways identified more closely with one other than they did with other people in the Chama. I argue below that new identities were created through coalescence at a larger scale as well, new identities of the Chama Valley, as the Tewa began to form their historic and modern identities.

The dynamic nature of these villages was probably not restricted to ongoing coalescence. Anschuetz's (2007a) discussion of the relationship between big and small villages throughout the Tewa Basin, and patterns of short-term sedentism, are intriguing. Again, it was likely the ma:tu'in who continually traveled between the large central villages and the farmsteads in the uplands or visited their friends and families at other pueblos (Ford 2018). Summers were likely spent away from the villages until harvest, when the community came back to join in the work of preparing for winter and the busy ceremonial schedule of the new year. While the village remained an inalienable center of the cosmos, the people would come and go and continually remake their world.

THE SIXTEENTH CENTURY

The final push of population coalescence in the Rio Chama watershed occurred at the turn of the sixteenth century when the area's villages experienced widespread building events. The villages of Posi'owingeh, Hupovi'owingeh, and Te'ewi'owingeh all have tree-ring cutting dates between 1490 and 1502 (Smiley 1951; Smiley et al. 1953; Stallings 1937). Elsewhere in the Chama other Classic period sites, including Ku'owingeh and Hilltop Pueblo, appear to have become mostly depopulated by 1500. People living in the Rio Chama watershed around 1500 either continued the process of coalescence and moved into a neighboring village or began to move out of the drainage entirely. Based on my demographic model that shows a drop-off in population in the area around this time, we can assume that leaving the area must have been an option that at least some of the people chose.

The causes for continued population coalescence in the Late Classic period are multivalent and based partially on declining climatic conditions (Orcutt 1991). The threat of violence and conflict, real or perceived, must have played a role as well. This was a time of strife, as large villages experienced site burning and homicide. Te'ewi'owingeh, Pesede'owingeh, and Poshu'owingeh were burned. At Pesede'owingeh multiple years of stored maize cobs and kernels— the lifeblood of the community—went up in flames (Jeançon 1912). The bodies of thirteen adolescent males were found killed and burned in Kiva 4 of Te'ewi'owingeh (Wendorf 1953). Poshu'owingeh was burned completely and thoroughly (Jeançon 1923). Possible attackers include other ancestral Tewa people and neighboring Pueblo groups. However, we cannot rule out contact and competition with non-Pueblo people, such as Athabaskan-speaking people from the north and west, a topic in the next chapter.

While the specific causes of population coalescence remain unclear, the years from 1500 to 1550 were obviously turbulent with residential upheaval. With large populations, competition over land and resources must have become a factor, as demonstrated in the southern Tewa Basin (Snead 2008) and the Pajarito Plateau (Kohler et al. 2004). The threat of violence may have acted as a mechanism to keep fiercely autonomous villages interconnected along shared watercourses.

Traditional culture history (Mera 1934) of the Chama explains that Tewa occupation of the valley ceased by the time the Spanish arrived in 1541. However, recent archaeological research demonstrates that multiple Tewa villages were inhabited both in 1541 and likely visited in 1591 (Schroeder 1979), with Tsama'owingeh being recorded in Juan de Oñate's 1602 census. In the next chapter I explore the Tewa experience through early colonial encounters and the Tewa's continued presence in the Chama through the Historic period. While the realities of the seventeenth and eighteenth centuries were certainly different, similar processes of movement and return to middle places continued to define and remake Tewa identity as it moved on a continuous path of becoming.

TEWA SPACE AND IDENTITY

In the previous section I explored how Tewa village life was constantly in flux, with people coming together, leaving, and returning to their center places. Throughout the Classic period, particularly through the processes of population coalescence, people must have continued to engage in seeking life through negotiating how to live with themselves and their landscape in an ever-changing world. Here, I make an argument that a similar process was happening on a larger scale: that the broad Tewa identity that emerged in the fourteenth century continued to grow and change, eventually leading to the diverse yet similar collection of Tewa identities encountered by the Spanish and ethnographers and lived by the Tewa people today.

For over a century the broad strokes of Tewa history, and its relationship to the larger Rio Grande region, have been understood by archaeologists. Kidder (1915) noted distinct geographic distributions of pottery across northern and central New Mexico in the Classic period (1350–1600), and Mera (1934) correlated these patterns with historic Pueblo ethnic and linguistic boundaries sketched by Harrington (1916). An emerging fourteenth-century Tewa identity was identified by the geographic extent of a unique whiteware tradition found along the Tewa Basin. These early arguments have been surprisingly resilient and continue to be supported by modern research that details the archaeology and geographic extent of ancestral Tewa architecture (Duwe 2011), agriculture

(Anschuetz 1998a, 2007a; Duwe and Anschuetz 2013; Eiselt 2019), rock art (Olsen 2004), and ritual landscapes (Anschuetz 1998a; Duwe 2011, 2016).

While archaeologists acknowledge that the Tewa of the Classic period were likely participating in the same ideational system represented by a singular pottery tradition (Graves and Eckert 1998), settlement histories and patterns of population coalescence vary greatly between the Rio Chama watershed and other areas of the Tewa Basin, particularly the Pajarito Plateau. There are also indications that during the Classic period these areas began to form distinct social relationships with the surrounding Rio Grande community, which may have influenced the eventual diversification of Tewa societies. Rio Grande glaze ware, produced by ancestral Keres and Tano potters from roughly Albuquerque to Santa Fe and the central and southern Pajarito Plateau (Habicht-Mauche 1993:33–36; Shepard 1942), is found in very low frequencies at villages in the Tewa Basin (Gauthier 1987; Mera 1934). This is particularly true for the Chama, where pueblos have 1–3 percent glaze ware and little additional nonlocal pottery, indicating economic and social isolation (Duwe 2011:Appendix B). Villagers on the Pajarito Plateau, however, maintained closer ties with glaze ware producers south of the Tewa Basin, as demonstrated by both larger proportions of glaze ware in ceramic assemblages (Duwe 2006) and high frequencies of Pajarito-produced biscuitware pottery distributed to sites such as Pecos Pueblo (Shepard 1936). In fact, the glaze ware found at Puye was produced locally, suggesting migration of Tano-speaking people into the Tewa Basin in the sixteenth century (Olinger 1991; Peckham and Olinger 1990). While the differences in regional interaction between the Chama and the Pajarito Plateau are likely related to geographic proximity (villages on the Pajarito Plateau were closer to glaze ware–producing potters), the correlation of geographic extents of pottery traditions with historic ethnic boundaries suggests the possibility of emerging Tewa identities. How were these emerging and dissimilar Tewa communities interacting with one another and what can their interactions tell us about the development of Tewa societies?

My recent provenance analysis of Tewa pottery begins to address these questions by demonstrating how Tewa pottery dating from 1250 to 1600 was produced using distinct geochemical clay sources in both the Pajarito Plateau and the Chama Basin (Duwe 2019). Patterns of production and distribution of this pottery indicate a fluidity in social connectivity between the two areas through time and the emergence of unique Tewa identities. Table 4 displays the observed frequencies of Chama-made pottery found at

TABLE 4 Observed frequencies of analyzed pottery from sites in the Rio Chama watershed and on the Pajarito Plateau (Duwe 2019)

TYPE	CHAMA TO PAJARITO	PAJARITO TO CHAMA
Santa Fe B/w (1200–1350)	NA	0.80
Wiyo B/w (1300–1400)	NA	0.13
Abiquiu B/g (1350–1450)	0.65	0.01
Bandelier B/g (1400–1500)	0.59	NA
Potsuwi'i Incised (1500–1600)	0.40	NA
Sankawi B/c (1500–1600)	0.06	NA

Pajarito Plateau sites and Pajarito-made pottery found at Chama sites for each ceramic period.

The two areas appear to be linked through shared histories in the Coalition period. At least some of the settlers of the Rio Chama watershed were from the Pajarito Plateau, based on similarities in architecture and sacred geographies (chapter 4). Although the early settlers of the Chama manufactured their own pots using local clays, substantial quantities of Santa Fe Black-on-white (80 percent) and Wiyo Black-on-white pottery (13 percent) were imported from the Pajarito Plateau. The importation of pottery suggests either direct population movement from the Pajarito to the Chama or some other type of interaction stemming from interconnected social networks.

The interconnectedness between the Pajarito Plateau and the Chama continues into the early years of the Classic period, again likely based on the movement of people between the areas from south to north. Large quantities of Chama-made pottery are found at villages in the northern Pajarito Plateau, particularly in the fourteenth and fifteenth centuries. Over half of the biscuitware (Abiquiu Black-on-gray and Bandelier Black-on-gray) in Pajarito villages of the period was imported from the Rio Chama watershed, implying a strong economic relationship based on shared settlement histories. Interestingly, the flow of pottery didn't travel the other direction, as potters in the Chama almost exclusively produced and used their own decorated pottery (Abiquiu Black-on-gray, Bandelier Black-on-gray, Sankawi Black-on-cream, and Potsuwi'i Incised). Given the evidence of imbalances between population and agricultural lands noted by Sunday Eiselt (2019) for the Classic period Rio Chama, this pattern of pottery movement may imply the increased flow of other products, such as cotton (Camilli et al. 2019), in the opposite direction, from the Pajarito to the Chama.

In the sixteenth century, economic bonds between the two areas appear to have weakened. While people in the Chama continued to exclusively use locally produced pots, Pajarito villagers imported fewer Chama-made pots through time, with only 6 percent of Sankawi Black-on-cream coming from the north. If we assume that the distribution of pottery represents some sort of social connectedness, this pattern of decreased interaction suggests the Chama and the Pajarito Plateau were becoming increasingly isolated from each other on the eve of the Historic period. These patterns raise questions: Why do villages in the Chama show increasing isolation while the Pajarito Plateau remained economically intertwined with both the Chama and the surrounding Rio Grande region? And why did the flow of pottery from the Chama to the Pajarito Plateau decrease over time? Perhaps differences in settlement histories between the two regions, and particularly the process of population coalescence, contributed to these patterns of change (Duwe 2019).

The Chama had become a population center of the Tewa world by the fifteenth century (Ortman 2016a), as climatic instability encouraged people from the Pajarito Plateau and elsewhere in the region to settle along its the relatively fertile river valleys. Social and economic systems were developed to accommodate this large and diverse population (Cruz and Ortman 2019; Duwe 2016; Duwe and Anschuetz 2013). Chama residents appear to have produced nearly all their pots, including enough to distribute to people on the Pajarito Plateau. I make the argument (Duwe 2019) that the lack of nonlocal pottery in the Chama may reflect self-sufficiency, spurred on by a sense of economic security (Ortman 2016b) and driven by favorable environmental factors and high populations. On the other hand, the lack of nonlocal pottery may reflect a high level of interdependency, where pots and other manufactured goods from the Chama flowed to the Pajarito, and other goods flowed in the opposite direction.

The history of the Chama contrasts greatly with that of the villages on the Pajarito Plateau. By the beginning of the Classic period, the population on the Pajarito Plateau began a gradual decline as people left for other locales. The villages that remained were highly coalesced towns that in comparison with sites in the Chama were much more socially connected with their neighbors. These ties, represented through higher quantities of glaze ware pottery, extended both north into the Chama and south into ancestral Keres and Tano communities. The correlation of population loss with increased social interaction is a common theme in Pueblo history. Ford (1972b) describes how villages that suffered from epidemics in the nineteenth and twentieth centuries reached out widely to find potential mates and replace the loss of ceremonial leaders and knowledge. The increased cultural contact of the Pajarito Plateau, opposed to the isolation of the Chama, may have contributed to the development of unique Tewa identities. In fact, Harrington (1916) discusses the village of Tyuonyi, in Frijoles Canyon (the traditional linguistic boundary between the Tewa and Keres people), as being the location of a peace treaty between the Tewa, Keres, and Jemez people.

Why economic relationships between the Chama and the Pajarito Plateau declined through time is still an open question. The population in the Chama began to decline by the sixteenth century as people either left the valley to join relatives along the Rio Grande or continued to coalesce into a handful of remaining villages. And though the connection between the Chama and the Pajarito Plateau may have begun to weaken in the fifteenth century as the Chama became more isolated (as demonstrated by frequencies of Bandelier Black-on-gray pottery), the upheaval caused by unfavorable climate changes and the arrival of the Spanish may have further disrupted the social and economic networks between the two areas in the last years of the occupation in the Chama.

Although preliminary, patterns suggest that Tewa identities and social networks were inherently fluid and connected to changing locations of center places and the conceptual boundaries of worlds. The Tewa world of today is not a monolith but a composite landscape of six related but distinct homelands within the Tewa Basin. It should be no surprise, then, that looking into the past shows us even greater diversity in how people interacted with one other and their landscapes in the many paths of becoming Tewa.

OF MOIETIES AND MADE PEOPLE

Bandelier (1892) easily noted the similarities between Posi'owingeh and other villages in the Rio Ojo Caliente valley to the Tewa living in the Rio Grande valley. In the 130 years since Bandelier's work, archaeologists have had few qualms about assigning a Tewa cultural affiliation to these Classic period places. An important contribution of this book is the demonstration that through building and living in these massive pueblos, the Tewa began to express material traces of a cosmos and village organization similar to the ethnographic era. In this section I outline how two fundamental elements of this world—the Summer and Winter People and the social and ceremonial hierarchy—are identifiable through architectural, settlement pattern, and ritual landscape analyses.

My interpretations of large-scale settlement patterns and social interactions rely on patterns of temporal change, particularly the fluidity of population movement over two centuries of the Classic period, but a lack of excavation and the poor chronological control associated with the ritual landscape survey make it difficult to understand how these patterns changed through time. I identify patterns of variability throughout the Chama, however, that speak of diverging social and ceremonial identities. I then synthesize the data with larger historical trends to speculate on a fundamental question of this volume—how the Tewa people become both united and divided—a process that is clearly linked to the continual coalescence and fluidity of the people during this crucial period of Tewa history.

SUMMER AND WINTER PEOPLE

As discussed in chapter 2, the social and ceremonial organization of the ethnographic Tewa revolves around the principle of duality. The entire population of a Tewa village is divided into the Summer People and the Winter People. The chiefs and staffs of each semiannually alternate ceremonial control of the pueblo (Ortiz 1969). Although the village is rarely spatially segregated based on moiety affiliation, historically this organization was often manifested by two large kivas, one for the Summer People and one for the Winter people, at a single village (e.g., San Ildefonso Pueblo; Parsons 1929). The historic Tewa appear, however, to have been pragmatic in their architectural preferences. Ceremonial life at Ohkay Owingeh, the prototype for Tewa life in the ethnographic and historic eras, centers on a single kiva that was alternately used by both moieties (Parsons 1996[1939]).

Although patterns of dual social organization are difficult to see in the archaeological record (but see Fowles 2005 and Lowell 1996), Tewa tradition dictates that the peoples came together to live in one village at Posi'owingeh. And based on my above analysis, they came together at other large Classic period pueblos in the Chama. We should therefore expect to see some evidence of moiety organization. This is clearly documented in a shift in kiva size and function in the Classic period. Florence Hawley Ellis (Hawley 1950) parsed the variability of kiva sizes into two classes, "big" and "small," and applied her analysis to the Rio Grande region. Small kivas, reflecting clan-based social organization, were generally phased out in favor of big kivas, which are the center for all dual organization among all Rio Grande pueblos (Parsons 1996[1939]). In the Classic period, small kivas represent the gathering place of potential sodalities and social groups, which Parsons (1929) documents among the Pueblos in the twentieth century.

Every Classic period village in the Rio Chama watershed has evidence of both big and small kivas, and there is a general increase in both kiva classes from the Coalition period to the Classic period (table 5). All Classic period villages have at least one big kiva over 10 m in diameters, with eight sites having two or more. Does the appearance of big kivas signal social organization akin to the historic Pueblos, likely with the dualities expressed by the historic Tewa? Possibly. But only four Classic period kivas have been excavated and reported in the Rio Chama watershed, all from the site of Te'ewi'owingeh (Wendorf 1953). Without excavated contexts it is difficult to understand the function and use of the big kivas at Classic period sites in the Chama, although Classic period kiva use looks very similar to that of the historic and ethnographic periods (Lakatos 2007).

TABLE 5 Small and big kivas at Coalition and Classic period village in the Rio Chama watershed

SITE	ROOMS	DATES (AD)	"BIG" KIVA	"SMALL" KIVA
Coalition period				
Maestas Pueblo	43	1250–1425	0	0
Tsama'owinge	199	1231–1500	0	3
Kap'owingeh	140	1275–1325	0	?
Palisade Ruin	42	1312–1335	0	1
Tsipin'owingeh	500	1312–1350	1	12
Riana Ruin		1335–1350	0	1
Classic period				
Cerro Colorado	550	1300–1425	2	0
Ponshipa'akedi'owingeh	1536	1312–1550	2	5
Pesede'owingeh	631	1365–1600	0 (disturbed)	1
Tsama'owingeh	1156	1324–1550	2	3
Posi'owingeh	2410	1344–1500	2	5
Hupovi'owingeh	1209	1363–1550	2	2
Te'ewi'owingeh	892	1365–1600	2	9
Sapa'owingeh	2541	1385–1526+	2	5
Ku'owingeh	600	1366–1500	2	1
Poshu'owingeh	1144	1375–1500	1	1
Howidi'owingeh	1697	1375–1537	2	4

The most impressive display of Tewa duality is the geographic placement of paired villages, such as Ohkay Owingeh and Yunque'owingeh, encountered by the Spanish in 1541 (Hammond and Rey 1940:244). A similar pattern exists in the Chama with the villages of Howidi'owingeh and Hupovi'owingeh (figure 24). The sites were contemporaneous, and both were occupied until the sixteenth century (Duwe 2011). Located on the northern frontier of the Tewa world, only 15 km from the northern Tiwa homeland, these two villages on opposite sides of the Rio Ojo Caliente would have been a stunning sight for a traveler journeying downriver. The villages mirror each other not only through their architecture but also through the shrines surrounding each village, possibly acting as the manifestation of the warrior twins, or Towa é (Ortiz 1969), guarding an entrance to the Tewa world.

Without additional excavated contexts it is difficult to interpret social organization with the available material culture, especially when my data were collected primarily from the modern ground surface. However, hints of a Classic period Tewa dual organization are found in ritual landscapes (see below).

THE SOCIAL AND CEREMONIAL HIERARCHY

Based on limited research, the ancestral Northern Tiwa (Fowles 2009, 2013), Tewa (Anschuetz 1998a), and Keresan (Snead 2008; Snead and Preucel 1999) Pueblo people began to differentiate themselves from one another through the construction of ritual landscapes in the fourteenth century. The resulting Classic period villages each have a complex and nuanced sacred geography that is composed of many shrines of multiple shrine types. Anschuetz (1998a) proposes that the Tewa process of becoming had matured into a cosmology similar to that of the ethnographic era by the Classic period in the Rio del Oso valley. Within this cosmography are places where the various members of Tewa social and ceremonial life interact with their world, indicating the emergence of elements of Pueblo organization discussed in twentieth-century ethnography and practiced today.

All of the Classic period villages that I surveyed have complex landscapes that include both village shrines and shrines in the hills surrounding the village. In general, both the placement and types of shrines are similar to twentieth-century Tewa landscapes recorded in the ethnographic literature (Douglass 1917; Harrington 1916; Ortiz 1969; Parsons 1929). These include *xayeh* represented by cupule, ground-slick, and nonground shrines. Although village shrines are

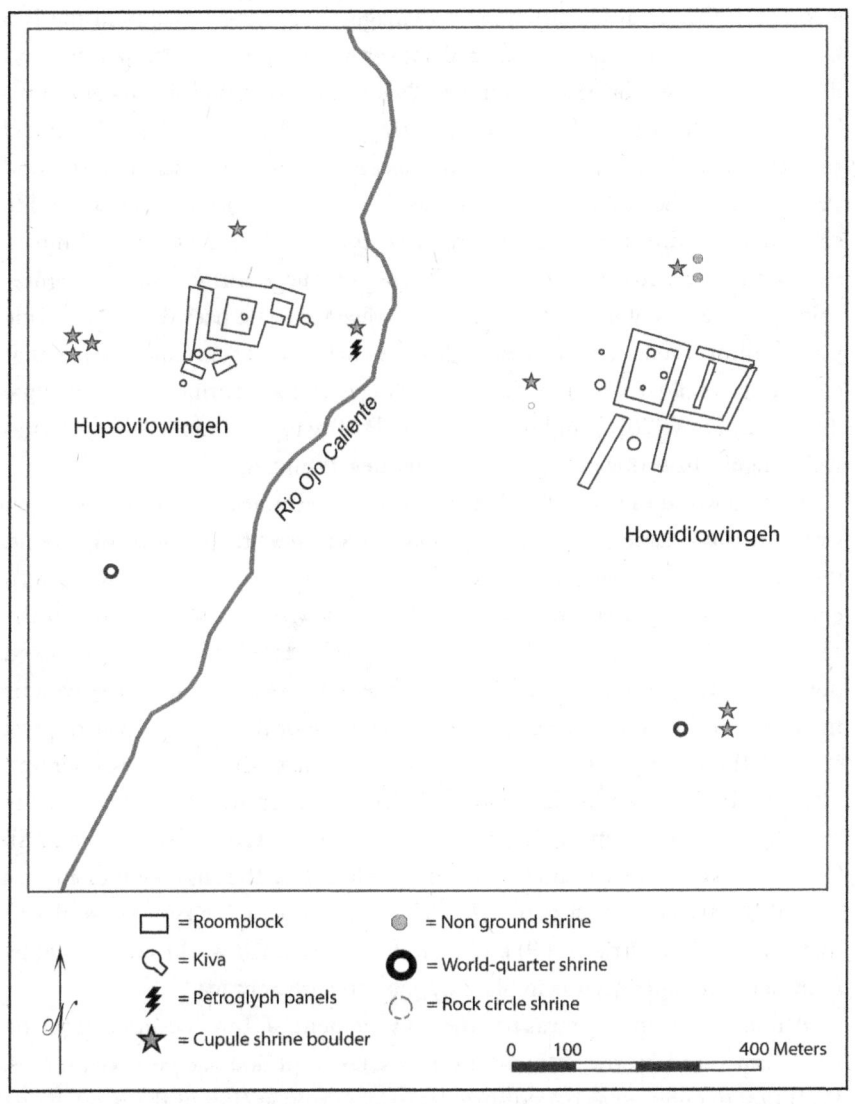

FIGURE 24 Schematic of the architecture and sacred geographies of Howidi'owingeh and Hupovi'owingeh.

a common feature at Coalition period villages (chapter 4), villages in the Rio Chama watershed founded after 1350 appear to have both a great quantity and diversity of village shrines. Additionally, some Classic period shrines appear to be placed at the cardinal directions. Ortiz (1969) described these directional shrines where the spirits of deceased nonceremonial specialists, or Dry Food People, travel and reside in their journey back to the place of emergence. He states that the directional shrines are often composed of small, indiscriminate stones; therefore, many of these special types of village shrines are unrecognizable to the archaeologist. However, all surveyed Classic period villages (aside from Hilltop Pueblo) have cupule, ground-slick, and nonground shrines that are strong candidates for the Xayeh T'a Pingeh (village shrines of the cardinal directions; Duwe 2016), and three villages (Posi'owingeh, Hupovi'owingeh, and Ku'owingeh) have obvious contenders (figures 25 and 26).

Tewa landscapes began to materially express a connection to a much larger world in the Classic period. Besides placing xayeh at the cardinal directions, the villagers of Ku'owingeh situated four large cupule shrines on the western edge of the village that are in direct alignment with Tsikumu, 22 km to the southwest. The cupule boulders were tentatively dated (based on associated pottery) to the Classic period. Tsikumu, the Tewa sacred peak of the west, is the home of the rain-bearing Oxua and the place of the *nan sipu* (earth-navel shrine). The mountain is one of the most dangerous, but also most important, places in the Tewa world (see chapter 2). The Tewa continue to the present day to make pilgrimages up the Rio del Oso valley to the top of Tsikumu to fulfill ceremonial obligations (Anschuetz 2014; Walt 2014). The alignment of shrines toward the sacred peak suggests that a Tewa cosmographic system, similar to that described by Ortiz (1969) and including a bounded world surrounded by four sacred mountains, was in place by the fifteenth century.

A four-tiered universe was not the only element of Tewa cosmology (Ortiz 1969) expressed by the reorientation of Classic period sacred geographies. Dualities, manifested as paired shrines, are common at sites in the Rio Chama watershed. Ku'owingeh, Tsama'owingeh, and Posi'owingeh all have pairs of large cupule or nonground shrines located at (or close to) cardinal directions. These shrines are located to the north and east (Ku'owingeh), west (Tsama'owingeh), and south (Posi'owingeh) of each village and are also located at the likely formal entrances to each pueblo. A similar pattern was observed by Fowles (2009), who recorded two large nonground boulders marking the western entrance to T'aitöna. Interpreting these paired shrines is pure speculation; however, it is

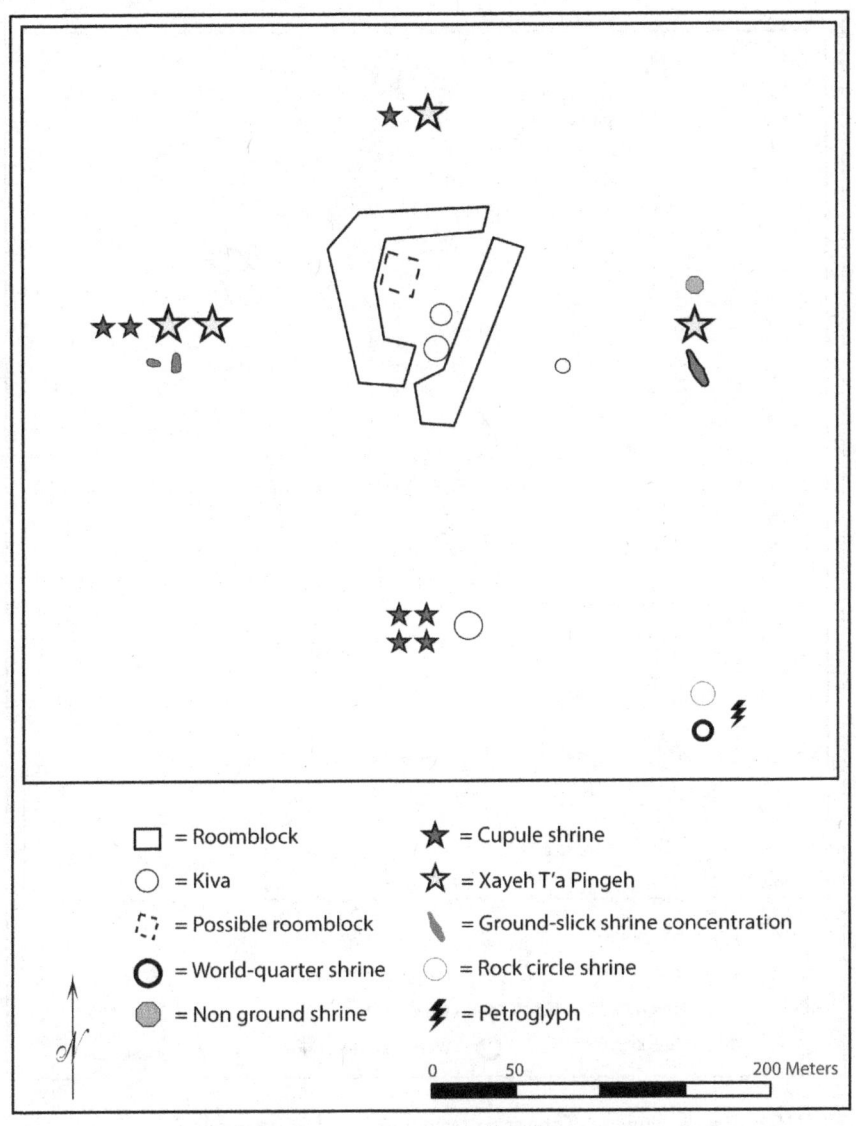

FIGURE 25 Schematic of the sacred geography of Ku'owingeh.

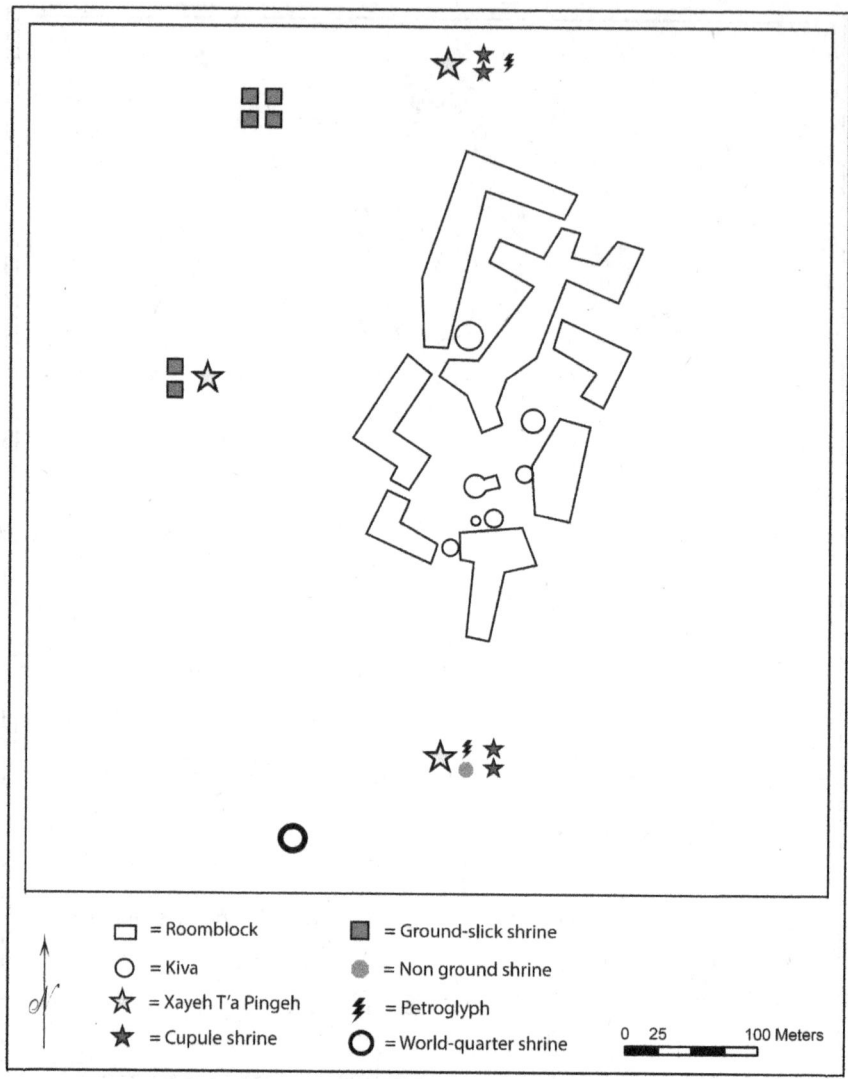

FIGURE 26 Schematic of the sacred geography of Posi'owingeh.

possible these groupings may represent the Towa é, or Tewa warrior twins, that guard the Tewa world. Based on the Tewa origin tradition, the Towa é stand guard as protectors on both the sacred peaks and the *tsin* surrounding each village (Parsons 1929). The placement of these paired shrines on the edges of the village, near the tsin, adds further weight to this interpretation.

Concurrent with the reorientation of village shrines was the construction of multiple types of shrines in the hills, or tsin, surrounding each village. Although the development of the world-quarter shrine was a Wiyo phase phenomenon, this shrine type became standard across the Rio Chama watershed in the early Classic period. Nearly every Classic period village in the Rio Chama, and every site I surveyed, appears to have an associated world-quarter shrine (figure 27). The world-quarter shrines at each village are standardized in their placement (to the south or southwest of the primary village architecture), size (10–12 m in diameter), and orientation (a single entrance facing east). Variability exists in construction material; however, this variability can be explained by available stone sources (either granite or basalt). The world-quarter shrine at Howidi'owingeh is bound by two concentric rings of upright slabs. Understanding if this is a pattern based on identity or chronology requires future research in world-quarter shrine morphology but does point to a seeming standardization of practice.

In chapter 4 I make the argument that the development of the world-quarter shrine at Tsipin'owingeh may signal a transformation in the social and ceremonial organization of the village. This transformation appears to have been complete by the Classic period. Above, I argued that the appearance of one or more "big kivas" (Hawley 1950) at each village likely is the manifestation of village-wide ceremonial organization that is probably similar to the Summer/Winter moieties of the ethnographic-era Tewa. The fact that historically a world-quarter shrine was maintained and used by a village's ceremonial leaders, including the chiefs of both Tewa moieties (Jeançon 1923), suggests that a similar village-wide organization was in place by the late fourteenth century.

The world-quarter shrine is only one type of shrine located in the second tier (the tsin) of Ortiz's model of the Tewa cosmos. Also included are rock circles (found at Howidi'owingeh and Ku'owingeh), reservoirs (recorded at Ku'owingeh and Posi'owingeh), and petroglyphs (Duwe 2011). Rock circles are likely analogous to the hunting shrines used by the Hunting Society (Parsons 1929:56), and reservoirs are a metaphorical symbol of emergence and fertility (Anschuetz 1998a). Petroglyphs are typical of the Rio Grande style defined by Polly Schaafsma (2000) and are predominately composed of shield-bearer and awanyu (feathered serpent) motifs. Each type of shrine has only tentative analogies with elements of ethnographic-era Tewa cosmology and identity, but together they appear to represent a landscape similar to the ones recorded in the twentieth century.

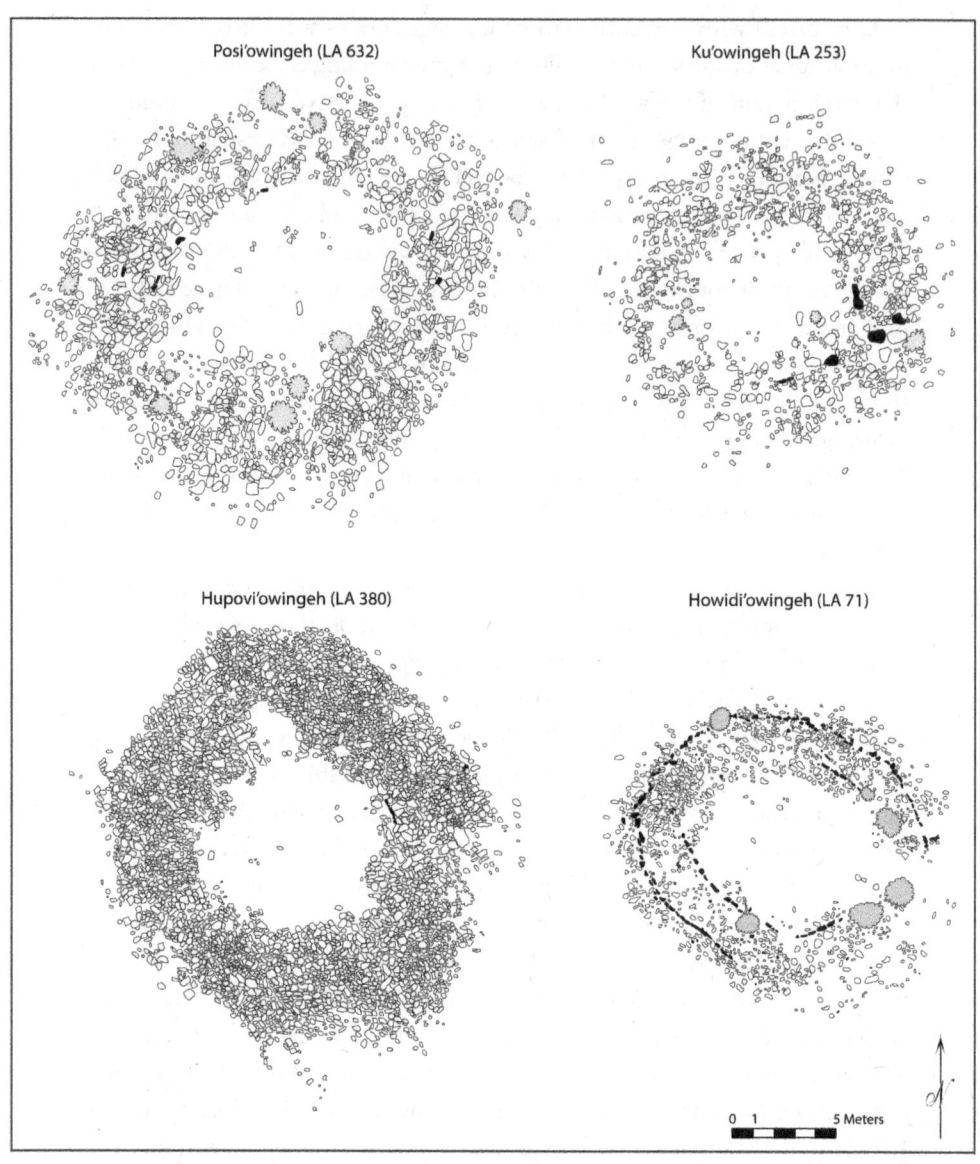

FIGURE 27 A selection of world-quarter shrines located at Posi'owingeh, Ku'owingeh, Hupovi'owingeh, and Howidi'owingeh.

The sacred geographies surrounding Classic period villages suggest that much of the social and ceremonial hierarchy described by Ortiz was in place by the fourteenth or fifteenth century. This includes the Dry Food People through the use of the directional shrines, the Towa é represented by twin shrines, and the Made People through the construction of world-quarter shrines. I can also speculate that the gendered landscape described in *The Tewa World* (Ortiz 1969) also existed through the hunting and agricultural shrines in the hills (the domain of men) and the complex landscape and architecture of the village (the domain of women). These sacred geographies also reveal an expansive cosmos where the village is the center of a world that is bounded by sacred peaks. And while I cannot temporally resolve the construction and use of these places beyond the rough confines of the Classic period, and therefore cannot understand how this cosmos changed through the fluidity of the era, there are indications that even within the Chama this was not a monolithic world.

VARIABILITY AND IDENTITY IN THE TEWA COSMOS

All Classic period villages in the Rio Chama watershed appear to have sacred geographies similar to those described by Ortiz (1969) for the ethnographic-era Tewa. However, variability exists in the types and contexts of shrines both between villages and between tributary valleys. The best example of landscape variability between river valleys is at Classic period villages along the Rio Ojo Caliente.

Although both cupule and ground-slick shrines are ubiquitous in the Rio Chama watershed and are found in every time period, very few ground-slicks were found in the valley and all were located at Posi'owingeh (figure 26). Because my survey coverage included four of the six Classic period villages in the Rio Ojo Caliente valley, I am confident in the strength of this pattern. Additionally, the five ground-slick shrines recorded at Posi'owingeh were all located on the west side of the village and were associated with only one cupule shrine. The remaining five cupule shrines are located to the east of the site.

The meaning of the dearth of ground-slick shrines in the Rio Ojo Caliente valley is difficult to understand. Ground-slicks are most likely a type of xayeh, or village shrine, and are found at sites along the Rio del Oso and Rio Chama. The ethnographic record does not record the activities and meaning associated with ground-slick shrines. Fowles (2009) suggests that ground-slick and cupule shrines may form a gendered dichotomy among the northern Tiwa in the thirteenth century, based on the activities that were likely associated with each shrine. Cupule shrines are traditionally associated with women (Parsons 1929) and ground-slick shrines may have begun as places to sharpen agricultural instruments (Anschuetz 1998a), a traditional male activity. However, the Tewa origin tradition provides hints that perhaps the absence of ground-slick shrines in the Rio Ojo Caliente valley is a proxy for social or cosmological identity.

In the Tewa origin tradition, the Summer and Winter People traveled separately south from the lake of emergence along both sides of the Rio Grande. The two groups coalesced in the Rio Ojo Caliente valley and built the village of Posi'owingh (Ortiz 1969). Because the absence of ground-slick shrines is a pattern found at the earliest identified ritual landscapes in the valley (e.g., Sandoval Pueblo), the first ground-slick shrines along the Rio Ojo Caliente were likely built in the mid-thirteenth century. Posi'owingeh was an important center for population coalescence in the early Classic period, based on both archaeological evidence and Tewa cosmogony. Although speculative, it is possible that the ground-slick shrines at Posi'owingeh represent non–Rio Ojo Caliente ideas of space and placemaking that were introduced during population coalescence.

If identity is related not only to how landscapes are constructed but also to the types of shrines found at ancestral Tewa villages, then the study of ritual landscapes is useful to understand intervillage identity and interactions. As mentioned earlier, the Tewa tie themselves to their larger landscape through associations with riverine umbilical cords that flow from the sacred peaks to their villages (Anschuetz 2007a). An example includes the pilgrimage pathway taken by the Made People of Ohkay Owingeh up the Rio del Oso valley, where stops are made at shrines, ancestral sites, springs, and, finally, at Tsikumu (Richard Ford, personal communication 2009). A similar sort of waterway-based conception of identity is found at Santa Clara Pueblo, where residents actively maintain a ceremonial relationship with shrines and ancestral villages along Santa Clara Creek (Kurt Anschuetz, personal communication 2010). If this same sort of conception can be projected onto the past, then perhaps ancestral villages along major waterways identified more closely with one another than with other people in the Rio Chama watershed. Fowles (2004b) makes a similar argument in his discussion of site clusters in the Tewa Basin. The lack of ground-slick shrines in the Rio Ojo Caliente valley can possibly be interpreted as representing a valley-wide identity, with Posi'owingeh acting as a mother-village.

Although Classic period villages in the Rio Chama may have been unified by common identities, my ritual landscape study has demonstrated that each pueblo was an autonomous entity. The villages of Hupovi'owingeh and Howidi'owingeh, located on either side of the Rio Ojo Caliente, are separated by only 400 m. The sites were occupied contemporaneously. Both tree-ring dates and my ceramic analysis suggest that the villages were built in the mid-fourteenth century and depopulated in the early sixteenth century (Duwe 2011). Previous archaeologists have questioned whether the villages were autonomous sites (Beal 1987). However, when the ritual landscapes were mapped and compared (figure 24), it's revealed that each village has its own independent assemblage of both village and hill shrines, including a world-quarter shrine. The mirror-image nature of the ritual landscapes surrounding Hupovi'owingeh and Howidi'owingeh suggests that each village was a unique center, with shrines that were used by each village's households and Made People. The inherent duality of the two villages may also represent the dual-division of Tewa society and cosmogony, where the Summer and Winter People journeyed down the east and west sides of the Rio Grande, respectively.

Regardless of my interpretations of Classic period ritual landscapes, a quantifiable transformation occurred beginning in the mid-fourteenth century. The number and diversity of shrines increased from those found at Coalition period sites, and a number of landscape features have clear or similar analogies with Tewa cosmography recorded in the ethnographic literature. Although the process of Tewa becoming was and is ongoing (Naranjo 2008), the consequences of this cosmological transformation was the formation of a historic Tewa conception of the world.

THE EMERGENCE OF THE TEWA COSMOS

A perennial question in understanding the Pueblo IV transition is why Pueblo people created new forms of social and ceremonial organization—and a fundamentally different type of village life—in the crucible of migration and population coalescence. This is also a fundamental question in this volume: How did the Tewa world described by Ortiz come to be? In the past thirty years southwestern archaeologists have often favored explanations based on Gregory Johnson's (1982) discussions of scalar stress, which suggest that the diversity and interconnectedness of ritual sodalities present at these large villages was an adaptation to the new demands of living in large communities (Adler 1993; Bernardini 1996; Crown and Kohler 1994). Large populations make communication difficult, leading to the segmentation of communities into integrated subgroups to effectively share information and reach consensus. For the Pueblos, these subgroups include clans, moieties, and other sodalities and kinship groups. In this view, the transformation of village life was the outgrowth of the demands of aggregation and Pueblo ceremonialism served to foster community integration to maintain a diverse amalgamation of people.

Certainly, as demonstrated above, the Tewa villages of the Classic period were both large (relatively, even accounting for Anschuetz's critique) and the result of intense population coalescence. And concurrent with these changes arose what appears to be fundamental elements of Tewa life recorded by Ortiz (1969) and others: a village that is both divided and united and that achieves this balance through an integrated system of crosscutting ties between its numerous parts (chapter 2). The challenges of living in large communities must have been very real, as can be seen in the fluid breaking apart and coming together of people throughout the Classic period and as Hill (1982) shows ethnographically through the factionalism at Santa Clara Pueblo. One way to ameliorate the tensions inherent in a diverse community is to spread people's loyalties and connections throughout the village in a sequential hierarchy, a system that James Moore and Jeffrey Boyer (2009) explain as the outgrowth of increasing population size and scalar stress in the fourteenth and fifteenth centuries.

But Fowles (2005, 2013) cautions against relying too heavily on functionalist explanations. While the challenges of large and diverse populations are real, attributing the development of new social and ceremonial systems as a form of adaptation dismisses social complexities. He also warns that integration is a red herring, arguing that what has classically been termed *religion* and *politics* can act as much as a mechanism for disintegration in a community as it can for integration (Fowles 2013). We should therefore rely on historical explanations to understand how diverse people came together to interact and negotiate their worlds.

A central question of this volume is how Tewa society became both divided and united. The answer to questions of division are found in Tewa tradition: in ancient times the people were split into two groups, the Summer and Winter People. In the previous chapter I demonstrated that these two peoples have unique histories expressed in the archaeological record as they took separate paths from the place of emergence to their eventual homes in the Rio Grande valley. The two groups also appear to have settled the Chama independently, beginning in the thirteenth century. Upon meeting, they joined at Posi'owingeh and the other massive villages in the latter half of the fourteenth century. But instead of subverting their differences, they instead emphasized them through the fundamental organizing principle of village life, and this pattern continues to define the Tewa today.

The Tewa did not invent dual organization. John Ware (2014) demonstrates its deep history across the Southwest. And forms of dualistic thinking, if not types of dual organization, are present among all of the Pueblos today (Parsons 1996[1939]). Ellis (1964:51) hypothesized a proto-Tanoan moiety system present by the twelfth century. Fowles (2005) identifies the earliest overt forms of dual-division in the Rio Grande valley among the northern Tiwa. And Ortman (2018) argues that dual-division social organization may have existed among the thirteenth-century Mesa Verde migrants. The Tewa, however, must have shaped these existing and ancient traditions in the immediate realities of fourteenth-century Tewa Basin: of many disparate yet related people coming together to live in close quarters. While the Summer and Winter People have their origins in the generalized encounters of migrants and first-comers, I argue in the previous chapter that the process is more important than the event. Instead, Tewa moieties may reflect a philosophy of constant negotiation and renegotiation of people who met, left, and returned again in a process of seeking life.

Curiously, understanding Tewa dual organization is the key to understanding unity, and one group of people cannot exist without the other. This is expressed most cogently in Rina Swentzell's (1993) discussion of Tewa thought that values complementarity over competition. Embracing the dualities of the world—summer and winter, female and male, life and death—is vital to the health of a community. This sentiment is expressed in the Tewa saying "be a woman, be a man"—a phrase that embodies the value that leaders should seek to represent both male and female life forces (Ortiz 1969:36). This is not to say that finding this balance is without tension. From materially recognizable acts of violence at turbulent moments in Tewa history, such as occurred at the end of the Wiyo phase and end of the Classic period, or the outright factionalism in the twentieth century (Dozier 1966; Hill 1982), seeking life can be and was traumatic. Factionalism is one way to achieve an eventual balance, but there are more desirable ways to attain this goal. This is best demonstrated in Ortiz's (1969) discussion of the roles of the Tewa's social and ceremonial hierarchy.

Ortiz emphasizes the roles of the Made People in achieving balance between the Summer and Winter People. Because the Made People are recruited from both moieties and govern independently (aside from the Summer and Winter chiefs), they transcend these divisions "in the middle of the structure" (Ortiz 1969:91) and hence work together for the benefit of the village as a whole. The social and ceremonial hierarchy described by Ortiz likely dates back to the Classic period, based on our available material evidence, as do the Summer and Winter People divisions of village life. And as with concepts of dualities, these ceremonial leaders and their associated societies may be much more ancient. In the Tewa migration traditions all of the Made People were created prior to the splitting of the people into Summer and Winter, and they traveled with the people to their eventual homes. Ortman (2018) makes the case that many of the leaders and associated sodalities (such as the Kossa and the Hunt chief) may have been present in the Mesa Verde region prior to migration, with the caveat that little is known about Rio Grande Developmental and Coalition social and ceremonial organization. Regardless, the elements of Tewa life, which possibly also included the Dry Food People and the Towa é, were ancient and may have extended back hundreds, if not thousands, of years. How these elements were ordered and emphasized and became uniquely Tewa is what changed in the Classic period.

Unfortunately, with current archaeological evidence I cannot describe the nature of these specific negotiations or the ways that Tewa village life were created upon coalescence. We lack excavation data and chronological control to address the relationships between the moieties and ceremonial hierarchy, when they were established, and the dynamics of coalescing groups. Certainly the challenges of large coalescing populations cannot be ignored, but the process of coming together that led to complex organization must have been an ongoing negotiation of various people in an ever-changing world rather than the "natural" result of adapting to the pressures of scalar stress. While Ortiz's model demonstrates an integrated whole, it was probably at any one time more of an ideal rather than the reality, because "the achievement of harmony is transitory," and the world and its interconnectedness are in a state of "constant re-creation and transformation" (Swentzell 1993:141). In fact, Ortiz (1969:108–110) himself discusses the inherent tensions within the system, and these tensions, based on the fluidity shown during and after the Classic period, demonstrate the reshaping of relationships between the Summer and Winter People, between the peoples and the ceremonial hierarchy, and between the Tewa and their larger cosmos.

The data presented in this chapter make three pertinent points regarding the questions of ethnogenesis and becoming that were raised at the beginning of this book. First, the elements of Tewa society are very old and were reordered and reemphasized in the Classic period. Second, the Classic period villages demonstrate material correlates to ethnographic and modern Tewa villages that suggest an organizational system similar to Ortiz's model was practiced in the fourteenth or fifteenth centuries. And third, Tewa life was hardly static and was constantly in flux, as is demonstrated through the fluidity of village life at both center places and social boundaries and in the diversity of sacred geographies across the Chama Basin. The constant process of searching for harmony and balance, or seeking life, defines the Tewa more than any specific historic event. Therefore, while it is tempting to view the Classic period as a type of ethnogenesis, the period is best seen as a point on a continuum that extends deep into the past and to the present, and into the future.

The balance and harmony of the Tewa world was again challenged in the midsummer of 1541, as hundreds of residents from the Rio Grande valley journeyed up the Chama to seek shelter with their kin. The catalyst for the migration was a foraging party from Francisco Vásquez de Coronado's expedition, the first Europeans to enter the Rio Grande valley, who were traveling north into Tewa country. Within the next sixty years the Spaniards would visit multiple villages in the Chama and found the first capital of New Mexico at Yunque'owingeh, establishing a permanent colonial presence that continues through to the present day.

CHAPTER 6

The Walls Are Never Vagrant

In the summer of 1598 Juan de Oñate traveled north under the dark green canopy of cottonwoods that lined the Rio Grande del Norte. Carrying his official papers from the Spanish crown authorizing colonization of New Mexico, Oñate moved quickly ahead of his two-mile long train of five hundred colonists, wagons, livestock, and artillery. His goal was to establish the capital of the crown's new kingdom in "the center of the realm" (Simmons 1991:109), or the Española valley north of modern-day Santa Fe, where previous entradas had observed large Tewa villages that produced bountiful crops of maize (Hammond and Rey 1940:244). Oñate had selected a route north of Mexico that roughly followed the Rio Grande, a path that would later be known as the Camino Real. Oñate's route, and his eventual destination, were informed by over a half century of sporadic contact with the Pueblo people, beginning with Coronado's entrada (1540–1542). In the years between Coronado's entrada and Oñate's, parties of Spaniards had ventured north to prospect for minerals, save souls, and attempt to colonize the Pueblo province. Through these initial contacts the Spanish were learning much about the Pueblos. And the inverse was also true; the Pueblos quickly realized that contact meant trouble. This was likely why the villages of Ohkay Owingeh and Yunque'owingeh were hastily left when Coronado's foraging party arrived in 1541. The Pueblos' embrace of movement in these cases was a strategy for survival. In other instances, however, the Pueblos accepted the Spaniards into their villages and began a centuries-long process of negotiation between two very different worlds—a dramatic form of seeking life.

Oñate arrived at Ohkay Owingeh on July 11, 1598. He and his party were apparently warmly welcomed. According to a friar who was present, these were "the best infidel people" he had ever seen (Simmons 1991:112). Ortiz (1979), however, questions the genuineness of this accommodation, particularly under the threat of steel and harquebuses (primitive muskets). Regardless, the Spaniards were there to stay. Oñate christened the village and his new camp San Juan de los Caballeros, and a makeshift church was dedicated in September of the same year. Over the next year the Spanish moved across the river to the sister village of Yunque'owingeh, situated on prime farmlands at the confluence of the Rio Chama and the Rio Grande and renamed the San Gabriel. It was here that the first Spanish capital of New Mexico was established. It marked the beginning of a permanent colonial presence on the Rio Chama and its valley, one that would span the Pueblo Revolt and last through two more governments and continue to the present day.

In this chapter I explore how the arrival of the Spanish fundamentally changed the course of Tewa history, even as Tewa identity and culture persisted through intense colonial encounters. As I do throughout this volume, I focus on the archaeology and history of the Rio Chama valley. Examining the relationship between the Tewa and Spanish in the Chama may seem like an unusual choice. While many of the large Classic period villages discussed in the last chapter were likely visited by sixteenth-century Spanish expeditions, the traditional history of the valley, according to both archaeologists and historians, posits that there was no full-time occupation of these pueblos after the turn of the seventeenth century, concurrent with the establishment of San Gabriel (but see Ramenofsky and Feathers 2002). There are no ruins of grand churches like those of Pecos Pueblo, and there is little evidence of Spanish material culture. In fact, while the timing and causation of the abandonment of the Chama is debated, the general consensus is that these shifts in settlement stemmed from the direct or indirect consequence of Spanish incursion. However, recent archaeological investigation, in concert with ethnohistoric literature, has revealed an unexpected long-term presence in the valley after Spanish contact. I explore Tewa conceptions of mobility and village life to reframe ideas of occupation and abandonment and highlight how Western ideas of settlement and land use vary dramatically from those held by the Pueblos. In short, the Chama was never abandoned by the Tewa people, and examining how the valley has been inhabited by the Tewa through the centuries speaks to long-term continuities in the face of great change.

ABANDONMENT

Today the great villages of the Chama look significantly different from how they would have looked some five centuries ago. Earthen mounds lie where towering multistory houses once stood. For archaeologists and historians these places mark an important period of history where the Tewa people once thrived and prospered. According to most Euro-American scholars, these villages were abandoned around the time of the establishment of San Gabriel, as was the Chama Valley as a whole. The center of the Tewa world was then focused on the mission villages on the Rio Grande.

The apparent abandonment of the Chama was part of a larger process of settlement and demographic change that occurred during the early years of Spanish colonialism. Historian Elinore Barrett (1997, 2002), using both ethnohistorical sources and archaeological data, shows that while the number of Pueblo villages throughout the Rio Grande valley was largely unaffected during Spanish contact in the sixteenth century, their numbers dramatically decreased in the seventeenth century. The introduction of the mission system and the feudal practices of taxation (impuesto and encomienda) and forced labor (repartimiento) limited Pueblo mobility and created severe hardships during a time when crops were failing from drought. The effects of disease reduced the Pueblo population by roughly two-thirds in the 1630s and is reflected in the decreased number of villages along the tributaries of the Rio Grande (Barrett 2002). Barrett concludes that based on direct and indirect Spanish action—exactions of labor and goods, expansion of Spanish settlement, drought, epidemics, and resulting attacks from Apachean tribes—these villages were permanently abandoned and that territory was lost. While the Pueblo people continued to endure before and after the Pueblo Revolt and to the present day, there was a "catastrophic decline in the number of pueblos, one from which they never recovered" (Barrett 2002:153).

From this perspective it would appear that the Pueblos and their larger worlds were dramatically and permanently altered by Spanish colonialism. While ancestral landscapes and sites were visited, these visits were intermittent and did not constitute a full-time occupation. The Pueblos were increasingly restricted to their mission villages along the Rio Grande and some of its major tributaries and were deeply affected by both secular and Catholic policy.

But how can we square this with how the Pueblos view their larger cosmos, both historically and today? One only has to look at the ethnographic literature, such as Harrington's (1916) atlas of Tewa place names, or talk to Tewa people to understand that ancestral villages, shrines, and topographic features continue to be vitally important in their cosmography. These places are viewed as much more than historical waypoints. They are seen as living places, or nodes, in a complex network of movement of people, animals, spirits, and blessings (see chapter 2). How can we reckon the continuity embodied in Pueblo traditions and practice with the great change recorded in the historical record?

The answers to these questions hinge on the concept of abandonment, a perennial and somewhat loaded concept in southwestern archaeology. It has long been understood that the Pueblo world is inherently dynamic, with periods of large-scale population movement. Famous examples include the twelfth-century reorganization of the Chaco world (Lekson and Cameron 1995) and the thirteenth-century exodus from the Mesa Verde region (Ortman 2012). When viewing Pueblo history from a bird's-eye view of settlement patterns over time, it becomes quickly apparent that the size and shape of the Pueblo world, based on full-time occupation of sites, decreased continually from the thirteenth century to the Historic period (Adams and Duff 2004). The upshot is that to move, people had to leave their previously occupied villages, and understanding how and why this process occurred has engrossed archaeologists for over a century.

In the last chapter I explored the creation of Tewa village life and noted that when archaeologists impose Western ideas of full-time occupation and permanence on Pueblo villages, they lose sight of the inherent fluidity of Pueblo life. Movement is the rule rather than the exception, and villages are but a stop along a continuous path. These same Western biases pervade the understanding of abandonment. From the viewpoint that the permanence of settlement equates to success, then leaving these places equates to failure. An abandonment-equals-failure narrative is seen in discussions of environmental degradation and mismanagement of resources (Dean et al. 1985; Hunter-Anderson 1979; Kohler and Matthews 1988), an inability to adapt to environmental change (Matson et al. 1988; Stuart and Gauthier 1981), conflict (Haas and Creamer 1996; Kelley 1952), and lack of cohesive social structure and internal dissent (Titiev 1944). The implication is that rational people do not plan to fail, and therefore abandonment behaviors were "'last-ditch' efforts to salvage life and limb when faced with untenable local or regional conditions" (Adler et al. 1996:400). Michael Adler and colleagues point out that this inherently negative view of abandonment as systemic failure contrasts with how movements such as migration and coalescence are portrayed—as organizational strategies designed by people who were making rational decisions. But what if we afford the same agency to Pueblo people leaving areas as we do for people making new homes?

In the past two decades southwestern archaeologists have begun to view abandonment of villages and landscapes not as a failure but as a choice. It is a normal part of residential mobility (Schiffer 1972), and under a processual framework abandonment was the consequence of strategic decision-making that spreads risk, people, and social obligations across the landscape (Adler et al. 1996; Cameron 1993). While this dissolves the problem of the failure narrative, it ignores the crucial role of movement in Pueblo thought (Preucel and Duwe 2019). According to Tessie Naranjo (1995), movement is one of the "big ideological concepts" of Pueblo thought because it is necessary for the perpetuation of life. Movement is not just normal; it represents the right way to live on the earth. Recent collaborative work between the Pueblos and archaeologists is starting to synthesize Pueblo belief with archaeological data to reinterpret histories of movement across the Southwest (see papers in Duwe and Preucel 2019). This research reframes interpretations of Pueblo history from being about a series of adaptations to external forces (such as drought) to being about the relationships between people and their worlds as they seek balance and harmony. The most important aspect of this work is that it demonstrates a continuous history from time immemorial to the present day and continuing into the future and shows that movement is forever ongoing.

The bias toward favoring permanence of occupation over movement is also seen in the way abandonment implies that the Pueblo people forsook their previous homelands—that those places were somehow given up and forgotten. While the long history of ethnographic research is filled with accounts of twentieth-century Pueblo people having a deep understanding of the greater Southwest, recent collaborative research has demonstrated that Pueblo history literally "is the land" (Ferguson and Colwell-Chanthaphonh 2006). Pueblo memory is inherently linked to place and space, and landscapes, even those very far away from their modern homes, are revered as "footprints" (Kuwanwisiwma and Ferguson 2002) and "memory pieces" (Ferguson and Colwell-Chanthaphonh 2006:162). These ancient homes are never devoid of life, and spiritual ancestors still reside in the places that archaeologists call sites (Tosa and Seowtewa 2019).

The critiques of the abandonment perspective are beginning to change the way archaeologists view Pueblo movement, particularly in the Chama, where, as I describe below, there was a Tewa presence in the valley throughout the Historic period. However, even when acknowledging this continued presence, an implied notion of abandonment exists in the historical and archaeological literature. Namely, understanding the relationship of the Tewa people with the Chama Valley, both during Spanish contact and colonization, rests on the concept of occupation. There appears to be a bias that places more historical importance on villages that were occupied year-round, such as the mission villages (and villages that were occupied before contact) and less on villages that were, as the historian Barrett (1997:21) describes, "of a limited or intermittent sort." The latter includes villages with small populations or that were reoccupied during the turn of the seventeenth century and suffered Spanish pressure, long-term drought, and increasingly hostile Apache raiding. In fact, Barrett (1997:21) questions whether many of these villages were still occupied at all or were "just used from time to time for purposes such as defense, ceremonials, a base for resource exploitation or, as on that occasion, as a refuge." The implication, of course, is that a Tewa presence in the valley was severely diminished and that the true center of social and economic importance was at villages on the Rio Grande.

Archaeologists, too, have made the distinction between full-time agricultural communities and villages that were reoccupied or only lived in by a remnant of their original population. An enduring debate revolves around whether the sixteenth- and seventeenth-century Chama villages were in fact occupied as full-time agricultural settlements (Schroeder 1979; Wozniak 1992) or were reused for seasonal resource gathering and eventual sheepherding (Schaafsma 2002). This distinction between types of occupation can be carried through to the seventeenth century as well, as I and others have tended to privilege centers of sustained population over small reoccupations in understanding the effects of Spanish colonialism. In this thinking we are divorcing the past from the present and the future and negating the very nature of the Pueblo village.

What if we reframe our discussion of Pueblo village life by placing the abandoned and reoccupied villages on the same plane of historical importance as occupied towns? What if an abandoned site, a reoccupied village, and a full-time settlement all have the same central importance, no matter the number of residents or time between occupations? According to Rina Swentzell, this is how the Tewa people view the village. A village is the metaphorical and the physical center place, and it is the place that connects human existence with the energies of the cosmos (Swentzell 1988:15). It is a nexus point, or node, where the interconnected beings of the world come to dwell. Because the world is in constant flux, so are its inhabitants. And the village, rather than existing in a state of stasis, is constantly evolving and changing. We often regard movement (such as abandonment) as an anomalous disruption of village life. Severin Fowles (2011) has recently proposed that we begin to flip this idea on its head and view Pueblo history as Pueblo people do—with the understanding that movement, rather than stasis, is the desired and normal way of life.

The Tewa believe that within the village "walls are alive and participate in contexts and cycles of life and death. *They are never vagrant*" (Swentzell 1993:147; emphasis mine). In this way the pueblo is inalienable, and although its walls may crumble, the adobe can be remixed with water and used to raise up other walls in its place. This means, of course, that a center place never ceases to become a center, and the village continues to be a living place. To "reoccupy" a village is to return home.

In the following pages I recount the history of the Chama from Spanish contact through the Historic period. This discussion is in two sections. The first section details Spanish contact and the great changes of the sixteenth and seventeenth century and the "abandonment" of the valley. The second section explores the enduring Tewa presence in the valley through to the modern day. I take Swentzell's view seriously in rethinking the connections between inalienable villages and the people and how these connections to place were maintained in the face of Spanish, Mexican, and American colonialism.

"FOUR STRONG PUEBLOS IN THE CRAGGY LANDS"

In 1598 the Spanish were no strangers to the Tewa and other Pueblos of northern New Mexico. In fact, beginning with Rodrigo de Barrionuevo's expedition to the north in 1541, the Tewa and other Pueblo people had multiple brief encounters with small Spanish exploratory parties almost sixty years before Governor Oñate arrived at Ohkay Owingeh. The coming of the Spanish coincides with a dramatic population restructuring that began in the fifteenth century and led to what has previously been interpreted as the full-scale abandonment of the valley. Was this a coincidence? What else would have led to the depopulation of the Chama? And what did life in the Chama look like at Spanish contact?

Traditionally, issues of contact and colonization in the Chama were virtually ignored because archaeologists like Harry Mera (1934) believed that the large villages of the Classic period were abandoned by the early sixteenth century, well before the Spanish entered the region. His assertion was based on the presence of biscuitware, which he believed was not produced after around 1500. The abandonment of the Chama prior to Spanish contact was echoed in Fred Wendorf and Eric Reed's (1955) seminal chronology of the northern Rio Grande and hence was cemented into the canon. In the mid-twentieth century, however, a number of documents from the earliest Spanish entradas into the region were translated and published, offering new insights on the extent of Spanish activities and what the Pueblo world looked like at contact. This information has given pause to archaeologists, who began to rethink sixteenth-century life in the Chama. Perhaps there was a significant Tewa occupation in the Chama at contact, one that would continue through to the establishment of San Gabriel.

FIRST CONTACT

Francisco Vázquez de Coronado's entrada signaled the first strong arm of Spanish imperialism northward in the Americas. His aim was similar to that of his contemporaries: to find and acquire riches for himself, his men, and the realm. In relative terms, Coronado's expedition was contemporaneous with other famous expeditions; it occurred nineteen years after Hernán Cortés destroyed the Aztec capital of Tenochtitlán and only seven years after Francisco Pizarro entered Cuzco as victor. All used similar tactics. Coronado's party was essentially an army, with 350 soldiers and over a thousand *indios amigos* (Mexican Indians), as well as a support staff, friars, and porters (Riley 1999:30). Coronado forged a path northward somewhere along the boundary between the modern states of Arizona and New Mexico, leading him to Cibola.

The fervor of finding golden cities, like his contemporaries found, drove Coronado north (Riley 1995:149). Upon reaching the Zuni village of Hawiku, he found no gold, but he did find a fight. The conflict destroyed the village (Flint and Flint 2005). The Zuni told Coronado that the fabled golden cities of Cibola did exist but farther east, sending the Spanish to the Rio Grande. There, in early 1541, Coronado engaged in battle with Tiwa villages. His three-month siege and occupation of the area became known as the Tiguex War (Flint 2008). While camped north of Albuquerque, Coronado sent out multiple foraging and exploratory parties. Francisco Barrionuevo led one up the Rio Grande and into Tewa country.

In the midsummer of 1541 Barrionuevo reached the confluence of the Rio Chama and the Rio Grande, and the Spanish discovered that news of their approach had preceded them (Hammond and Rey 1940:244). Two large villages, Yunque'owingeh and Ohkay Owingeh, were filled with "many provisions and very beautiful pottery" but were entirely devoid of people. Before plundering these villages and returning to the main expedition in the south, the party discovered, through inquiries to other Pueblo people, that the residents had fled to "four strong pueblos in the craggy lands." This would not be the only time the Spanish witnessed the Pueblo people pragmatically "abandoning" their villages to avoid incoming soldiers. Castaño de Sosa witnessed a similar scene at Pecos in 1591 (Hammond and Rey 1966; Schroeder and Matson 1965), as did Oñate among the Piro- and Tiwa-speaking villages in 1598 (Simmons 1991). The Puebloans' residential flexibility frustrated and bewildered the Spanish and, as we will see shortly, continues to confound archaeologists and historians today.

Barrionuevo never ventured up the Chama to see these villages for himself. There are also points of doubt in the description, and the interpretation of his expedition, chronicled by Pedro de Castañeda, was written twenty years after the events (Ramenofsky and Vaughan 2003) and then copied thirty years after that, leading to discrepancies (Winship 1896). However, it does appear that at mid-sixteenth century four pueblos were occupied. Whether they were permanent settlements or refuges for the fleeing villagers from Yunque'owingeh remains unknown. Albert Schroeder's pioneering research (1979:250) places the villages in the "craggy lands" in the Chama Valley, some five to fifteen miles northwest of the Rio Grande. Schroeder, based on his extensive archaeological and geographic knowledge, suggested that the "strong pueblos" may have referred to either Sapa'owingeh, Pesede'owingeh, Te'ewi'owingeh, Tsama'owingeh, or Ku'owingeh. All of these villages were occupied in the Classic period, and the first four have evidence of dating to at least the mid-sixteenth century, suggesting that these were the four villages described to Barrionuevo (map 6). Te'ewi'owingeh, located approximately five miles from Ohkay, has a kiva that was built in 1529 and likely was occupied, at least sporadically, through the end

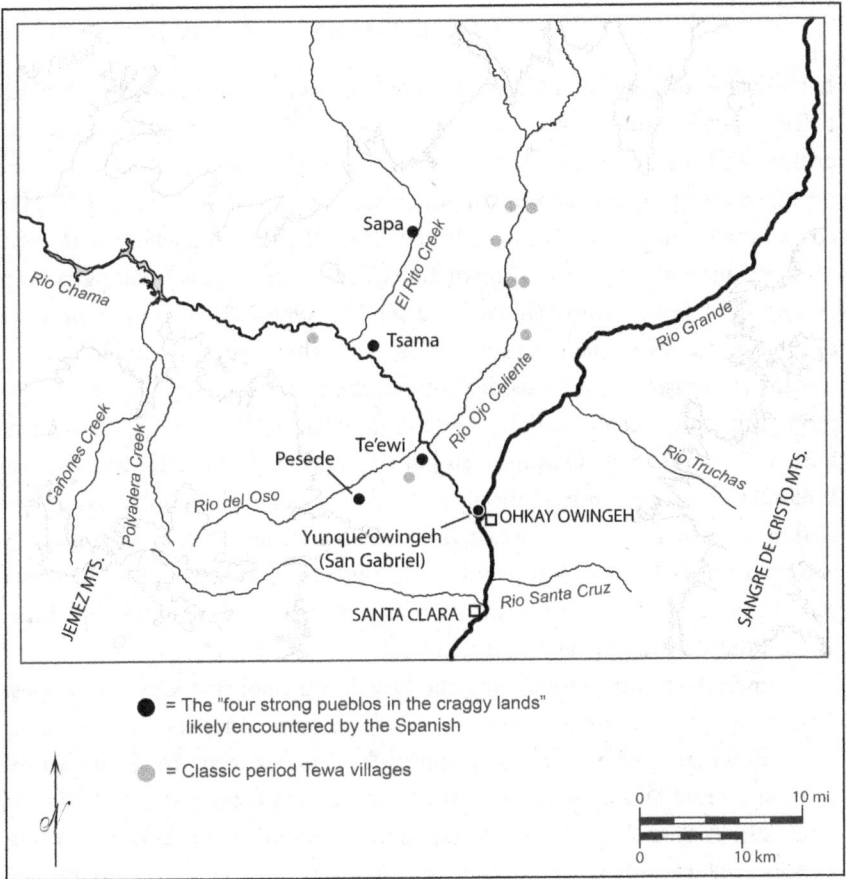

MAP 6 Map of possible sixteenth-century Tewa villages encountered by the Spanish in the Chama Valley.

of the century (Wendorf 1953). Recent ceramic analysis at Pesede'owingeh and Sapa'owingeh shows evidence of Glaze E and F pottery (1550–1700; Eiselt and Darling 2013), as does Tsama'owingeh (Shure 1973).

A number of other smaller Spanish parties continued to venture north up the Rio Grande in the latter half of the sixteenth century (Riley 1999:32–36), including the Rodriguez-Chamuscada expedition into Tewa country in 1580, but none journeyed to the "craggy lands" until 1591, when the first Spanish boots touched the verdant soil of the Chama Valley.

INTO THE CHAMA

In the winter of 1590–1591 Gaspar Castaño de Sosa of Nuevo León, tired of his failed efforts to gain the support of the Spanish crown to colonize New Mexico, decided to lead an illegal expedition northward. He followed the Pecos River north, where upon reaching the mountains, he stumbled on Pecos Pueblo. He coaxed the fleeing citizens of the village back to their homes, where he insisted they become followers of the crown and Christ, then led his small party west and north to Tewa country (Hammond and Rey 1966:283). This time the Tewa did not retreat from their villages as they had when Barrionuevo entered the territory, but instead they defended their maize and belongings. After encountering numerous Keres- and Tewa-speaking villages (Flint 2017), Castaño de Sosa arrived at Ohkay Owingeh on January 12, 1591 (Schroeder and Matson 1965:121). After appointing officials and erecting a cross, he and his party traveled into the mountains to the east, likely visiting Picuris Pueblo on January 13, and returning to Ohkay (or the surrounding environs) on January 14, where they stayed the night. The next morning Castaño de Sosa and his small expedition crossed the Rio Grande and ventured west.

Historical accounts chronicling the expedition note that Castaño de Sosa visited two villages on the west bank of the river. The first was certainly Yunque'owingeh, where the party stayed for about two hours, enough time to raise a cross and secure obedience to the crown (Schroeder and Matson 1965:129). Archaeologists are less certain of the identity of the second village. The documents explain that "we went to another pueblo, a league from this one, and we slept in it. They gave their obedience to His Majesty, a governor, *alcades*, and *aguacil* were appointed; a high cross was set up to the sound of trumpets and arguebuses." Dorothy Hull (1916) proposed that this second village was Santa Clara. However, based on the geographic description of the village as being a league (four miles) away from Yunque'owingeh and their knowledge of the valley's archaeology, Albert Schroeder and Dan Matson (1965:131) postulated that the second village may have been Te'ewi'owingeh. Te'ewi'owingeh is located five miles from the confluence of the Rio Chama and Rio Grande, at the junction of the Chama and the Rio del Oso. It was also likely part of the "four strong pueblos" recorded by the Barrionuevo expedition. If it was Te'ewi, the village appears to have had a substantial population to warrant the full ceremonies that Castaño de Sosa bestowed. The village most certainly was not founded by Tewa populations fleeing the Rio Grande, because Castaño de Sosa's party was based at Ohkay Owingeh and was "received well by them" (Schroeder and Matson 1965:121).

Te'ewi'owingeh likely dates to at least the late sixteenth century, as suggested by a small percentage of Kapo Black-on-white, a pottery type that dates to 1550–1700 (Wendorf 1953). And although Castaño de Sosa only recorded a handful of villages, it is likely others were occupied during this period as well. Pesede'owingeh, a village that was modified and occupied by seventeenth-century Hispanic residents (Anschuetz 1998a; Eiselt and Darling 2013), has evidence of Posuwi'i Incised, a type of pottery that dates to the sixteenth century, in Spanish colonial vessel forms (Ford and Anschuetz 1995). Nineteen Glaze F sherds were recorded at Sapa'owingeh that date to 1550–1700, as well as one sherd of a Spanish cup form (Eiselt and Darling 2013:2.12). Glaze F pottery was found at Tsama'owingeh, which is unsurprising because the village, according to Spanish documents, had a substantial occupation through the first decade of the seventeenth century (Shure 1973:12).

Castaño de Sosa's expedition did not end well. Later in the year he was hauled back to Mexico City in chains for embarking on an illegal colonization attempt. It would be another seven years before the Spanish ventured back into the Chama, and this time they stayed.

OÑATE AND SAN GABRIEL DEL YUNQUE

During the last sixty years of the sixteenth century the Spanish were concerned primarily with exploration and understanding what riches and people lay at the far northernmost extent of their expanding empire. What they found both disappointed and intrigued them. There were no cities of gold, but there were numerous small, relatively peaceful communities of agriculturalists whose souls they could save. There was also a very real possibility that the Pueblo people were unwittingly living along skirts of mountains filled with veins of gold and silver that rivaled the rich ore deposits to the south. And there were murmurs that other nations, such as England, were also looking to expand inland (Simmons 1991:63). To procure this wealth—of minerals and salvation—the Spanish began to think of establishing a colony in the heart of the Pueblo province.

This was no easy task. Upon taking moral inventory of the atrocities of conquest in Mexico and Peru, and acknowledging global geopolitical opinion, Spain began to shift its policy of action in New Spain in the 1540s. Conquest was no longer in vogue, and colonization and missionization became, at least on paper, the main impetuses for imperial expansion (Riley 1999:32). All colonial activity was ultimately under the discretion of the king of Spain, and it was a burdensome process that required playing politics at multiple scales to be granted colonial opportunities. This red tape was altogether too much for Castaño de Sosa, and he chose to pursue his colonial endeavors illegally in 1591. Others in the 1590s shared this colonial dream and were jockeying for the chance to lead sanctioned expeditions of their own. One of these men was Juan de Oñate, the son of a wealthy family from Zacatecas, in New Spain, whose father had established the family fortune through the mining of silver. Upon recommendation from the viceroy, Juan de Oñate was given permission to undertake his colonial endeavor. His task was to recruit five hundred men and their families and equip them out of his own funds (Simmons 1991).

Oñate departed for what would become New Mexico in the spring of 1598, with Ohkay Owingeh as his destination. His journey would take him north to the Rio Grande, and he would more or less follow the river into the heart of the Pueblo world. Oñate reached Ohkay in July and soon set up a base of operations there. As he waited for the rest of his slow caravan to arrive, he drafted 1,500 Pueblo people from Ohkay Owingeh and neighboring villages to begin to dig a large Iberian-style canal system, or *acequia madre*, to irrigate the fertile land at the confluence of the Rio Chama and Rio Grande for the planting of winter wheat (for Catholic communion) and other newly introduced crops (Simmons 1991:114). This system of irrigation expanded on the existing small-scale ditch-based irrigation and is still used today (Ford 1987; Ford and Swentzell 2015). When the colonists arrived in August, they quickly occupied the adobe houses and built a makeshift church, which was consecrated on September 8, 1598 (Riley 1999:75).

Oñate quickly sought to explore the vast expanse of the new colony and to seek the submission of other Pueblo people. One of the most well-known, and most disastrous, encounters between the Spanish and the Pueblos was at Acoma Pueblo (Simmons 1991). Oñate sent his nephew, Juan de Zaldívar, to the village. Upon demanding and being denied food, the Spanish instigated a fight that left Zaldívar and eleven of his men dead. Oñate's reaction was to send Zaldívar's brother, Vicente, to Acoma to punish the citizens. Vicente and his men, using cannon, massacred some five hundred warriors and three hundred women and children and took five hundred villagers as prisoners. Punishments were heinous and included sentencing many of the prisoners to enslavement and cutting off the right foot of the men. The captives eventually escaped and Acoma was soon rebuilt. The actions of Oñate and his men were eventually too much even for Spain and led to Oñate's recall to Mexico City in 1608 and his life-long banishment from New Mexico in 1614 (Simmons 1991:178). The massacre at Acoma set the stage for many crises to come.

Meanwhile, while the timing and circumstances are unclear, in 1599 Oñate and the rest of the colony left Ohkay and resettled in a nearby village called Yunque'owingeh, on the west bank of the Rio Grande (Simmons 1991). Located on a fertile triangle of land west of the Rio Grande and north of the Chama, Yunque'owingeh was evacuated by its Tewa inhabitants, who moved to Ohkay Owingeh, and the village was reoccupied by the Spanish. This removal of people was the first act of *reducción*, the Spanish policy of moving dispersed groups into fewer settlements for proselytization and governance, in the Pueblo world. Documents do not record why Oñate made this move, but Yunque'owingeh was situated in prime farmland and would have been an ideal place to build (and feed) his colony. Also, it may have been in the Tewa's best interests to put distance between themselves and the Spanish; living as close neighbors likely created a stressful situation (Simmons 1987). This colonial action of reducción is remembered at Ohkay Owingeh as the seminal event of coming together of the people. The people of Yunque'owingeh (the Summer People) ceded their village to the Spanish and joined with their new neighbors at Ohkay (the Winter People) (Ellis 1987). Oñate christened Yunque'owingeh "San Gabriel" and made it his new capital. The new occupants built a permanent church and remodeled the village to Oñate's standards. Oñate thus established the second Spanish occupation in the modern United States (San Augustin, along the Atlantic coast of Florida, was established in 1565).

San Gabriel, and the colony as a whole, was plagued with crises from the start. Although much of the capital's woes stemmed from Oñate's poor administrative decisions and the brutal acts that led to his eventual recall, the colonists were also very unlucky. Tree-ring records indicate that by 1598 the region had entered a five-year period of an unfortunate combination of a sustained drought and extreme cold (Van West et al. 2013). In the summers of 1600 and 1601 even irrigated maize crops failed. Even if they had survived the scorching summer months, the crops were certainly destroyed by the early frosts (White 2014). Starvation and hardship were a startling reality for the colonists. In a letter dated October 1, 1601, Fray Juan de Escalona wrote the following about the direness of the situation.

As I was writing this letter, a frost scorched the fields of the Indians. Before this time there had been a shortage of rain, and as a result the greater portion of the cornfields had dried up. Your lordship's chaplains, the royal alferez, and all the other captains and soldiers reflected on the fact that *we had consumed all the corn that the Indians had saved during the preceding six years*, because there has not been a week since we came here that we have not used up from fifty to sixty fanegas of corn, and when the governor and the rest of the people were here we consumed upwards of eighty fanegas. (Hammond and Rey 1966:1953; emphasis mine)

The Spaniards had it hard, but the Tewa had it much worse. The citizens of Ohkay Owingeh had stored years worth of corn for situations just like this, and without Spanish interference they would have weathered the storm. The temperatures dropped so low in the winter of 1600–1601 that horses could cross the frozen Rio Grande and the communion wine "had to be heated to be drunk" (Carlin et al. 2013:20). Besides a lack of food, the intense cold meant a severe shortage of turkey-feather cloaks and cotton blankets, which the Spanish took off the backs of the villagers (White 2014). Tensions grew, both between the colonists and the Tewa and among the colonists themselves, leading to the defection of half the colony back to Mexico in 1601 (Simmons 1991). The villagers of Ohkay Owingeh had no such recourse, and these experiences led to the first of many hardships that culminated in the Pueblo Revolt. The cold and drought began to ease in 1602, but by then the damage had been done.

The history of San Gabriel is shockingly short; in less than a decade the capital would be moved to Santa Fe and Oñate would be removed. Spanish documents reveal surprisingly little about what life was like at the village. However, the material remains at Yunque'owingeh document approximately nine years of intense contact between the Pueblo and Spanish people and the beginning actions of colonization that would lay the foundation of conflict and the blending of traditions.

Today, Yunque'owingeh is a quiet place, marked by a cross and a plaque (figure 28). A house sits on one of the housemounds, and the area of Spanish occupation is farmed for alfalfa. But the village has never been forgotten. Richard Ford remembers hearing stories from people at Ohkay who grew up climbing on the stone foundations of the first church. And some at the pueblo trace their history to the west side of the Rio Grande (personal communication May 2018). The site was tested in 1944 (Tichy 1944), but the most significant

FIGURE 28 Yunque'owingeh, July 2018.

excavations were called for by the government of Ohkay because of a concern about impacts to the site (mining for adobe and cultivation). Thus began the University of New Mexico's work at Yunque'owingeh, directed by Florence Hawley Ellis from 1959 to 1962.

Ellis brought her field school to excavate three area of the village. Stratigraphically, she observed three components. The lowest layer of the site dated to the Late Coalition and Classic periods and was thus contemporaneous with ancestral villages of the Chama, between the fourteenth and sixteenth centuries. Pottery ranged from Santa Fe Black-on-white to Sankawi Black-on-cream. The village, approximately four hundred rooms arranged around a central plaza, would have looked similar to villages in the craggy lands (Sapa'owingeh, Pesede'owingeh, Te'ewi'owingeh, Tsama'owingeh). The top layer yielded culture material dating to the eighteenth through twentieth centuries and represents both Tewa and Hispanic farmsteads and agricultural features. Between these two layers was the main event and the focus of the field school: Oñate's occupation of San Gabriel del Yunque.

Unfortunately little was ever written on Ellis's research. However, within a few scant reports a story begins to emerge about culture contact within the first years of the colony. In the course of her excavations Ellis was able to identify the church, the officer apartments, the soldiers' barracks, and possible houses for Tewa people who aided the Spanish (Ellis 1987, 1989).

Far from being the great city that Oñate envisioned, San Gabriel was in many ways simply a remodeling of the village of Yunque'owingeh. While the unmarried Spanish soldiers likely reoccupied Tewa houses in the western portion of the village for use as barracks (Ellis 1987:25), the officers and officials lived in relatively spacious apartments, based on obvious signs of renovation such as plastering floors, removing walls, and cutting windows and doors. It was likely Tewa women who were commissioned (or forced) to do this work (Ellis 1989:78). Even with these slight modifications it is important to note that Oñate and his men were essentially living in a Tewa village, on the plaza, and were surrounded by local adobe crafted by local hands. Immediately adjacent to their houses were fields that had been farmed for twenty generations, and beyond the fields were the *tsin* and sacred peaks. It's intriguing to think of how living within the Tewa's architectural and cosmological landscape shaped the colonizers' view of this new world.

As the Spanish were being molded in the Pueblo world, culture contact appeared to quickly have worked the other way as well. Though Yunque'owingeh may have been conceded to Oñate and his colonists to free the Tewa of the burden of living cheek by jowl with the Spanish, Tewa people may have lived in the eastern portion of the village, perhaps employed by the Spanish. There is evidence that at least some individuals began to embrace this new form of life. The church was built by Tewa hands, but likely with great resistance. But buried in the north transept of the church were found the remains of two individuals, identified as Native Americans, presumably Tewa, who had ox bones engraved with crosses laid on top of their bodies (Ellis 1989:67–68). Could these have been neophytes, and some of the earliest Tewa converts to Catholicism? It is also tempting to think that these conversions could be evidence of the beginning of the Fiscales, part of the Towa é who are elected annually by the Summer and Winter chiefs today.

The fruits, quite literally, of colonization were also quickly adopted. Sweet-tasting native plants are rare in the Southwest, and the monotony of maize must have been real. Many of the staples of the modern spread at a Pueblo feast day were introduced by Oñate's party, including wheat and fruit trees and the beef, pork, mutton, and chicken that make up green chili stew and other dishes. Melons were such a delicacy that they spread in advance of the entradas and were possibly mentioned in early Spanish documents (Flint and Flint 2005:305–306). Interestingly, in the Pueblo Revolt, when all things brought by the Spanish were to be cast off, these food stuffs stayed. Ford (1972a, 1987) argued that while the Spanish bitterly complained about the unproductive nature of New Mexico farming, the Pueblo people successfully integrated a multitude of Old World domesticates into their agricultural and cosmological systems. The Tewa were able to expand their resource base and secure against risk without changing their cultural values and principles (Bernstein et al. 2019).

As the colonists were attempting to hold on at San Gabriel, Oñate embarked on a series of adventures to the Plains (modern-day Kansas) and modern-day Arizona. The latter mission was to assess for precious minerals and to find the Strait of Anián (the Colorado River). He failed in both. Shortly after returning to New Mexico in 1608, Oñate was called back to Mexico City and in 1614 was charged with a number of crimes, including those stemming from his actions at Acoma (Simmons 1991:184). He was forbidden to return to New Mexico and was exiled from New Spain. He returned to Spain and lived out his remaining days as a mining inspector, dying in 1626.

Before he left New Mexico, Oñate appears to have begun preparations to establish a new capital in an area of northern New Mexico not lived in by Pueblo people, on the east side of the Rio Grande and at the flanks of the Sangre de Cristo Mountains (Simmons 1991:182). This new capital, called La Villa Real de la Santa Fé de San Francisco de Asís (normally shortened to Santa Fe), was christened by the new governor, Pedro de Peralta, in 1610. In the years between the Oñate and Peralta governments, the fate of the colony hung in the balance because of its lack of silver and food and its harsh winters. But there were Catholic neophytes among the Pueblos and other Native peoples, and to ensure that the crown did not forsake them, the Franciscans embarked on a campaign to baptize thousands (Simmons 1991:183–184). Missionization became the primary purpose for naming New Mexico a crown colony in 1608.

It is unclear what remained of the Spanish occupation at San Gabriel following the transfer of the capital to Santa Fe. Some Spanish citizens may have remained in the village for another few years, as the place is mentioned until 1617 (Simmons 1987:44), but most likely many moved to Santa Fe. The church, whose foundations many generations of children played on and were formally uncovered by Ellis in 1962, was probably destroyed during the Pueblo Revolt of 1680. It is likely that after a short stay away from the village when the Spanish were present, the former residents of Yunque began to return. But the process of intense culture contact remained and was sowed deep in the hearts of the Tewa people and included the adoption and valuation of many aspects of Spanish material life and governance. It also included fear, distrust, and anger toward the Spanish. One of Ohkay's most famous residents, Po'pay, planned and led the Pueblo Revolt some seventy years after Oñate left Yunque.

Yunque'owingeh is now under alfalfa fields, or in the archaeological collections housed at the Maxwell Museum in Albuquerque and at Ghost Ranch. Some of the site has been lost to the activities of adobe mining, agriculture, and house construction. In her account, Ellis (1987:36) takes a somewhat mournful tone that the site was not better preserved, as it is an important historical and cultural site that should be counted as one of the jewels of our national heritage. While I empathize with this sentiment, I cannot help but remember Rina Swentzell's (1993) description of Pueblo walls as never being vagrant. One of the main causes of site destruction—digging the earth for adobe for use in new home construction—is also a kind of rebirth. The walls of Yunque'owingeh continue to vitalize the community of Ohkay Owingeh.

WHAT HAPPENED IN THE CHAMA?

Regardless of the timing of settlement shifts in the Chama, the questions remain: When and why did people leave their homes and join their brethren at Ohkay Owingeh and Yunque'owingeh? For the question of when, based on ethnohistoric and archaeological information, we know that at least one village in the Chama was occupied into the seventeenth century. One of the first orders of business Oñate conducted at Ohkay was a census (Hammond and Rey 1953, 1966). Oñate's cartographer, Enrico Martínez, recorded three Tewa pueblos in the uplands, including the named village of Sama (Tsama'owingeh) and an unnamed pueblo on the northern Pajarito Plateau that was likely Tsirege'owingeh (Barrett 2002). The Tewa pueblos recorded by Martínez dated to at least the late sixteenth century (Breternitz 1966; Duwe 2006). Tsama'owingeh apparently had a sizable enough population to be assigned a priest (Hammond and Rey 1953:346). Frank Wozniak (1992:50) postulates that the three other villages likely noted in 1541 (Sapa'owingeh, Te'ewi'owingeh, and Pesede'owingeh) were probably still occupied during Oñate's occupation, and this is supported by the archaeological evidence cited earlier for Castaño de Sosa's expedition. However, based on Fray Lazaro Ximenez's descriptions of Apache raids on Tewa villages in 1608 and the lack of references to Tsama'owingeh or any other Chama village in later documents, it's likely that these late-occupation villages were burned and destroyed (Hammond and Rey 1953:1059). Intriguingly, both

Te'ewi'owingeh (Wendorf 1953) and Pesede'owingeh (Jeançon 1912) have evidence of intense burning.

Why this depopulation in the Chama occurred is a complex question because it appears to have happened there significantly earlier than it did at other places in the northern Rio Grande region, where historians (Barrett 1997, 2002), using ethnohistoric documents, suggest that the majority of villages were depopulated beginning in the 1630s, almost a century after those in the Chama. These great changes in the number and location of Pueblo settlements in the larger region, recorded in Spanish census records, may have been due to epidemics that reduced the population by perhaps two-thirds. Additionally, Spanish secular and mission policy required Pueblo people to live in centralized villages. Outlying locations became hinterlands to the mission pueblos. But why did this process begin in the Chama a century earlier than it did in the northern Rio Grande region?

Based on the discussion in the last chapter, one could make the argument that similar, if not identical, processes of coalescence that began at the end of the thirteenth century extended through Spanish contact and colonization. Jeffrey Dean and colleagues (1994) make the argument that beginning with the Four Corners migration and the reorganization of the Pueblo Southwest, the following centuries can best be defined by different scales of village and population coalescence. Beginning around 1350 a similar pattern follows in the Chama, where many of the small villages or hamlets occupied during the Coalition period were left as people coalesced at other small villages and eventually built large pueblos like that of Posi'owingeh. Further population coalescence occurred beginning in the early fifteenth century (going from places like Cerro Colorado to Sapa'owingeh) as these large villages continued to grow in size. Coalescence was still continuing by the turn of the sixteenth century. Half of the eleven Classic period villages do not have much evidence of sixteenth-century pottery or tree-ring dates and Spanish raiding and exploratory parties likely encountered (or at least heard about) the other half. Eventually the people from the towns described to Barrionuevo in 1541 joined their kin at Ohkay and Yunque'owingeh.

While there are most likely errors in how we (Duwe 2011; Duwe et al. 2016; Ortman 2012, 2016a) estimate momentary population through time, village chronology and geographic location suggest that this general pattern of coalescence was very real. In the last chapter I proposed multiple reasons for why this process occurs, ranging from climatic variability, real and perceived threats of competition, and the requirements of an emerging social and ceremonial system. Similar catalysts likely occurred through the sixteenth century as well, but with an important difference: coalescence was happening much faster than before. Perhaps the appropriate question, therefore, is not why people left the Chama but rather why the ongoing process of population coalescence rapidly increased in the sixteenth century?

Certainly the climate was a factor. Northern New Mexico and the larger Southwest have always been relatively dry, but it's the unpredictability and variability of precipitation and temperature that make the climate challenging for farmers (Van West et al. 2013). The Tewa in the Chama adapted to the challenging climate by developing a social and ceremonial system that emphasized mobility and flexibility, allowing them to move freely between villages and the upland and lowland areas of the valley (Anschuetz 2007a; Duwe and Anschuetz 2013). The weather in the sixteenth century must have made farming particularly difficult. The 1530s were exceptionally dry (Towner and Salzer 2013) and may be the reason why half of the Classic period villages were unoccupied by Barrionuevo's arrival. The second half of the century experienced a megadrought believed to be the most intense drought in the last two millennium (Stahle et al. 2000). Felt by the entire continent from the 1550s to the 1590s, the megadrought particularly affected northern New Mexico and may have been a significant contributing factor in the decision to move to the well-watered environs along the Rio Grande (Schroeder 1968).

The Tewa give another reason for the depopulation of the Chama. In Ohkay's tradition, the Summer and Winter People came together at the village of Posi'owingeh, located in the Rio Ojo Caliente valley. After a long and prosperous time, the village suffered an epidemic and the residents left, subsequently building the six historic Tewa pueblos that replicate the new Summer-Winter People organization (Ortiz 1969:15). It is tempting to equate the epidemic in the origin tradition with the European-introduced diseases that ravaged the New World (Ramenofsky 1988), especially because regional demographic histories (Barrett 2002; Ortman 2016a) show a large decrease in Tewa Basin populations beginning in the sixteenth century. While major Eurasian diseases were known to affect the region by the 1630s (Barrett 2002), perhaps their impact was felt much earlier and was a factor in the Tewa's decision to move.

By the beginning of the seventeenth century the Spanish documented increased Apachean harassment in the valley. Fray Lazaro Ximenez, in 1608, reported that the Apache were destroying and burning pueblos and stealing horses (Hammond and Rey 1953:1059). Wozniak (1992:51) believes that this may have been the reason why the residents of the final occupied villages, such as Tsama'owingeh, finally moved to Ohkay and Yunque'owingeh, where they could seek protection in the mission villages. However, the dates of Apache migration into the region have been steadily pushed backward, possibly into the thirteenth century (Fowles 2018; Fowles and Eiselt 2019), and competition with non-Pueblo people may have occurred throughout the 1500s, if not before. The ties between Pueblo and non-Pueblo people were historically complex and involved shifting patterns of trading and raiding, alliance and warfare (Ford 1972b). Through recent work by Sunday Eiselt (2012) we have learned much about the Apache in the Historic period, but earlier interactions offer great research potential for understanding Tewa coalescence back into the Classic period.

Last, soon after the establishment of the colony, the Spanish imposed the policy of reducción to concentrate the Tewa and other Pueblo people at the mission villages. The policy was formalized in the 1610s (Hammond and Rey 1953:1090; Schroeder 1984:285) and may have been a critical factor for why villages that were temporarily left because of drought or raiding were never reoccupied in a substantial way. Within the mission villages, such as Ohkay, the Tewa people were required to submit to taxation (*impuesto*) of cotton mantas (blankets) or bushels of maize, a difficult if not impossible burden (Camilli et al. 2019). They were also subject to the needs of the church, which included raising wheat, herding sheep, and, in the early years, constructing the building at Yunque'owingeh.

So why did the Tewa's settlement patterns shift in the sixteenth century? It was likely a combination of all of these factors, with a return back to the Chama restricted by Spanish secular and mission policy. But, as detailed in the next section, the Tewa never left the Chama in any real way—a conclusion that makes most sense when viewed through Tewa ideas of mobility, landscape, and village life.

AN ENDURING PRESENCE

The history of the Tewa in the Chama has largely been written off. Either the Tewa are seen as abandoning their villages (and their landscape) in the sixteenth century, or, more recently, their limited presence in the valley after 1598 is viewed as largely inconsequential to the larger colonial project. This latter view is so pervasive, in fact, my earlier work (Duwe 2011) largely focused on the Classic period with only a small discussion of the seventeenth century and later. In some ways this makes sense. For historians, the center of Spanish action, and its effects on Pueblo people, was located at the missionized villages. And the archaeology of the Historic period is tenuous, with little evidence of either Spanish or Tewa presence in the valley.

Archaeologists are left with a gap in our knowledge of landscape production and propagation between the sixteenth century and the ethnographic period. Surely, based on the discussion in the previous chapter, the Tewa people not only lived in the Chama in large numbers but also became inherently tied to its landscape and history. And the plethora of place names recorded at the beginning of the twentieth century by Harrington (1916), as well as those places revered and visited by residents of Ohkay today, attest to deep and unbroken connections with the valley that have been maintained over three centuries of colonization.

Unlike in other areas of the northern Rio Grande, such as the Jemez province (Liebmann 2012) and the heights above Cochiti (Snead and Preucel 1999), there are few overt signs of historic Tewa presence in the Chama. This can be partly attributed to the fact that archaeologists largely dismissed a significant Tewa presence in the Chama after colonization and that few researchers have sought proof to challenge this claim. However, recent research by myself and others is beginning to find evidence that supports the claims of Ohkay Owingeh, both past and present that the Chama has always been an integral part of their world. It's important to keep in mind the local geography: it's only a half-day's walk from Ohkay Owingeh to many of the large ancestral villages in the valley. Instead of a vast and faraway hinterland, the Chama is in Ohkay's backyard. And this is reflected in a number of actions the people of Ohkay have taken in the Chama, historically and through the modern day, including pilgrimage, refuge, and resource gathering (map 7). However, it would be folly to ignore a dynamic colonial environment, and we are beginning to understand how the Tewa people practiced both continuity and change in their connections with the landscape of the Chama Valley.

THE SEVENTEENTH CENTURY

Although their mobility was constrained in the first decades of the colonial era, there is evidence the Tewa maintained a strong presence in the Chama Valley. While the people's primary residence during the seventeenth century was along

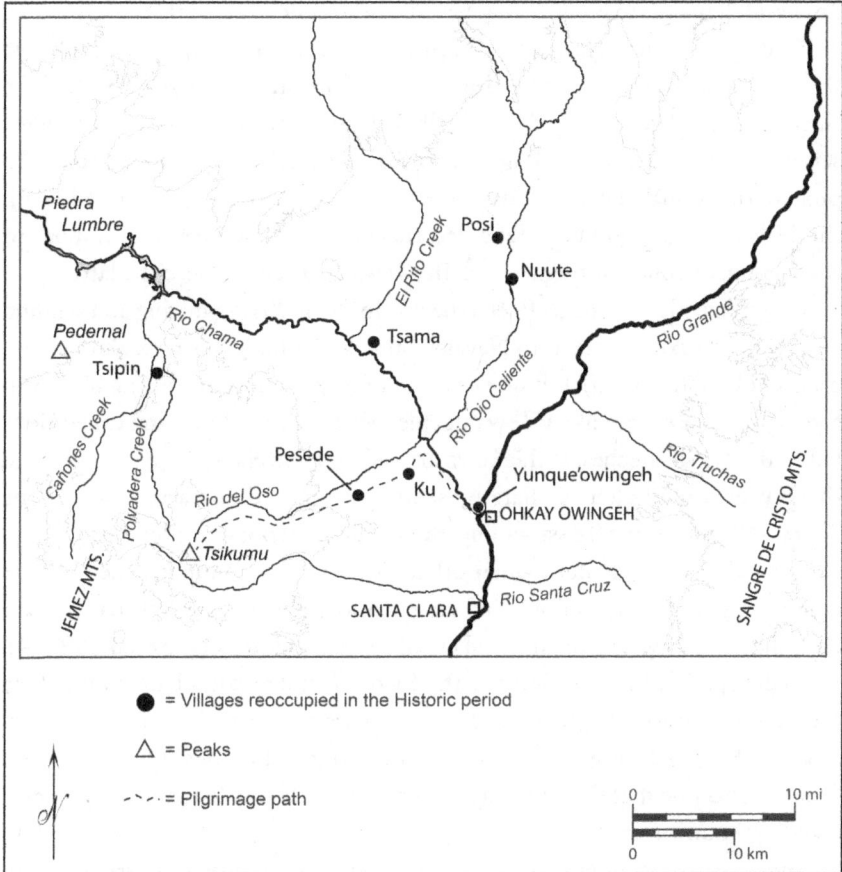

MAP 7 Map of the Tewa presence in the Chama Valley, including reoccupied villages, paths of pilgrimage, and resource areas.

the Rio Grande, the Chama was part of the larger "Yungue-Yungue" province and was viewed by the Spanish as Ohkay's homeland (Hammond and Rey 1940).

Unfortunately, Spanish documents do not mention Pueblo people from 1629 to 1676, or the Tewa specifically from 1730 to 1780 (Wozniak 1992:51). However, Wozniak (1992:51–54) describes a fascinating picture of Tewa presence in the Chama in the early part of the seventeenth century by focusing on a mineral resource valued by both the Pueblo and the Navajo Apaches who lived to the west of modern-day Abiquiú: alumbre, or rock alum. The mineral was used by Pueblo people to dye cloth, and it was particularly valued because of Spanish impuesto demands to produce mantas. The nearest deposits of the shiny mineral are found in the vicinity of what is now known as the Piedra Lumbre, just past the northwestern frontier of the Tewa world (Forrestral and Lynch 1954:45). In the mountains surrounding the valley lived Navajos who had positioned themselves to engage in both trading and raiding with the Rio Grande pueblos. To procure this valuable commodity, the Pueblos would either have to trade with the Navajo, who vigorously defended this valuable resource as an important trade good, or collect it themselves. The Tewa apparently chose the latter.

Fray Benavides described Pueblo people in the 1620s organizing and sending large military expeditions into Navajo country to gather this rock alum (Forrestal and Lynch 1954:45). Because of geographic proximity and a long history in the region, these were likely Tewa people (Wozniak 1992:53). The expeditions led to deadly skirmishes. If the Tewa arrived and the Navajo were not present, the Navajo would later retaliate by sending large raiding parties against the Tewa. Why were the Tewa willing to sacrifice warriors (and endure Navajo wrath) to obtain rock alum when other Pueblo people simply traded for the commodity? Perhaps it was within living memory that Tewa people had lived in the valley and they had an ancestral claim to their territory (Wozniak 1992:54). Tewa occupation in the vicinity of the Piedra Lumbre dates back to the early fourteenth century (chapter 4), and other minerals, such as chert from the skirts of Cerro Pedernal, have been an important resource since possibly before then. One can imagine that the Tewa's aggressiveness was a way to maintain the long-standing boundaries of the Tewa world.

The Tewa also maintained a strong presence in the valley, and particularly in the Piedra Lumbre area, because of Spanish-sanctioned sheepherding. While Spanish herds were small in the early seventeenth century, they continued to grow dramatically (Carrillo 1992:323). By the 1660s the governor of the colony ordered Spanish friars to pay Pueblo herders to care for the flocks (Wozniak 1992:55), and the Chama Valley was an ideal location to graze livestock. While controversial, there appears to be archaeological evidence for Tewa sheepherding in the region. When conducting survey prior to the construction of the Abiquiu dam and resulting reservoir, Curtis Schaafsma (1979, 2002) defined the Piedra Lumbre phase (1640–1710). Sites consisted of round and square single-room structures with associated corrals and faunal assemblages of sheep and goat. Schaafsma believe that these sites were built by the Navajo, but based on an abundance of historic Tewa pottery, very little Navajo pottery, and no historic references to Navajo pastoralism in the sixteenth century, many researchers attribute the sites to a Tewa occupation (Carrillo 1992; Eiselt and Darling 2013:2.30; Kemrer 1992; Wozniak 1992) or perhaps a hybrid Navajo-Tewa community. This assertion is supported by historic accounts of Tewa taking refuge in the area during the Second Pueblo Revolt in 1696 (see below).

Besides not living full time in the Chama, it is becoming more difficult to say that the Tewa abandoned the Chama upon Spanish colonization. The Tewa traveled through the valley extensively for resource procurement and pilgrimage (see below) and had substantial seasonal occupation in the form of sheepherding camps. While it is difficult to determine, many of their ancestral sites may have also been lived at during this time. We do have evidence, however, of a reoccupation of these places in the latter half of the seventeenth century and during and after the Pueblo Revolt.

REFUGE AND REVOLT

In 1541 the people at Ohkay Owingeh and Yunque'owingeh, upon hearing of incoming strangers who had caused so much pain in the south, decided to temporarily leave their homes. Their natural destination was refuge with their brothers and sisters and cousins and friends at the villages in the Chama. Tewa mobility was hardly new, but this dramatic response to the Spanish presence would set a precedent for the colonial era. The Chama became a place of refuge and resistance, particularly during the Pueblo Revolt and its aftermath.

The "reverse abandonment" of the mission (or soon to be missionized) villages for refuge at ancestral villages and landscapes became an established pattern for the entire Pueblo world when faced with Spanish oppression. When Oñate traveled up the Rio Grande in 1598, he found that many of the Piro- and Tiwa-speaking villages near Albuquerque were ghost towns, completely devoid of people and food stores. The people had been deeply scarred by Coronado's actions a half century prior and so they packed up and temporarily moved to more out of the way places to avoid a similar fate (Simmons 1991). The people of Pecos left in much the same way when Castaño de Sosa arrived in 1591 (Schroeder and Matson 1965). These acts of fluidity were not undertaken as permanent migrations. Rather they leveraged one of the Pueblos' greatest assets—movement—to protect themselves in times of uncertainty.

Movement wasn't the only form of Pueblo resistance, however. When Castaño de Sosa reached Ohkay and Yunque in 1591, the Tewa chose to fortify their villages for defense to protect their maize and belongings rather than leave

(Schroeder and Matson 1965). In the seventeenth century the Pueblos showed a willingness to engage the Spanish in combat, with revolts at Jemez, Zuni, and Taos in the 1620s and 1630s. The reasons for resistance were many. Beginning with Governor Peralta's administration in 1610, policies of taxation and forced labor imposed serious economic hardships on the Pueblo people. Children were enslaved to work the silver mines of Northern Mexico (Wilcox 2009). And a severe drought in the 1670s increased tensions (Towner and Salzer 2013). But the last straw was the persecution of Pueblo ceremonial leaders and their doings, led by the church beginning in the 1660s, which culminated in the arrest of forty-seven ceremonial leaders for "sorcery" in 1675. The Spanish hanged three of the men and one died of suicide (Knaut 1995). Pueblo pressure led to the release of one of these captured men, Po'pay, who was from Ohkay Owingeh.

Po'pay, along with other ceremonial leaders, became the center of the resistance. Taking up residence at Taos Pueblo, these men planned to unify all of the Pueblos, from Hopi to Zuni, in rebellion. As leader, Po'pay preached a fiery millennial message that called for the expulsion of the Spanish and their culture and for the return to a traditional way of life (Knaut 1995). On August 10, 1680, a unified Pueblo world rose up and overthrew the Spanish, killing four hundred Spanish citizens and twenty-one of the thirty-three Franciscan missionaries in New Mexico. They destroyed churches and Spanish settlements and laid siege to Santa Fe (Hackett and Shelby 1942:2:234–239). By August 21 the current governor, Antonio de Otermin, retreated from the capital and fled to El Paso.

On multiple occasions the Spanish attempted to take back their lost territory. Eager to regain his honor, Otermin returned in November of 1681 with approximately three hundred Spanish and Mexican Indian soldiers (Knaut 1995). The pre-Spanish paradise that Po'pay envisioned never came to pass, and the Pueblo world, composed of autonomous villages, became increasingly fractured, based on an unwillingness to adopt Po'pay's dramatic worldview and the lack of a common enemy. However, in 1681 the remains of the Pueblo alliance, led by Don Luis Tupata, a Picuris man living at Ohkay, were intact enough to turn back the Spaniards at Cochiti and prompt Otermin's return to El Paso (Hackett and Shelby 1942:2:295). Other attempts to recapture New Mexico were made in 1687 and 1689, which resulted in battles that claimed both Pueblo and Spanish lives.

In 1692 Diego de Vargas, the new governor of New Mexico appointed to reconquer and pacify the territory for the Spanish, arrived at the colony and proceeded to reclaim Santa Fe (Kessell and Hendricks 1994:385). Although considered a "bloodless reconquest," this was only true initially. When Vargas returned in 1693, this time with troops and colonists, many of the Pueblos actively resisted. By this time the pan-Pueblo alliance had collapsed and old animosities had returned, leading Pueblo villages to take sides with either the Spanish or the resistance. Many of the Rio Grande villages were temporarily depopulated because of their vulnerability and the people took refuge in the highlands and mountain areas of their larger worlds. These newly built mesa-top villages incorporated people from many different Pueblo groups, likely including members of *ma:tu'in* from many places (Ford 2018), who were actively resisting Vargas's assaults (Preucel and Aguilar 2018). These villages were built in the Jemez region (Liebmann 2012; Liebmann and Preucel 2007), the area north of Cochiti (Preucel 2000, 2006; Wilcox 2009), and on Tunyo (Black Mesa) at San Ildefonso (Aguilar and Preucel 2019). While the Chama is not specified in historical documents, it was likely another place of refuge. Through a protracted military campaign and by laying economic siege, Vargas successfully overcame this resistance, ending the Pueblo Revolt with the surrender of Tewa forces at Tunyo in September 1694 (Hendricks 2007).

Seeking refuge in the mountains and on mesa tops had a strategic importance—these places were easier to defend compared with the vulnerable mission villages. But Joseph Aguilar and Robert Preucel (2019) note that traveling and occupying these places also had a deeper meaning to the Tewa people. The mountains and mesa tops were their ancestral homes. They were places where the Tewa could pay reverence to those who came before them and draw on their strength and protection. While male warriors made their stand at Tunyo, women and children took refuge at the Late Coalition period village of Nake'muu, located in a highly inaccessible and protected area on the Pajarito Plateau. The same principles appear to have informed the decisions of people from Ohkay Owingeh and other Tewa villages when they reoccupied villages in the Chama.

While violence was quelled in 1694, deep-seated resentment was not. This resentment led to the Second Pueblo Revolt of 1696, where fourteen Rio Grande Pueblos once again rose up against the Spanish. Retaliation by Vargas was harsh and swift, and once again the Tewa and other Pueblo people took refuge away from their mission villages (Espinosa 1942:244–246). The Tewa headed to multiple places, including north up the Rio Grande into the gorge near Embudo, south to Cochiti Mesa, and into the Chama Valley. Aside from at Embudo, where the Spanish engaged the Pueblos in combat, Vargas implemented a strategy of starving the Pueblos out of hiding (Espinosa 1942). Spanish documents tell of Tewa encamped at the foot of Cerro Pedernal. They had probably returned to this area of the Tewa world to protect the livestock and find pasture, gather plants, and seek aid from the Navajo (Wozniak 1992:59). By late summer the Tewa were suffering food shortages, and by the winter of 1696–1697 most of the refugees had returned to their villages and the revolt was over (Espinosa 1942:296–303).

Although it is difficult to pinpoint exactly when the Tewa were in the Chama, archaeologists generally use the term *Revolt era* to designate the period between 1680 and 1700. In recent years we have begun to identify a reoccupation of ancestral villages akin to how San Ildefonso took strength and refuge on the Pajarito Plateau (Aguilar and Preucel 2019). For example, oral tradition from Ohkay Owingeh states that the villages of Pesede'owingeh, Tsama'owingeh, and Ku'owingeh were reoccupied during the Revolt era (Walt 2014:72). Pesede'owingeh is a complex archaeological site that was inhabited through the Classic period and was likely visited by Castaño de Sosa in 1591 (Schroeder 1979). Based on the reanalysis of pottery excavated by Jeançon (Ford and Anschuetz 1995), including a European vessel form of Potsuwi'i Incised and Sankawi Black-on-cream, we know that the village of Pesede'owingeh must have been lived at during the Historic period. Ellis (1968:16) notes that Pesede'owingeh and the adjacent San Lorenzo valley were important for farming, and it is likely that wheat was grown sometime before Spanish homesteaders arrived in the 1730s (Eiselt and Darling 2013:2.29). The village was occupied by Spanish from 1730 to 1747 (Darling and Eiselt 2017), and this adds another complex layer of material culture on top of the Tewa village, including walls that were built using Tewa shrines (Duwe 2011) and the construction of a torreon and additional structures (Eiselt and Darling 2013).

Although there is scant evidence for a Revolt-era occupation at Pesede'owingeh proper, recent research has identified an occupation 300 m northeast of the village dating to the late seventeenth and early eighteenth centuries (Darling and Eiselt 2014:2.48–51). The site includes two stone foundations, a rock cluster (a probable horno), and a rock wall. Additionally, there are the remains of a jacal structure with associated kitchen midden containing ash, bone, pottery, and flaked stone. The majority of the pottery is historic and includes Tewa red, buff, and brown pottery, much of it micaceous and probably produced at Ohkay Owingeh. Mean ceramic dates place this assemblage around the turn of the eighteenth century, or the time of the Revolt era. When corroborated with Ohkay tradition, this is occupation is probably a place where the Tewa lived when life became dangerous on the Rio Grande. It is also likely representational of what other Revolt-era occupations looked like in the Chama: nuanced and short-term encampments at or near ancestral villages.

Another place that Ohkay Owingeh maintains was lived at during the Revolt era is Tsama'owingeh, the earliest-dated village in the Chama and one of the last villages to be fully occupied during Spanish colonization. Stephen Shure (1973) identified Kapo Black and other historic Tewa pottery at the village, and I found evidence of Historic period occupation when mapping the village (Duwe 2011:547–48). I mapped a concentration of double-coursed wall foundations on top of the house mounds (figure 29), and Ford believes these foundations represent the footing stones of a jacal or adobe superstructure (personal communication June 2018). While the dating of these structures is inconclusive, they were likely built after the depopulation of Tsama'owingeh in the early seventeenth century. I can imagine that Tsama'owingeh has continued to be a central place in the Tewa world since its founding in the 1230s. Additionally, I

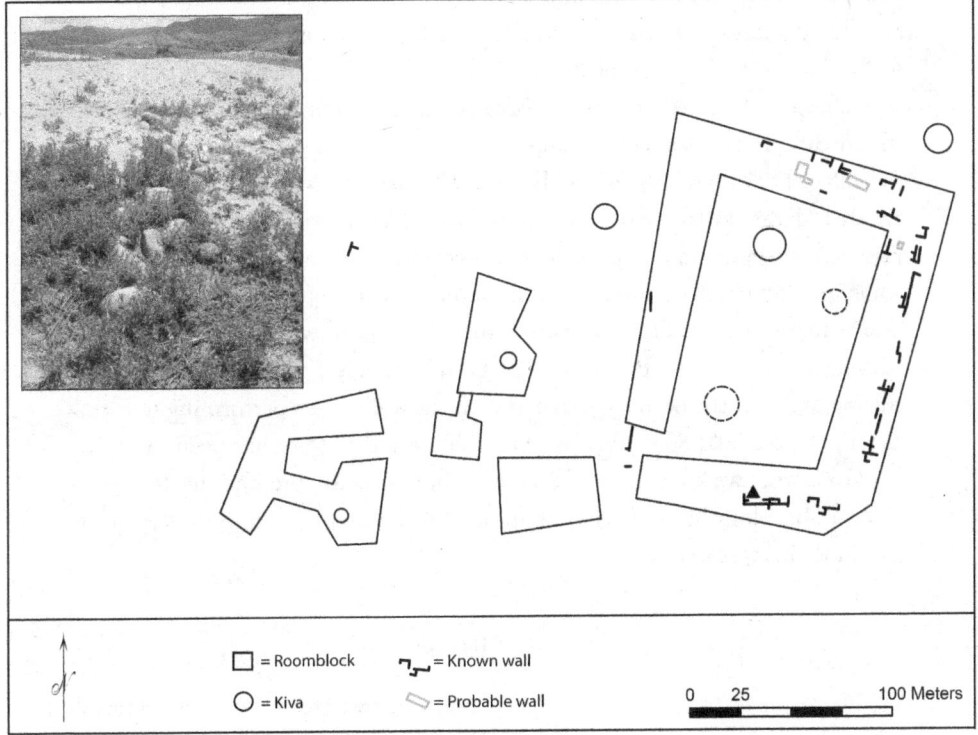

FIGURE 29 Parallel coursed-stone adobe foundations at Tsama'owingeh.

and colleagues believe there are possible Historic period traces in both footing stones and pottery at Ponshipa'akedi'owingeh, Ku'owingeh, and Poshu'owingeh (Kurt Anschuetz, personal communication May 2019), although thought sites are not as well preserved as Tsama'owingeh, and at Little Sapawe, near the modern town of El Rito (Anschuetz 1998b).

We also have additional hints of Revolt-era occupation. For example, Ann Ramenofsky and James Feathers (2002) examined the village of Nuute'owingeh, located in the Rio Ojo Caliente valley, and found a relatively high proportion of Historic period pottery. When subjected to luminescence dating, the pottery produced dates ranging from the sixteenth century to the nineteenth century. Evidence of sheepherding during the Second Pueblo Revolt and the Tewa's general mobility through the Chama at the end of the seventeenth century suggest that there is much more to discover of refuge and return in the Chama.

Last, we know that from 1696 to 1697 the Tewa sought refuge with their livestock in the area north and west of Abiquiú, near the skirts of Cerro Pedernal. The nearby village of Tsipin'owingeh, a place dating to the Late Coalition and Early Classic periods (Chapter 4), may have been a place that was visited or lived at. The village is located on a defendable high mesa with only three access points. Located at each of these points are high walls of stacked rocks (figure 30). These walls do not appear to be associated with the occupation of the village but rather look to have been created at a considerably later date. Why are there large walls guarding the mesa? These walls could have been built by Hispanic sheepherders to protect their livestock from wandering off the mesa when grazing (Richard Ford, personal communication June 2018). They might also be fortifications of high mesa tops to protect the Tewa from hostile Spanish advances in the Second Pueblo Revolt. Unfortunately, I was not able to procure cutting dates for the beams associated with the walls when performing tree-ring dating (Duwe 2011:503). And no Historic period pottery has been observed. But from what we know now of a nuanced but pervasive presence of Revolt-era Tewa archaeology in the Chama, Tsipin'owingeh remains an important place to continue this research.

PILGRIMAGE

With respect to the ferocity and persistence of seventeenth-century Spanish military pursuits, it is surprising that the eventual loss of Tewa access to the Chama came not by Spanish guns and steel but rather by homesteaders and

FIGURE 30 The walls at Tsipin'owingeh.

land grants. Around 1714, Hispanic settlers and ranchers began to rapidly colonize the Chama Valley and effectively cut off access between the Rio Grande and the people's ancestral homeland (Wozniak 1992:61). While this curtailed the mobility that the Tewa had experienced for hundreds of years, it did not divorce the people from their valley. Ortiz's work, and that of Rina Swentzell, Tessie Naranjo, and Gregory Cajete, has demonstrated that the Tewa world is not simply a collection of places embodied with memory and sacredness. Instead, the Tewa perspective also emphasizes the connections between these places, the living people, and the larger world. This interconnectedness is the basis for understanding the "whole" (Swentzell 1991), and it ties all beings together in a complex web of causality and consequence. I have emphasized that the Chama was never abandoned, but the more obvious question is: How could it be?

While the Chama can be traversed through song and story, these connections are often manifested physically as movement through their ancestral landscape to visit spiritually charged places. These places are described in chapter 3 and include places deeply associated with spiritual beings, societies, and genders. While these places are sites of major shrines and topographic features (such as Tsikumu, see below), they are also ancestral villages that are themselves seen as crucial nexus points between living people and the spiritual world. To visit all these places is to commune with the ancestors, pray for blessings, and remember history and its lessons to apply to the present and future.

Historic, ethnographic, and modern documentation reveal that visiting these places was not done in isolation but rather by specialized groups and it emphasized movement through the landscape. Along these paths, which are deeply established and have been used for centuries, are many stops to visit important places. These paths trace the emergence and migration of the Tewa people from the north and emulate the flow of blessings and life-giving water given by spiritual beings to the people of the village. They are journeys unto themselves, multiday excursions that cover the vast depth of time and geographic breadth of Tewa history.

One particular story stands out. In 1925 society members and war chiefs from Ohkay made an extended trek on horseback over much of the ancestral Tewa world (Walt 2014:52). Their path traced the migration tradition and was spurred on by the need to collect medicinal plants. The pilgrimage began at Yunque'owingeh. The party then traveled to Echo Amphitheater, Pagosa Springs, and the shrine of Chimney Rock in Colorado. The party then journeyed down the La Plata River and into the San Juan drainage and back through Jicarilla Apache country. On their return trip their path took them down the Rio Chama, where they stopped at Tsipin'owingeh, Tsama'owingeh, Ku'owingeh, and Te'ewi'owingeh, and eventually Yunque'owingeh and the kiva at Ohkay Owingeh. While this type of pilgrimage has not happened since, because of private land and fences, Naranjo (2009:2) recounts a similar journey that she and her nephew, Porter Swentzell, took up to Colorado by car from Santa Clara. As Porter gave the name of a specific mesa, she felt "a jolt, that kind of astonishment that makes one remember something for the rest of their life. I was astonished that so far away from Santa Clara (that is, if you were walking) there was evidence of a place that spoke directly to our ancestors' movement around and within what Ortiz calls 'the Tewa world.'"

Pilgrimage also expresses the connectedness of the Tewa world. Of particular importance to Tewa people is the journey to Tsikumu, the Tewa sacred peak of the west. On its bald summit sits the earth navel (*nansipupinge*) that is directly responsible for gathering rain and blessings and directing these to the Pueblo villages (Curtis 1926; Douglass 1912, 1917; Ellis 1968; Ford 1968; Ortiz 1969;

Parsons 1929). This shrine has historically been visited by village leaders from not just the Tewa villages of Ohkay Owingeh, Santa Clara, and San Ildefonso but also from Taos, Cochiti, and Jemez. In fact, because of the sacredness of this place and its importance to many of the Pueblo people of northern New Mexico, historically it was forbidden to engage in conflict at the summit (Parsons 1929:29).

The shrine has been visited annually to sweep out the "rain roads" that direct moisture to the village and to make offerings to the ancestral spirits who bring rain, fertility, and good fortune. The results of this work are manifest in the towering cumulus clouds that build over the mountain in the summer months and eventually unleash torrents of rain that engulf the peak. These rain-laden clouds descend into small creeks that form on the mountains skirts and quench the parched grid gardens and gravel-mulched fields found on the alluvial benches that line the upland areas. This rain fills the creek and this water from the clouds and river race down the valleys. These blessings take many courses. For San Ildefonso, the water races down Los Alamos Canyon and a number of small rivers, eventually reaching the village on the Rio Grande. Santa Clara is connected to the mountain by Santa Clara Creek. And for Ohkay Owingeh, the Rio del Oso flows into the Rio Chama and from there these blessings reach the Rio Grande. It is at the confluence of these two great rivers that the village and the fields await the fruits of these pilgrimages. It is no wonder then that these rivers are seen as an "umbilical cord" (Anschuetz 2014) that ties the Tewa villages with Tsikumu. The course that moisture and blessings take is hardly metaphysical. It is real in the form of a torrent of water and dark gray thunderheads that charge down the valleys. These paths are also the natural courses for Tewa pilgrimage to the sacred peak and to their ancestral villages.

The best-known pilgrimage route from a Tewa village to Tsikumu is that of Ohkay Owingeh's journey up the Rio del Oso. The pilgrimage route, as described by Walt (2014:61), begins at Ohkay Owingeh and crosses the Rio Grande to stop at Yunque'owingeh. From there the path follows the Chama to the confluence of the Rio del Oso. One of the first stops is at the ancestral village of Ku'owingeh. The path continues upstream to the village of Pesede'owingeh, where at least six shrines are visited. From there the party separates and follows society-specific trails, each with associated society shrines. One of the important trail stops is at Tsin Tsineh (San Lorenzo Springs), the headwater of the Oso on the skirts of Tsikumu. Analogous with Tewa philosophy, the paths of the separated factions (in this case societies) come back together at the summit of Tsikumu and the path proceeds to the Ohkay Owingeh rain road of the earth naval. After performing their doings, the party returns to the village along the Rio del Oso, bending plants toward Ohkay on their way to encourage the rain and blessings to follow them back to the people (Ford 1968:143). Also, plants are collected from the mountains and tied into bundles, or "water stops," and then placed in the maize fields to attract water and blessings from the mountains (Ford 1968:143–144).

The pilgrimage path up the Rio del Oso, and the reverence of Tsikumu, is likely very old. The accounts of these places recorded by Harrington (1916) in 1910 embodied the living memory of these journeys a century prior. And as described in chapter 4, the Rio del Oso valley has some of the earliest Tewa villages in the Chama, some dating to the thirteenth century. Based on these sites, and the later large Classic period villages such as Te'ewi'owingeh, Ku'owingeh, and Pesede'owingeh, I am confident that the pilgrimage trail was traveled for at least seven hundred years. When we account for the fact that people had been living in the region for thousands of years prior, then the sacredness of Tsikumu likely extends to time immemorial.

Archaeological research over the past twenty-five years has begun to trace Ohkay Owingeh's pilgrimage path well into the past. Kurt Anschuetz (1993, 1998a) was the first to explore the history of Tewa landscapes in the Oso, and he recorded sites, agricultural fields, and shrines. The shrines were particularly illuminating, as he observed marked differences between Coalition and Classic period shrine assemblages surrounding ancestral villages, a pattern that I confirmed throughout the Chama Valley, reflecting the Tewa's active reconstruction of their world in the crucible of becoming (chapters 4 and 5). But most important for this discussion, Anschuetz also observed shrines that postdate the Classic period. He noted (Anschuetz 1998a; also see Duwe 2011; Duwe et al. 2016) that at Ku'owingeh, nine Tewa shrines sit on the massive mounds of adobe that represent the collapsed walls and roofs of a five-hundred-room village (Duwe et al. 2016). Composed of small boulders, eight that have cupules and one with a ground-slick, these shrines resemble those *xayeh* (household shrines) that typically surround a Tewa village. However, their placement *on top* of the collapsed architecture suggests they were used after Ku'owingeh ceased to be occupied by a large number of people. Based on the ceramics found on the ground surface, I estimate that the village dates from 1350 to 1500 (Duwe 2011:632). Therefore, these shrines date to the sixteenth century *at the earliest* and continue to be visited today by leaders from Ohkay Owingeh on their pilgrimage path to Tsikumu (Walt 2014:47).

While it is impossible to date the first usage of these shrines, they must have been consecrated within the past four hundred years. There is evidence, however, that the pilgrimage to Tsikumu extends centuries earlier. While mapping the sacred geography of Ku'owingeh, I noticed that some of the village's shrines, presumably dating to the Classic period occupation of the site, formed a curious alignment. When mapped in GIS, and later confirmed in the field, it became apparent that four shrines formed a line that pointed directly to Tsikumu. This suggests that Oso has been a lifeline connecting Tsikumu to the many Tewa communities since at least the fourteenth century.

Similar evidence of an enduring Tewa historic presence in the Chama is also found at the next stop on the pilgrim's path: the ancestral village of Pesede'owingeh. In a recent report Eiselt and Darling (2013) observed two rock circle shrines near the village that would have overlooked the fields in the valley below. These shrines are associated with both historic and earlier Tewa pottery and likely date to the nineteenth century (Eiselt and Darling 2013:6.37). And at the village proper there are two historic rock circle shrines overlooking the fields. Associated historic Tewa pottery date this pilgrimage to the eighteenth and nineteenth centuries.

We know much about the Rio del Oso because of large archaeological projects with a landscape focus. But the Tewa today and historically have made pilgrimages to many other places in the Chama, including ancestral villages, springs, and shrines (Walt 2014), and these journeys likely extend an unbroken tradition to before Spanish contact. However, this is not to say that there haven't been impediments to pilgrimage. The establishment of Spanish land grants and homesteading in the valley brought great changes in land use in the early part of the eighteenth century. Even with these challenges the Tewa people maintained their deep connections in the Chama and to their past and future by visiting important places physically or through story and song.

RESOURCE GATHERING

Closely associated with pilgrimage is the gathering of resources, which includes medicinal plants, game, and minerals. Farming and sheepherding were also vitally important. The Rio Chama valley, like all of the upland areas surrounding the modern Rio Grande pueblos, has been a place to gather resources to sustain the people, from time immemorial to the present day.

In his retelling of the 1925 pilgrimage, Henry Walt (2014:52) describes plant gathering as the impetus for the trip. The collecting and harvesting of wild plants has deep medicinal and spiritual value for the Tewa, and plants growing in the hills and mountains are associated with water and rainfall (Ford 1972a:142). The plants are often gathered on pilgrimage, such as to Tsikumu (Ford 1968:141). In the winter months evergreen boughs are gathered, specifically for the Turtle Dance (Walt 2014:80). Piñon firewood is hauled from the hills and ponderosa pine for vigas brought down from the mountains (Ford 1968:103). In the fall, families venture together into the hills to harvest piñon nuts (Ford 1968:198, 1972b:35).

Traditionally, archaeologists have associated "subsistence activities" as being in a sphere outside of the ceremonial realm. However, a source of meat for the Tewa (and a primary source before Spanish contact) is game. Hunting is a ritually sanctioned activity controlled by the Hunt chief, and the hunting of large game is to occur only in the fall and winter months after the crops have been harvested (Ford 1972a:36). The season begins with the ceremonial cleaning of shrines (Ortiz 1969:112), followed by a communal rabbit hunt. Walt (2014:84) describes elders from Ohkay telling of trips they or their relatives had taken to the highlands of the Chama, including Comanche Canyon, Petaca, Cerritos, the area north of El Rito, and the landscape north and west of Abiquiú. I can imagine that shrines and ancestral villages were stayed in during these winter trips, and old hearths were warmed once more.

In the previous chapters I described the importance of clay and stone material to the Tewa who made the ubiquitous pottery and flakes found at every one of the Chama's ancestral villages. These minerals continue to have a vital importance to the community. Earlier I told of the value that the rock alum of the Piedra Lumbre had to the Tewa, so much so that they were willing to go to war to ensure access to the valuable rock. These minerals could be seen as "pieces of place" representing ancient ties to the valley. The minerals include red ochre for facial paints used in dances, gypsum for whitewashing house walls, sillimanite for ceremonial axes, quartzite for mortars, and mica for decorating pottery (Walt 2014:77–80). Rhyolite, found at Tsikumu, is found at shrines across the Chama watershed (Walt 2014:80), and Pedernal chert, from the skirts of Cerro Pedernal (Tsipin, or "Flaking Stone Mountain") continues to be prized. Salt was gathered in the Estancia Basin to the south (Ford 1968:99). Probably the most utilized mineral of all is the ample clay found in the valley, used for making painted and micaceous pottery. In a recent study Sunday Eiselt and Andrew Darling (2013) demonstrate that micaceous clay from the northern parts of the Chama Valley was heavily used between 1300 and 1600. Ethnographic documentation shows that it is still procured today (Walt 2014:76). Procuring the raw material to make pottery was a family affair. Women gathered clay from close sources but traveled with men to gather more temper from farther away. Only men would travel into the distant hills to gather wood for firing (Ford 1968:179).

During the Second Pueblo Revolt the Tewa were in part protecting their sheep herds from the Spanish when they took refuge in the area near Abiquiú. While Hispanic settlement likely curtailed sheepherding, there are stories of members of Ohkay Owingeh traveling through the Chama, particularly around Abiquiú and up to Ojo Caliente, to graze their flocks (Walt 2014:82). There are also hints that the Chama was farmed historically. A vast field system is located in the fields west of Pesede'owingeh, one that Harrington (1916:152) named Pesede'owikejinaba, "the place at Pesede where crops are raised." According to accounts from members from Ohkay Owingeh, this was a place where wheat was grown prior to the Hispanic settlement in the valley, beginning in the 1730s (Eiselt and Darling 2013:6.29).

The use of resources in the Chama can be seen as both ceremonial and subsistence based, but for the Tewa these are one in the same. The Chama has provided, sustained, and protected the Tewa for the past eight centuries through multiple periods of upheaval and prosperity. And along the way the people visit their ancestral villages in the same ways they have for countless generations.

DISCUSSION

We now have good evidence that the Tewa ancestors had a substantial presence in the Chama Valley during Spanish contact and colonization and that they did not forsake their ancestral homeland after the establishment of San Gabriel in 1598. Based on this information alone, it becomes folly to think of the Chama as ever having been abandoned, before or after Spanish contact, as similar patterns of land use are practiced at Ohkay today.

This chapter began with a curious paradox: the Chama was seemingly abandoned yet it lives in both the memories and lives of the Tewa people today. I argue that archaeologists and historians are hung up on permanent occupation being a meaningful concept. While this concept has purchase in the West, it likely doesn't apply to the Tewa world. For example, I was struck by the similarities in historian Elinore Barrett's distinction between an "occupied" village and one that is abandoned and Rina Swentzell's description of the *bupingeh*, or plaza, within a modern Tewa pueblo.

> This information from the Castaño de Sosa and Oñate expeditions indicates there was probably some late contact period settlement in the Chama Basin of a limited or intermittent sort. Whether it was related to possible earlier settlement in Coronado's time cannot be known. Because Barrionuevo did not visit the four "mountain" pueblos, it is not known if they were in the Chama Basin or on the Pajarito Plateau; *or whether they were still occupied or abandoned, or just used from time to time for purposes such as defense, ceremonials, a base for resource exploitation or, as on that occasion, as a refuge.* (Barrett 1997:21; emphasis mine)

> The bupingeh, then, is empty so that it may be full of everything—the sacred and the everyday. It is where the heat of the sun soaks into the walls and packed earth surface to make the space usable for wintertime tasks. It is where—when outside danger loomed, as during the Navajo raids—the people retreated for safety. It is where cooking and sleeping traditionally happened on the roof terraces, which are an extension of the bupingeh space. It is where the harvest was brought and then distributed. It is where young men who are not yet married serve the public in general. They go after firewood, and pile it up in the court or plaza, where the women go to get it for use in their houses. (Swentzell 1988:18–19)

In Swentzell's telling, the village and its plaza is a flexible and dynamic place. In matters of defense and conflict the village can be both a place of protection and a place to leave to seek refuge elsewhere. The plaza may fill with people from many pueblos for certain feasts and doings, and the people may go to other villages for their celebrations. It may be a place to stay when gathering resources or a place to return to after a trip into the mountains. However, while people come and go according to the situation, these places never cease to be center places, or nodes, where the various beings and spirits of the world stop to dwell. Even though an ancestral village may just be "used from time to time," the meaning of the place, and the activities that take place within its walls, is no different than that of any other village. Besides, these places are never abandoned, because these are the homes of the ancestors.

Perhaps "abandoned" villages differ from their "occupied" brothers not in nature but in the intensity of connections that pass through them. According to Ortiz (1991), the Tewa, who value space over time, can always return to the places and renew their connections with them no matter the interval between occupations.

Once we begin to move beyond valuing permanent occupation, the answer to this chapter's central paradox becomes clearer. The ancestral villages in the Chama, and across the larger Tewa world, do not exist in Tewa memory or tradition just to be sung about or remembered. Rather the villages are part of a larger network of villages that far outnumber the six modern villages discussed by anthropologists and historians. In the Tewa world there are hundreds of villages, connected by the movement of people, spirits, animals, and breath. To ignore these places is to deny the very shape and nature of the Tewa world.

CHAPTER 7

Seeking Life

"It belongs to me," the artist Georgia O'Keeffe once remarked of Tsipin (Cerro Pedernal). "God told me if I painted it enough, I could have it" (Halverson 2004:14). In 1929, at the same time that anthropologists were busy defining the Tewa world, O'Keeffe's train rolled into Santa Fe. She was immediately taken by the landscape and earthen architecture and soon made northern New Mexico her home. The land she found was deeply personal, becoming at once her subject and muse, leading her to capture in paint the places listed in Harrington's (1916) atlas. Her many subjects included the distinct flat-topped Tsipin and the Piedra Lumbre, for which the Tewa risked their lives to defend some 250 years prior (figure 31, cover image). While it might be easy to dismiss O'Keeffe's quote as an artist's whimsy, this sentiment was part of a larger process. The landscape of northern New Mexico was becoming increasingly appropriated by new colonizers, the Americans, who discovered the splendor and beauty of the region and chose to define the land of enchantment by mapping their own desires and meaning onto it.

This process—the contestation of the landscape by an increasingly diverse population—began much earlier, of course. Since the coming of Pueblo migrants from the north, the history of the Rio Grande valley is one of tension and complementarity, and these negotiations between opposing forces have defined people's interactions with others and their worlds. The arrival of Spaniards in the sixteenth century dramatically reconfigured Tewa lives, not

FIGURE 31 Tsipin (Cerro Pedernal) viewed from Tsipin'owingeh. Photograph by Kate Newton.

only physically through the imposition of labor but also politically, ceremonially, and economically. Spanish policies and actions limited Tewa mobility and access to their homelands, but the Tewa people continued to return to the Chama and other ancestral lands for strength and protection, even through encounters with Apache and Navajo people. It wasn't until the early eighteenth century that this freedom of movement became restricted as Hispanic families began to homestead in the upland valleys. And in the early twentieth century another great shift occurred when the United States, through institutions like the Forest Service and Los Alamos National Laboratory, took control of the mountains and highlands. The ownership of many Tewa sacred places was now in the hands of the federal government, and by extension the American public (Gordon-McCutchan 1995). It is stunning to think that an atomic bomb was built at Los Alamos, twelve miles from San Ildefonso atop the Pajarito Plateau, years before electricity was run to the village. And that San Ildefonso's ancestral villages, living places to be cared for, were now surrounded with barbed wire and signs demanding NO TRESPASSING—BY ORDER OF THE UNITED STATES DEPARTMENT OF ENERGY.

But through all this change the Tewa have never forgotten or forsaken their larger world. In the previous chapter I demonstrated the myriad ways the Tewa people remain connected to their history and the cosmos. A landscape focus is instructive in that it shows just how accretional space and place really are, as layers of memories and meaning are inscribed by countless individuals from a multitude of backgrounds and identities. A perusal of Harrington's atlas proves this point: each place has many names recorded in different Tewa village dialects, neighboring Pueblo languages, Spanish, and English. If "history is the land" (Ferguson and Colwell-Chanthaphonh 2006), then it is through the landscape that we see histories of deep relationships that continue to be negotiated.

The purpose of this book is to demonstrate how the Tewa world, described and mapped by twentieth-century anthropologists and lived by the Tewa today, has a deep history. This history provides archaeologists, land managers, and the public with an appreciation of the interconnectedness of the Tewa people today with their larger homeland, which I hope will lead to efforts to afford access to and protection of these places. I also believe that by taking Pueblo philosophical and historical concepts seriously we can write more robust histories that cause us to reexamine many of our traditional archaeological perspectives, assumptions, and biases.

In this final chapter I summarize my central argument. However, while I've drawn from the critiques and written experiences of modern Tewa scholars, the majority of this book has focused on deep Tewa history through the Spanish colonial experience, with little discussion of the twentieth century and beyond. This is a mistake, according to Ortiz (1977:22), because archaeologists' and historians' "near exclusive preoccupation with the distant past continues to render Indian experiences of the present or Indian aspirations for the future opaque." Now is not the place to explore the complex ways the Tewa people have sought life in the modern world. But in response to Ortiz's critique, we can return to the discussion of landscape. Much of what we know of the Tewa world, both historically and today, was recorded through an anthropological lens, and archaeologists in particular have been as much involved with the appropriation and redefinition of the land as any other colonizing force. The relationship between the Tewa people and the field of anthropology is yet another series of ongoing negotiations and tensions. Therefore, I conclude this chapter, and this book, with a discussion of anthropology and its role in contemporary Tewa life and the ongoing creation of Tewa history.

BEING AND BECOMING TEWA

This project, at its heart, presents a culture history of the Rio Chama valley, a history that exists, in written form, as a few scant publications and many badly photocopied pages in the Archaeological Records Management Section (ARMS) files in Santa Fe. The Chama, with its massive villages and striking landscape, has for the past century fascinated archaeologists and the general public. But it has never really received sustained archaeological attention, and the work that has been performed has focused on the Classic period villages, leaving earlier and later stories largely untold. These untold stories are what first drew me to the valley, with the particular goal of addressing a question long asked by archaeologists in the northern Rio Grande region, and in the Southwest more generally: Why and how did people come together to create a new form of village life (chapter 5)?

Along the way I became interested in the earlier history of the Chama and the settlement of the valley in the thirteenth century. In the first decade of the twenty-first century archaeologists began to passionately debate questions regarding Tewa ancestors as either originating in the Mesa Verde region or as continuing indigenous Rio Grande traditions. The Chama provides a unique opportunity to understand how *both* migrants and first-comers settled the valley and began to negotiate their eventual Tewa identities. I began to take Tewa oral tradition seriously and found that the thirteenth and early fourteenth centuries are best understood as the coming together of Winter and Summer People, two distantly related groups who constitute complementary halves of Tewa society. Tewa migration traditions are not descriptions of historical events only, however; they are also vital historical processes of negotiation, a process that continues today (chapter 4).

The bright line between prehistory and history has a long tenure in southwestern archaeology and continues to this day. In fact, my early discussions (2011) ended with the arrival of Juan de Oñate and the founding of San Gabriel. This is not to say that archaeologists do not acknowledge that contemporary Pueblo people are direct descendants of the pre-Hispanic people we study. Rather, the cultural and historical connections are poorly understood, and therefore researchers are rightly cautious of connecting the present to the past. There is also the pervasive belief that the Pueblo people of the Historic period practiced a less pristine way of living, corrupted by colonialism. The unfortunate result, from an archaeological perspective, is that we have virtually ignored or discounted all but the most obvious traces of Pueblo life outside the mission village in the colonial era. But they are there! My implicit view that the Chama was abandoned in the sixteenth century was fundamentally challenged by evidence of historic occupation and revisitation of the Chama recorded by others (Anschuetz 2008a; Eiselt and Darling 2013), as well as by historic documentation and my own observations. I began to understand that new colonial realities caused the Tewa to maintain and transform their connections with their larger world (chapter 6). Because ancestral villages never lose their importance as middle places, these old homes have been revisited time and again, particularly in times of refuge, resource gathering, and pilgrimage.

The archaeology of the Chama does not tell a story of fits and starts, static living punctuated by events of great change, but rather it tells of eight centuries of unbroken, yet changing, Tewa history. And this history, recorded in the land, is lived by the Tewa people today. I came to the realization that one of the fundamental problems of southwestern anthropology, the gulf between 140 years of archaeological research and the complex and nuanced ethnographic descriptions recorded in the twentieth century, can be best addressed by emphasizing the continuity between past and present through the writing of holistic histories. This continuity comes not from the continuation of older ways of living, although this was sometimes the case, but rather by the antiquity of the Pueblo philosophy of *continuity through change*. To requote Paul Tosa and Octavius Seowtewa (2019:255): "While our clothing and pottery have changed over time, our culture remains the same."

My perspective has been heavily influenced by two sources. The first is a group of Indigenous and non-Indigenous scholars engaging in collaborative archaeologies, in both the Pueblo Southwest and across the globe. This work is transformative in that it brings together Indigenous and archaeological knowledge for the expressed goal of benefiting Native communities. The second is more unconventional. Instead of theorizing Tewa history through the lens of anthropology, I draw from the writings of Pueblo scholars and artists who discuss Pueblo concepts of history, philosophy, ontology, cosmology, and epistemology. These ideas challenge archaeologists to rethink many of our previous assumptions about the Pueblo past, assumptions based on an inherent Western bias.

In the first chapter I explored Pueblo concepts of history and philosophy through the sculpture by Santa Clara Pueblo artist Nora Naranjo Morse, titled *Always Becoming*. I also defined four basic principles of an archaeology of becoming. To recapitulate my argument, the following is a brief discussion of how the archaeology of the Rio Chama valley informs and is influenced by these principles.

THE WORLD IS ALWAYS IN A STATE OF FLUX

Tewa history, like the history of all Pueblo people, is one of continual movement in an ever-transforming world. This movements involve a dynamism in space and through time as the people re-create their relationships with the cosmos. Archaeologist, however, have imposed a very different view of Pueblo history by privileging periodic cultural transformation over transformative continuity, including divorcing the past from the present. While *continuity through change* is an idiom that runs through this entire book, it is particularly relevant when reframing two processes important in discussions of southwestern archaeology: origins and ethnogenesis.

I began by asking who and when are the Tewa. For many archaeologists this is a hotly debated topic, and researchers have argued that Tewa origins can be mostly attributed to either indigenous Rio Grande people present since the tenth century *or* to migrants from the Mesa Verde region in the 1200s. Archaeologists have also had to explain when, why, and how large settlements grew with new forms of social and ceremonial organization a century later, a process defined as ethnogenesis, or the creation of new ethnic (Tewa) identities. While archaeologists debate the details, the questions of origins and ethnogenesis are themselves founded on the underlying assumption that Pueblo history is divided chronologically by relatively static periods of time. When change does occur (say, the depopulation of the northern Southwest), it is often attributed to externally forced revolutions. Pueblo history is seen as a punctuated equilibrium of sorts. But this isn't how Tewa scholars have defined their own history. Instead, Tewa history relates the journeys of two related groups, the Summer and Winter People, who were split asunder and then rejoined in the Rio Grande valley to find their center places. And also, Tewa history is continually being written.

When viewed through the perspective of Tewa history and philosophy, our understanding of Tewa history becomes more nuanced. For instance, I observed a heterogeneity in material culture traces left by the settlers of the Chama, suggesting that both first-comers (Winter People) and migrants (Summer People) sought new lives, and futures, in the valley, and both contributed to the formation of Tewa culture through contributing ideas of center and edge (chapter 4). This wasn't a single event but a process that occurred over a century. I also discussed how a similar history of the coming together of diverse people happened both earlier and later as people sought multiple center places. I argue that Tewa origins are best seen as a metaphorical process rather than a single transformative event, as diverse people continued to negotiate new identities and seek life in a dynamic social landscape. The search for Tewa origins is problematic because the Tewa have always been Tewa and they can trace their ancestry through many lineages. Instead our focus should be on the myriad ways Tewa ancestors negotiated their worlds.

The people didn't become Tewa somewhere along the journey—they have always been Tewa, forever in a process of becoming. In chapter 5 I demonstrated that while the large villages were built (or expanded) by the coalescence of diverse populations in the mid-fourteenth century, a significant step in Tewa becoming, the subsequent two centuries of the Classic period were hardly static. There was a dynamic fluidity, some of which can be seen in the archaeological record, in movement and settlement, social interaction, and an ongoing development of the relationship with the cosmos. Like origins, ethnogenesis is an ongoing process. The histories of the Summer and Winter People and the Made People likely extend deep in time. And the Classic period Tewa villages are not a carbon copy of historic and modern Tewa villages, for change continued through the Historic period and continues today. I argue that ethnogenesis has often been used by archaeologists to emphasize a step-wise change inherent in archaeological classification systems but that Pueblo history can better be viewed as what Clive Gamble (2007) describes as a gradient with an uneven surface that encapsulates both continuity and change. What drives this history is the process of seeking life in an interconnected world.

THE INTERCONNECTEDNESS OF THE WORLD

Ortiz (1969) demonstrated how the many aspects of Tewa society and the cosmos are an interconnected and balanced whole, including the inherent division of summer and winter and the levels of being in the social and supernatural hierarchy (chapter 2). However, archaeologists and the Tewa themselves acknowledge that the Tewa world of the twentieth century defined by Ortiz was the product of a complex history of migration, coalescence, and colonialism. The dualities that underlie the Tewa world—summer and winter, female and male, center and edge—are both complementary and a source of tension. Tewa history is one of seeking life to find balance between opposing forces, with the understanding that these dualities complement each other as part of larger wholes (Naranjo and Swentzell 1989:258). To seek life is to avoid stasis and to embrace movement and the transformation of life that results from the tension of opposites (Swentzell 1993:45). Seeking life also requires finding the balance between common Tewa and ceremonial leaders, the world of the living and the supernatural plane, and the practicalities of making a living as agriculturalists and a semiarid and often unforgiving environment.

Tewa history must have been replete with tensions and attempts to find balance and harmony. Two particular examples from the present study stand out. One is the coming together of the Summer and Winter People, which in the Chama and elsewhere took the form of first-comers and migrants negotiating an eventual village life. While the specifics of these negotiations are yet to be determined, we know that they occurred. Elements of both groups, including Rio Grande concepts of center (ancient architectural traditions) and the migrants' ideas of edge (represented by the introduction of novel place-making practices), were incorporated into a Tewa identity. The two groups influenced each other in a dynamic process of movement and transformation. A village, and a people, would be incomplete without both groups, and the cosmos recorded by Harrington (1916), Ortiz (1969), and Ford (1968) demonstrate how these oppositions were rectified in a united yet divided form of village life.

Another example that stands out is the arrival of the Spanish in the sixteenth century, an experience that dramatically reshaped Tewa life (chapter 6). Amidst the brutality of conquest and colonization the Tewa sought balance for their own cultural survival in three ways. The first was accepting Spanish municipal government that allowed the Tewa (and other Pueblos) to engage with outsiders (the Spanish, then Mexicans and Americans) and successfully manage threatening external influences (Ortiz 1969:62–72). The second was adopting elements of the outside world, such as foreign crops and livestock, but segregating them from traditional ontologies (Bernstein et al. 2019; Ford 1968). And the third is the Tewa's ongoing connection to their landscape, even in the face of colonial policies that restricted movement or access to their larger world.

Archaeologists are beginning to understand that for the Pueblos, life was, and is, never restricted to occupied villages but extends to shrines, hills, springs, sacred peaks, and old homes where their ancestors dwell. This connectedness to the cosmos, above all, helped the Tewa culture to endure (Ortiz 1994).

STEWARDSHIP AND RENEWAL

One of the most important lessons from reading Tewa ethnography and the writings of modern scholars, as well as talking to the Tewa people today, is the necessity to rethink how we conceptualize what we call *archaeological sites*. For the Tewa (and all Pueblos), these old homes, fields, and shrines are not just places of remembrance—they are also moral lessons that are passed through generations. Although archaeological sites were made in the past and represent the actions of ancestors, their significance and meaning exists in the present and into the future. Also, these places can never be abandoned, because a middle place never ceases to lose its connectedness to the people and to the larger cosmos. These are places where the spirits dwell and are continually cared for.

Both archaeologists and historians have claimed that soon after the Spanish arrived in New Mexico in the sixteenth century, the Tewa abandoned much of their ancestral homeland. Tewa life was necessarily focused on the newly missionized villages along the Rio Grande, where both secular and church policies required a centralized population. In chapter 6 I argue that the villages along the Rio Chama and its tributaries were never abandoned in any sense of the word. Rather, new colonial realities caused the Tewa to maintain and transform their connections with their larger world. Because ancestral villages never lose their importance as middle places, these old homes were revisited time and again, in times of refuge, particularly during the Pueblo Revolt, and for resource gathering. Additionally, the Tewa ethic of stewardship and renewal is manifested through pilgrimage to ancestral villages and blessing places, practices that not only foster remembrance of the past but also provide guidance for the future.

Although the Tewa's homelands have been threatened since the arrival of the Spanish, the twentieth century brought with it the new challenges of home and infrastructure construction and increased visitation. The need to protect ancestral places is important to both archaeologists and Pueblo communities and offers a middle ground. Also, archaeologists and land managers should appreciate the importance of the landscape as an extension of the living community and understand that it is our ethical obligation to strive to ensure access to these places.

BECOMING IS NEVER COMPLETE

There is no end date in Tewa history, not with the coming of the Spanish, or the Americans, or the modern age. This book has told a history of the past eight centuries, but Tewa ancestors extend to time immemorial. So too does the future, reflected in a landscape of blessing places that look to impart the same lessons for generations to come. We can expect the same principles of seeking life to carry on, for it is in "this long-demonstrate ability to, as one Tewa metaphor states it, reinvigorate decaying vines from nearby vital ones, lies the strength of the Pueblo people and their prime hope for the future. From my reading of the evidence here I would like to conclude that, for Americans, the Pueblos, like the poor, you shall have always with you" (Ortiz 1994:305).

In an essay on Pueblo cultural adaptability and survival, Ortiz expands this argument. I quote in full because he, in an economy of words, summarizes this book's argument of a history of becoming Tewa.

> That the Pueblos, most of them, have survived is obvious to anyone who knows them. That they can revitalize is also obvious, for revitalization is a way of life for them. It is not just a challenge of the present or the recent past, but something that they have had to do regularly for as long as we can trace their presence on the peculiar landscape we know today as the American Southwest. When they came up out of their caves as Basketmakers early in the European Christian era and began to adapt themselves to life as village-building, pottery-making, maize-growers they had to revitalize; when they had to abandon their great towns in Chaco Canyon and Mesa Verde during the thirteenth century and move to areas of more dependable water sources they had to revitalize; when Coronado cut a wide swath through them in the middle of the sixteenth century they had to revitalize; after their great revolution of 1680, when they cast off the yoke of Spanish oppression, they had to revitalize; after a widespread epidemic of smallpox sharply decimated their numbers in 1781–82 they had to revitalize; when there were threats to their remaining land base late in the last century and during the first two decades of this century they had to revitalize; since at least 1960, with renewed threats to their sovereignty and to their land

and water rights they have again had to revitalize, and even now they are in the process of doing so. Those numerous revitalization efforts have simply not attracted much attention among scholars because most of their efforts have proceeded quietly and without fanfare. (Ortiz 1994:304–305)

That the Pueblos are continually revitalizing and reshaping their ancient traditions in the face of contemporary challenges will come as no surprise to even those with a casual appreciation for the cultural heritage of the Southwest. On a recent visit to the Pueblo of Acoma's San Esteban Feast Day I witnessed people of all walks of life climbing the ancient staircase to the top of the mesa, respectfully watching the dances, and being invited to sit down and eat at long tables in residents' homes. The atmosphere was festive. Children whose fingers were stained red by "Kool-Aid pickles" ran among the crowd with while their parents laughed and talked and perused booths featuring pottery and jewelry. But in the air hung a certain seriousness and importance. The dances are not for show but are intended to do the critical work of the community, to encourage blessings and to commemorate the harvest. It's striking—or maybe not—that the pueblo continues to open its doors to Anglos, Hispanics, and anyone who want to come, on the same ground where 420 years earlier Oñate's men dragged a cannon through the streets and massacred eight hundred souls. This celebration of survivance in the face of colonialism, performed with grace and openness, is a remarkable, but hardly unusual, illustration of seeking life as the Pueblos continue to maintain their traditional ways in the modern world.

SEEKING LIFE AND THE FUTURE OF ARCHAEOLOGY

In 1880 a spur off the mainline of the Atchison, Topeka and Santa Fe Railway reached Santa Fe. Its cars would bring all manner of visitors to northern New Mexico, including tourists, artists, and anthropologists, who began to define the Land of Enchantment (figure 32). For Pueblo people, however, it brought something very different, including "danger, shattered quiet, confusion, resentment, the invasion of outsiders, the insults to natures, and sacrilege to native religion" (Frost 2016:27).

Pueblo people once again were on the front lines of a new entrada, and their communities soon became tourist destinations marketed by savvy promoters. An advertisement in 1900 read that Taos Pueblo was "compared favorably to

FIGURE 32 "Picnicking in Caliente Canon, Near Ojo Caliente, New Mexico," by Dana B. Chase (1884–1892?). Courtesy of the Palace of the Governors Photo Archives (NMHM/DCA), 118552.

a trip to Egypt, while not taking up so much time and being less expensive" (Weigle 1989:117). In the mid-1920s Pueblo ethnotourism was perfected by the Fred Harvey Company, which offered Indian Detours. Seven-passenger Packards were dubbed "Thunderbirds" and were driven by "cowboys," highly trained drivers who were silent and stoic and wore 10-gallon hats. Leading the tours were "couriers," young women dressed in bright Navajo prints. The tourists, called "dudes," would travel a circuit familiar to many readers: up to Taos, over to Puye and Bandelier, back to Santa Fe. Along the way they would stop at other Pueblo communities, such as San Ildefonso and Tesuque (Weigle 1990). Heavy promotion reached people throughout the United States, not just those who could afford to stay at a Harvey House, who learned of the mystique of the Pueblos and the arid lands of the Southwest (Frost 1980), an image that continues today.

In the previous chapters I have discussed and critiqued some of the ways that southwestern anthropology has acted as a colonial institution. Early twentieth-century ethnography was a direct response to the consequences of American expansionism and the dawn of modernity. Extracting information before the Pueblos assimilated or went extinct was used to justify poor ethics (Strong 1996). Anthropological writings also increased the flood of tourism to the

Pueblos (e.g., Benedict 1934[1989]). And archaeologists furthered the colonial project by writing Pueblo histories in which they divorce the past from the present and impose Western concepts. But anthropologists took an active role in the redefinition of New Mexico as well. Their work transcended the dusty, inaccessible libraries of academia and helped to fundamentally shape the identity of the region.

Tourism and southwestern anthropology boosted Santa Fe's fortunes, as it was a small city of five thousand people that was bypassed by the main rail line. In the 1910s archaeologists and others at the Museum of New Mexico, including anthropologists, drew from local vernaculars, including architecture found in Pueblo communities, and created a Santa Fe style, which was widely adopted and boosted awareness of the uniqueness of the city (Wilson 1997). And in 1925 the Indian Arts Fund was founded in Santa Fe to collect and develop a market for traditional Pueblo pottery. Among the trustees were artists and archaeologists, who saw an opportunity to create a distinctive regional identity and generate tourist dollars (Dauber 1990).

Through the work of archaeologists and anthropologists the citizens of Santa Fe began to leverage one of its two great assets, Pueblo culture (the other being the remarkable landscape), to mold the Pueblo Southwest into a twentieth-century American image, a mixture of authenticity and familiarity. Others saw the allure of ruins and began to promote Pueblo archaeology for economic benefits as well as to make a case for admission into statehood (1912). Leading this charge was Edgar Lee Hewett, a self-trained archaeologist and the first director of the Museum of New Mexico and what is now the School for Advanced Research. He widely promoted his and others' excavations in the Southwest and drafted the Antiquities Act of 1906, which protected Mesa Verde (1906), Chaco Canyon (1907), and Bandelier (1916) by bringing them into the eventual National Park System. While affording protection to these ancestral places has undoubtably yielded benefits as a defense against the continuing encroachment of American progress, protection too was a form of colonization because access and policy increasingly fell under federal jurisdiction.

Hewett's relationship with Pueblo people was complex and embodies many of the tensions between archaeologists and the Pueblos today. He practiced an archaeology that purposefully obscured the connection between living Pueblo people (whom he employed as workmen on his digs) and their ancestral homes for the purpose of constructing and promoting a more noble culture with high morals that could inspire the public (Snead 2001:130–131). His ideas were largely rejected, but a similar sentiment of the division between the present and the past continues to live on, as does a fascination with ancestral Pueblo places. But Hewett also forged meaningful connections with Pueblo people that had lasting benefits. For example, in 1908, after finishing a season of excavation on the Pajarito Plateau, he urged María Martinez, the wife of one of his workmen from San Ildefonso and a well-regarded potter, to try to craft a pot based on a sherd he had recovered. She succeeded with the help of her husband Julián, who painted the designs, and together their family would revive an old pottery tradition and create a new one (Marriot 1948). This process, creating something new from the wellspring of ancient tradition, must have happened countless times in the history of Pueblo potting traditions, but the immense skill of Martinez, combined with a burgeoning Native crafts market encouraged and sponsored by Hewett and his associates, made her world famous (figure 33). Hewett and others encouraged and financially backed her early work, and her success catalyzed an appreciation for Pueblo pottery that has brought money into communities and helped to preserve some traditional ways (Ortiz 1994). Her story, and that of Hewett's, provide an example of the complicated relationship between archaeologists and Pueblo people, and the present and the past.

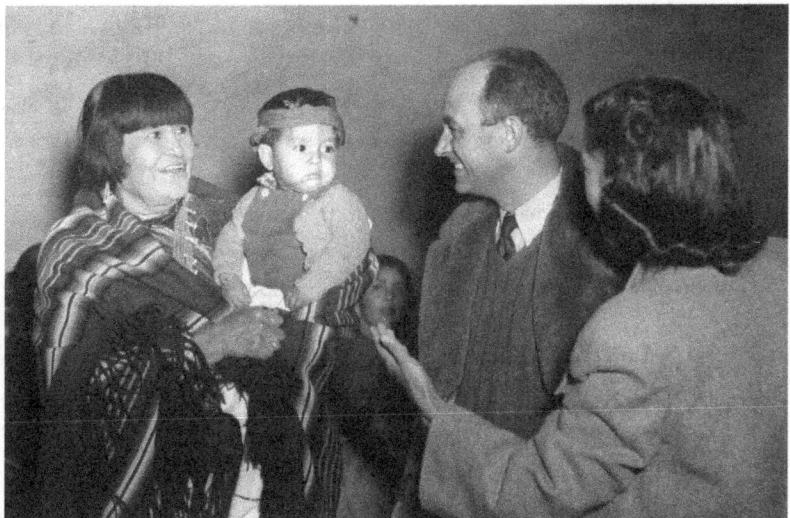

FIGURE 33 San Ildefonso potter María Martinez talking with physicist Enrico Fermi, the creator of the world's first nuclear reactor. Martinez was a welcoming figure to soldiers and scientists and their families who visited from Los Alamos National Laboratory. Courtesy of the Atomic Heritage Foundation.

I do not have the space to continue to explore the relationships between anthropologists and the Pueblos beyond the brief histories recounted in chapters 1 and 2. Suffice it to say that two important things have happened over the past century. The first is that the ethnographers were wrong and the Pueblo people have endured. The second is that the American colonization of the landscape and its identity, with the help of anthropologists, has succeeded. Bandelier National Monument is as popular as ever and has recently started a shuttle bus service to ferry visitors into Frijoles Canyon to reduce vehicle congestion. The New Mexico State Tourism Department's magazine, *New Mexico True*, recently featured an article titled "Authentic Culture: Experience Ancestral History and Rich Multiculturalism." And one can pick up a *Native Adventure Guide* to visit the Pueblos.

My understanding of the Tewa view of history is one of a world and its interconnectedness that is in a state of constant re-creation and transformation, driven by the never-ending process of searching for harmony and balance between opposites. Perhaps the coming of anthropologists, and in extension Western modernity, is another example of tensions between opposites, like the dualities of summer and winter, male and female, Tewa tradition and Spanish politics and religion. This is what Rina Swentzell implied when she wrote about tensions between archaeologists and Pueblo people (requoted from chapter 1).

> My questions: Is it possible for both the Pueblo people and the archaeologists to uncover, in a partnership mode and a creative act, the pattern of human existence in the prehistoric Southwest? Is it possible for both reason and intuition to be used simultaneously? For such to happen, however, archaeologists, because they are presently in charge of digging and interpretation, must use "feminine" aspects of their beings to include Pueblo people in the process of linking present Pueblo knowledge with scientific evidence for a more holistic sense of Anasazi life and culture. Unexpected patterns and truths might even emerge. (Swentzell 1991:180)

When Swentzell wrote those words, the histories of archaeologists and Pueblos had been intertwined for over a hundred years. But in the last three decades these questions remain unanswered. In recent years the relationship between anthropologists and Tewa communities has begun to change, and the balance has shifted slightly. This is due in no small part to the Native American Graves Protection and Repatriation Act (NAGPRA) and the mandatory consultation process that provides a Tewa voice in any archaeological research on federal lands. Three villages (Santa Clara, San Ildefonso, and Pojoaque) now have tribal historic preservation offices to field permitting inquiries, protect their sacred places, and educate its citizens about their heritage. Most important, where for much of the twentieth century anthropology exploited the Tewa for their knowledge, the Tewa are now actively using anthropology for the benefit of their communities. Tewa community members have received advanced degrees in anthropological archaeology (Aguilar 2019; Cruz 2018), hired archaeologists and anthropologists as expert witnesses in legal cases to secure land and water rights, and used ethnography, a painful part of their history, to bolster their long tenure in the Rio Grande valley and to protect their sacred landscape. Anthropological knowledge is also contributing to cultural revitalization through educating youth (Cajete 1994) and reconnecting the people with their language and landscape (Jacobs et al. 1998).

Yet the majority of Tewa (and Pueblo) archaeology is still performed by outsiders in the realms of academic research and cultural resource management. And articles and books (like this one) addressing Pueblo history are mostly written by non-Pueblo archaeologists. At the same time there continues to be resistance among archaeologists to embrace the synthesis of archaeological and Native knowledge. Stephen Lekson (2018:159) recently declared that "archaeology is not Indigenous." He writes that "many Indigenous people and more than a few non-Indigenous archaeologists are uncomfortable with that provenance, so they are trying to change archaeology, to make it Indigenous. But then it would no longer be archaeology." Lekson proposes a clear separation between history (what happened in the past as understood in Western terms, founded on empirical evidence and universal principles) and heritage (the uses of the past in the present). Archaeologists should focus on writing history and Native people on understanding their heritage, as "ships that pass in the night, hopefully steered away from collision" (Lekson 2018:162).

But the collision is happening, and has been happening. It's just now that archaeologists are feeling the crunch. I sense a sea change at the national meeting and through talking with my students. The separation of archaeology from Indigenous concerns is not tenable, politically, ethically, or intellectually. I am sympathetic to one aspect of Lekson's argument though. Elsewhere in the book he convincingly makes a case for the idea of Pueblo Space, an ahistorical conception of the Pueblos as egalitarian, small-scale, and autonomous communities derived from both twentieth-century ethnography and the "mystique" generated by early archaeologists and promoters (Lekson 2018:13). Southwestern archaeology is often interpreted through this generalized caricature that limits our appreciation of discontinuities between the past and present. I don't think it's fair to characterize all Indigenous archaeology in the Pueblo Southwest as operating in Pueblo Space, but it is a good critique to ensure that archaeologists emphasize both continuity *and* change. However, I cannot accept Lekson's (2018:161) view of an archaeology where "we are the authorities" and therefore should not have to give up control of archaeological narratives to Native people. But, if not this type of archaeology, then what type?

Many Indigenous and non-Indigenous scholars, some referred to in the first chapter, have written eloquently on this topic. I was inspired, however, by Swentzell's questions as a model moving forward of seeking life, or rather, seeking a Pueblo archaeology. She argues that for real partnership to happen, archaeologists must embrace "feminine" aspects of their beings to connect present Pueblo knowledge with scientific evidence. By *feminine* she means that "dichotomies are recognized but not in an either/or sense. Opposites are brought together to complement each other rather than to create a power struggle. In that sense, the traditional pueblo world is a world *focused* on equalitarianism, inclusiveness, and linkages" (Swentzell 1991:179–180). For me this has meant privileging Pueblo understandings of the world over generalized social theory, challenging my preconceived notions of the Pueblo past, understanding that I am not an inherently objective researcher, keeping an open but critical mind when thinking of the many ways to understand history, and accepting that I might have gotten things wrong.

For this last point especially I find solace in that seeking life is both a goal and a process and is never complete. With these principles, archaeologists can continue to form meaningful and creative partnerships with the Pueblo people, and together both can embrace both tensions and complementarities and recognize that, perhaps, they too are part of a larger whole.

REFERENCES

Acklen, John C. 1991. *Data Recovery Plan for the Ojo Line Extension Project*. Report prepared for the Public Service Company of New Mexico, Albuquerque. Mariah Associates, No. 5271, Albuquerque, New Mexico.

Adams, E. Charles. 1991. *The Origins and Development of the Pueblo Katsina Cult*. University of Arizona Press, Tucson.

Adams, E. Charles, and Andrew I. Duff. 2004. Settlement Clusters and the Pueblo IV Period. In *The Protohistoric Pueblo World, A.D. 1275–1600*, edited by E. Charles Adams and Andrew I. Duff, pp. 3–16. University of Arizona Press, Tucson.

Adler, Michael A. 1993. Why Is a Kiva? New Interpretations of Prehistoric Social Integrative Architecture in the Northern Rio Grande Region of New Mexico. *Journal of Anthropological Research* 49(4):319–346.

Adler, Michael A., Todd Van Pool, and Robert D. Leonard. 1996. Ancestral Pueblo Population Aggregation and Abandonment in the North American Southwest. *Journal of World Prehistory* 10(3):375–438.

Agoyo, Herman. 2002. The Holy War. In *Archaeologies of the Pueblo Revolt*, edited by Robert W. Preucel, pp. xi–xiv. University of New Mexico Press, Albuquerque.

Agoyo, Herman. 2005. The Tricentennial Commemoration. In *Po'pay: Leader of the First American Revolution*, edited by Joe S. Sando and Herman Agoyo, pp. 93–106. Clear Life, Santa Fe.

Aguilar, Joseph. 2019. *Asserting Sovereignty: An Indigenous Archaeology of the Pueblo Revolt Period at Tunyo, San Ildefonso Pueblo, New Mexico*. PhD dissertation, Department of Anthropology, University of Pennsylvania, Philadelphia.

Aguilar, Joseph, and Robert W. Preucel. 2019. Seeking Strength and Protection: Tewa Mobility During the Pueblo Revolt Period. In *The Continuous Path: Pueblo Movement and the Archaeology of Becoming*, edited by Samuel Duwe and Robert W. Preucel, pp. 149–165. University of Arizona Press, Tucson.

Alberti, Benjamin. 2016. Archaeologies of Ontology. *Annual Review of Anthropology* 45:163–179.

Anschuetz, Kurt F. 1993. Preliminary Report for the 1992 Field Season: The University of Michigan Rio del Oso Archaeological Survey, Española Ranger District, Santa Fe National Forest. Submitted to Española Ranger District, Santa Fe National Forest, Española. Manuscript on file, Santa Fe National Forest, Southwestern Region, USDA Forest Service, Santa Fe.

Anschuetz, Kurt F. 1998a. Not Waiting for the Rain: Integrated Systems of Water Management by Pre-Columbian Pueblo Farmers in North-Central New Mexico. PhD dissertation, Department of Anthropology, University of Michigan, Ann Arbor.

Anschuetz, Kurt F. 1998b. Pre-Columbian Pueblo Agricultural Plots (AR-03-02-02-0460 [LA114161]) within the proposed Las Clinicas del Norte Special-Use Permit Parcel, El Rito Ranger District, Carson National Forest, Rio Arriba County, New Mexico. Community and Cultural Landscape Contribution II, Rio Grande Foundation for Communities and Cultural Landscapes, Santa Fe, New Mexico.

Anschuetz, Kurt F. 2007a. Room to Grow with Room to Spare: Agriculture and Big-Site Settlements in the Late Pre-Columbian Tewa Basin Pueblo Landscape. *Kiva* 73(2):173–194.

Anschuetz, Kurt F. 2007b. Becoming the Tewa World: Pueblo, Place, and Time in North-Central New Mexico, A.D. 1250–1600. Prepared for the symposium "Demographic, Social, and Ideological Perspectives on Population Movement: Papers in Honor of Linda S. Cordell." Presented at the 72nd Annual Meeting of the Society for American Archaeology, Austin, Texas.

Anschuetz, Kurt F. 2014. Toward an Archaeology of Pueblo Ritual Landscapes: A Forthcoming NMAC Continuing Education Program. *NewsMAC: Newsletter of the New Mexico Archaeological Council* 2014(1):9–15.

Anschuetz, Kurt F. 2015. Las Bocas Canyon: A Contested Landscape at the Intersection of the Tewa, Keres, Tano, and Spanish Colonial Homelands. In *The Multifaceted Forester: Papers in Honor of John Hayden*, edited by Emily J. Brown, Karen Armstrong, Carol J. Condie, and Helen K. Crotty, pp. 17–34. The Archaeological Society of New Mexico 41. Archaeological Society of New Mexico, Albuquerque.

Anschuetz, Kurt F., Eileen L. Camilli, and Christopher D. Banet. 2017. Agricultural Landscapes. In *Oxford Handbook of Southwest Archaeology*, edited by Barbara Mills and Severin Fowles, pp. 697–714. Oxford University Press, Oxford.

Anschuetz, Kurt F., and Richard I. Ford. 2018. Earning Their Living: Ideation, Ritual, and Agricultural Practice in the Southwestern Pueblo Cultural Landscape. Prepared for the symposium "Ritual Ecologies of Food Production in the Ancient World." Presented at the 83rd Annual Meeting of the Society for American Archaeology, Washington, D.C.

Anschuetz, Kurt F., and Cherie L. Scheick. 2006[1996]. The Española Basin Geographic Subdivision. In *A Study of Pre-Columbian and Historic Uses of the Santa Fe National Forest: Competition and Alliance in the Northern Middle Rio Grande*, edited by Cherie J.

Scheick, pp. 169–234. Report No. 18, United Stated Department of Agriculture, Forest Service, Southwestern Region.

Anschuetz, Kurt F., Richard H. Wilshusen, and Cherie Scheick. 2001. An Archaeology of Landscapes: Perspectives and Directions. *Journal of Archaeological Research* 9(2):157–211.

Anschuetz, Kurt F., and Richard H. Wilshusen. 2011. Ensouled Places: Ethnogenesis and the Making of the Dinétah and Tewa Basin Landscapes. In *Movement, Connectivity and Landscape Change in the Ancient Southwest*, edited by Margaret C. Nelson and Colleen Strawhacker, pp. 321–344. University Press of Colorado, Boulder.

Arakawa, Fumiyasu, Scott G. Ortman, M. Steven Shackley, and Andrew I. Duff. 2011. Obsidian Toolstone Procurement in the Central Mesa Verde. *American Antiquity* 76:773–795.

Atalay, Sonya. 2012. *Community-Based Archaeology: Research with, by, and for Indigenous and Local Communities*. University of California Press, Berkeley.

Baker, Craig, and Joseph C. Winter (editors). 1981. *High Altitude Adaptations Along Redondo Creek: The Baca Geothermal Project*. Office of Contract Archeology, University of New Mexico, Albuquerque.

Bandelier, Adolph. 1890. *The Delight Makers*. Dodd, Mead and Company, New York.

Bandelier, Adolph. 1892. *Final Report of Investigations Among the Indians of the Southwestern United States, Carried on Mainly in the Years from 1880 to 1885: Part II*. Papers of the Archaeological Institute of American, American Vol. IV. Cambridge University Press, Cambridge.

Barrett, Elinore M. 1997. *The Geography of Rio Grande Pueblos Revealed by Spanish Explorers, 1540–1598*. Latin American Institute Research Paper Series No. 30, University of New Mexico, Albuquerque.

Barrett, Elinore M. 2002. The Geography of the Rio Grande Pueblos in the Seventeenth Century. *Ethnohistory* 49(1):123–169.

Basso, Keith H. 1979. A History of Ethnological Research. In *Handbook of North American Indians, Vol. 9, Southwest*, edited by Alfonso Ortiz, pp. 14–21. Smithsonian Institution Press, Washington, D.C.

Basso, Keith H. 1996. *Wisdom Sits in Places: Landscape and Language Among the Western Apache*. University of New Mexico Press, Albuquerque.

Baugh, Timothy G., and Fred W. Nelson. 1987. New Mexico Obsidian Sources and Exchange on the Southern Plains. *Journal of Field Archaeology* 14(3):313–329.

Beal, John D. 1987. *Foundation of the Rio Grande Classic: The Lower Chama River, A.D. 1300–1500*. Report Submitted to the Office of Cultural Affairs, Historic Preservation Division, by Southwest Archaeological Consultants, Albuquerque.

Benedict, Ruth. 1934[1989]. *Patterns of Culture*. Houghton Mifflin, Boston.

Benjamin, Rebecca, Regis Pecos, and Mary Eunice Romero. 1996. Language Revitalization Efforts in the Pueblo de Cochiti: Becoming "Literate" in an Oral Society. In *Indigenous Literacies in the Americas: Language Planning from the Bottom Up*, edited by Nancy H. Hornberger, pp. 115–136. Mouton de Gruyter, Berlin.

Bernardini, Wesley. 1996. Transitions in Social Organization: A Predictive Model from Southwestern Archaeology. *Journal of Anthropological Archaeology* 15:1–31.

Bernardini, Wesley. 2011. North, South, and Center: An Outline of Hopi Ethnogenesis. In *Religious Transformation in the Late Pre-Hispanic Pueblo World*, edited by Donna M. Glowacki and Scott Van Keuren, pp. 196–220. University of Arizona Press, Tucson.

Bernardini, Wesley. 2018. Visual Prominence and the Stability of Cultural Landscapes. In *Footprints of Hopi History: Hopihiniwtiput Kukveni'at*, edited by Leigh J. Kuwanwisiwma, T. J. Ferguson, and Chip Colwell, pp. 73–89. University of Arizona Press, Tucson.

Bernardini, Wesley, and Severin M. Fowles. 2011. Becoming Hopi, Becoming Tiwa: Two Pueblo Histories of Movement. In *Movement, Connectivity, and Landscape Change in the Ancient Southwest*, edited by Margaret C. Nelson and Colleen Strawhacker, pp. 253–274. University Press of Colorado, Boulder.

Bernstein, Bruce. 2012. *Santa Fe Indian Market: A History of Native Arts and the Marketplace*. Museum of New Mexico Press, Albuquerque.

Bernstein, Bruce, Erik Fender, and Russell Sanchez. 2019. Moving Ideas, Staying at Home: Change and Continuity in the Mid-Eighteenth-Century Tewa Pottery. In *The Continuous Path: Pueblo Movement and the Archaeology of Becoming*, edited by Samuel Duwe and Robert W. Preucel, pp. 195–221. University of Arizona Press, Tucson.

Biella, Jan V. 1979. Changing Residential Patterns Among the Anasazi, A.D. 750–1525. In *Adaptive Change in the Northern Rio Grande Valley*, edited by Jan V. Biella and Richard C. Chapman, pp. 103–144. Archeological Investigations in Cochiti Reservoir, New Mexico, Vol. 4. Office of Contract Archeology, University of New Mexico, Albuquerque.

Biella, Jan V. 1992. LA70029: An Archaic/Basketmaker II and Coalition Phase Site on the Pajarito Plateau. Southwest Archaeological Consultants Research Series No. 266, Santa Fe.

Binford, Lewis R. 1962. Archaeology as Anthropology. *American Antiquity* 28(2):217–225.

Boyer, Jeffrey L. 1998. Preliminary Results of Archaeological and Ethnohistoric Data Recovery Efforts at Twelve Sites Along U.S. 285. Letter on file, Archaeological Records Management Section, New Mexico State Historic Preservation Division, and Museum of New Mexico, Santa Fe.

Boyer, Jeffrey L., James L. Moore, Steven Lakatos, Nancy J. Akins, C. Dean Wilson and Eric Blinman. 2010. Remodeling Immigration: A Northern Rio Grande Perspective on Depopulation, Migration, and Donation-Side Models. In *Leaving Mesa Verde: Peril and Change in the Thirteenth-Century Southwest*, edited by Timothy A. Kohler, Mark D. Varien and Aaron M. Wright, pp. 285–322. University of Arizona Press, Tucson.

Bradley, Bruce A. 1996. Pitchers to Mugs: Chacoan Revival at Sand Canyon Pueblo. *Kiva* 61(3):241–255.

Brandt, Elizabeth. 1980. On Secrecy and the Control of Knowledge: Taos Pueblo. In *Secrecy: A Cross-Cultural Perspective*, edited by Stanton K. Tefft, pp. 123–146. Human Sciences, New York.

Brandt, Elizabeth. 2002. The Climate for Ethnographic/Ethnohistoric Research in the Southwest. In *Traditions, Transitions, and Technologies: Themes in Southwestern Archaeology*, edited by Sarah H. Schlanger, pp 113–126. University Press of Colorado, Boulder.

Bremer, J. Michael. 1995a. AR-03-10-06-1230. Site form on file, Archaeological Records Management System, Historic Preservation Division and Museum of New Mexico, Santa Fe.

Bremer, J. Michael. 1995b. AR-03-10-06-1231. Site form on file, Archaeological Records Management System, Historic Preservation Division and Museum of New Mexico, Santa Fe.

Breternitz, David A. 1966. *An Appraisal of Tree-Ring Dated Pottery in the Southwest*. Anthropological Papers of the University of Arizona No. 10. University of Arizona Press, Tucson.

Bugé, David E. 1978. *Preliminary Report: 1978 Excavations at NM-01–1407, Ojo Caliente, New Mexico*. Manuscript on file, Laboratory of Anthropology, Museum of New Mexico, Santa Fe.

Buge, David E. 1984. Prehistoric Subsistence Strategies in the Ojo Caliente Valley, New Mexico. In *Prehistoric Agricultural Strategies in the Southwest*, edited by Suzanne K. Fish and Paul R. Fish, pp. 27–34. Anthropological Research Papers No. 33, Arizona State University, Tempe.

Bunzel, Ruth L. 1932. Introduction to Zuñi Ceremonialism. In *47th Annual Report of the Bureau of American Ethnology for the Years 1929–1930*, pp. 467–544. Government Printing Office, Washington, D.C.

Cajete, Gregory. 1994. *Look to the Mountain: An Ecology of Indigenous Education*. Kivaki Press, Durango, Colorado.

Cameron, Catherine M. 1993. Abandonment and Archaeological Interpretation. In *Abandonment of Settlements and Regions: Ethnoarchaeological and Archaeological Approaches*, edited by Catherine M. Cameron and Steve A. Tomka, pp. 3–10. Cambridge University Press, Cambridge.

Cameron, Catherine M. 1999. *Hopi Dwellings: Architecture at Orayvi*. University of Arizona Press, Tucson.

Camilli, Eileen L., Kurt F. Anschuetz, Susan Smith, and Christopher Banet. 2019. Pre-Hispanic Pueblo Cotton Cultivation and Gravel Mulch Technology in the Northern Rio Grande Region. In *Reframing the Northern Rio Grande Pueblo Economy*, edited by Scott G. Ortman, pp. 31–48. University of Arizona Press, Tucson.

Carlin, A. Roberta, Barbara Demarco, Jerry Craddock, and John H. R. Polt. 2013. Archivo General de Indias, Sevilla, Audiencia de Mexico, Legajo 26, 48-E, Fol. 40r, "Investigation Carried Out by Order of the Viceroy." In *Desertion of the Colonists of New Mexico 1601, Part 3*, pp.1–40, English translation section. Research Center for Romance Studies, University of California at Berkeley. Available online: https://escholarship.org/uc/item/452289m6.

Carrillo, Charles M. 1992. Where Were the Sheep: The Piedra Lumbre Phase Revisited. In *Current Research on the Late Prehistory and Early History of New Mexico*, edited by Bradley J. Vierra. Special Publication No. 1. New Mexico Archaeological Council. Albuquerque, New Mexico.

Catanach, Samuel Villarreal, and Mark R. Agostini. 2019. Toward the Center: Movement and Becoming at the Pueblo of Pojoaque. In *The Continuous Path: Pueblo Movement and the Archaeology of Becoming*, edited by Samuel Duwe and Robert W. Preucel, pp. 222–241. University of Arizona Press, Tucson.

Clark, Joelle, and George Gumerman IV. 2018. Hopi Footprints: What Really Matters in Cultural Preservation. In *Footprints of Hopi History: Hopihiniwtiput Kukveni'at*, edited by Leigh J. Kuwanwisiwma, T. J. Ferguson, and Chip Colwell, pp. 178–197. University of Arizona Press, Tucson.

Colwell-Chanthaphonh, Chip. 2010. *Living Histories: Native Americans and Southwestern Archaeology*. AltaMira Press, Lanham, Maryland.

Colwell-Chanthaphonh, Chip, and T. J. Ferguson. 2008. Introduction: The Collaborative Continuum. In *Collaboration in Archaeological Practice: Engaging Descendant Communities*, edited by Chip Colwell-Chanthaphonh and T. J. Ferguson, pp. 203–223. AltaMira Press, Lanham, Maryland.

Colwell, Chip, and Stewart B. Koyiyumtewa. 2018. Traditional Cultural Properties and the Hopi Model of Cultural Preservation. In *Footprints of Hopi History: Hopihiniwtiput Kukveni'at*, edited by Leigh J. Kuwanwisiwma, T. J. Ferguson, and Chip Colwell, pp. 16–38. University of Arizona Press, Tucson.

Cordell, Linda S. 1979. Prehistory: Eastern Anasazi. In *Southwest*, edited by Alfonso Ortiz, pp. 131–151. Handbook of North American Indians, Vol. 9, William C. Sturtevant, general editor. Smithsonian Institution, Washington, D.C.

Cordell, Linda S. 1996. Big Sites, Big Questions: Pueblos in Transition. In *The Prehistoric Pueblo World, AD 1150–1350*, edited by Michael A. Adler, pp. 228–240. University of Arizona Press, Tucson.

Creamer, Winifred. 1993. *The Architecture of Arroyo Hondo Pueblo, New Mexico*. Arroyo Hondo Archaeological Series, Vol. 7. School of American Research Press, Santa Fe, New Mexico.

Creamer, Winifred. 1996. Developing Complexity in the American Southwest: Constructing a Model for the Rio Grande Valley. In *Emergent Complexity: The Evolution of Intermediate Societies*, edited by Jeanne E. Arnold, pp. 91–106. International Monographs in Prehistory, Ann Arbor, Michigan.

Crotty, Helen K. 1995. *Anasazi Mural Art of the Pueblo IV Period, A.D. 1300–1600: Influences, Selective Adaptation, and Cultural Diversity in the Prehistoric Southwest*. PhD dissertation, Department of Anthropology, University of New Mexico, Albuquerque.

Crown, Patricia L. 1994. *Ceramics and Ideology: Salado Polychrome Pottery*. University of New Mexico Press, Albuquerque.

Crown, Patricia L., and Timothy A. Kohler. 1994. Community Dynamics, Site Structure, and Aggregation in the Northern Rio Grande. In *The Ancient Southwestern Community: Models and Methods for the Study of Prehistoric Social Organization*, edited by

W. H. Wills and Robert D. Leonard, pp. 103–117. University of New Mexico Press, Albuquerque.

Crown, Patricia L., Janet D. Orcutt and Timothy A. Kohler. 1996. Pueblo Cultures in Transition: The Northern Rio Grande. In *The Prehistoric Pueblo World: A.D. 1150–1350*, edited by Michael A. Adler, pp. 188–204. University of Arizona Press, Tucson.

Cruz, Patrick. 2018. *Landscape Memory and Authority: How Perceptions of Landscape Played a Part in Pueblo Migrations to the Northern Rio Grande*. Master's thesis, Department of Anthropology, University of Colorado, Boulder.

Curewitz, Diane C., and Franklin F. Foit. 2018. Shards in Sherds: Identifying Production Locations and Exchange Patterns Using Electron Microprobe Analysis of Volcanic Ash Temper in Northern Rio Grande Biscuit Ware. *Journal of Archaeological Science: Reports* 18:487–498.

Cruz, Patrick, and Scott G. Ortman. 2019. Revisiting Settlement Clusters: Political Organization and Economic Cooperation. In *Reframing the Northern Rio Grande Pueblo Economy*, edited by Scott G. Ortman, pp. 61–74. Anthropological Papers of the University of Arizona 80, University of Arizona Press, Tucson.

Curtis, Edward S. 1926. *The North American Indian*. Vol 17, The Tewa The Zuni. Johnson Reprint, New York.

Cushing, Frank H. 1883. Zuñi Fetiches. In *2nd Annual Report of the Bureau of American Ethnology for the Years 1880–1881*, pp. 3–45. Government Printing Office, Washington, D.C.

Cushing, Frank Hamilton. 1890. Preliminary Notes on the Origin, Working Hypothesis, and Primary Research of the Hemmingway Southwestern Archaeological Expedition. *Compte-Rendu de la Septieme Session, Congres International de Americanistes, Berlin* 1888:152–194.

Darling, J. Andrew. 1998. Mass Inhumation and the Execution of Witches in the American Southwest. *American Anthropologist* 100(3):732–752.

Darling, J. Andrew, and B. Sunday Eiselt. 2017. Aquí Me Quedo: Vecino Origins and the Settlement Archaeology of the Rio del Oso Grant, New Mexico. In *New Mexico and the Pimeria Alta: The Colonial Period in the American Southwest*, edited by John G. Douglass and William M. Graves, pp. 187-211. University Press of Colorado, Boulder.

Dauber, Kenneth. 1990. Pueblo Pottery and the Politics of Regional Identity. *Journal of the Southwest* 32(4):576–596.

Dean, Jeffrey S., William H. Doelle, and Janet Orcutt. 1994. Adaptive Stress: Environment and Demography. In *Themes in Southwest Prehistory*, edited by George Gumerman, pp. 53–86. School of American Research Press, Santa Fe, New Mexico.

Dean, Jeffrey S., Robert C. Euler, George J. Gumerman, Fred Plog, Richard H. Hevly, and Thor N. V. Karlstrom. 1985. Human Behavior, Demography, and Paleoenvironment on the Colorado Plateau. *American Antiquity* 50(3):537–554.

Dickson, D. Bruce. 1975. Settlement Pattern Stability and Change in the Middle Northern Rio Grande Region, New Mexico: A Test of Some Hypotheses. *American Antiquity* 40(2):159–171.

Dongoske, Kurt, Leigh Jenkins, and T. J. Ferguson. 1993. Understanding the Past Through Hopi Oral History. *Native Peoples* 6(2):24–31.

Dougherty, Julia D. 1980. An Archaeological Evaluation of Tsiping Ruin (AR-03-10-01-01). Cultural Resources Report No. 1. Santa Fe National Forest, Southwestern Region, USDA Forest Service, Santa Fe, New Mexico.

Douglass, William B. 1912. A World-Quarter Shrine of the Tewa Indians. *Records of the Past* XI(IV):159–173.

Douglass, William B. 1917. Notes on the Shrines of the Tewa and Other Pueblo Indians of New Mexico. In *Proceedings of the Nineteenth International Congress of Americanists*, edited by Frank W. Hodge, pp. 344–378, Government Printing Office, Washington, D.C.

Dozier, Edward P. 1954. *The Hopi-Tewa of Arizona*. University of California Publications in American Archaeology and Ethnology, Vol. 44, No. 3. University of California Press, Berkeley.

Dozier, Edward P. 1961. Rio Grande Pueblos. In *Perspectives in American Indian Culture Change*, edited by Edward H. Spicer, pp. 94–186. University of Chicago Press, Chicago.

Dozier, Edward P. 1966. Factionalism at Santa Clara Pueblo. *Ethnology* 5(2):172–185.

Dozier, Edward P. 1970. *The Pueblo Indians of North America*. Waveland Press, Prospect Heights, Illinois.

Duff, Andrew I. 2002. *Western Pueblo Identities: Regional Interaction, Migration, and Transformation*. University of Arizona Press, Tucson.

Duwe, Samuel. 2006. Ceramic Analysis and Interpretation of Classic Period Pueblos on Los Alamos National Laboratory Land Collected by the Pajarito Archaeological Research Project (PARP). ESH-20 Cultural Resources Team, Ecology Group, Los Alamos National Laboratory.

Duwe, Samuel. 2009. Making Villages out of Adobe Hills: Micro-Topographic Mapping of Ancestral Tewa Sites in the Tewa Basin, New Mexico. In *Between the Mountains, Beyond the Mountains: Papers in Honor of Paul R. Williams*, edited by Emily J. Brown, pp. 49–56. Papers of the Archaeological Society of New Mexico, No. 35. Archaeological Society of New Mexico, Albuquerque.

Duwe, Samuel. 2011. *The Prehispanic Tewa World: Space, Time, and Becoming in the Pueblo Southwest*. PhD dissertation, School of Anthropology, University of Arizona, Tucson.

Duwe, Samuel. 2013. Appendix 4: Site Descriptions of 10 Ancestral Ohkay Owingeh Sites in the Rio Chama Watershed. In *Population History, Agricultural Land Use and Cultural Continuity in the Ohkay Owingeh Homeland, Rio Chama Watershed*, edited by B. Sunday Eiselt and Andrew Darling. Southwest Heritage Research Report No. 2102–1, Dallas, Texas.

Duwe, Samuel. 2014. Of Moieties and Made People: The Development of Tewa Pueblo Society. Prepared for the symposium "Integration and Disintegration: The Role of Public Architecture in the Prehispanic American Southwest." Presented at the 79th Annual Meeting of the Society for American Archaeology, Austin, Texas.

Duwe, Samuel. 2016. Cupules and the Creation of the Tewa Pueblo World. *Journal of Lithic Studies* 3(3):147–168.

Duwe, Samuel. 2017. Re-excavation of Palisade Ruin (LA 3505). Manuscript on file, Albuquerque District, U.S. Army Corps of Engineers, Albuquerque, New Mexico.

Duwe, Samuel. 2019. The Economics of Becoming: Population Coalescence and the Production and Distribution of Ancestral Tewa Pottery. In *Re-Framing the Northern Rio Grande Pueblo Economy*, edited by Scott G. Ortman, pp. 104–118. University of Arizona Press, Tucson.

Duwe, Samuel, and Kurt F. Anschuetz. 2013. Ecological Uncertainty and Organizational Flexibility on the Prehispanic Tewa Landscape: Notes from the Northern Frontier. In *From Mountaintop to Valley Bottom: Understanding Past Land Use in the Northern Rio Grande Valley, New Mexico*, edited by Bradley J. Vierra, pp. 95–112. University of Utah Press, Salt Lake City.

Duwe, Samuel, and Patrick J. Cruz. 2019. Tewa Origins and Middle Places. In *The Continuous Path: Pueblo Movement and the Archaeology of Becoming*, edited by Samuel Duwe and Robert W. Preucel, pp. 96–123. University of Arizona Press, Tucson.

Duwe, Samuel, B. Sunday Eiselt, J. Andrew Darling, Mark D. Willis, and Chester Walker. 2016. The Pueblo Decomposition Model: A Method for Quantifying Architectural Rubble to Estimate Population Size. *Journal of Archaeological Science* 65:20–31.

Duwe, Samuel, and Robert W. Preucel (editors). 2019. *The Continuous Path: Pueblo Movement and the Archaeology of Becoming*. University of Arizona Press, Tucson.

Eggan, Fred. 1950. *Social Organization of the Western Pueblos*. University of Chicago Publications in Anthropology. University of Chicago Press, Chicago.

Eiselt, B. Sunday. 2012. *Becoming White Clay: A History of Archeology of Jicarilla Apache Enclavement*. University of Utah Press, Salt Lake City.

Eiselt, B. Sunday. 2019. New Perspectives on the Regional Agricultural Economy in the Ohkay Owingeh Homeland. In *Reframing the Northern Rio Grande Pueblo Economy*, edited by Scott G. Ortman, pp. 17–30. University of Arizona Press, Tucson.

Eiselt, B. Sunday, and Andrew Darling. 2013. Population History, Argricultural Land Use and Cultural Continuity in the Ohkay Owingeh Homeland, Rio Chama Watershed. Southwest Heritage Research Report No. 2102–1, Dallas, Texas.

Eiselt, B. Sunday, J. Andrew Darling, Samuel Duwe, Mark Willis, Chester Walker, William Hudspeth, and Leslie Reeder-Meyers. 2017. A Bird's-Eye View of Proto-Tewa Subsistence Agriculture: Making the Case for Floodplain Farming in the Ohkay Owingeh Homeland, New Mexico. *American Antiquity* 82(2):397–413.

Ellis, Florence Hawley. 1964. *A Reconstruction of the Basic Jemez Pattern of Social Organization: With Comparisons to Other Tanoan Social Structures*. No. 11. University of New Mexico Press, Albuquerque.

Ellis, Florence Hawley. 1968. San Juan Pueblo's Water Use. Bound copy of 27-page draft with bibliography. Catalogue No. 2010.41.1968f, Maxwell Museum, University of New Mexico, Albuquerque.

Ellis, Florence Hawley. 1974. Nambe: Their Past Agricultural Use of Territory. Prepared for the USDI, Bureau of Indian Affairs. Manuscript on file, New Mexico Office of the State Engineer, Santa Fe.

Ellis, Florence Hawley. 1975. Highways to the Past: The Valleys of the Rio Chama and Rio Gallina. *New Mexico Magazine* 53(5):18–25, 38–40.

Ellis, Florence Hawley. 1987. The Long Lost "City" of San Gabriel del Yungue, Second Oldest European Settlement in the United States. In *When Cultures Meet: Remembering San Gabriel del Yunge Oweenge*, pp. 10–38. Papers from the October 20, 1984 conference held at San Juan Pueblo, New Mexico. Sunstone Press, Santa Fe.

Ellis, Florence Hawley, and L. Hammack 1968. The Inner Sanctum of Feather Cave, a Mogollon Sun and Earth Shrine Linking Mexico and the Southwest. *American Antiquity* 33(1):25–44.

Ellis, Florence Hawley. 1989. *San Gabriel del Yungue as Seen by an Archaeologist*. Sunstone Press, Santa Fe.

Espinosa, J. Manuel. 1942. *Crusaders of the Rio Grande*. Institute of Jesuit History, Chicago.

Fallon, Denise, and Karen Wening. 1987. Howiri: Excavations at a Northern Rio Grande Biscuit Ware Site, Laboratory of Anthropology Notes 261b. Museum of New Mexico Research Section, Santa Fe.

Ferguson, T. J., Roger Anyon, and Edmund J. Ladd. 1996. Repatriation at the Pueblo of Zuni: Diverse Solution to Complex Problems. *American Indian Quarterly* 20(2): 251–273.

Ferguson, T. J., and Roger Anyon. 2001. Hopi and Zuni Cultural Landscapes: Implications of History and Scale for Cultural Resources Management. In *Native Peoples of the Southwest: Negotiating Land, Water, and Ethnicities*, edited by Laurie Weinstein, pp. 99–122. Bergin and Garvey, Westport, Connecticut.

Ferguson, T. J., and Chip Colwell-Chanthaphonh. 2006. *History Is in the Land: Multivocal Tribal Traditions in Arizona's San Pedro Valley*. University of Arizona Press, Tucson.

Ferguson, T. J., Leigh J. Kuwanwisiwma, Micah Loma'omvaya, Patrick Lyons, Gregson Schachner, and Laurie Webster. 2013. Yep Hisat Hoopoq'yaqam Yesiwa [Hopi Ancestors Were Once Here]: Repatriation Research Documenting Hopi Cultural Affiliation with the Ancient Hohokam of Southern Arizona. In *Global Ancestors: Understanding the Shared Humanity of Our Ancestors*, edited by Margaret Clegg, Rebecca Redfern, Jelena Bekvalac, and Heather Bonney, pp. 103–144. Oxbow Books, London.

Fetterman, Jerry, and Linda Honeycutt. 1987. *The Mockingbird Mesa Survey, Southwestern Colorado*. Bureau of Land Management, Albuquerque, New Mexico.

Fewkes, Jesse W. 1900. Tusayan Migration Traditions. *19th Annual Report of the Bureau of American Ethnology of the Years 1897–1898*, Pt. 2. pp. 573–634. Government Printing Office, Washington, D.C.

Fewkes, Jesse W. 1906. Hopi Shrines Near the East Mesa, Arizona. *American Anthropologist* 8(2):346–375.

Fewkes, Jesse W. 1922. Ancestor Worship of the Hopi Indians. In *Annual Report of the Board of Regents of the Smithsonian Institution Showing the Operations, Expenditures, and Condition of the Institution for the Year Ending June 30, 1921*, pp. 485–506. Government Printing Office, Washington, D.C.

Flint, Richard. 2017. Ditch-Irrigated Agriculture Noted by Spaniards at Santo Domingo Pueblo in 1591: Evidence from Dating Anomalies in the *Memoria de Castaño de Sosa*. *New Mexico Historical Review* 92(2):157–180.

Flint, Richard, and Shirley Cushing Flint. 2005. *Documents of the Coronado Expedition, 1539–1542*. University of New Mexico Press, Albuquerque.

Flint, Richard. 2008. *No Settlement, No Conquest: A History of the Coronado Entrada*. University of New Mexico Press, Albuquerque.

Ford, Richard I. 1968. An Ecological Analysis Involving the Population of San Juan Pueblo, New Mexico. PhD dissertation, Department of Anthropology, University of Michigan, Ann Arbor.

Ford, Richard I. 1972a. An Ecological Perspective on the Eastern Pueblos. In *New Perspectives on the Pueblos*, edited by Alfonso Ortiz, pp. 1–18. University of New Mexico Press, Albuquerque.

Ford, Richard I. 1972b. Barter, Gift, or Violence: An Analysis of Tewa Intertribal Exchange. In *Social Exchange and Interaction*, edited by Edwin N. Wilmsen, pp. 21–45. Anthropological Papers, Museum of Anthropology, University of Michigan, Ann Arbor.

Ford, Richard I. 1980. The Color of Survival. *Discovery*: 17–29.

Ford, Richard I. 1987. The New Pueblo Economy. In *When Cultures Meet: Remembering San Gabriel del Yunge Oweenge*, pp. 73–91. Papers from the October 20, 1984 conference held at San Juan Pueblo, New Mexico. Sunstone Press, Santa Fe.

Ford, Richard I. 2018. *Ma:tu'in*: The Bridge Between Kinship and "Clan" in the Tewa Pueblos of New Mexico. In *Puebloan Societies: Homology and Heterogeneity in Time and Space*, edited by Peter M. Whiteley, pp. 25–49. School for Advanced Research Press, Santa Fe.

Ford, Richard I., and Kurt F. Anschuetz. 1995. Pesedeuinge Pueblo Pottery Identifications. J.A. Jeançon Collection, Colorado Springs Pioneers Museum. Manuscript on file, Museum of Anthropology, University of Michigan, Ann Arbor.

Ford, Richard I., Albert H. Schroeder, and Stewart L. Peckham. 1972. Three Perspectives on Puebloan Prehistory. In *New Perspectives on the Pueblos*, edited by Alfonso Ortiz, pp. 19–39. University of New Mexico Press, Albuquerque.

Ford, Richard I., and Roxanne Swentzell. 2015. Precontact Agriculture in Northern New Mexico. In *Traditional Lands Agriculture: Understanding the Past for the Future*, edited by Scott F. Ingram and Robert C. Hunt, pp. 330–357. University of Arizona Press, Tucson.

Forrestral, Peter P., and Cyprian J. Lynch. 1954. *Benavides Memorial of 1630*. Academy of American Franciscan History, Washington, D.C.

Fowler, Don D. 2000. *A Laboratory for Anthropology: Science and Romanticism in the American Southwest, 1846–1930*. University of New Mexico Press, Albuquerque.

Fowles, Severin M. 2004a. The Making of Made People: The Prehistoric Evolution of Hierocracy Among the Northern Tiwa of New Mexico. PhD dissertation, Department of Anthropology, University of Michigan, Ann Arbor.

Fowles, Severin M. 2004b. Tewa Versus Tiwa: Northern Rio Grande Settlement Patterns and Social History, A.D. 1275 to 1540. In *The Protohistoric Pueblo World: A.D. 1275–1600*, edited by E. Charles Adams and Andrew I. Duff, pp. 17–25. University of Arizona Press, Tucson.

Fowles, Severin M. 2005. Historical Contingency and the Prehistoric Foundations of Moiety Organization Among the Eastern Pueblos. *Journal of Anthropological Research* 61(1):25–52.

Fowles, Severin M. 2009. The Enshrined Pueblo: Villagescape and Cosmos in the Northern Rio Grande. *American Antiquity* 74(3):448–466.

Fowles, Severin M. 2010. The Southwest School of Landscape Archaeology. *Annual Review of Anthropology* 39:453–468.

Fowles, Severin M. 2011. Movement and the Unsettling of the Pueblos. In *Rethinking Anthropological Perspectives on Migration*, edited by Graciela S. Cabana and Jeffrey J. Clark, pp. 45–67. University of Florida Press, Gainesville.

Fowles, Severin. 2012. The Pueblo Village in an Age of Reformation. In *Oxford Handbook of North American Archaeology*, edited by Timothy Pauketat, pp. 631–644. Oxford University Press, London.

Fowles, Severin M. 2013. *An Archaeology of Doings: Secularism and the Study of Pueblo Religion*. School for Advanced Research, Santa Fe, New Mexico.

Fowles, Severin M. 2018. Taos Social History: A Rhizomatic Account. In *Puebloan Societies: Homology and Heterogeneity in Time and Space*, edited by Peter M. Whiteley, pp. 75–101. School for Advanced Research Press, Santa Fe, New Mexico.

Fowles, Severin M., and B. Sunday Eiselt. 2019. Apache, Tiwa, and Back Again: Ethnic Shifting in the American Southwest. In *The Continuous Path: Pueblo Movement and the Archaeology of Becoming*, edited by Samuel Duwe and Robert W. Preucel, pp. 165–194. University of Arizona Press, Tucson.

Fowles, Severin M., and Barbara Mills. 2017. On History in Southwest Archaeology. In *Oxford Handbook of Southwest Archaeology*, edited by Barbara Mills and Severin Fowles, pp. 3–71. Oxford University Press, Oxford.

Fowles, Severin M., Leah Minc, Samuel Duwe, and David V. Hill. 2007. Clay, Conflict, and Village Aggregation: Compositional Analyses of Pre-Classic Pottery from Taos, New Mexico. *American Antiquity* 72(1):125–152.

Fox, Robin. 1967. *The Keresan Bridge*. London School of Economics Monographs in Social Anthropology 35. Athlone Press, London.

Frost, Rochard H. 1980. The Romantic Inflation Pueblo Culture. *The American West* 17(1)5–9, 56–60.

Frost, Richard H. 2016. *The Railroad and the Pueblo Indians: The Impacts of the Atchison, Topeka and Santa Fe on the Pueblos of the Rio Grande, 1880–1930*. University of Utah Press, Salt Lake City.

Futrell, Mary E. 1998. Social Boundaries and Interaction: Ceramic Zones in the Northern Rio Grande Pueblo IV Period. *Migration and Reorganization: The Pueblo IV Period in the American Southwest*, edited by Katherine A. Spielmann. Arizona State University Anthropological Research Papers, Tempe.

Gabler, Brandon M. 2009. *Panarchy on the Plateau: Modeling Prehistoric Settlement Pattern, Land Use, and Demographic Change on the Pajarito Plateau, New Mexico*. PhD dissertation, School of Anthropology, University of Arizona, Tucson.

Gamble, Clive. 2007. *Origins and Revolutions: Human Identity in the Earliest Prehistory*. Cambridge University Press, Cambridge.

Garcia, Damian, and Kurt F. Anschuetz. 2019. Movement as an Acoma Way of Life. In *The Continuous Path: Pueblo Movement and the Archaeology of Becoming*, edited by Samuel Duwe and Robert W. Preucel, pp. 37–59. University of Arizona Press, Tucson.

Gauthier, Rory. 1987. Ceramics. In *Howiri: Excavation at a Northern Rio Grande Biscuit Ware Site*, edited by Denise Fallon and Karen Wening, pp. 35–58. Laboratory of Anthropology, Santa Fe.

Glowacki, Donna M., and Scott Van Keuren (editors). 2011. *Religious Transformation in the Late Pre-Hispanic Pueblo World.* University of Arizona Press, Tucson.

Glowacki, Donna M. 2015 *Living and Leaving: A Social History of Regional Depopulation in Thirteenth-Century Mesa Verde.* University of Arizona Press, Tucson.

Gordon-McCutchan, R. C. 1995. *The Taos Indians and the Battle for Blue Lake.* Red Crane Books, Santa Fe.

Graves, William M., and Suzanne L. Eckert. 1998. Decorated Ceramics and Ideological Developments in the Northern and Central Rio Grande Valley, New Mexico. In *Migration and Reorganization: The Pueblo IV Period in the American Southwest*, edited by Katherine A. Spielmann, pp. 263–283. Arizona State University Anthropological Research Papers, Tempe.

Greenlee, Robert. 1933. Archaeological Sites in the Chama Valley, and Report on the Excavations at Tsama, 1929–1933. Manuscript on file, Laboratory of Anthropology, Museum of New Mexico, Santa Fe.

Gutiérrez, Ramón A. 1996. Introduction. In *Pueblo Indian Religion*, Vol. 2, by Elsie Clews Parsons. University of Nebraska Press, Lincoln.

Haas, Jonathan, and Winifred Creamer. 1996. The Role of Warfare in the Pueblo III Period. In *The Prehistoric Pueblo World, A.D. 1150–1350*, edited by Michael A. Adler, pp. 205–213. University of Arizona Press, Tucson.

Habicht-Mauche, Judith A. 1993. *The Pottery from Arroyo Hondo Pueblo, New Mexico: Tribalization and Trade in the Northern Rio Grande.* School of American Research Press, Santa Fe.

Habicht-Mauche, Judith A., Suzanne Eckert, and Deborah L. Huntley (editors). 2006. *The Social Lives of Pots: Glaze Wares and Cultural Dynamics in the Southwest, AD 1250–1680.* University of Arizona Press, Tucson.

Hackett, Charles W., and Charmion C. Shelby (editor and translator). 1942. *Revolt of the Pueblo Indians of New Mexico, and Otermín's Attempted Reconquest, 1680–1682.* 2 vols. Coronado Cuarto Centennial Publications. University of New Mexico Press, Albuquerque.

Hagstrum, Melissa B. 1985. Measuring Prehistoric Ceramic Craft Specialization: A Test Case in the American Southwest. *Journal of Field Archaeology* 12(1):65–75.

Halverson, Cathryn. 2004. *Maverick Autobiographies: Women Writers and the American West, 1900–1936.* University of Wisconsin Press, Madison.

Hammond, George P., and Agapito Rey. 1940. *Narratives of the Coronado Expedition, 1540–1542.* University of New Mexico Press, Albuquerque.

Hammond, George P., and Agapito Rey. 1953. *Don Juan de Oñate, Colonizer of New Mexico, 1595–1628.* University of New Mexico Press, Albuquerque.

Hammond, George P., and Agapito Rey. 1966. *The Rediscovery of New Mexico, 1580–1592.* University of New Mexico Press, Albuquerque.

Harlow, Francis H. 1973. *Matte-Paint Pottery of the Tewa, Keres, and Zuni Pueblos.* School of American Research Press, Santa Fe.

Harrington, John P. 1910. A Brief Description of the Tewa Language. *American Anthropologist* 12:497–504.

Harrington, John P. 1916. *The Ethnography of the Tewa Indians*. 29th Annual Report of the Bureau of American Ethnology, pp. 29–636. Government Printing Office, Washington, D.C.

Haury, Emil W. 1935. Tree Rings. The Archaeologist's Time-Piece. *American Antiquity* 1(2):98–108.

Hawley, Florence. 1950. Big Kivas, Little Kivas, and Moiety Houses in Historical Reconstruction. *Southwestern Journal of Anthropology* 6:286–302.

Hays-Gilpin, Kelley, and Dennis Gilpin. 2018a. Becoming Hopi: Exploring Hopi Ethnogenesis Through Architecture, Pottery, and Cultural Knowledge. In *Footprints of Hopi History: Hopihiniwtiput Kukveni'at*, edited by Leigh J. Kuwanwisiwma, T. J. Ferguson, and Chip Colwell, pp. 123–140. University of Arizona Press, Tucson.

Hays-Gilpin, Kelley, and Dennis Gilpin. 2018b. Archaeological Expressions of Ancestral Hopi Social Organization. In *Puebloan Societies: Homology and Heterogeneity in Time and Space*, edited by Peter M. Whiteley, pp. 157–174. School for Advanced Research Press, Santa Fe.

Hays-Gilpin, Kelley, and Jane H. Hill. 1999. The Flower World in Material Culture: An Iconographic Complex in the Southwest and Mesoamerica. *Journal of Anthropological Research* 55(1):1–37.

Hedquist, Saul L., Maren P. Hopkins, Stewart B. Koyiyumptewa, Lee Wayne Lomayestewa, and T. J. Ferguson. 2018. Tungwniwpi nit Wukwlavayi (Named Places and Oral Traditions): Multivocal Approaches to Hopi Land. In *Footprints of Hopi History: Hopihiniwtiput Kukveni'at*, edited by Leigh J. Kuwanwisiwma, T. J. Ferguson, and Chip Colwell, pp. 52–72. University of Arizona Press, Tucson.

Henderson, Junius, and John P. Harrington. 1914. Ethnozoology of the Tewa Indians. In *Annual Report of the Bureau of American Ethnology for the Years 1910–1911*. Government Printing Office, Washington, D.C.

Hendricks, Rick. 2007. Pueblo-Spanish Warfare in Seventeenth-Century New Mexico: The Battles of Black Mesa, Kotyiti, and Astialakwa. In *Archaeologies of the Pueblo Revolt: Identity, Meaning, and Renewal in the Pueblo World*, edited by Robert W. Preucel, pp. 180–197. University of New Mexico Press, Albuquerque.

Hewett, Edgar L. 1906. *Antiquities of the Jemez Plateau, New Mexico*. Bureau of American Ethnology Bulletin No. 32. Government Printing Office, Washington, D.C.

Hewett, Edgar L. 1938. *Pajarito Plateau and Its Ancient People*. Handbook of Archaeological History, 2nd ed., revised 1953. University of New Mexico Press and School of American Research, Albuquerque and Santa Fe.

Hibben, Frank C. 1937. *Excavation of the Riana Ruin and Chama Valley Survey*. Anthropological Series Bulletin 300. University of New Mexico Press, Albuquerque.

Hill, James N., William N. Trierweiler, and Robert W. Preucel. 1996. The Evolution of Cultural Complexity: A Case from the Pajarito Plateau, New Mexico. In *Emergent Complexity: The Evolution of Intermediate Societies*, edited by Jeanne E. Arnold, pp. 107–127. International Monographs in Prehistory, Madison.

Hill, W. W. 1982. *An Ethnography of Santa Clara Pueblo, New Mexico*. University of New Mexico Press, Albuquerque.

Hu, Di. 2013. Approaches to the Archaeology of Ethnogenesis: Past and Emergent Perspectives. *Journal of Archaeological Research* 21:371–402.

Hull, Dorothy. 1916. *Castaño de Sosa's Expedition to New Mexico in 1590*. Master's thesis, University of California, Berkeley.

Hunter-Anderson, Rosalind D. 1979. Explaining Residential Aggregation in the Northern Rio Grande: A Competition Reduction Model. In *Archaeological Investigations in the Cochiti Reservoir, New Mexico, Vol. 4. Adaptive Change in the Northern Rio Grande Valley*, edited by Jan V. Biellaand Richard Chapman, pp. 56–67. Office of Contract Archaeology, University of New Mexico, Albuquerque.

Huxley, Aldous. 1932. *Brave New World*. Chatto and Windus, London.

Ingold, Tim. 2011. *Being Alive: Essays on Movement, Knowledge and Description*. Routledge, London.

Jacobs, Sue-Ellen, Siri G. Tuttle, and Esther Martinez. 1998. Multimedia Technology in Language and Culture Restoration Efforts at San Juan Pueblo. *Wicazo Sa Review* 13(2):45–58.

Jeançon, Jean A. 1912. Ruins at Pesedeuinge. *Records of the Past* 11:28–37.

Jeançon, Jean A. 1923. *Excavations in the Chama Valley, New Mexico*. Bureau of American Ethnology Bulletin 81. Government Printing Office, Washington, D.C.

Jeançon, Jean A. 1925. Primitive Coloradoans. *The Colorado Magazine* 2(1):35–40.

Jenks, Kelly L. 2013. Building Community: Exploring Civic Identity in Hispanic New Mexico. *Journal of Social Archaeology* 13(3):371–393.

Jerome, Kathryn. 2018. Coalescence and Transition: The Painted Ceramics at Palisade Ruin. Student paper on file, Department of Anthropology, University of Oklahoma.

Johnson, George. 1997. Alfonso Ortiz, 57, Anthropologist of the Pueblo, Dies. *New York Times* January 31, 1997.

Johnson, Gregory A. 1982. Organizational Structure and Scalar Stress. In *Theory and Explanation in Archaeology*, edited by Colin Renfrew, M. J. Rowlands, and B. A. Segraves, pp. 389–421. Academic Press, New York.

Jojola, Ted. 1997. A Tribute to Alfonso Ortiz (1939–97). *Wicazo Sa Review* 12(2):9–11.

Kelley, J. Charles. 1952. Factors Involved in the Abandonment of Certain Peripheral Southwestern Settlements. *American Anthropologist* 54:356–397.

Kelley, Vincent C. 1979. Geomorphology of the Española Basin. In *Guidebook of Santa Fe Country*, edited by Raymond V. Indersoll, pp. 281–288. 30th Field Conference, New Mexico Geological Survey, Socorro, New Mexico.

Kemp, Brian M., Kathleen Judd, Cara Monroe, Jelmer W. Eerkens, Lindsay Hilldorger, Connor Cordray, Rebecca Schad, Erin Reams, Scott G. Ortman, and Timothy A. Kohler. 2017. Prehistoric Mitochondrial DNA of Domesticate Animals Supports a 13th Century Exodus from the Northern U.S. Southwest. *PLOS ONE* 12(7):e0178882.

Kemrer, M. F. 1992. An Appraisal of the Piedra Lumbre Phase in North Central New Mexico. In *History and Ethnohistory Along the Rio Chama*, prepared by J. D. Schelberg and R. R. Kneebone, pp. 66–108. U.S. Army Corps of Engineers, Albuquerque District, Albuquerque, New Mexico.

Kessell, John L., and Rick Hendricks. 1994. *By Force of Arms: The Journals of Don Diego de Vargas, New Mexico 1691–1693*. University of New Mexico Press, Albuquerque.

Kidder, Alfred V. 1915. *Pottery of the Pajarito Plateau and of Some Adjacent Regions in New Mexico*. Memoirs of the American Anthropological Association. Vol. 2, pp. 407–462. American Anthropological Association, Washington, D.C.

Kidder, Alfred V. 1924. *An Introduction to the Study of Southwestern Archaeology with a Preliminary Account of the Excavations at Pecos*. Yale University Press, New Haven, Connecticut.

Kidder, Alfred V. 1927. Southwestern Archaeological Conference. *Science* 66(1716): 489–491.

Kidder, Alfred V. 1936. *The Pottery of Pecos*. Papers of the Southwest Expedition, no. 7. Yale University Press, New Haven.

Kidder, Alfred V. 1958. *Pecos, New Mexico: Archaeological Notes*. Papers of the Robert S. Peabody Foundation for Archaeology 5. Phillips Academy, Andover, Massachusetts.

Klager, Karol J. 1980. Archaeological Survey of Remaining Corps of Engineers Project Lands at Abiquiu Dam, New Mexico. Manuscript on file, U.S. Army Corps of Engineers, Albuquerque.

Knaut, Andrew L. 1995. *The Pueblo Revolt: Conquest and Resistance in Seventeenth-Century New Mexico*. University of Oklahoma Press, Norman.

Kohler, Timothy A. 2004. *Archaeology of Bandelier National Monument: Village Formation on the Pajarito Plateau, New Mexico*. University of New Mexico Press, Albuquerque.

Kohler, Timothy A., Sarah Herr, and Matthew A. Root. 2004. The Rise and Fall of Towns on the Pajarito (A.D. 1375–1600). In *Archaeology of Bandelier National Monument: Village Formation on the Pajarito Plateau, New Mexico*, edited by Timothy A. Kohler, pp. 215–264. University of New Mexico Press, Albuquerque.

Kohler, Timothy A., and Meredith H. Matthews. 1988. Long-Term Anasazi Land Use and Forest Reduction: A Case Study from Southwest Colorado. *American Antiquity* 53:537–564.

Kohler, Timothy A., and Matthew A. Root. 2004. The First Hunter/Farmers. In *Archaeology of Bandelier National Monument: Village Formation on the Pajarito Plateau, New Mexico*, edited by Timothy A. Kohler, pp. 117–172. University of New Mexico Press, Albuquerque.

Kroeber, Alfred L. 1919. *Zuñi Kin and Clan*. Anthropological Papers of the American Museum of Natural History Vol. 18(2):39–204. American Museum of Natural History, New York.

Kuwanwisiwma, Leigh J. 2018. The Collaborative Road: A Personal History of the Hopi Cultural Preservation Office. In *Footprints of Hopi History: Hopihiniwtiput Kukveni'at*, edited by Leigh J. Kuwanwisiwma, T. J. Ferguson, and Chip Colwell, pp. 1–15. University of Arizona Press, Tucson.

Kuwanwisiwma, Leigh J., and T. J. Ferguson. 2002. Ang Kukota. *Expedition* 46(2): 24–29.

Lakatos, Steven. 2007. Cultural Continuity and the Development of Integrative Architecture in the Northern Rio Grande Valley of New Mexico, A.D. 600–1200. *Kiva* 73(1):31–66.

Lang, Richard W. 1980. Archaeological Investigations at a Pueblo Agricultural Site, and Archaic and Puebloan Encampments on the Rio Ojo Caliente, Rio Arriba County, New Mexico. Contract Archaeology Program Report 007. School of American Research, Santa Fe, New Mexico.

Lang, Richard W. 1988. The First Six Millennia: Early Foragers of the Upper Pecos. In *Pecos, Gateway to Pueblos and Plains: The Anthology*, edited by John V. Bezy and Joseph P. Sanchez, pp. 20–25. Southwest Parks and Monuments Association, Tucson.

Lang, Richard W. 1992. *Archaeological Excavations at Dos Griegos, Upper Cañada de Los Alamos, Santa Fe County, New Mexico: Archaic through Pueblo V*. Southwest Archaeological Consultants Research Series 283, Santa Fe, New Mexico.

Laski, Vera. 1958. *Seeking Life*. Memoirs of the American Folklore Society 50. American Folklore Society, Philadelphia.

Lekson, Stephen H. 2009. *A History of the Ancient Southwest*. School for Advanced Research Press, Santa Fe, New Mexico.

Lekson, Stephen H. 2012. Chaco's Hinterlands. In *Oxford Handbook of North American Archaeology*, edited by Timothy Pauketat, pp. 597–607. Oxford University Press, London

Lekson, Stephen H. 2018. *A Study of Southwestern Archaeology*. University of Utah Press, Salt Lake City.

Lekson, Stephen H., and Catherine M. Cameron. 1995. The Abandonment of Chaco Canyon, the Mesa Verde Migrations, and the Reorganization of the Pueblo World. *Journal of Anthropological Archaeology* 14:184–202.

Liebmann, Matthew. 2012. *Revolt: An Archaeological History of Pueblo Resistance and Revitalization in the 17th Century, New Mexico*. University of Arizona Press, Tucson.

Liebmann, Matthew, T. J. Ferguson, and Robert W. Preucel. 2005. Pueblo Settlement, Architecture, and Social Change in the Pueblo Revolt Era, A.D. 1680–1696. *Journal of Field Archaeology* 30:1–16.

Liebmann, Matthew, and Robert W. Preucel. 2007. The Archaeology of the Pueblo Revolt and the Formation of the Modern Pueblo World. *Kiva* 73:197–219.

Liebmann, Matthew, and Uzma Z. Rizvi (editors). 2010. *Archaeology and the Postcolonial Critique*. AltaMira Press, Lanham, Maryland.

Lipe, William D. 2006. Notes from the North. In *The Archaeology of Chaco Canyon: An Eleventh-Century Pueblo Regional Center*, edited by Stephen H. Lekson, pp. 261–314. School of American Research Press, Santa Fe, New Mexico.

Lowell, Julia C. 1996. Moieties in Prehistory: A Case Study from the Pueblo Southwest. *Journal of Field Archaeology* 23(1):77–90.

Lowie, Robert H. 1929a. Notes on Hopi Clans. *Anthropological Papers of the American Museum of Natural History* 30(6):303–360. American Museum of Natural History, New York.

Lowie, Robert H. 1929b. Hopi Kinship. *Anthropological Papers of the American Museum of Natural History* 30(7):361–387. American Museum of Natural History, New York.

Luebben, Ralph A. 1953. Leaf Water Site. In *Salvage Archaeology in the Chama Valley, New Mexico*, edited by Fred Wendorf, pp. 9–33. Monographs of the School of American Research, School of American Research Press, Santa Fe, New Mexico.

Luebben, Ralph A., and David Brugge. 1953. Physiographic Environment of the Lower Chama Valley. In *Salvage Archaeology in the Chama Valley, New Mexico*, edited by Fred Wendorf, pp. 1–4. Monographs of the School of American Research, School of American Research Press, Santa Fe, New Mexico.

McKenna, Peter J. 1970. Excavation of West Plaza, North Mound: Anthropology Field School, University of New Mexico. Unpublished manuscript on file at ARMS, Museum of New Mexico, Santa Fe.

McKenna, Peter J., and Judith Miles. 1996. Pecos Archaeological Survey 1996 Ceramic Typology: Field Manual. Manuscript on file, Laboratory of Anthropology, Santa Fe.

McNutt, Charles H. 1969. *Early Puebloan Occupation at Tesuque By-Pass and in the Upper Rio Grande Valley*. Anthropological Papers No. 40. Museum of Anthropology, University of Michigan, Ann Arbor.

Marcus, George E., and Michael M. J. Fischer. 1986. *Anthropology as Cultural Critique: An Experimental Moment in the Human Sciences*. University of Chicago Press, Chicago.

Marriott, Alice. 1948. *María: The Potter of San Ildefonso*. University of Oklahoma Press, Norman.

Marshall, Michael P. 1997. The Chacoan Roads: A Cosmological Interpretation. In *Anasazi Architecture and American Design*, edited by Baker H. Morrow and V. B. Price, pp. 63–75. University of New Mexico Press, Albuquerque.

Marshall, Michael P., John R. Stein, R. W. Loose and J. E. Novotny. 1979. *Anasazi Communities of the San Juan Basin*. Public Service Company of New Mexico, Albuquerque and New Mexico State Historic Preservation Bureau, Santa Fe.

Marshall, Michael P., and Henry Walt. 2007. The Eastern Homeland of San Juan Pueblo: Tewa Land and Water Use in the Santa Cruz and Truchas Watersheds: An Archaeological and Ethnogeographic Study. Cibola Research Consultants Report No. 432, Corrales, New Mexico.

Martinez, Esther. 1982. *San Juan Pueblo Tewa Dictionary*. San Juan Pueblo, New Mexico: SJP Bilingual Program.

Mathien, Frances Joan. 1994. History of Archaeological Investigations on the Pajarito Plateau. Manuscript on file, Southwest Cultural Resources Center, Southwest Region, National Park Service, Santa Fe, New Mexico.

Matson, R. G. 1991. *The Origins of Southwestern Agriculture*. University of Arizona Press, Tucson.

Matson, R. G., William D. Lipe, and William R. Haase IV. 1988. Adaptational Continuities and Occupational Discontinuities: The Cedar Mesa Anasazi. *Journal of Field Archaeology* 15:245–264.

Maxwell, Timothy D. 1994. Prehistoric Population Change in the Lower Rio Chama Valley, Northwestern New Mexico. Paper Presented at the 59th Annual Meeting of the Society for American Archaeology, Anaheim, California.

Mera, Harry P. 1932. *Wares Ancestral to Tewa Polychrome*. Technical Series, Bulletin No. 4. Laboratory of Anthropology, Santa Fe, New Mexico.

Mera, Harry P. 1934. *A Survey of the Biscuit Ware Area in Northern New Mexico*. Technical Series, Bulletin No. 6. Laboratory of Anthropology, Santa Fe, New Mexico.

Mera, Harry P. 1935. *Ceramic Clues to the Prehistory of North Central New Mexico*. Laboratory of Anthropology Technical Series Bulletin No. 8. Santa Fe, New Mexico.

Mills, Barbara J. (editor). 2000. *Alternative Leadership Strategies in the Prehispanic Southwest*. University of Arizona Press, Tucson.

Mills, Barbara J. 2007. Performing the Feast: Visual Display and Superhousehold Commensalism in the Puebloan Southwest. *American Antiquity* 72(2):210–240.

Mills, Barbara J., Jeffery J. Clark, Matthew A. Peeples, W. R. Haas Jr., John M. Roberts Jr., J. Brett Hill, Deborah L. Huntley, Lewis Borck, Ronald L. Breiger, Aaron Clauset, and M. Steven Shackley. 2013. Transformation of Social Networks in the Late Pre-Hispanic U.S. Southwest. *PNAS* 110(15):5785–5790.

Mindeleff, Cosmos. 1900. *Localization of Tusayan Clans*. Annual Report of the Bureau of American Ethnology, No. 19. Smithsonian Institution, Government Printing Office, Washington, D.C.

Mindeleff, Victor. 1891. *A Study of Pueblo Architecture: Tusayan and Cibola*. Annual Report of the Bureau of American Ethnology, No. 8. Smithsonian Institution, Government Printing Office, Washington, D.C.

Moore, James L., and Jeffrey L. Boyer. 2009. Too Many People: How Tanoan Social Organization Coped with Late Prehistoric Village Aggregation. In *Between the Mountains, Beyond the Mountains: Papers in Honor of Paul R. Williams*, edited by Emily J. Brown, pp. 125–138. Papers of the Archaeological Society of New Mexico, No. 35. Archaeological Society of New Mexico, Albuquerque.

Moore, Jerry D. 2009. The Archaeology of Plazas and the Proxemics of Ritual: Three Andean Traditions. *American Anthropologist* 98(4):789–802.

Morley, Sylvanus G. 1910. The South House at Puye, New Mexico. *Papers of the School of American Archaeology*, No. 7. Santa Fe, New Mexico.

Munson, Marit K. 2002. *On Boundaries and Beliefs: Rock Art and Identity on the Pajarito Plateau*. PhD dissertation, Department of Anthropology, University of New Mexico, Albuquerque.

Naranjo, Tessie. 1995. Thoughts on Migration by Santa Clara Pueblo. *Journal of Anthropological Archaeology* 14:247–250.

Naranjo, Tessie. 2008. Life as Movement: A Tewa View of Community and Identity. In *The Social Construction of Communities: Agency, Structure, and Identity in the Prehispanic Southwest*, edited by Mark D. Varien and James M. Potter, pp. 251–262. AltaMira Press, Lanham, Maryland.

Naranjo, Tessie. 2009. Some Recent Thoughts About Tewa Ancestral Movement. Paper presented at the New Mexico Archaeological Council Fall Conference, November 14, 2009, Albuquerque.

Naranjo, Tito, and Rina Swentzell. 1989. Healing Places in the Tewa Pueblo World. *American Indian Culture and Research Journal* 13(304):257–265.

Naranjo-Morse, Nora, Gail Joice, and Kelly McHugh. 2012. Always Becoming. American Institute for Conservation of Historic and Artistic Works Objects Specialty Group Postprints, Vol. 19:147–157.

Naroll, Raoul. 1962. Floor Area and Settlement Population. *American Antiquity* 27(4): 587–589.

Nelson, Nels. 1916. Chronology of the Tano Ruins, New Mexico. *American Anthropologist* 18(2):159–180.

Norcini, Marilyn. 2007. *Edward P. Dozier: The Paradox of the American Indian Anthropologist*. University of Arizona Press, Tucson.

Olinger, Bart. 1991. Glaze Decorated Pottery of Puye and Picuris Pueblo. In *Puebloan Past and Present: Papers in Honor of Steward Peckham*, edited by Meliha S. Duran and David T. Kirkpatrick, pp. 133–139. The Archaeological Society of New Mexico, Vol. 17. Albuquerque.

Olsen, Nancy H. 2004. Rock Art on the Pajarito Plateau. In *Archaeology of Bandelier National Monument: Village Formation on the Pajarito Plateau, New Mexico*, edited by Timothy A. Kohler, pp. 265–292. University of New Mexico Press, Albuquerque.

Orcutt, Janet D. 1991. Environmental Variability and Settlement Changes on the Pajarito Plateau, New Mexico. *American Antiquity* 56(2):315–332.

Orcutt, Janet D. 1999. Demography, Settlement, and Agriculture. In *The Bandelier Archaeological Survey*, edited by Robert P. Powers and Janet D. Orcutt, pp. 219–308. Vol. 1, Anthropology Projects, Cultural Resources Management, Intermountain Region, National Park Service, Department of the Interior, Santa Fe, New Mexico.

Ortiz, Alfonso. 1965. Dual Organization as an Operational Concept in the Pueblo Southwest. *Ethnology* 4:389–396.

Ortiz, Alfonso. 1969. *The Tewa World: Space, Time, Being, and Becoming in a Pueblo Society*. University of Chicago Press, Chicago.

Ortiz, Alfonso. 1972. Ritual Drama and the Pueblo World View. In *New Perspectives on the Pueblos*, edited by Alfonso Ortiz, pp. 135–162. University of New Mexico Press, Albuquerque.

Ortiz, Alfonso (editor). 1972. *New Perspectives on the Pueblos*. University of New Mexico Press, Albuquerque.

Ortiz, Alfonso. 1977. Some Concerns Central to the Writing of "Indian" History. *The Indian Historian* 10(1):17–22.

Ortiz, Alfonso. 1979. San Juan Pueblo. In *Southwest*, edited by Alfonso Ortiz, pp. 278–295. Handbook of North American Indians, Vol. 9, W. G. Sturtevant, general editor. Smithsonian Institution Press, Washington, D.C.

Ortiz, Alfonso (editor). 1979. *Southwest*. Handbook of North American Indians, Vol. 9, W.G. Sturtevant, general editor. Smithsonian Institution Press, Washington, D.C.

Ortiz, Alfonso. 1991. Through Tewa Eyes: Origins. *National Geographic* 180(4):6–13.
Ortiz, Alfonso. 1994. The Dynamics of Pueblo Cultural Survival. In *North American Indian Anthropology: Essays on Society and Culture*, edited by Raymond J. DeMallie and Alfonso Ortiz, pp. 296–306.
Ortman, Scott G. 2010. Evidence of a Mesa Verde Homeland for the Tewa Pueblo. In *Leaving Mesa Verde: Peril and Change in the Thirteenth-Century Southwest*, edited by Timothy A. Kohler, Mark D. Varien, and Aaron M. Wright, pp. 222–261. University of Arizona Press, Tucson.
Ortman, Scott G. 2011. Bowls to Gardens: A History of Tewa Community Metaphors. In *Religious Transformation in the Late Pre-Hispanic Pueblo World*, edited by Donna M. Glowacki and Scott Van Keuren, pp. 84–108. University of Arizona Press, Tucson.
Ortman, Scott G. 2012. *Winds from the North: Tewa Origins and Historical Anthropology*. University of Utah Press, Salt Lake City.
Ortman, Scott G. 2016a. Uniform Probability Density Analysis and Population History in the Northern Rio Grande. *Journal of Archaeological Method and Theory* 23(1):95–126.
Ortman, Scott G. 2016b. Discourse and Human Securities in Tewa Origins. *Archaeological Papers of the American Anthropological Association* 27:74–94.
Ortman, Scott G. 2018. The Historical Anthropology of Tewa Social Organization. In *Puebloan Societies: Homology and Heterogeneity in Time and Space*, edited by Peter M. Whiteley, pp. 75–102. School for Advanced Research Press, Santa Fe, New Mexico.
Parsons, Elsie Clews. 1923. Notes on San Felipe and Santo Domingo. *American Anthropologist* 25(4):485–494.
Parsons, Elsie Clews. 1924. Tewa Kin, Clan, and Moiety. *American Anthropologist* 26(3):333–339.
Parsons, Elsie Clews. 1925. *The Pueblo of Jemez*. Papers of the Phillips Academy Southwestern Expedition, Yale University Press, New Haven, Connecticut.
Parsons, Elsie Clews 1929. *The Social Organization of the Tewa of New Mexico*. Memoirs of the American Anthropological Association No. 36. American Anthropological Association, Menasha, Wisconsin.
Parsons, Elsie Clews. 1933. *Hopi and Zuñi Ceremonialism*. Memoirs of the American Anthropological Association No. 39. American Anthropological Association, Menasha, Wisconsin.
Parsons, Elsie Clews. 1994[1926]. *Tewa Tales*. University of Arizona Press, Tucson.
Parsons, Elsie Clews. 1996[1939]. *Pueblo Indian Religion*. University of Nebraska Press, Lincoln.
Peckham, Stewart L. 1981. The Palisade Ruin. In *Collected Papers in Honor of Erik Kellerman Reed*, edited by Albert H. Schroeder, pp. 113–147. Vol. 6. Archaeological Society of New Mexico, Albuquerque.
Peckham, Stewart L., and Bart Olinger. 1990. Postulated Movements of the Tano or Southern Tewa, A.D. 1300–1700. In *Collected Papers in Honor of William M. Sundt*, edited by Meliha S. Duran and David T. Kirkpatrick, pp. 203–215. Papers of the Archaeological Society of New Mexico, No. 16, Albuquerque.

Phillips, David A., Christine E. Vanpool, and Todd L. Vanpool. 2007. The Horned Serpent Tradition in the North American Southwest. In *Religion in the Prehispanic Southwest*, edited by Christin S. Vanpool, Todd L. Vanpool, and David A. Phillips, pp. 17–30. AltaMira Press, Lanham, Maryland.

Post, Stephen. 1994. Archaeological Testing and Treatment Plan for a Late Archaic Period Site and Three Coalition-Early Classic Period Sites, Estates V and Other Areas, Las Campanas de Santa Fe, Santa Fe County, New Mexico. Archaeology Notes 140. Office of Archaeological Studies, Museum of New Mexico, Santa Fe.

Post, Stephen S. 2013. Transitional Archaic and Emergent Agricultural Settlement in the Lowland-Upland Settings of the Northern Rio Grande, New Mexico. In *From Mountaintop to Valley Bottoms: Understanding Past Land Use in the Northern Rio Grande Valley, New Mexico*, edited by Bradley J. Vierra, pp. 80–94. University of Utah Press, Salt Lake City.

Preucel, Robert W. 1987. Settlement Succession on the Pajarito Plateau, New Mexico. *Kiva* 53(1):3–33.

Preucel, Robert W. 1988. *Seasonal Agricultural Circulation and Residential Mobility: A Prehistoric Example from the Pajarito Plateau, New Mexico.* Unpublished doctoral dissertation, University of California, Los Angeles.

Preucel, Robert W. 2000. Living on the Mesa: Hanat Kotyiti, a Post-revolt Cochiti Community in the Northern Rio Grande. *Expedition* 42:8–17.

Preucel, Robert W. 2005a. Ethnicity and Southwestern Archaeology. In *Southwestern Archaeology in the Twentieth Century*, edited by Linda S. Cordell and Don D. Fowler, pp. 174–193. University of Utah Press, Salt Lake City.

Preucel, Robert W. 2005b. The Journey from Shipap. In *The Peopling of Bandelier: New Insights from the Archaeology of the Pajarito Plateau*, edited by Robert P. Powers. School for Advanced Research Press, Santa Fe, New Mexico.

Preucel, Robert W. 2006. *Archaeological Semiotics*. Blackwell, Oxford.

Preucel, Robert W. 2013. Review of *Winds from the North: Tewa Origins and Historical Anthropology*, by Scott G. Ortman. *New Mexico Historical Review* 88(3):364–365.

Preucel, Robert W., and Joseph Aguilar. 2018. From Mission to Mesa: Reconstructing Pueblo Social Networks during the Pueblo Revolt Period. In *Puebloan Societies: Homology and Heterogeneity in Time and Space*, edited by Peter M. Whiteley, pp. 207–236. School for Advanced Research Press, Santa Fe, New Mexico.

Preucel, Robert W., and Samuel Duwe. 2019. Engaging with Pueblo Movement: An Introduction. In *The Continuous Path: Pueblo Movement and the Archaeology of Becoming*, edited by Samuel Duwe and Robert W. Preucel, pp. 1–33. University of Arizona Press, Tucson.

Preucel, Robert W., Loa P. Traxler, and Michael Wilcox. 2002. "Now the God of the Spaniards Is Dead": Ethnogenesis and Community Formation in the Aftermath of the Pueblo Revolt of 1680. In *Traditions, Transitions, and Technologies: Themes in Southwestern Archaeology*, edited by Sarah H. Schlanger, pp. 71–93. University Press of Colorado, Boulder.

Quintela, Daniel. 2018. *Late Coalition Period Tewa Pueblos in the Rio Chama Valley: Understanding Cultural Coalescence Through Lithic Artifacts.* Poster presented at 83rd Annual Meeting of the Society for American Archaeology, Washington, D.C.

Ramenofsky, Ann F. 1988. *Vectors of Death: The Archaeology of European Contact.* University of New Mexico Press, Albuquerque.

Ramenofsky, Ann F., and C. David Vaughan. 2003. Jars Full of Shiny Metal: Analyzing Barrionuevo's Visit to Yuque Yunque. In *The Coronado Expedition: From the Distance of 460 Years*, edited by Richard Flint and Shirley Cushing Flint, pp. 116–139. University of New Mexico Press, Albuquerque:

Ramenofsky, Ann F., and James K. Feathers. 2002. Documents, Ceramics, Tree Rings, and Luminescence: Estimating Final Native Abandonment of the Lower Rio Chama. *Journal of Anthropological Research* 58:121–159.

Reed, Eric K. 1949. Sources of Rio Grande Culture and Population. *El Palacio* 56:163–184.

Reed, Paul F. 2000. Fundamental Issues in Basketmaker Archaeology. In *Foundations of Anasazi Culture: The Basketmaker-Pueblo Transition*, edited by Paul F. Reed, pp. 1–18. University of Utah Press, Salt Lake City.

Reid, J. Jefferson, Michael B. Schiffer, Stephanie M. Whittlesey, Madeline J. Hinkins, Alan P. Sullivan III, Christian E Downum, William A. Longacrea, and H. David Tuggle. 1989. Perception and Interpretation in Contemporary Southwestern Archaeology: Comments on Cordell, Upham, and Brock. *American Antiquity* 54:802–814.

Riggs, Charles R. 2001. *The Architecture of Grasshopper Pueblo.* University of Utah Press, Salt Lake City.

Riley, Carroll L. 1987. *The Frontier People: The Greater Southwest in the Protohistoric Period.* University of New Mexico Press, Albuquerque.

Riley, Carroll L. 1995. *Rio del Norte: People of the Upper Rio Grande from Earliest Times to the Pueblo Revolt.* University of Utah Press, Salt Lake City.

Riley, Carroll L. 1999. *The Kachina and the Cross: Indians and Spaniards in the Early Southwest.* University of Utah Press, Salt Lake City.

Robbins, Wilfred W., John P. Harrington, and Barbara Freire-Marreco. 1916. *Ethnobotany of the Tewa Indians.* Bulletin 55, U.S. Bureau of American Ethnology, Washington, D.C.

Rocek, Thomas R. 1995. Sedentarization and Agricultural Dependence: Perspectives from the Pithouse-to-Pueblo Transition in the American Southwest. *American Antiquity* 60(2):218–239.

Rose, Martin R., Jeffrey S. Dean, and William J. Robinson. 1981. The Past Climate of Arroyo Hondo, New Mexico, Reconstructed from Tree Rings. Arroyo Hondo Archaeological Series Vol. 4. School of American Research, Santa Fe, New Mexico.

Saitta, Dean J. 1997. Power, Labor, and the Dynamics of Change in Chacoan Political Economy. *American Antiquity* 62(1):7–26.

Sando, Joe S. 1979. The Pueblo Revolt. In *Southwest*, edited by Alfonso Ortiz, pp. 194–197. Handbook of North American Indians, Vol. 9. Smithsonian Institution Press, Washington, D.C.

Schaafsma, Curtis F. 1978. Archaeological Studies in the Abiquiu Reservoir District. *Discovery (Santa Fe: School of American Research)*:41–69.

Schaafsma, Curtis F. 1979. *The Cerrito Site (AR-4), a Piedra Lumbre Phase Settlement at Abiquiu Reservoir*. School of American Research, Santa Fe, New Mexico.

Schaafsma, Curtis F. 2002. *Apaches de Navajo: Seventeenth-Century Navajos in the Chama Valley of New Mexico*. University of Utah Press, Salt Lake City.

Schaafsma, Polly. 2000. *Warrior, Shield, and Star*. Western Edge Press, Santa Fe, New Mexico.

Schachner, Gregson. 2018. Forging New Intellectual Genealogies in Southwest Archaeology. In *Footprints of Hopi History: Hopihiniwtiput Kukveni'at*, edited by Leigh J. Kuwanwisiwma, T. J. Ferguson, and Chip Colwell, pp. 214–229. University of Arizona Press, Tucson.

Scheick, Cherie L. 2003. Archaeological Investigations of a Middle to Late Developmental Period Site Adjacent to Fort Marcy Hill, Santa Fe, New Mexico. Southwest Archaeological Consultants Research Series 454d, Santa Fe.

Scheick, Cherie L. 2005. Coalition Period Remains Under the West Alcove, U.S. Federal Courthouse, Santa Fe, New Mexico. Southwest Archaeological Consultants Research Series 477c, Santa Fe.

Schiffer, Michael B. 1972. Cultural Laws and the Reconstruction of Past Lifeways. *Kiva* 37:1489–157.

Schiffer, Michael B. 1986. Radiocarbon Dating and the "Old Wood" Problem: The Case of the Hohokam Chronology. *Journal of Archaeological Science* 13:13–30.

Schillaci, Michael A., and Steven A. Lakatos. 2016. Refiguring the Population History of the Tewa Basin. *Kiva* 82(4):364–386.

Schillaci, Michael A., and Steven A. Lakatos. 2017. The Emergence of Kwahe'e Black-on-white Pottery in the Tewa Basin, New Mexico. *Journal of Field Archaeology* 42(2):152–160.

Schillaci, Michael A., Steven A. Lakatos, and Logan D. Sutton. 2017. Tewa Place Names for Early Habitation Sites in the Northern Rio Grande Valley, New Mexico. *Journal of Field Archaeology* 42(2):142–151.

Schmidt, Peter R., and Stephen A. Mrozowski. 2013. The Death of Prehistory: Reforming the Past, Looking to the Future. In *The Death of Prehistory*, edited by Peter R. Schmidt and Stephen A. Mrozowski, pp. 1–28. Oxford University Press, Oxford.

Schroeder, Albert H. 1968. Shifting for Survival in the Spanish Southwest. *New Mexico Historical Review* 43(4):291–310.

Schroeder, Albert H. 1979. Pueblos Abandoned in Historic Times. In *Southwest*, edited by Alfonso Ortiz, pp. 236–254. Handbook of North American Indians, Vol. 9. Smithsonian Institution Press, Washington, D.C.

Schroeder, Albert H. 1984. The Tewa Indians of the Rio Grande and Their Neighbors, A.D. 1450–1689. In *Guidebook to the 35th Field Conference of the New Mexico Geological Society*, edited by W. Scott Baldridge, Patricia W. Dickerson, Robert E. Riecker, and Jiri Zidek, pp. 283–286. New Mexico Geological Society, Socorro, New Mexico.

Schroeder, Albert H., and Dan S. Matson. 1965. *A Colony on the Move: Gaspar Castaño de Sosa's Journal, 1590–1591*. University of New Mexico Press, Albuquerque.

Shackley, M. Steven. 2011. Sources of Archaeological Dacite in Northern New Mexico. *Journal of Archaeological Science* 38:1001–1007.

Shepard, Anna O. 1936. The Technology of Pecos Pottery. In *The Pottery of Pecos*, edited by Alfred V. Kidder. Yale University Press, New Haven, Connecticut.

Shepard, Anna O. 1942. *Rio Grande Glaze Paint Ware: A Study Illustrating the Place of Ceramic Technological Analysis in Archaeological Research*. Contributions to American Anthropology and History, No. 39. Carnegie Institution of Washington, Publication 528, pp. 129–262, Washington, D.C.

Shure, Stephen William. 1973. Site LA908 (Tsama Ruin) Report. Manuscript on file, Maxwell Center for Archaeological Research, University of New Mexico, Albuquerque.

Silko, Leslie Marmon. 1995. Interior and Exterior Landscapes: The Pueblo Migration Stories. In *Landscape in America*, edited by George F. Thompson, pp. 155–169. University of Texas Press, Austin.

Simmons, Marc. 1987. The Spaniards of San Gabriel. In *When Cultures Meet: Remembering San Gabriel del Yunge Oweenge*, pp. 39–62. Papers from the October 20, 1984 conference held at San Juan Pueblo, New Mexico. Sunstone Press, Santa Fe, New Mexico.

Simmons, Marc. 1991. *The Last Conquistador: Juan de Oñate and the Settling of the Far Southwest*. University of Oklahoma Press, Norman.

Smiley, Terah L. 1951. *A Summary of Tree-Ring Dates from Some Southwestern Archaeological Sites*. University of Arizona Bulletin 22, Laboratory of Tree-Ring Research Bulletin 5, Laboratory of Tree-Ring Research, Tucson.

Smiley, Terah L., Stanley A. Stubbs, and Bryant Bannister. 1953. *A Foundation for Dating of Some Late Archaeological Sites in the Rio Grande Area, New Mexico: Based on Studies in Tree-Ring Methods and Pottery Analyses*. University of Arizona Bulletin 24(3), Laboratory of Tree-Ring Research Bulletin 6, Laboratory of Tree-Ring Research, Tucson.

Smith, Claire, and H. Martin Wobst (editors). 2005. *Indigenous Archaeologies: Decolonizing Theory and Practice*. Routledge, London.

Smith, Gary A., and Bruce B. Huckell. 2005. The Geological and Geoarchaeological Significance of Cerro Pedernal, Rio Arriba County, New Mexico. *New Mexico Geological Society Guidebook, 52nd Field Conference, Geology of the Chama Basin*, edited by Spencer G. Lucas, Kate E. Zeigler, Virgil W. Lueth, and Donald E. Owen, pp. 425–431. New Mexico Geological Survey, Albuquerque.

Snead, James E. 2001. *Ruins and Rivals: The Making of Southwest Archaeology*. University of Arizona Press, Tucson.

Snead, James E. 2008. *Ancestral Landscapes of the Pueblo World*. University of Arizona Press, Tucson.

Snead, James E., and Robert W. Preucel. 1999. The Ideology of Settlement: Ancestral Keres Landscapes in the Northern Rio Grande. In *Archaeologists of Landscape: Contemporary Perspectives*, edited by Wendy Ashmore and A. Bernard Knapp, pp. 169–200. Blackwell Publishing, Oxford.

Speirs, Randall Hannaford 1966. *Some Aspects of the Structure of Rio Grande Tewa*. PhD dissertation, State University of New York, Buffalo.
Spielmann, Katherine A. 2005 Ethnographic Analogy and Ancestral Pueblo Archaeology. In *Southwest Archaeology in the Twentieth Century*, edited by Linda S. Cordell and Don D. Fowler, pp. 194–203. University of Utah Press, Salt Lake City.
Stahle, D. W., E. R. Cook, M. K. Cleaveland, M. D. Therrell, D. M. Meko, and H. D. Grissino-Mayer. 2000. Tree-Ring Data Document 16th Century Megadrought over North America. *Eos, Transactions, American Geophysical Union* 81:121–125.
Stallings, William A. 1937. Southwest Dated Ruins. *Tree-Ring Bulletin* 4(2):3–5.
Steen, Charlie R. 1977. Pajarito Plateau: Archaeological Survey and Excavations. Los Alamos Scientific Laboratory, Los Alamos, New Mexico.
Steen, Charlie R. 1982. Pajarito Plateau Archaeological Surveys and Excavations II. Los Alamos National Laboratory, LA-8860-NERP, Los Alamos, New Mexico.
Stein, John R., and Stephen H. Lekson. 1992. Anasazi Ritual Landscapes. In *Anasazi Regional Organization and the Chaco System*, edited by David E. Doyel, pp. 87–100. Anthropological Papers No. 5. Maxwell Museum of Anthropology, University of New Mexico, Albuquerque.
Steponaitis, Vincas P., and Keith W. Kintigh. 1993. Estimating Site Occupation Spans from Dated Artifact Types: Some New Approaches. In *Archaeology of Eastern North America: Papers in Honor of Stephen Williams*, edited by J. B. Stoltman, pp. 349–361. Archaeological Report, No. 25. Mississippi Department of Archives and History, Jackson.
Strong, Pauline Turner. 1996. Introduction. In *Pueblo Indian Religion, Vol. 1*, by Elsie Clews Parsons, pp. v–xxvii. University of Nebraska Press, Lincoln.
Stuart, David E., and Rory P. Gauthier. 1981. *Prehistoric New Mexico: Background for Survey*. Office of Cultural Affairs, Historic Preservation Division, State of New Mexico, Santa Fe.
Stubbs, Stanley A., and William A. Stallings. 1953. *The Excavation of Pindi Pueblo, New Mexico*. Monographs of the School of American Research and the Laboratory of Anthropology 18. School of American Research Press, Santa Fe, New Mexico.
Suina, Joseph H. 1992. Pueblo Secrecy: Result of Intrusion. *New Mexico Magazine* 70(1):60–63.
Suina, Joseph H. 2019. Getting Accustomed to the Light. In *The Continuous Path: Pueblo Movement and the Archaeology of Becoming*, edited by Samuel Duwe and Robert W. Preucel, pp. 242–253. University of Arizona Press, Tucson.
Sweet, Jill. 2004. *Dances of the Tewa Pueblo Indians: Expressions of New Life*. 2nd ed. School of American Research Press, Santa Fe, New Mexico.
Swentzell, Porter. 2018. Place-Based Education and Sovereignty: Traditional Arts at the Institute of American Indian Arts. PhD dissertation, School of Social Transformation, Arizona State University, Tempe.
Swentzell, Rina. 1988. Bupingeh: The Pueblo Plaza. *El Palacio* 94(2):14–19.
Swentzell, Rina. 1989. The Butterfly Effect: A Conversation with Rina Swentzell. *El Palacio* 95(1):24–29.

Swentzell, Rina. 1990. Pueblo Space, Form, and Mythology. In *Pueblo Style and Regional Architecture*, edited by Nicholas C. Markovich, Wolfgang F. R. Preiser, and Fred Sturm, pp. 23–30. Van Nostrand Reinhold, New York.

Swentzell, Rina. 1991. Levels of Truth: Southwest Archaeologists and Anasazi/Pueblo People. In *Puebloan Past and Present: Paper in Honor of Stewart Peckham*, pp. 177–181. Archaeological Society of New Mexico, Albuquerque.

Swentzell, Rina. 1993. Mountain Form, Village Form: Unity in the Pueblo World. In *Ancient Land, Ancestral Places: Paul Logsdon in the Pueblo Southwest*, edited by Stephen H. Lekson and Rina Swentzell, 139–147. Museum New Mexico Press, Albuquerque.

Tichy, Marjorie F. 1944. Exploratory Work at Yunque Yunque. *El Palacio* L1:11:22–24.

Titiev, Mischa. 1944. *Old Oraibi: A Study of the Hopi Indians of Third Mesa*. Papers of the Peabody Museum of American Archaeology and Ethnology Vol. 22, No. 1, Harvard University, Cambridge, Massachusetts.

Tosa, Paul, Matthew J. Liebmann, T. J. Ferguson, and John R. Welch. 2019. Movement Encased in Tradition and Stone: Hemish Migration, Land Use, and Identity. In *The Continuous Path: Pueblo Movement and the Archaeology of Becoming*, edited by Samuel Duwe and Robert W. Preucel, pp. 60–77. University of Arizona Press, Tucson.

Tosa, Paul, and Octavius Seowtewa. 2019. Movement and Becoming: A Pueblo Perspective. In *The Continuous Path: Pueblo Movement and the Archaeology of Becoming*, edited by Samuel Duwe and Robert W. Preucel, pp. 254–259. University of Arizona Press, Tucson.

Towner, Ronald H., and Mathew W. Salzer. 2013. Dendroclimatic Reconstruction of Precipitation for the Northern Rio Grande. In *From Mountaintop to Valley Bottom: Understanding Past Land Use in the Northern Rio Grande Valley, New Mexico*, edited by Bradley J. Vierra, pp. 54–68. University of Utah Press, Salt Lake City.

Trott, J. James, and Michael Taylor. 1994. Tsiping Ruin: Stabilization Assessment and Preservation Plan. Report No. 1994-10-010, Manuscript on file, National Park Service, Southwest Regional Office, Santa Fe, New Mexico.

Upham, Steadman. 1987. The Tyranny of Ethnographic Analogy in Southwestern Archaeology. In *Coasts, Plains and Deserts: Essays in Honor of Reynold J. Ruppé*, edited by Sylvia Gaines and G. A. Clark, pp. 265–279. Anthropological Research Paper No. 38. Arizona State University, Tempe.

Van Dyke, Ruth M. 2008. *The Chaco Experience: Landscape and Ideology at the Center Place*. School of Advanced Research Press, Santa Fe, New Mexico.

Van West, Carla R., Thomas C. Windes, Frances Levine, Henri D. Grissimo-Mayer, and Matthew W. Salzer. 2013. The Role of Climate in Early Spanish-Native American Interactions in the U.S. Southwest. In *Native and Spanish New Worlds: Sixteenth-Century Entradas in the American Southwest and Southeast*, edited by Clay Mathers, Jeffrey M. Mitchem, and Charles M. Haecker, pp. 81–98. University of Arizona Press, Tucson.

Vélez de Escalante, Silvestre. 1778. Letter to Fray Juan Augustin Morfi, August 2. Reprinted in *The Land of Sunshine*, vol. XII (December 1899–May 1900), edited by Charles Lummis. Land of Sunshine, Los Angeles.

Vélez de Escalante, Silvestre, and Ted J. Warner. 1995. *The Dominguez-Escalante Journal: Their Expedition Through Colorado, Utah, Arizona, and New Mexico in 1776*. University of Utah Press, Salt Lake City.

Vierra, Bradley J. 2005. Ancient Foragers of the High Desert Country. In *The Peopling of Bandelier: New Insights from the Archaeology of the Pajarito Plateau*, edited by Robert P. Powers, pp. 19–26. School of American Research Press, Santa Fe, New Mexico.

Vierra, Bradley J., and Richard I. Ford. 2007. Foragers and Farmers in the Northern Rio Grande Valley, New Mexico. *Kiva* 73(2):117–130.

Voss, Barbara L. 2008. *The Archaeology of Ethnogenesis: Race and Sexuality in Colonial San Francisco*. University of California Press, Berkeley.

Voss, Barbara L. 2015. What's New? Rethinking Ethnogenesis in the Archaeology of Colonialism. *American Antiquity* 80(4):655-670.

Walker, William H. 1998. Where Are the Witches of Prehistory? *Journal of Archaeological Method and Theory* 5(3):245–308.

Walker, William H., Vincent M. LaMotta, and E. Charles Adams. 2000. Katsinas and Kiva Abandonment at Homol'ovi: A Deposit-Oriented Perspective on Religion in Southwest Prehistory. In *The Archaeology of Regional Interaction*, edited by Michelle Hegmon, pp. 341–360. University Press of Colorado, Boulder.

Walsh, Michael R. Lines in the Sand: Competition and Stone Selection on the Pajarito Plateau, New Mexico. *American Antiquity* 63(4):573–593.

Walt, Henry. 2014. The Western Homeland of Ohkay Owingeh: The Use and Ancestral Occupation of the Chama Watershed. Prepared for Ohkay Owingeh (San Juan Pueblo. New Mexico vs. Aragon).

Ware, John A. 2014. *A Pueblo Social History Kinship, Sodality, and Community in the Northern Southwest*. School for Advanced Research Press, Santa Fe, New Mexico.

Warren, A. Helene. 1974. The Ancient Mineral Industries of Cerro Pedernal, Rio Arriba County, New Mexico. *New Mexico Geological Society Guidebook, 25th Field Conference, Ghost Ranch (Central-Northern N.M.)*, edited by Charles T. Siemers, Lee A. Woodward, and Jonathan F. Callender, pp. 87–93. New Mexico Geological Survey, Albuquerque.

Watkins, Joe. 2000. *Indigenous Archaeology: American Indian Values and Scientific Practice*. AltaMira Press, Lanham, Maryland.

Weber, M. 1978. *Economy and Society: An Outline of Interpretive Sociology*. University of California Press, Berkeley.

Weigle, Marta. 1989. From Desert to Disney World: The Santa Fe Railway and the Fred Harvey Company Display in the Indian Southwest. *Journal of Anthropological Research* 45(1):115–137.

Weigle, Marta. 1990. Southwest Lures: Innocents Detoured, Incensed Determined. *Journal of the Southwest* 32(4):499–540.

Weik, T. M. 2014. The Archaeology of Ethnogenesis. *Annual Reviews in Anthropology* 43:291–305.

Wendorf, Fred. 1953. Excavations at Te'ewi. In *Salvage Archaeology of the Chama Valley, New Mexico*, edited by Fred Wendorf. School of American Research Press, Santa Fe, New Mexico.

Wendorf, Fred. 1954. A Reconstruction of Northern Rio Grande Prehistory. *American Anthropologist* 56(2):200–227.

Wendorf, Fred, and Erik K. Reed. 1955. An Alternative Reconstruction of Rio Grande Prehistory. *El Palacio* 62(5–6):131–173.

White, Leslie A. 1935. *The Pueblo of Santo Domingo, New Mexico*. Memoirs of the American Anthropological Association 43. American Anthropological Association, Washington, D.C.

White, Leslie A. 1942. *The Pueblo of Santa Ana, New Mexico*. Memoirs of the American Anthropological Association 44. American Anthropological Association, Washington, D.C.

White, Leslie A. 1962. *The Pueblo of Sia, New Mexico*. Bureau of American Ethnology Bulletin 184, Washington, D.C.

White, Sam. 2014. Cold, Drought, and Disaster: The Little Ice Age and the Spanish Conquest of New Mexico. *New Mexico Historical Review* 89(4):425–458.

Whiteley, Peter. 1993. The End of Anthropology (at Hopi)? *Journal of the Southwest* 35(2):125–157.

Whiteley, Peter M. 1999. Alfonso Ortiz (1939–1997). *American Anthropologist* 101(2): 392–395.

Whiteley, Peter M. 2004. Social Formations in the Pueblo IV Southwest: An Ethnological View. In *The Protohistoric Pueblo World: A.D. 1275–1600*, edited by E. Charles Adams and Andrew I. Duff, pp. 144–156. University of Arizona Press, Tucson.

Whiteley, Peter. 2015. Chacoan Kinship. In *Chaco Revisited: New Research on the Prehistory of Chaco Canyon, New Mexico*, edited by Carrie C. Heitman and Stephen Plog, pp. 272–304. University of Arizona Press, Tucson.

Whiteley, Peter (editor). 2018. *Puebloan Societies: Homology and Heterogeneity in Time and Space*. School for Advanced Research Press, Santa Fe, New Mexico.

Whitman, William. 1947. *The Pueblo Indians of San Ildefonso: A Changing Culture*. Columbia University Contributions to Anthropology 34, New York.

Wilcox, Michael V. 2009. *The Pueblo Revolt and the Mythology of Conquest an Indigenous Archaeology*. University of California Press, Berkeley.

Wilson, Chris. 1997. *The Myth of Santa Fe: Creating a Modern Regional Tradition*. University of New Mexico Press, Albuquerque.

Wilson, Gordon P. 2007. *Guide to Ceramic Identification: Northern Rio Grande Valley and Galisteo Basin to A.D. 1700*. 2nd ed. Laboratory of Anthropology Technical Series Bulletin No. 12. Laboratory of Anthropology, Santa Fe, New Mexico.

Windes, Thomas C. 1970. Report on Excavation at Tsama LA 908 Near Abiquiu, New Mexico, Summer 1970, West Mound West Rooms and West Mound Kiva W-4. Unpublished manuscript on file at ARMS, Museum of New Mexico, Santa Fe.

Windes, Thomas C. 1978. Stones Circles of Chaco Canyon, Northwestern New Mexico. Reports of the Chaco Center No. 8. Division of Cultural Research, National Park Service, Albuquerque, New Mexico.

Windes, Thomas C., and Peter J. McKenna. 2006. The Kivas of Tsama (LA 908). In *Southwestern Interludes: Papers in Honor of Charlotte J. and Theodore R. Frisbie*, Vol. 32, edited by Regge N. Wiseman, Thomas C. O'Laughlin, and Cordelia T. Snow, pp. 233–253. Archaeological Society of New Mexico, Albuquerque.

Winship, George Parker. 1896. The Coronado Expedition, 1540-1542. In *Fourteenth Annual Report of the Bureau of Ethnology, 1892–93*. Government Printing Office, Washington, D.C.

Wissler, Clark. 1917. *The American Indian: An Introduction to the Anthropology of the New World*. Douglas C. McMurtrie, New York.

Woodbury, Richard B. 1979. Zuni Prehistory and History to 1850. In *Handbook of North American Indians: Volume 9, Southwest*, edited by Alfonso Ortiz, pp. 474–481. Smithsonian Institution Press, Washington, D.C.

Woodbury, Richard. 1993. *Sixty Years of Southwestern Archaeology: A History of the Pecos Conference*. University of New Mexico Press, Albuquerque.

Wozniak, Frank E. 1992. Ethnohistory of the Abiquiu Reservoir Area. In *History and Ethnohistory Along the Rio Chama*, prepared by John D. Schelberg and Ronald Kneebone. Manuscript on file at the U.S. Army Corps of Engineers, Albuquerque District.

INDEX

f denotes a figure, and *t* denotes a table.

abandonment: critique, 190; Historic period, 211; relation to concept of occupation, 191; traditional southwestern archaeology views, 24, 189–190; villages in Rio Grande, 188
Abiquiú, 70, 80, 117, 209, 216, 222, 223
Abiquiu Black-on-gray: correlation with identity, 83; description, 84*t*, 122, 137, 159; observed frequencies of exchange between the Chama and Pajarito Plateau, 167
Abiquiu Reservoir, 29, 125, 129, 131, 133, 210
acequia madre, 198
Acoma Pueblo: collaborative archaeology, 15; kinship, 9; landscape concepts, 24; massacre, 8, 198–99; San Esteban feast day, 236
Adler, Michael, 190
aggregation. *See* coalescence
Agoyo, Herman, 57
Aguilar, Joseph, 69, 213
alumbre. *See* rock alum

Always Becoming, 3–5, 17, 18, 231
Anschuetz, Kurt, 24, 64, 65, 73, 89, 97, 107–108, 119, 120, 147 151–152, 163, 172, 220
Apache, 8, 39; hostility with Pueblos, 188, 191; Tewa oral tradition, 39; trading and raiding, 204, 206–207; Western Apache landscapes, 28
Archaeological Institute of America, 11
Archaeological Records Management Section (ARMS), 229
archaeology: collaborative, 15, 26–27; historical approaches, 13–14, 16; Indigenous, 14; New Archaeology, 12; post-colonial critique, 14; processualism, 13; surface, 76
Archaic period, 64
Arroyo Hondo, 116
ash pile, 54–55, 82, 92, 93
awanyu, 95, 177
axis mundi, 53

Bandelier, Adolph, 11, 12, 32, 61, 72, 77, 142, 152, 169

Bandelier Black-on gray, 85*f*; correlation with identity, 83; description, 84*t*, 122; observed frequencies of exchange between the Chama and Pajarito Plateau, 167
Bandelier National Monument, 12, 154, 240
Barrett, Elinore, 188, 223–24
Barrionuevo, Rodrigo de, 192, 194, 196, 205, 206, 224
Basso, Keith, 28
Bernardini, Wesley, 109, 147
Bernstein, Bruce, 69
Binford, Lewis, 13
biscuitware, 122; ethnic and linguistic boundaries, 67; production and distribution between Chama and Pajarito Plateau, 166. *See also* Abiquiu Black-on-gray, Bandelier Black-on-gray, biscuitware area
biscuitware area, 72, 77, 83
Black Mesa. *See* Tunyo
Boyer, Jeffrey, 182
Bureau of American Ethnology, 11, 28
Burnt Corn Pueblo, 93, 94, 137

Cajete, Gregory, 56, 217
Cañones Creek, 123, 136
Castañeda, Pedro de, 194
Castaño de Sosa, Gaspar, 194, 196–97, 204, 211, 214, 224
Catholic Church, 41, 44, 69, 189, 198, 202, 203,
Ceramic: analysis, 83–86; provenance study, 98–99, 158
Cerro Colorado (LA 370), 74*f*, 75*t*, 153*f*, 156*f*, 159, 171*t*, 205
Cerro Pedernal. *See* Tsipin
Chaco: Chaco Culture National Historic Park, 238; great houses architecture, 116; Phenomenon, 146, 148; shrines, 94, 120; twelfth-century reorganization, 189
channel shrines, 94–95, 133, 134

chert, 64, 129 210, 222. *See also* Tsipin (Cerro Pedernal)
Chimayó, 60
circular shrine, 52, 97, 177. *See also* hunt shrine
Classic period, 63*f*; architecture and settlement patterns, 155–58; coalescence, 152–164; identity, 179–181; sacred geographies, 172–79; summary in the northern Rio Grande, 67–68
classification, 19; critiques of, 62
climate: fourteenth-century drought; microclimate and maize agriculture, 89; severe drought in 1670s, 212; sixteenth-century megadrought, 206; Tewa Basin, 29
clowns (Kosa and Kwirana), 10, 39, 46, 136
coalescence: catalysts, 161–62, 164–65; Classic period, 152–164; definition, 67; Pueblo III-Pueblo IV transition, 103; serial coalescence, 112; sixteenth century in Chama, 205
Coalition period, 63*f*; summary in the northern Rio Grande, 65–66
Cochiti Pueblo, 51, 154, 208, 212, 213, 219
Coronado, Francisco Vasquez de, 8, 30, 159, 185, 186, 193, 211, 224,
Cruz, Patrick, 111
cupule shrines: Classic period, 172–76; description, 91–93; Galisteo Basin, 120; gendered, 179-180; Tsama'owingeh, 119; Tsipin,owingeh, 131, 133; LA 142926, 120; LA 142927, 131; Sandoval Pueblo, 133; Taos area, 120
Cushing, Frank Hamilton, 11, 21

D-shaped kiva, 116–17
dacite, 129
Darling, Andrew, 82–83
dendrochronology, 19, 74, 86, 154
Developmental period, 63*f*; summary in the northern Rio Grande, 65
directional shrines (xayeh t'a pingeh), 44, 55, 93, 107, 120, 174, 179,

doings, 14
Douglass, William, 50, 96
Dozier, Edward, 13, 32, 34
Dry Food People, 93; Classic period shrines, 174; description/organization, 43–44; ethnographic shrine use, 54–55, 93; initiation, 42
Dry Food People Who Are No Longer, 43, 44
Dry Food People Who Never Did Become, 43, 47, 51
Duff, Andrew, 147

earth mother earth naval middle place, 54, 82, 90
earth naval (nan sipu), 50, 51, 96, 174, 218
Eggan, Fred, 34
Eiselt, Sunday, 82
El Rito Creek, 155, 159, 163
Ellis, Florence Hawley, 32–33, 40, 72, 110, 111, 112, 115, 170, 183, 201, 203, 204, 214
encomienda, 188
epidemics, 40, 168–69, 206
Escalona, Juan de, 88, 199–200
Española, 186
ethnogenesis, 146, 232; critique, 147–48
factionalism, 32, 33, 34, 162–63, 182, 183

Fewkes, Jesse Walter, 11
Fiscales, 41, 44–45; evidence at Yunque'owingeh, 202
repartimiento, 188
Ford, Richard, 31, 32, 69, 90, 163
Forked Lightning, 117
Fowles, Severin, 10, 14, 68, 92f, 109, 137, 146, 151, 162, 174, 179, 180, 182
Fox, Robin, 151
Fred Harvey Company, 237
Frijoles Canyon, 12, 127, 240

Galisteo Basin, 29, 120
Gallina, 113
Gamble, Clive, 105, 232

Garcia, Damian, 24
Garcia, Jason, 26
glaze ware, Rio Grande, 166; Historic period, 195, 197; Keres and Tanoan homelands, 67; Pajarito Plateau, 67; Puye, 166
Greenlee, Robert, 127
ground-slick shrines: Chaco Canyon, 94; Classic period, 172–76; description, 93–94; directional shrines, 174; gendered, 179–180; Historic period shrines at Ku'owingeh, 220; Kapo'owingeh, 131; LA 3851, 134; LA 142926, 120; LA 142927, 131; Maestas Pueblo, 119–120; Posi'owingeh, 179; Tsama'owingeh, 119; Tsipin'owingeh, 133

Hano, 29, 34
Harrington, John P., 28, 31, 32, 33, 61, 89
Hewett, Edgar Lee, 61, 72, 238–39
Hibben, Frank, 72, 121–22
Hill, Willard, 32
Hilltop Pueblo (LA 66288), 74f, 75t, 114f, 153f; architecture, 156f; depopulation, 164; sacred geography, 174
Historic period, 63f; refuge and revolt, 211–16; resource gathering, 221–23; Spanish colony, 197–204; Spanish contact, 193–97; summary in the northern Rio Grande, 68–70; pilgrimage, 216–221
Hispanic: engagement with Pueblo archaeology, 60; farmsteads at Yunque'owingeh, 201; homesteaders in the Chama, 217
Hopi, 51: collaborative archaeology, 15; dualism, 22; early anthropology, 11; ethnogenesis, 147; ethnography, 12; footprints, 24; katsinas, 51; kinship, 9; language, 9; oral tradition, 109, 147; Pueblo Revolt, 212; stewardship, 25
Howidi'owingeh (LA 71), 74f, 75t, 95, 97, 114f, 153f; architectural plan and chronology 155, 156f, 158; dualism (with

Howidi'owingeh (LA 71) (*continued*) Hupovi'owingeh), 172, 181; history of research, 72; kivas, 171*t*; settlement pattern, 163; sacred geography, 173*f*; world-quarter shrine, 177, 178*f*

Hunt chief, 46, 222; origins in Mesa Verde region, 184; Tewa origin tradition, 38–40

Hunt shrine, 54, 55, 97, 177, 179, 222

Hunt Society, 46. *See also* Hunt chief

Hupovi'owingeh (LA 380), 74*f*, 75*t*, 114*f*, 153*f*; architectural plan and chronology, 155, 156*f*; directional shrine, 174; dualism (with Howidi'owingeh), 172, 181; final coalescence, 164; kivas, 171(table); sacred geography, 173*f*, 174; settlement pattern, 163; world-quarter shrine, 178*f*

impuesto, 188, 207, 210

Jeançon, J. A., 32, 71, 72, 80, 91, 92, 96, 136, 214

Jemez Black-on-white, 129

Jemez Mountains, 29; ethnic boundary, 71; obsidian, 64, 129; Tewa oral history, 40, 50, 51,

Jemez province, 208

Jemez Pueblo: seventeenth-century revolt, 212; Tsikumu, 51

Jerome, Kathryn, 126, 130

Johnson, Gregory, 181

Kapo Black pottery, 84*t*, 197, 215

Kap'owingeh (LA 300), 74*f*, 75*t*, 80, 114*f*, 158; architecture, 124*f*; depopulation, 137; history of research, 72; kivas, 171*t*; Wiyo phase, 122; sacred geography, 131; similarities with Palisade Ruin, 127

katsinas, 51

Ke (medicine men/Bear Medicine), 39, 46

Ke Pin (San Antonio Peak), 50

Keres Pueblos: boundary with Tewa, 86, 191; ethnography, 12; glaze ware, 67, 166, 168; language, 9; Oku Pin, 50; sacred geography, 172; Spanish contact, 196; Tsikumu, 51

Kidder, Alfred V., 12, 26, 83, 145, 165

kiva: architectural differences between Mesa Verde and Rio Grande, 121; big and small, 68, 170; burning, 164; Classic period, 170–72; middle place, 82; Pindi phase, 115–17; Tewa moieties, 41, 82, 170–72; Wiyo phase, 123, 126, 127, 128*f*. *See also* D-shaped kiva, Kiva W-4

Kiva House (near Cochiti Pueblo), 117

Ku Sehn Pin (Truchas Peak), 50

Ku'owingeh (LA 253), 74*f*, 75*t*, 97, 114*f*, 153*f*; architectural plan and chronology, 155, 156*f*; depopulation, 164; directional shrines, 174; Historic period pilgrimage, 220; kivas, 171; sacred geography, 173, 174*f*; world-quarter shrine, 178*f*

Kwahe'e Black-on-white, 110, 113

LA 142926, 74*f*, 75*t*, 114*f*, 117; sacred geography, 118*f*, 120

LA 142927, 74*f*, 75*t*, 114*f*, 122; architecture, 124*f*; sacred geography, 131

LA 3851, 134

Laboratory of Tree-Ring Research, 86, 136

Lakatos, Stephen, 104, 121

Lake Peak, 50–51

landscape: integrated Pueblo worlds, 23; survey, 90–92; Tewa cosmography, 48–55

Lang, Richard, 65

Lekson, Stephen, 241–42

Los Alamos National Laboratory, 227

ma:tu'in (relatives), 76, 163, 213

Made People (Patowa): description/organization, 46; mediating force, 48; retreat for rain, 96–97; use of world-quarter shrine, 136; Wiyo phase, 136; works, 162. *See also* Bear Medicine, Clowns (Kossa and Kwirana), Hunt society, Scalp

society, Summer and Winter chiefs, Women's society
Maestas Pueblo (LA 90844), 74f, 75t, 114f; Classic period coalescence, 158; dating and settlement, 117; kivas, 171t; sacred geography, 118f, 119–120
maize, 89; crop failure at Yunque'owingeh, 199–200; land-extensive agriculture, 89; overplanting and storage of, 88; Pueblo economy, 8
Martínez, Enrico, 204
Martinez, Esther, 57
Martinez, María, 239
mean ceramic dating, 75t, 86, 115, 155, 159, 214
Mera, Harry P., 61, 77, 80, 115, 147, 158–59, 165, 193
mesa-top villages (Pueblo Revolt-era), 213. *See also* Cochiti, Nuke'muu, Tunyo
Mesa Verde, 50, 146; American discovery, 10; dualism, 183; ethnogenesis, 148; kiva architecture, 116, 127; Made People, 184; migration, 66, 103, 105; rejection of previous lifeways, 147; sacred geography, 107; Summer People, 111; Tewa place-names, 50, 104
midden. *See* ash pile
middle place, 17, 48, 53, 77, 80
moieties, 36, 40, 41–44 *passim*, 46, 48, 162, 170
Moore, James, 182
Morgan, Henry Lewis, 11
movement: avoiding Spanish expeditions, 211; juxtaposed to abandonment, 190; Pueblo philosophy, 18, 20–21

nah poeh meng (the continuous path), 31
Nake'muu, 213
Nambé, 29, 40, 50, 51, 110, 111
Naranjo Morse, Nora, 3, 5, 21, 26, 231
Naranjo, Tessie, 56, 139–141, 190, 217, 218
Naranjo, Tito, 56
National Museum of the American Indian, 3

Native American Graves Protection and Repatriation Act (NAGPRA), 15, 240–41
Navajo, 51, 210; pastoralism, 210–211; Tewa alliance with, 214
New Mexico v. Aragon, 76
nonground shrine: across the northern Rio Grande, 120; Classic period, 172-176; description, 117; Tsama'owingeh, 119
Nuute'owingeh (LA 298), 74f, 75t, 114f, 153f, 209f; architecture, 156f, Pueblo Revolt-era reoccupation, 216; settlement pattern, 163

O'Keeffe, Georgia, 226
obsidian, 64, 129, 130
Ohkay Owingeh, 29, 30, 50, 69, 88, 111–12, 159; arrival of Castaño, 196; arrival of Oñate, 198; Barrionuevo expedition, 194; dualism (with Yunque'owingeh), 172; Made People, 162
Oku Pin (Sandia Crest), 50
Oñate, Juan de, 8, 69; arrival at Ohkay Owingeh, 186–187; San Gabriel del Yunque, 199; journey to New Mexico, 198
ontological turn, 22–23
Orcutt, Janet, 152, 176
Ortiz, Alfonso, 13, 31, 34, 62, 107, 217, 228; criticism, 34–35; mediation of dualities, 183–84; structuralism, 37; understanding of history, 100
Ortman, Scott, 66, 104, 110, 117, 147, 148, 183–84
Otermin, Antonio de, 212
Oxua, 47–48, 51, 79, 174

Pajarito Plateau, 29, 64–65, 71; Classic period, 67; coalescence, 154; Developmental period, 65; ethnic boundaries, 67; interaction with Chama Valley, 167–69; migrant settlement; movement to the Chama, 158; Pindi phase architecture, 117; Pueblo Revolt, 213–14; Summer

Pajarito Plateau (*continued*)
  People; shrines, 94; similarities with Tsipin'owingeh, 127
Paleoindian period, 64
Palisade Ruin (LA 3501), 74*f*, 75*t*, 76, 114*f*; architecture, 124*f*; description, 123–25; kivas, 171; role in defining Wiyo phase, 122
Parsons, Elsie Clews, 12, 31, 32, 33, 93
path (poeh), 42, 218
Pecos Classification, 19, 62, 63*f*
Pecos Pueblo, 83, 166, 194
Peralta, Pedro de, 203, 212
Pesede'owingeh (LA 299), 72, 74*f*, 75*t*, 114*f*, 153*f*, 195*f*, 209*f*; architecture, 156*f*; evidence for burning, 164; Historic period pilgrimage, 221, 223; Pueblo Revolt-era reoccupation, 213–15; kivas, 171*t*; Barrionuevo expedition, 194–195
Petroglyphs: Kap'owingeh, 131; Classic period, 177
Picuris Pueblo, 110
Piedra Lumbre, 210, 226
Piedra Lumbre phase, 210
Pilgrimage: Ohkay Owingeh to southern Colorado, 218; Ohkay Owingeh to Tsikumu, 218–220; Tewa in the Chama, 221
Pindi Black-on-white, 127
Pindi phase: definition, 114; architecture and settlement patterns, 115–118 *passim*; sacred geographies, 118–21 *passim*
Pindi Pueblo, 114, 116–17
plaza (bupingeh), 8, 23, 49*f*, 53–54, 82, 146, 224
Po'pay, 31, 212
Pojoaque Pueblo, 29, 30, 50, 65, 241
Pojoaque Grant Site, 65
Polvadera Peak, 129
Polvedera Creek, 123, 136
Ponshipa'akedi'owingeh (LA 297), 74*f*, 75*t*, 95, 114*f*, 122, 153*f*; architectural plan and chronology, 155, 156*f*, 157*f*; coalescence, 163; kivas, 171*t*; Historic period footing stones, 216; history of research, 72; settlement pattern, 163; Wiyo phase component, 122
population estimates: critique, 88–89, 161; methodology, 87–88; room estimates, 82–83
Pose-yemu, 142
Poshu'owingeh (LA 274), 74*f*, 75*t*, 80, 96, 114*f*, 153*f*; architectural plan and chronology, 155, 156*f*; ethnographic shrine use, 92–93, 96; burning, 164; history of research, 72, 80; kivas, 171*t*; Historic period footing stones, 216
Posi'owingeh (LA 632), 74*f*, 75*t*, 94, 114*f*, 142, 144, 153*f*, 209*f*; architectural plan and chronology, 155, 156*f*; directional shrines, 174; kivas, 171*t*; final coalescence, 164; founding (archaeological evidence), 154, 158; ground-slick shrines, 179; oral tradition, 40, 64, 67; maximum room size, 159; sacred geography, 174, 176*f*; settlement pattern, 163; traditional place of coming together of the Peoples, 112; world-quarter shrine, 178*f*
Post, Stephen, 113
Potsuwi'i Incised, 84*t*, 85*f*; European vessel forms, 214
Potsuwi'owingeh (LA 169), 74*f*, 75*t*, 154
Powaha, 4, 22, 25, 54, 68 151,
Powell, John Wesley, 11
prehistory, 12; construction of, 19; critique, 20, 25
Preucel, Robert 151, 213
Pueblo III period, 19, 147
Pueblo III-Pueblo IV tradition, 147, 181
Pueblo IV period, 19, 21, 145, 146, 147
Pueblo philosophy: antiquity, 17; balance and harmony, 22; becoming, 20; complementarity, 22; continuity through change, 16–17, 19, 231; dualism, 22; emergence and migration traditions, 17, 21; movement, 18; ongoing nature of becoming, 26; stewardship, 24, 234

Pueblo Revolt, 8, 212; era, 69, 214; ethnogenesis, 147–48
Pueblo Space, 241
Pueblo: architecture, 81–82; demographics, 9; ethnographic understanding, 9; kinship, 9; language families, 8
Putnam, Frederic Ward, 11
Puye, 67, 68, 154, 166

Quintela, Daniel, 126

Reconquest, 212–13; Pueblo resistance to, 213
reducción, 199, 207
Reed, Erik, 62, 114, 149
reservoirs, 177
resource gathering: clay and minerals, 222–23; firewood and architectural timbers, 222; hunting, 222; wild plants, 222
revitalization: Mesa Verde migration, 111, 116; language, 26; Pueblo cultural, 235–36, 241
Riana Ruin, 114*f*, 137, 153, 158; architecture, 124*f*; end of the Wiyo phase, 137; history of research, 72; kivas, 171; role in defining Wiyo phase, 122
Rio Chama valley: association with Ohkay Owingeh, 71; earliest settlers, 115; geography, 70; history of research, 72–73; interaction with Pajarito Plateau, 167–69; Pueblo Revolt era 214–16. *See also* Coalition period, Classic period, Historic period, Pindi phase, Wiyo phase
Rio del Oso, 70, 71, 73; field systems, 94; pilgrimage path, 219–220; research in valley, 73, 117, 119–120, 122, 131, 158, 172, 174, 221; site clusters, 163
Rio Grande Gorge, 213
Rio Ojo Caliente, 70, 169; identity, 179–181; research in valley, 122, 131, 133, 142, 163, 172; Historic period occupation, 216. *See also* Posi'owingeh
rock alum, 209–210

Sacred peaks, 50–52
San Gabriel del Yunque. *See* Yunque'owingeh
San Ildefonso Pueblo, 29, 50, 69, 111, 154, 170, 214, 227, 241; resistance against Spanish reconquest, 213
San Juan Basin, 65, 95
Sandoval Pueblo (LA 98319), 74*f*, 75*t*, 114*f*, 122–23, 133, 153*f*; architecture, 156*f*; sacred geography, 131, 132*f*
Sandy Lake Place, 38
Sangre de Cristo Mountains: Developmental period, 65, environment, 29; Pindi Black-on-white, 127; Tewa oral tradition, 40, 51; Tewa cosmography, 50, 51; Winter People, 110
Sankawi Black-on-cream, 84*t*; European vessel forms, 214; observed frequencies of exchange between the Chama and Pajarito Plateau, 167
Santa Clara Pueblo, 3, 6, 29, 50, 56, 67–68, 154, 218, 241; factionalism, 162
Santa Cruz watershed, 65, 113, 126, 137
Santa Fe Black-on-white, 65, 67, 83, 84*t*, 116, 117, 122, 130; observed frequencies of exchange between the Chama and Pajarito Plateau, 167
Santa Fe: boosters, 238; establishment by Spanish, 203; railroad, 236
Sapa'owingeh (LA 306), 74*f*, 75*t*, 114*f*, 153*f*, 195*f*; architectural plan and chronology, 155, 156*f*; history of research, 72; kivas, 171; maximum room size, 159; Barrionuevo expedition, 194–95; pottery, 85*f*; settlement pattern, 163
Sapawe Micaceous, 85*f*
scalar stress, 181–82
Scalp chief, 39, 46
Schaafsma, Curtis, 177, 210
Scheick, Cherie, 64
Schillaci, Michael, 104
School of American Research, 72
Schroeder, Albert, 194, 218

Second Pueblo Revolt, 213–14
secrecy: Pueblo, 33
seeking life, 5, 10, 22, 233
Seowtewa, Octavius, 17, 25, 230
serial coalescence, 112
serpent shrines, 94–95; Pajarito Plateau, 127; Tsipin'owingeh, 134;
sheephearding 73, 210, 216
shrine: Dry Food People, 44; hills, 52–53; identification, 91; mountains, 50–51; Pueblo cosmology, 22–23; recording methodology, 90; Tewa cosmography, 49f; village, 54–55. *See also* channel shrine, cupule shrine, ground-slick shrine, nonground shrine, serpent shrine, soul-dwelling middle place, world-quarter shrine
sipofene, 38, 64
Snead, James, 11, 119
soul-dwelling middle place (xayeh t'a pingeh), 55, 93, 174
southwestern ethnography: analogies and homologies, 16; Boasian perspectives, 12; critiques of ethnographic analogy, 16; "death" of field, 13; ethical critique, 13
Spain: Castaño, 196; colonial policies, 197–98, 207; Coronado, 193–94; Escalante expedition, 59; introduced domesticated plants and animals, 202–203; Mexican independence from, 10; Oñate and Yunque'owingeh, 197–204; Pueblo oppression and restriction, 212–14
Speirs, Randall, 32
Summer and Winter people: archaeologically identifiable groups, 109–112; creation of chiefs, 39; migration tradition, 108–109; organization, 40–42. *See also* Pueblo philosophy: dualism, Posi'owingeh
Swanso, Aniceto, 96
Swentzell, Porter, 56, 218
Swentzell, Rina, 6, 11, 14, 18, 27, 56, 99, 183, 217, 224, 240, 242

T'aitöna, 93, 95, 174; shrines, 137
Tanoan, 67–68
Taos Pueblo, 5, 110, 236–37; dualism, 22; San Geronimo feast day, 10; seventeenth-century revolt, 212
Te'ewi'owingeh (LA 252), 74f, 75t, 80, 114f, 153f, 195f; architectural plan and chronology, 155, 156f, 158; evidence for burning -164; final coalescence, 164; history of research, 72; kivas, 171; Castaño, 196–97; Barrionuevo expedition, 194–95
Tekhe'owingeh, 40, 111, 139
Tesuque Pueblo, 29, 50, 237
Tewa: cosmography, 48–55; debate about origins, 102–108; dual organization, 40–42; history of ethnographic research, 32–36; history of archaeological research, 61–70; oral tradition, 38–40; social organization, 42–48. *See also* abandonment, coalescence, ethnogenesis, revitalization
Tewa Basin; environment, 29; geography, 28–29
Tewa Polychrome, 84
Tewa Red, 84t, 214
The Tewa World, 34, 36–38
Tiguex province, 88
Tiguex War, 194
Tiwa: dual organization, 183; language, 9; migration from the north, 59, 65, 110; Northern Tiwa sacred geography, 120, 172; Oku Pin, 50; T'aitöna, 93; Tewa Winter People, 103, 109, 111; Spanish contact, 194, 211. *See also* Picuris Pueblo, Taos Pueblo, Tiguex War
Tosa, Paul, 17, 25, 230
Towa é: cosmography, 50, 52–53; description/organization, 44; Fiscales, 44; governor, 44; manifestation in Classic period through architecture, 172; Classic period sacred geography, 176; mythical, 39; selection, 41–42, 45; Towa é, 44
Tsama'owingeh (LA 908/909), 74f, 75t, 91, 95, 114f, 127, 153f, 195f, 209f; architecture,

156*f*; Barrionuevo expedition, 194–95; contact by Spanish, 165; dating, 115; history of research, 72; identity of settlers, 116; Kiva W-4, 116–17; kivas, 121, 171; location and context, 115; Onate's census, 204; Pueblo Revolt-era reoccupation, 215–16; sacred geography, 119, 174

Tsave Yoh, 53

Tse Shu (Conjilon Peak), 50

Tshirege'owingeh (LA 170), 74*f*, 75*t*; Onate's census, 204

Tsikumu, 50–51, 96; importance to the Pueblos of northern New Mexico, 218–19; pilgrimage, 174, 221; Classic period sacred geographies, 174

Tsin, 52–53

Tsin Tsineh (San Lorenzo Springs), 219

Tsipin (Cerro Pedernal), 64, 129, 210, 213–14, 216, 222, 226

Tsipin'owingeh (LA 301), 74*f*, 75*t*, 97, 114*f*, 123, 153*f*, 154, 209*f*; architecture, 124*f*, 156*f*; building sequence, 134; description, 123, 125–26; Revolt-era reoccupation, 216; kivas, 128*f*, 171; sacred geography, 133–34; shrines, 94–95; world-quarter shrine, 135–36

Tunyo, 69, 213

University of New Mexico field school. *See* Ellis, Florence Hawley

University of Oklahoma field school, 76–77

unmanned aerial vehicle, 82

Vallecitos Black-on-white, 127

Vargas, Diego de, 212–13

Vélez de Escalante, Silvestre, 59, 61, 102

vecino, 148

Walker, Chester, 83

Ware, John, 183

Wendorf, Fred, 62, 114, 145, 149

wheat agriculture, 69

Whitman, William, 32

Willis, Mark, 83

Wissler, Clark, 12

witchcraft, 39, 46, 138

Wiyo Black-on-white, 84*t*, 121–22, 130, 133; observed frequencies of exchange between the Chama and Pajarito Plateau, 167

Wiyo phase: definition, 121–22; architecture and settlement patterns, 121–28 *passim*; lithic assemblage, 129; pottery, 130; sacred geographies, 130–138 *passim*

Wiyo Pueblo, 60, 97, 126, 137

Women's society, 39, 46

world-quarter shrine, 95–96; Classic period, 177, 178*f*; evidence of Made People in Classic period, 177; Tewa cosmography, 52–53, 95–97; Tsama'owingeh, 119; Tsiping'owingeh, 126, 135*f*, 135–37

Wozniak, Frank, 204, 209

xayeh, 54–55, 93, 172, 176

Ximenez, Fray Lazaro, 204, 206

Yucca House, 50

Yunque'owingeh (LA 59), 40, 45, 69, 112, 159, 195*f*, 209*f*; archaeological investigations, 200–202; arrival of Castaño, 196; Barrionuevo expedition, 194; dualism (with Ohkay Owingeh), 172; establishment of San Gabriel del Yunque; pottery, 85*f*

Yunque-Yunque province, 209

Zuni, 51; cosmology, 21; encounter with Coronado, 193; Hawiku, 193; memory pieces, 180; seventeenth-century revolt, 212

ABOUT THE AUTHOR

Samuel Duwe is an assistant professor in the Department of Anthropology at the University of Oklahoma. He is co-editor of *The Continuous Path: Pueblo Movement and the Archaeology of Becoming*.